THEOLOGY OF THE OLD TESTAMENT

THEOLOGY OF THE
OLD TESTAMENT

EDMOND JACOB

Doctor of Theology
Professor of the University of Strasbourg

Translated by
ARTHUR W. HEATHCOTE and PHILIP J. ALLCOCK

London
HODDER & STOUGHTON

FIRST PUBLISHED IN GREAT BRITAIN 1958
SECOND IMPRESSION 1961

Printed in Great Britain
for Hodder & Stoughton Ltd., London
by Lowe & Brydone (Printers) Ltd., London

CONTENTS

5

PART TWO

THE ACTION OF GOD ACCORDING TO THE OLD TESTAMENT

PART THREE

OPPOSITION TO AND FINAL TRIUMPH OF GOD'S WORK

LIST OF ABBREVIATIONS

ATD	Das Alte Testament deutsch.
AOTB	Altorientalische Texte und Bilder zum Alten Testament, 2nd ed.
ARW	Archiv für Religionswissenschaft.
BZAW	Beihefte der Zeitschrift für die alttestamentliche Wissenschaft.
DBS	Supplément au Dictionnaire de la Bible (Letouzey, Paris).
Eph. th. lov.	Ephemerides theologicae lovanienses.
EThR	Etudes théologiques et religieuses (Montpellier).
FRL	Forschungen zur Religion und Literatur des A.u.N.T.
JBL	Journal of Biblical Literature.
JTS	Journal of Theological Studies.
LVT	Lexicon Veteris Testamenti (Koehler-Baumgartner).
NKZ	Neue kirchliche Zeitschrift.
NRTh	Nouvelle revue théologique (Louvain).
RB	Revue biblique.
RHR	Revue de l'histoire des religions.
RHPR	Revue d'histoire et de philosophie religieuses.
RGG	Die Religion in Geschichte und Gegenwart (2nd ed.).
RScPhTh	Revue des sciences philosophiques et théologiques.
RThP	Revue de théologie et de philosophie.
TWBNT	Theologisches Wörterbuch zum N.T. (Kittel).
ThLitztg	Theologische Literaturzeitung.
ThStKr	Theologische Studien und Kritiken.
ThZ	Theologische Zeitschrift (Bâle).
UUA	Uppsala Universitets Arsskrift.
VT	Vetus Testamentum.
ZAW	Zeitschrift für die alttestamentliche Wissenschaft.
ZNW	Zeitschrift für die neutestamentliche Wissenschaft.
ZDMG	Zeitschrift der deutschen morgenländischen Gesellschaft.
ZThK	Zeitschrift für Theologie und Kirche.

INTRODUCTION

HISTORICAL
AND METHODOLOGICAL
CONSIDERATIONS

~~~~~~

I. OUTLINE OF THE HISTORY OF THE SUBJECT

THE theology of the Old Testament may be defined as the systematic account of the specific religious ideas which can be found throughout the Old Testament and which form its profound unity. This subject is relatively new, since only from the eighteenth century onwards can we see it developing as an autonomous science and diverging from dogmatics, to which it was until then indissolubly bound. But the reality is older than the name. Within the Old Testament itself it is already possible to speak of theology. The Old Testament counts among its authors several real theologians, of whom the most ancient, the one called the Yahwist by the critics, portrays the history of humanity and of Israel's earliest days as a succession of events according to the principle of grace (God's initiative), of punishment (man's disobedience) and of faith (God's requirement and man's normal attitude towards him); an analogous plan is adopted by the writer of Deuteronomy, who insists more strictly on the divine punishment for man's rebellion. The so-called Priestly writer presents Israel's history in the form of four successive covenants and the writer of Chronicles sets out to show how all history must confirm the promise made to king David that his dynasty would be everlasting. Similarly we could speak of the theology of each prophet. Among these second Isaiah is the one whose book is a real theological treatise based on the three themes of creation, redemption and final salvation. We recall these early outlines because we hold that, even in the twentieth century, a theology of the Old Testament should be able to draw inspiration from them so as not to fit the Old Testament into a modern scheme or explain it according to a dialectic that is fundamentally foreign to it. The New Testament too is a theology of the Old Testament, for its essential purpose is to show that Jesus of Nazareth is the Christ, the Messiah promised to Israel to whom all Scripture bears witness. Certain of the New Testament writings assume more especially the appearance of theological treatises: the Gospel of Matthew is an historical treatise meant to prove that Jesus is a new Moses, while the Epistle to the Romans and the Epistle to the Hebrews present the Old Testament from the point of view of the law and the promise in one case, and of priesthood in the other. The latter writing is particularly important for the exegetical methods of the early Church, it is not "the most finished specimen of allegory",[1] but a model of typological exegesis, for which the past is a preparation and an imperfect sketch of the future. According to this writing there is between the two Testaments the relationship of shadow to reality. In general, the Apostle Paul makes the same use of it, only giving up typology for allegory when he views the Old Testament apart from the general perspective of the fulfilment of Scripture in history.[2]

A theology of the Old Testament which is founded not on certain isolated verses, but on the Old Testament as a whole, can only be a Christology, for what was revealed under the old covenant, through a long and varied history, in events, persons and institutions, is, in Christ, gathered together and brought to perfection. Such a statement does not in any way mean that we should only consider the Old Testament in the light of its fulfilment, but a perfectly objective study makes us discern already in the Old Testament the same message of the God who is present, of the God who saves and of the God who comes, which characterizes the Gospel. Unless it is based upon the principle of the unity of the

---

[1] The expression is from P. Lestringant, *Essai sur l'Unité de la révélation biblique*, Paris 1943, p. 131.

[2] Galatians 4.21ff. is the clearest example of this.

two Testaments, and *a fortiori* on the internal unity of the Old Testament itself, it is not possible to speak of a theology of the Old Testament. The unity of the Old Testament is in no way incompatible with what critical and historical study has revealed about the very diverse elements that have gone to its composition, for the collections of books and traditions have not prevented the Old Testament from remaining as one book and the expression of one religion. That is an objective fact and consequently justifiable from scientific study.[1]

The theology of the Old Testament IS AN HISTORICAL SUBJECT; through neglecting this fundamental aspect and through becoming the vassal of dogmatics it did not make its appearance until a relatively recent date. From the earliest times of the Christian Church, the Old Testament could not, for dogmatic reasons, become the object of historical study. In its struggle against Gnosticism on the one hand and Judaism on the other, the Church could not do full justice to the Old Testament. Despite its ephemeral nature, the work of Marcion and the Gnostics was serious enough to perpetuate in the Church a reserved attitude towards the Old Testament and consequently a certain dualism in theological thought. In order to resist the perpetual currents of heresy which kept coming to light within the fold, the Church was glad to attenuate, even indeed to deny the differences between the two Testaments. A place apart, however, must be given to the work of Irenaeus of Lyons; in face of the Gnostic arguments, which were not without a certain force, it was impossible to maintain the naïve point of view of the identity of the Gospel and the Jewish scriptures, proved by means of an allegorical exegesis pushed to the extreme. By insisting on the fact of the incarnation Irenaeus shows salvation set in the framework of a history in which each initiative of God assumes the form of a covenant; the Mosaic law and the salvation of the New Testament were given, at appropriate times, for the salvation of humanity by one and the same God, knowledge of the creator God being the *principium evangelii*. Irenaeus shows its development with the help of the following comparison : just as an earthly sovereign may show more generosity

[1] The problem of the unity of the Bible has been most recently treated in a particularly profound manner by H. H. Rowley, *The Unity of the Bible*, 1953, which does full justice to the diversity of currents brought to light by historical and literary criticism.

at some times than at others, God has not always shown his generosity towards his subjects in the same way. This simile of the divine pedagogue is already found with the apostle Paul in the Epistle to the Galatians in particular, but Irenaeus replaces the notions of sin and grace by the less central ones, biblically speaking, of growth and education; in this way he manages to preserve against Marcionism the unity of the divine plan, while allowing the difference between the two Testaments to stand. But it is a difference of degree, not of two worlds that have no common measure, " now more or less are only said of two things which have something in common, like water with water or light with light or grace with grace ".[1]

Alexandrine theology, made famous by the exegetical prestige of Origen, has the purpose of finding in the Old Testament all the Christian dogmas in a figurative form. To this end it makes extensive use of allegorical exegesis, whose methods had held an honoured place in Alexandria since the time of Philo. According to Origen Scripture has three meanings which correspond to the three parts of the human body and to the three categories of believers: the body is the letter visible to all eyes, the soul is the hidden meaning contained in the letter, lastly, the spirit is the heavenly things which the letter represents. Obviously the spiritual meaning is the only true one, although that spiritual meaning is only accessible through the outer covering of the literal meaning, which, however, is speedily forgotten once the spiritual meaning is reached. It is not without reason that in the eyes of Origen the most important figure in the Old Testament is Moses: Moses is the man who saw God's glory. That is a spiritual and mystical experience in the light of which the Alexandrine school views the experiences of the prophets and the prophetic rôle of the Old Testament in general. For the man who sees the glory of God, the world and history have no other meaning than the one they take through reference to Christ, who is the reflection of the divine glory. Origen made the mistake of generalizing from this valid insight, finding a symbolic meaning in every detail of the Scriptures. Despite the absence of historical sense which is its chief weakness, the exegesis of the Alexandrine school is not devoid of greatness in its way of grasping Scripture as a whole or, as is

---

[1] *Adversus haereses*, IV, 9, 2.

frequently said to-day, in its plenary sense and of showing the convergence of all its parts towards the one who forms its centre.

The School of Antioch is generally opposed to the Alexandrine, and certain writings from these schools bring us an echo of this opposition; but perhaps it is fairer to speak of misunderstanding rather than of real opposition. The School of Antioch is incontestably superior to its rival in possessing an historical sense which is better able to grasp the Old Testament revelation. To ἀλληγορία, the theologians of Antioch oppose the θεωρία or ἐπιθεωρία that is contemplation, a term which Origen uses in a mystical sense only. Diodore of Tarsus (330-392)[1] wrote a treatise entitled: τίς διαφορὰ θεωρίας καὶ ἀλληγορίας; the *theoria* does not change history, but is superimposed upon it; thus in one and the same text certain features refer to events of the author's own time, others to Christ. The men of Antioch attach great importance to the historical study of a text and to the history of the people of Israel itself: for them the chief figure in Israelite history is David, the man who lived in advance the whole of his people's history. They try to satisfy a twofold requirement, the search for historical meaning and for the typological meaning if it has a place there. It is not without reason that one of their most illustrious representatives, Theodore of Mopsuestia, can from some of his ideas be considered a precursor of modern criticism.

In the West, the Alexandrine principles triumphed, thanks especially to St. Jerome and St. Augustine, but as Scripture was primarily regarded from a practical point of view developments in the meaning of the Scriptures as a whole held a very minor place. It must be noticed, however, that in several of his writings St. Augustine has clearly set out the historical progression from the Old to the New Covenant. In books XV-XVII of the *City of God* he divides the history of God's reign on earth into six successive periods: (*a*) from Adam to Noah—*infantia*; (*b*) from Noah to Abraham—*puerilitas*; (*c*) from Abraham to David—*adulescentia*; (*d*) from David to the Exile—*virilitas*; (*e*) from the Exile to Jesus Christ—*senectus*; (*f*) Time of the Church—*Novum Testamentum*. We have in the *City of God* a grandiose essay in the theology of history, but St. Augustine's picture goes beyond

---

[1] Cf. Ed. Schweizer, "Diodor von Tarsus als Exeget", *ZNW* 40, p. 33.

the Old Testament plan and is inspired more by apocalyptic motives than by historical considerations, the historical reality of Israel being viewed in a figurative way only.

In the course of the Middle Ages the Old Testament is almost completely viewed as a means of promoting the spiritual life and as an anthology of *dicta probantia* supporting the theocratic ideal of the Church. Exegesis is completely subordinated to dogma, whose task it is to decide between different interpretations. It is the open door to subjectivism, each one finding in the Old Testament his own doctrines, making of the Bible, to use a pungent expression of Geiler of Kaysersberg, a *nasus cereus* (*wächserne Nase*) which is adaptable to any form. St. Thomas Aquinas wrote many exegetical works, but he refers all biblical notions to the Scholastic norm, according to which the idea alone has value whereas history has none. It must not be supposed, however, that Old Testament study in the Middle Ages merely marked time. From that period the Old Testament opened the way to two new studies which could not fail to influence the way it was understood: the philosophy and history of religions. Between these two the Old Testament had, in the course of time, a lot of difficulty in maintaining its autonomy and it could not resist the temptation to become a philosophy or a history of religion. There also arose in the Middle Ages, as a result of Christianity's contact with the pagan religions, with Islam in particular, the problem of each religion's value, a problem which obliged Christians to examine the foundations of their faith.

If the Reformation was able to advance beyond the Middle Ages in interpretation of the Bible, it owes such progress in particular to the great humanist Reuchlin, who gave a new impetus to Hebrew which Christians, through anti-Semitism, had neglected to study and who, by returning to the sources, freed the Bible from the yoke of tradition. The Reformers did not, however, succeed in giving a coherent picture of the Old Testament: obliged to be obedient to two opposing views they were not in a position to grasp the organic unity of the Old Testament—the opposition between Law and Gospel drove them to accentuate the differences and to regard the Old Testament as superseded. In addition, in their desire to offer strong resistance to their Catholic and "spiritualist" opponents, they insisted on the unity of the Scriptures by putting both Testaments on the same plane by means of allegorical exegesis. The importance of the historical element did not, however, escape Luther. "Faith," he says, "should be built on history,"[1] and certain of his prefaces to the books of the Old Testament insist on a knowledge of the history and the precise circumstances in which these books were composed. Luther's position seems to be quite close to that of the School of Antioch; it differs from it, however, on the most important point, that of Christ's presence. While for the earlier writers Christ is only present symbolically, he is really present according to Luther's conception; he compares this presence of Christ with the presence of the ram which Abraham saw in the bushes when he turned round at the moment of Isaac's sacrifice. Though Luther insists on the notion of history, he separates it radically from the concept of development. In effect the Gospel does not succeed the Law but, after the old covenant, the Law and the Gospel are mingled together. Luther does not minimize the importance of the incarnation as an historical event, but that incarnation is totally outside the law of time and that is why it is discussed at the beginning, in the middle and at the end of Revelation; there is not then in the Old Testament a continuous development, but there are testimonies to Christ; that is why Luther insists especially on the prophets and on the great signs which are real events by which God proclaims his grace; and the man who, like Abraham, grasps that grace, through faith, makes the new covenant real already under the old: "*Idem Christus eademque fides ab Habel in finem mundi per varia saecula regnavit in electis, sed alia et alia ejusdem Christi et fidei signa fuerant, quae vere sacramenta gratiae dicuntur*", and again: "*externa variant, interna valent*".[2] Luther's Christological principle and his conception of time call for some correction; it is none the less true that Luther showed in a masterly way that the Old Testament represents "the swaddling clothes and cradle in which Jesus Christ was placed".[3]

According to Diestel,[4] Calvin brings together the complete

---

[1] *Ex historia aedificanda est fides*. The expression is found in the *Commentary on Isaiah* (1527-30); Luther certainly affirms revelation in history, but at the same time he understands that all external history should become the history of each believer.

[2] *Operationes in Psalmos*, 1519-20.

[3] *Preface to the O.T.*, 1523. Luther uses this image several times, particularly in the explanation of the Gospel of Christmas in the *Kirchenpostille* of 1522.

[4] *Geschichte des A.T. in der christlichen Kirche*, p. 269.

liberty of a Theodore of Mopsuestia with regard to the text and the spiritual depth of Luther, which gives him that intuitive perception which is one of the supreme qualities of a good exegete. He does not wish to Christianize the Old Testament at any cost and seems rather to come nearer to using a typological method, the theocracy of the Old Testament being for example a type and a model of the Kingdom of God which the Church should try to make real. He himself characterizes the unity and difference of the two Testaments in the following way: "The Church which was among the Jews was the same as ours, but as it was still in the weakness of childhood, God kept it under that legal tutelage without giving it clear knowledge of the spiritual promises, having presented them to it only in a shrouded form and veiled by material promises."[1] All the Reformers are agreed in recognizing only one dispensation from the Fall to the end of the present age in which the Law and the Gospel are proclaimed.

Those who followed the Reformers fall back into a new scholasticism and envisage the Bible only as a collection of *dicta probantia* meant to support their dogmatic utterances; at the same time the idea of inspiration takes on a progressively more rigid form. The Bible, being the absolutely infallible Book, could contain neither contradiction nor progress. Even what the Renaissance and the Reformation had established concerning the human character of the Bible's composition is subjected to the dogmatic preoccupation of the times, and even philology becomes a branch of dogmatics.

The seventeenth century bears the lasting imprint of the work of the Reformed theologian John Cocceius (1603-1669,)[2] whose name is coupled with that of covenant theology. Cocceius distinguishes the *foedus naturale* and the *foedus gratiae*, the second being the successor to the first, which was destroyed by the Fall. Consequently the covenant of grace is unfolded in the economy of the Old and the New Testament; it is not only the idea of the covenant which is presented historically, but also the idea of the Kingdom of God, the history of which becomes confused with the history of the Church—this provides Cocceius with the opportunity

---

[1] *Inst.* 2, 11.

[2] *Summa doctrinae de foedere ac testamentis Dei.* Cocceius underlines along with the covenant idea the importance of the idea of the Kingdom, as is pointed out by G. Schrenk, *Gottesreich und Bund*, 1923.

of a vast typology in which the whole history of the Church is foreshadowed from the beginnings to the time of Gustavus Adolphus. In spite of his weaknesses, due primarily to the presentation of the covenant according to the Zwinglian conception as a *foedus mutuum* —instead of seeing in it, as the Old Testament itself does, a gift to humanity—and to his concern in seeking in the Old Testament the description of contemporary events, Cocceius had the merit of giving a new impetus to biblical study and to syntheses of vast scope. The Bible is no longer the collection of sayings used to support theses, but a book capable of supplying an intrinsic answer to all questions about the faith. Moreover, Cocceius' success went far beyond Reformed circles; from it several Lutherans, in particular the founders of Pietism, Spener and Francke, drew to some extent their biblicism. In his *Pia Desideria* Spener had deplored the almost total absence in the Church of a serious study of the Bible and expressed the wish that it should be remedied. In the *Collegium Philobiblicum* of Halle the Bible was read in its original text and was freed from dogmatic shackles, but since individual edification was more important than the need for knowledge, study of the Bible was in the main concentrated on the New Testament. In the Catholic Church dogmatic prejudice with regard to the Bible was less strong and allowed a greater liberty of research and hypothesis, a preliminary condition for all research. So it is not surprising that it was in this Church that there appeared a work like Richard Simon's, which, however, fell far short of receiving unanimous approval.

The harmonizing of a serious study of the Bible with an historical and philological commentary on it characterizes the work in the eighteenth century of a man who more than any other deserves the title of biblical theologian—J. A. Bengel (1697-1752) of Würtemberg. Bengel sets out to show that there is in the Scriptures a scheme of dispensation in an historical form which culminates in an eschatological fulfilment: "*Tota religio tendit in futurum.*"[1] Bengel's famous formula "*opertum initio tenetur, quod deinde apertum cernitur*"[2] re-echoes St. Augustine's still more famous

---

[1] *Gnomon*, p. 528 (8th ed. as quoted by Schrenk, *op. cit.*, p. 311, the 8th edition of the *Gnomon* not being accessible to us).

[2] *Ordo Temporum*, 1741, p. 305. The work of Bengel, who is perhaps the greatest exegete of the eighteenth century, abounds in pertinent remarks about the unity of biblical revelation. From this interesting collection we may quote the definition to be found in a letter addressed to one of his pupils, Jér. Fr. Reuss: "Es stimmt

saying: *"Novum Testamentum in Vetere Testamento latet, Vetus Testamentum in Novo Testamento patet."*

Rationalism, under which the Bible was read with the aim of becoming not more pious but more reasonable, favoured the constitution of biblical theology as an independent science. The necessity of treating biblical theology from an historical point of view was first formulated by Johann Philipp Gabler in a slim volume whose title contains a programme of work: *Oratio de justo discrimine theologiae biblicae et dogmaticae regundisque recte utriusque finibus.*[1] The purpose of biblical theology is to describe what the authors of the Old Testament thought concerning divine things. In formulating this standpoint Gabler takes into account two results to which he had been led by a profound study of the Bible: (*a*) there are in the Old Testament diverse and sometimes contradictory statements; (*b*) dogmatics makes a selection from the contents of the Bible. By defining the boundaries between dogmatics and biblical theology, Gabler set up the latter as an indipendent science by removing the mortgage which until then had weighed so heavily upon it. The first theology of the Old Testament written according to Gabler's principles was G. L. Bauer's (1796).[2] While permitting the birth of a biblical theology Rationalism stamped it at the same time with the seal of its own philosophy and made it incapable of grasping the specific character of Hebrew mentality, to such an extent that the Old Testament was the object of criticism more frequently than of an effort of positive appreciation. In spite of the effort made by de Wette[3] to place himself on a higher plane than the dispute between orthodoxy and rationalism and to bring out the idea of God as holy will as a central principle of the Old Testament, biblical theology does not become dissociated

---

alles so schön zusammen (*omnia se quadrant*); wie man an einer Kugel sieht, dass sie rund und eben damit ganz ist, so sieht man's auch an der Heiligen Schrift, Altes und Neues Testament" (quoted from Burk, *Leben Bengels*, 1831, p. 64).

[1] In his short book—it is an academic lecture—given in 1787 (published in the *Opuscula academica*, II, pp. 179-198, Ulm 1831), he presents dogmatic theology as a philosophy concerning divine things in contrast to biblical theology, an historical science; the advice that he gives "that biblical theology is not *conficta ad nostros sensus*" remains perfectly valid.

[2] *Theologie des alten Testaments oder Abriss der religiösen Begriffe der alten Hebräer von der ältesten Zeit bis auf den Anfang der christlichen Epoche,* Leipzig 1796.

[2] *Biblische Dogmatik des alten und neuen Testaments oder kritische Darstellung der Religionslehre des Hebraismus, des Judentums und des Urchristentums,* Berlin 1813.

from a purely historical schema, as is shown by the division of that period's classic work, D. C. von Cölln's *Biblische Theologie* (1836), which arranges the material in two sections, Hebraism and Judaism, showing in each one the evolution from particularism towards universalism. The Romantic movement effected some progress in that it created a favourable climate for grasping the originality of the religious life. The Old Testament owes much to the work of Herder on Hebrew poetry, but the secularization that biblical books thus underwent did not take place without harm to their normative rôle in matters of faith. Schleiermacher, without adopting the extremist position of Marcion's disciples, gave much more emphasis to what separated Christianity from Judaism than to their fundamental unity. By declaring that what was best in the Old Testament could also be found in Greek philosophy, Schleiermacher[1] forgot that that best was neither monotheism, nor the immortality of the soul, but the holiness of God. For the theological study of the Old Testament, Hegel's influence was more valuable than Schleiermacher's, for, far from considering the religion of Israel as an historical accident, he secures for it a necessary place in the development towards absolute religion. The great advance of this tendency over rationalism was to show that development in religion was something other than a simple chronological sequence. The work most in keeping with the Hegelian system is the *Biblische Theologie* of Wilhelm Vatke (I *Die Religion des Alten Testaments*, 1835), to which Wellhausen acknowledges his debt for what is best in his synthesis. It is incontestable that, freed from dogmatic prejudice, the study of the Bible opened new possibilities to exegesis. But if theology wished to maintain its autonomy in the face of philosophy and history, it was necessary for it to make fresh contact with the Scriptures as a normative authority. Two names stand out in the movement directed towards a theological understanding of the Old Testament: Hengstenberg in his *Christologie de l'Ancien Testament*[2] recalled the unity of the two Testaments, but treated too lightly the elements which an historical study had brought to light. J. C. Hofmann deserves more attention for his work *Weissagung und Erfüllung*[3]

[1] In *Der christliche Glaube*, 1842, paragraph 12, p. 78, he says among other things: "Man kann das Christentum auf keine Weise als eine Umbildung oder eine erneuernde Fortsetzung des Judentums ansehen."
[2] *Christologie des Alten Testaments*, Berlin 1829-35.
[3] Also *Der Schriftbeweis*, Nordlingen 1852.

(1840-1844). In it he examines the relationship between history and prophecy, saying that all history is prophecy and all prophecy history; each period of history bears within it the germ of the period that follows and represents it in advance; it is thus that all history is a prophecy of the final and lasting relationship between God and man, the terminal phase of which is inaugurated by the coming of Christ, Christ being the goal of history and prophecy. Hofmann envisages biblical history in its entirety, and not merely the specifically Messianic prophecies, from the viewpoint of the history of salvation (*Heilsgeschichte*). This historical exposition is accompanied, in Hofmann's work, particularly in his *Schriftbeweis*, by a psychological confirmation which has with good reason been called a "biblical theosophy",[1] namely that the Christian rediscovers in his own life the course of sacred history: creation, fall, flood, promise, judgment. This considerable work, which O. Cullmann compares with the work of Irenaeus,[2] provided, despite some eccentricities, a solid basis for the construction of a theology of the Old Testament which could take account of history and of salvation and the highly important discovery that salvation is carried out through the course of history. Orthodox reaction, stamped, however, with Hegel's influence, is shown in a work that was for long a classic, the *Theology of the Old Testament* by G. F. Oehler.[3] The work is divided into three parts: Mosaism, prophetism, wisdom, the two first each containing an historical and a systematic section. In the preface the proposed aim is defined in the following way: "Biblical theology must never lose sight of the fact that its domain includes the whole of revelation; it must never forget that the stages through which revelation has passed are, so to speak, different limbs of one and the same body. And as a body can only be studied when it is fully grown, as an historical evolution can only be fully appreciated when it is completed, the theology of the Old Testament will take care to use the light that the Lord's appearing throws on the whole preparatory covenant" (French translation, p. 58). In spite of his conservative ideas on the history of Israel, Oehler fully grasped the fact that a theology of the Old Testament could not be other than a theology of

[1] Diestel, *op. cit.*, pp. 698ff.

[2] *Christ et le temps*, p. 131.

[3] The first edition appeared in 1873, a year after the author's death: *Theologie des Alten Testaments*, Tübingen; a French translation by H. de Rougemont appeared in Neuchâtel in 1875 (in two volumes); English translation 1874-93.

history. The end of the nineteenth century is dominated by the name of Wellhausen, whose ideas were to permit the presentation of Israel's history in a form acceptable to the mind of a generation moulded by Darwin and Hegel. As the new presentation of the history of Israel's religion, springing from the new discrimination of the sources, takes precedence over theology, works which bear this title are in reality only so many histories of the religion of Israel. Such is the case of the posthumous work of Augustus Kayser,[1] edited by Edouard Reuss in 1886, and of the work in French of the Strasbourg minister C. Piepenbring.[2] However, the latter author makes the praiseworthy effort of arranging his material in a systematic order under three headings: Mosaism, prophetism, Judaism. Germany witnessed the success of the *Alttestamentliche Theologie* of Hermann Schultz, which ran into five successive editions between 1869 and 1896 and which, while giving much importance to historical development, finds in the idea of the Kingdom of God on earth, the central principle of the whole of the Old Testament teaching; while the *Theology of the Old Testament* by A. B. Davidson (1904) does not succeed in freeing itself from an exclusively historical point of view.

The result of this state of things was that at the dawn of the twentieth century theology was almost excluded from the field of Old Testament studies. Eduard Koenig's manual which appeared in 1922[3] cannot be considered as the sign of the rebirth of this branch, but must rather be viewed as the last testimony of a scholar who had always remained refractory to Wellhausen's theories. The new approach has its starting-point in 1925 when, in an article entitled *Alttestamentliche Theologie und alttestamentliche Religionsgeschichte,*[4] Steuernagel declares for the maintenance and respective autonomy of the two studies which had become almost totally confused. A year later, in an article with an almost identical title,[5] Eissfeldt states the case in favour of the legitimacy

---

[1] *Die Theologie des Alten Testaments in ihrer geschichtlichen Entwicklung dargestellt*, 1886, 2nd ed. revised by K. Marti under the title (which shows the change of approach) *Geschichte der israelitischen Religion*, 1903.

[2] *Théologie de l'Ancien Testament*, Paris 1886; English translation by H. G. Mitchell, New York 1893.

[3] *Theologie des Alten Testaments kritisch und vergleichend dargestellt*, Stuttgart 1922.

[4] *BZAW* 41 (Martifestschrift), pp. 266ff.

[5] " Israelitisch-jüdische Religionsgeschichte und alttestamentliche Theologie ", *ZAW*, 1926, pp. 1ff.

of the theology of the Old Testament, but, according to him, this could not be the object of an historical investigation and could only be an account of what the religious or ecclesiastical attitude of the man conducting the enquiry finds in the Old Testament. This attitude, diametrically opposed to the one formerly advocated by Gabler, is explained by the concern to do justice to certain dogmatic and pneumatic tendencies, more or less stirred up by Barth's commentary on the Epistle to the Romans, and to allot a separate field to them where they would no longer trespass on the fields of history and exegesis. This partitioning could not, however, be retained; it was rightly and validly objected that, since in the Old Testament revelation is carried out through the course of history, there could be no divorce between historical research and theological interpretation. The next few years saw the almost simultaneous appearance of several works of biblical theology. Sellin[1] in a short, but compact book, arranges the material round the three classical themes: God—Man—Judgment and Salvation. L. Koehler[2] adopts the same scheme and finds in the notion of the kingship of God the unifying principle of the whole of the Old Testament. The most important work is the one by Walter Eichrodt,[3] professor at Bâle, which arranges the material not according to the classical scheme as borrowed from dogmatics, but round a specifically Israelite notion, that of the covenant regarded in a threefold way: the covenant of God with the people, with man, with the world. In choosing this notion Eichrodt tried to explain the Old Testament by its own dialectic and the schematization of which he can be accused does not detract from the value of his synthesis, the most notable of the first half of this century. Otto Procksch[4] gives, in a first section, a history of the religion of Israel and then arranges the "world of ideas" according to the tripartite scheme which Eichrodt admits to have borrowed from him.[5] The unity of the two Testaments is strongly stressed by both authors. "Every theology is a Christology",[6] writes Procksch, and the Dutch writer Th. C.

---

[1] *Theologie des Alten Testaments*, Leipzig 1933.
[2] *Theologie des Alten Testaments*, Tübingen 1936.
[3] *Theologie des Alten Testaments*, vol. 1, "Gott und Volk", Leipzig 1933; vol. 2, "Gott und Welt", 1935; vol. 3, "Gott und Mensch", 1939.
[4] *Theologie des Alten Testaments*, 1950, published after the author's death by G. von Rad.
[5] *ThAT*, vol. 1, p. 6, note.
[6] *ThAT*, p. 1.

Vriezen[1] states in the introductory part of his manual that the Old Testament can only be really understood by starting from Jesus Christ, and he strives in the main part to elucidate the central themes which are important to the Christian faith. On the Roman Catholic side, the *Theology* of Paul Heinisch[2] is a clear and well-documented statement following the classical plan borrowed from dogmatics. The two comprehensive works[3] published in the United States also have as a dominant theme the assertion of the unity of the two Testaments and of the unity of the Old Testament itself. Millar Burrows[4] succeeds in a masterly way, by treating in 380 pages the biblical theology of the whole Bible; these two works are conceived less as scientific studies than as practical contributions intended to put the substance of the Old Testament at the disposal of believers and especially of ministers. Even if it is not his immediate aim, the theologian of the Old Testament can only rejoice to see his efforts help towards a better use of the Old Testament in the life of the Church. In a quarter of a century the theology of the Old Testament, which had been reduced to the rank of a poor relation, has thus succeeded in taking the front of the stage in the domain of Old Testament studies. This interest is made plain by the publication, in addition to the comprehensive works already mentioned, of monographs dealing with certain central topics of the religion of the Old Testament. Works such as those of Haenel[5] on holiness, of Wheeler Robinson,[6] whom death prevented from producing a complete treatment of Old Testament theology, of N. H. Snaith[7] on the distinctive ideas of the Old Testament, of Hempel[8] on piety, of H. H. Rowley[9] on election and the unity of the Bible, of Baumgaertel[10] on the promise, of W.

---

[1] *Hoofdlijnen der Theologie van het Oude Testament*, Wageningen 1949.
[2] *Theologie des Alten Testamentes*, Bonn 1940.
[3] Otto J. Baab, *The Theology of the Old Testament*, Nashville 1949.
[4] Millar Burrows, *An Outline of Biblical Theology*, Philadelphia 1946.
[5] *Die Religion der Heiligkeit*, Gütersloh 1931.
[6] *The Religious Ideas of the Old Testament*, 1913, " The Theology of the Old Testament " in the composite work *Record and Revelation*, Oxford 1938. *Inspiration and Revelation in the Old Testament*, Oxford 1946.
[7] *The Distinctive Ideas of the Old Testament*, London 1944.
[8] *Gott und Mensch im Alten Testament*, 1926.
[9] *The Biblical Doctrine of Election*, London 1950; *The Unity of the Bible*, 1953; *The Rediscovery of the Old Testament*, 1946.
[10] *Verheissung. Zur Frage des evangelischen Verständnisses des Alten Testaments*, Gütersloh 1952.

Vischer[1] on the testimony to Christ in the Old Testament, of G. E. Wright[2] on the originality.of Israel's religion in relation to the surrounding world, are so many contributions to a deeper knowledge of the Old Testament and the elucidation of its specific and permanent value.[3]

[1] *Das Christuszeugnis des Alten Testaments*, Vol. 1: "Das Gesetz", Zurich 1934; Vol. 2: "Die früheren Propheten", Zurich 1942 (French trans. published by Delachaux et Niestlé, Neuchâtel and Paris 1949 and 1951).

[2] *The Challenge of Israel's Faith*, 1944. "The Old Testament against its Environment", *Studies in Biblical Theology*, no. 2, London. "God Who Acts. Biblical Theology as Recital", *Studies in Biblical Theology*, no. 8, 1952.

[3] We must also mention the articles in *TWBNT* which for the most part (especially in the first two volumes) give a big share to the prehistory of the words of the Old Testament and articles in the supplement to Pirot's *Dictionnaire de la Bible*. More modestly the *Vocabulaire biblique* (Delachaux et Niestlé, 1954; English edition in preparation) sets out to put before a wider public the theological contents of the key words of the Old Testament.

II. THE PLACE OF THEOLOGY IN RELATION TO OTHER BRANCHES OF OLD TESTAMENT STUDY

THEOLOGY is always placed last in lists of the different branches which constitute Old Testament study, which indicates that it is their conclusion and that it could not do without their results.

Granted that between the various branches there is the coherence that unites the members of one body, there can be no question of separating them and we cannot accept the point of view of those who separate the theology of the Old Testament, as depending on pneumatic or existential knowledge, from the other branches depending on historical knowledge. It is important, however, that within this unity the various branches should perform their parts in a fully autonomous way. The introductory study concerns the forming of the books, their composition, their authenticity, etc. Biblical theology could not without loss neglect taking them into account. The time of a book's composition is not irrelevant to its theological value, precisely because the Bible contains, not a timeless revelation, but a word of God for particular men in particular circumstances. One of the most unanimously recognized results of this introductory study is the progressive and collective composition of many books; the authors therefore represent a milieu, a school, and the book is not the result of the inspiration of one particular author, but the expression of the religion of a whole people. Such evidence can have important theological repercussions. Although light on the composition of the Pentateuch is far from complete, we adopt until further notice the Graf-Wellhausen theory; by accepting then that the Law is later than the prophets, we shall avoid defining the religion of the Old Testament as a legalistic religion in its earliest stages and we shall not choose the Law as the central unifying principle of the Old Testament. This example shows that a critical study of the Old Testament is not necessarily in opposition to a theological study and that the terms "history"

and "history of salvation" are not mutually exclusive. By applying to the Old Testament the methods of the profane branches of
learning, criticism only brings out more clearly, among the un-
enduring elements, the specifically religious element and allows us
a better grasp of what is God's word in it. Nor can the theology
of the Old Testament ignore the lessons of archaeology, using
the word in the wide sense of the examination of civilizations and
customs, for if theology is the study of the manifestations of God
it cannot be uninterested in the human environment in which these
saw the light of day. But though they may sometimes deal with
the same topic, theology and archaeology must confine themselves
each to its own field. Thus the study of the cultus depends at the
same time on archaeology and theology: it is archaeology's rôle
to supply the description of cultic places and objects, to study the
forms of priesthood and sacrifice, and from that description theology
will disentangle the meaning of the cult and will reconstruct its
symbolism. Archaeological work can show itself very useful, for
the frequency of such and such an object or of such and such a
rite is a clue pointing towards a certain form of worship which itself
is only the expression of an underlying attitude; if archaeology
succeeds in showing that the essential meaning of sacrifice is that
of gift or that of substitution, then the theological perspective for
the meaning of the cultus is considerably modified; but we are not
yet at the stage—and we shall probably never reach it—where
archaeology's findings will be able to do without the biblical texts.[1]
The third discipline with which the theology of the Old Testament
must of necessity collaborate is the history of the people of Israel.
To know the way in which the nation was moulded, the political
and social changes that it underwent, is as important as to know
how the Old Testament itself was formed, knowledge that is all
the more indispensable since theology does not work with ideas,
but with historical facts. Questions of the spirituality, of the unity
or of the foreknowledge of God are far less important for the faith
of ancient Israel than questions of the Exodus from Egypt, of the
Sinai covenant or of the conquest of Canaan. The "Credo"[2] of

---

[1] It would be unjust not to acknowledge the debt that Old Testament theology
owes to the work of Johs Pedersen, *Israel, its life and culture*, on Hebrew mentality;
in France Pedersen's works have received an original adaptation in those of A. Causse,
particularly in his last book *Du groupe ethnique à la communauté religieuse*, 1937.

[2] Cf. G. von Rad, *Das formgeschichtliche Problem des Hexateuchs*, 1938, and
Wright, *God who acts.*

the people was firmly based on the affirmation and remembrance of historical events. The Old Testament theologian therefore cannot have with regard to history that attitude of indifference or scepticism which is often shown towards historical questions by philosophers and dogmatists. It is then important to know—and it will only be known by virtue of the methods proper to historical study —whether the events which the Old Testament relates, and on which it bases its faith, really took place. This method cannot be applied, of course to the early chapters of Genesis, where we are in the presence of myths which give expression to supra-historical truths or to historical facts only in the eyes of a higher power, but we could not speak with the same authority of Abraham's faith if it were historically proved that the patriarch never existed. It is important, however, at the same time to state that it is not enough that an event should have taken place on a particular day in a particular place for it to be historical. In order to merit the title of "historical event", an event has to be conspicuous and that conspicuous quality is not necessarily a function of the event's primary importance in history: the death of Jesus passed unnoticed in Roman history and yet that historical event dominates world history and caused it to move in a new direction. Similarly, the Exodus of the Israelites must have been a quite trivial event, but that trivial event made its mark on the life of the Jewish people and, as a result, on universal history. We can grasp this significance of the historical event by considering the interpretation of history in the prophets and in the Psalms. We discover there that history is very freely used, that the sequence of events is sometimes reversed, as in Psalm 114 where the Jordan is mentioned before the Red Sea, and that the whole tendency is to set the principal themes in relief. Hence Old Testament theology, while remaining a descriptive subject, will not stop over details of history and will not be shackled by the chronological order of events, yet it will not launch into excesses of allegory.

So it is neither desirable nor possible to pose the dilemma: either the history of Israel's religion, or the theology of the Old Testament. Each has its proper function to fulfil while remaining in each case an historical and descriptive subject: the first will show the variety of the history and its evolution, the second will emphasize its unity. But can one legitimately speak of "theology" and would it not be better, as has been recently suggested, to be content to speak of the "phenomenology of the Old Testament"?[1] The objection would be valid if the history of Israel were not itself a part of the theology, that is to say a word and a revelation of God. And so we think it is better to use the word theology in a wide sense—one could speak of the theology of events and the theology of ideas—rather than to see in it only the expression of the piety and faith of the Church. In conclusion let it be said that there is no history without theology and no theology without history.

---

[1] N. W. Porteous, "The Old Testament and some theological thought-forms" in *Scottish Journal of Theology*, 1954, pp. 153ff.

III. THE PLACE OF OLD TESTAMENT THEOLOGY IN RELATION TO OTHER THEOLOGICAL STUDIES

ALTHOUGH it is a strictly historical subject, Old Testament theology is not without relationship to dogmatics, with which it lived in a kind of symbiosis until the time of Rationalism. The separation of the two subjects was salutary for both by allowing each to develop its potentialities. Dogmatics does not confine itself solely to the Bible, it takes much account of the contributions of philosophy and natural theology, as well as that of Church tradition; but if it wishes to remain "Christian" it will always have to make fresh assessments of its declarations by comparing them with the essential biblical data, the elucidation of which is precisely the task of biblical theology, itself based on well-founded exegesis. By supplying the raw material, biblical theology will remind dogmatics of its limits and will preserve it from falling into a subjectivism where the essential might be sacrificed to the accessory.

Among the other fields of study, the New Testament is obviously the one whose proper orientation depends on Old Testament knowledge. At the present time New Testament exegetes have very little sympathy for the opinion of Schleiermacher and Harnack, for whom the Jewish origin of Christianity was merely an accident. Knowledge of the Old Testament brings better understanding of the New Testament not through contrast alone, but on many points the New Testament message is completed by the Old Testament message. Christian ethics, piety and eschatology have found no better expression than the Decalogue, the Psalms and the words of the prophets. Yet it must not be forgotten that between the Old and the New Testament there is a theology represented by the apocryphal and pseudepigraphical literature whose influence on the New Testament could hardly be sufficiently emphasized. The inclusion of this literature in the study of Old Testament theology is admitted and widely practised by Catholic authors. In our opinion there should only be recourse to extra-canonical literature in altogether exceptional cases, for, either the apocryphal writers only reproduce in a less original and less clear form the affirmations of the Old Testament itself, and then it is pointless to refer to it, or they introduce into an idea, particularly in what concerns life after death, completely new elements which are no longer in agreement with the specific message of the Old Testament, and then they deserve treatment in a theology of Judaism.[1]

Old Testament theology will not be able to deal with all the questions that the Old Testament puts before us and it should not try to do so; drawing inspiration from all branches, it will not make the claim of being a possible substitute for them; faithful to its name, it will deal only with God and his relationship with man and the world. Piety, religious institutions and ethics are not part of Old Testament theology's specific domain.

This is the limitation which we have imposed in this present work, which makes no claim to be a "compendium" of the permanent or Christian values of the Old Testament. Two closely connected themes have come to our notice more forcibly than others, the themes of the *presence* and the *action* of God. The God of the Old Testament is a God who seeks to manifest his presence in order to be recognized as the sovereign Lord; that is why the fear of God is at the basis of all piety and all wisdom. But God also and especially seeks to manifest his presence in order to save man. A line not always straight, but none the less continuous, leads from the anthropomorphism of the earliest pages of the Bible, to the incarnation of God in Jesus Christ. God's action throws into relief the specifically Hebrew quality of that presence: the Old Testament does not bring us ideas about God, but acts of God, a God who leaves his transcendence to link his own destiny with the destiny of a people and through that people with the whole of humanity. A contemporary Jewish philosopher has given expression to this truth by saying that "the Bible is not the theology of

---

[1] This theology of Judaism will have to be written; at present the best synthesis in French is by J. Bonsirven, *Le judaïsme palestinien*, 2 vols., but the Qumran discoveries have brought to light fresh evidence on many doctrinal aspects of that period. The exclusion from our work of the apocryphal and pseudepigraphical writings does not imply that they have no place in the history of salvation. This subject goes beyond the framework of the Old Testament; thus the Essene sect of Qumran constitutes a very clear step towards the completion of that history, although the faith of this and of other similar groups was mainly nurtured by the books of the Old Testament.

man, but the anthropology of God "[1] a profound statement which, in our view, found its fulfilment in Christ and which will be made fully real at the time when there comes to pass what is said in that book of the last days, each term of the statement being drawn directly from the Old Testament: Ἰδοὺ ἡ σκηνὴ τοῦ θεοῦ μετὰ τῶν ἀνθρώπων, καὶ σκηνώσει μετ᾽ αὐτῶν, καὶ αὐτοὶ λαοὶ αὐτοῦ ἔσονται, καὶ αὐτὸς ὁ θεὸς μετ᾽ αὐτῶν ἔσται (Rev. 21.3).

BIBLIOGRAPHY

I. GENERAL WORKS

BAAB, O. J., *The Theology of the Old Testament*, Nashville 1949.

BURROWS, MILLAR, *An Outline of Biblical Theology*, Philadelphia 1946.

DAVIDSON, A. B., *The Theology of the Old Testament*, Edinburgh 1904.

DILLMANN, A., *Handbuch der alttestamentlichen Theologie*, ed. R. Kittel, Leipzig 1895.

EICHRODT, W., *Theologie des Alten Testaments*, 3 vols., Leipzig 1933-39.

GELIN, A., *Les idées maîtresses de l'Ancien Testament*, Paris 1948.

HEINISCH, PAUL, *Theologie des Alten Testamentes*, Bonn 1940.

HEMPEL, JOH., *Gott und Mensch im Alten Testament*, Stuttgart 1926.

IMSCHOOT, VAN P., *Théologie de l'Ancien Testament*, I. Dieu, Paris-Tournai 1954.

KOEHLER, L., *Theologie des Alten Testaments*, Tübingen 1936.

KOENIG, ED., *Theologie des Alten Testaments*, Stuttgart 1922.

OEHLER, G. F., *Theologie des Alten Testaments*, Tübingen 1873.

PIEPENBRING, C., *Théologie de l'Ancien Testament*, Paris 1886.

PROCKSCH, O., *Theologie des Alten Testaments*, Gütersloh 1950.

RIEHM, ED., *Alttestamentliche Theologie*, ed. K. Pahnke, Halle 1889.

ROBINSON, H. W., *The Religious Ideas of the Old Testament*, New York 1913.

ROWLEY, H. H., *The Unity of the Bible*, London 1953.

SCHULTZ, HERMANN, *Alttestamentliche Theologie. Die Offenbarungsreligion in ihrer vorchristlichen Entwicklungsstufe*, Frankfurt 1869.

SELLIN, E., *Alttestamentliche Theologie auf religionsgeschichtlicher Grundlage*. T.1, *Israelitisch-jüdische Religionsgeschichte*; T.2, *Theologie des Alten Testaments*, Leipzig 1933.

SNAITH, N. H., *The Distinctive Ideas of the Old Testament*, London 1944.

---

[1] Abraham Heschel, *Man is not alone. A philosophy of religion*. New York 1951, p. 129.

STADE, B., *Biblische Theologie des Alten Testaments*, Tübingen 1905.

TRESMONTANT, C., *Essai sur la pensée hébraïque*, Paris 1953.

VRIEZEN, T. C., *Hoofdlijnen der Theologie van het Oude Testament*, Wageningen 1949.

WRIGHT, G. E., *The Challenge of Israel's faith*, London 1946.
      God Who Acts, London 1952.

II. SPECIAL STUDIES

BAUMGÄRTEL, F., "Erwägungen zur Darstellung der Theologie des A.T." *ThLitztg*, 1951, p. 257.

BONWETSCH, N., "Das Alte Testament in der Geschichte der Kirche", *Allg. evang. luth. Kirchenzeitung*, 1923.

BORNKAMM, H., *Luther und das Alte Testament*, Tübingen 1948.

COPPENS, J., *Les harmonies des deux Testaments*, Paris 1949.

DANIÉLOU, J., *Sacramentum Futuri. Les origines de la typologie biblique*, Paris 1950.

DENTAN, R. C., *Preface to Old Testament Theology. Yale Studies in Religion*, New Haven 1950.

DIESTEL, L., *Geschichte des Alten Testaments in der christlichen Kirche*, 1869.

DODD, C. H., *The Bible To-day*, Cambridge 1946.
      According to the Scriptures, London 1952.

EICHRODT, W., "Hat die alttestamentliche Theologie noch selbständige Bedeutung innerhalb der alttestamentlichen Wissenschaft?" *ZAW*, 1929, p. 83.

EISSFELDT, O. ,"Israelitisch-jüdische Religionsgeschichte und alttestamentliche Theologie", *ZAW*, 1926, p. 1.

GOPPELT, L., *Typos* (Beiträge zur Förderung christlicher Theologie 43), 1939.

HEBERT, A. G., *The Authority of the O.T.*, London 1947.
      The Throne of David, London 1941.

IRWIN, W. A., "The reviving theology of the O.T.", *Journal of Religion*, 1945, p. 235.

LINDBLOM, J., *Zur Frage der Eigenart der alttestamentlichen Rel gion*, Werden u. Wesen des A.T., *BZAW* 66, 1936, p. 128.

NORTH, C. R., "Old Testament theology and history of the religion of Israel", *Scottish Journal of Theology*, 1949, p. 113.

PORTEOUS, N. W., "Towards a theology of the O.T.", *Scottish Journal of Theology*, 1947, p. 136.
      "Old Testament Theology" (in *The Old Testament and Modern Study*, edited by H. H. Rowley, Oxford 1951, p. 311).

RAD, VON G., "Grundprobleme einer biblischen Theologie des A.T." *ThLitztg*, 1943, p. 225.

ROST, L., "Zur Theologie des A. T. Eine Übersicht" *Christentum und Wissenschaft*, 1934, p. 121.

ROWLEY, H. H., *The Rediscovery of the Old Testament*, London 1945.

SMART, JAMES D., "The death and rebirth of Old Testament theology", *Journal of Religion*, 1943, pp. 1ff. and 125ff.

STAERK, W., "Religionsgeschichte und Religionsphilosophie in ihrer Bedeutung für die biblische Theologie des A.T.", *ZThK*, 1923, p. 289.

VISCHER, W., *Das Christuszeugnis des A.T.* French tr. vol. 1 La loi; vol. 2 Les premiers prophètes. English tr. vol. I, London 1949.

WEISER, A., *Die theologische Aufgabe der alttestamentlichen Wissenschaft*, Werden u. Wesen des A.T., *BZAW* 66, 1936, p. 207.

L'Ancien Testament et les chrétiens, ouvrage collectif (Rencontres 36), Paris 1951.

PART ONE

CHARACTERISTIC ASPECTS OF
THE GOD OF
THE OLD TESTAMENT

~~~~~~

I. THE LIVING GOD,
CENTRE OF REVELATION AND OF FAITH

WHAT gives the Old Testament its force and unity is the affirmation of the sovereignty of God. God is the basis of all things and all that exists only exists by his will. Moreover, the existence of God is never questioned; only fools can say, "There is no God" (Ps. 14.1; 53.2; Job 2.10); and even when the prophet Jeremiah speaks of the unfaithful Israelites who denied Yahweh by saying, "It is not he" (*lo hu*) (5.12) he does not intend to speak of those who disbelieve in God but of rebels who question his sovereignty. The passages which can be invoked as proofs of the existence of God are meant to lay stress on certain aspects which can be discussed, but the reality of God imposed itself with an evidence which passed beyond all demonstration. The knowledge of God in the sense of the awareness of divine reality—and not in the profounder sense the prophets will give to it—is to be found everywhere. The entire world knows God; not only Israel but all the peoples praise him; even nature has only been created to proclaim his power (Ps. 148.9-13). Even sin itself proclaims the existence of God by contrast, for it is either desertion from God or revolt against him; the sinner is a man who turns his back on God, but who does not dream of contesting his existence. The fact of God is so normal that we have no trace of speculation

37

in the Old Testament about the origin or the evolution of God:
whilst neighbouring religions present a theogony as the first step
in the organization of chaos, the God of the Old Testament is
there from the beginning. He does not evolve, and the various
names which are given him are those of originally independent gods
and do not mark phases of his development. The Old Testament
gives us no "history" of the person of Yahweh, who nevertheless
existed in another form before becoming the national God of the
Israelites, and the gods of the patriarchs only have a chronological
and not a genealogical connection with Yahweh. From the time
that Yahweh appears he is a major God whose eternity could be
affirmed (Ps. 90.2; 139.16), but the idea of eternity is secondary to
that of life. God is not living because he is eternal, but he is
eternal because he is living. The Israelite felt God as an active
power before positing him as an eternal principle. God is never a
problem, he is not the ultimate conclusion of a series of reflections;
on the contrary, it is he who questions and from whom the
initiative always comes. Strongly typical in this respect is the
sudden and unexpected appearance on the scene of history of the
prophet Elijah, who justifies his intervention simply by the words,
"Yahweh is living" (1 Kings 17.1). Just as life is a mysterious
reality which can only be recognized, so God is a power which
imposes itself on man and comes to meet him without his being
always prepared for it.

The expression "living God" ('el chay, 'elohim chayyim) has a
less deeply imprinted theological character than other formulae
such as holy God or God the King, and so we do not agree
with Baudissin[1] that it is of recent date and that it sprang into being
from the polemic of Yahwism against the cult of dying and rising
gods who claimed to have the monopoly of life, nor with L. Koehler[2]
that it sprang up as an answer to the criticism that God had neither
life nor power. To say of God that he was a living God was the
elementary and primordial reaction of man in face of the experience
of the power which, imposing itself on the entirety of his being,
could only be envisaged as a person, that is, as a living being. It
is to the power and succour of that person that the Israelites appeal

[1] In *Adonis und Eshmun*, Leipzig 1911, pp. 450ff. The expression "living God"
does not necessarily imply a relation to nature. Yahweh—to whom the title is given
more often than to El or Elohim—is living because he is bound to a social group,
which is a living reality *par excellence*.

[2] L. Koehler, *Theologie des A.T.*, p. 35.

when they are menaced in their own personal life, *chay Yahweh*,
and when Yahweh himself wishes to confirm by an oath the
dependability of his threats or promises he introduces it by the
affirmation of his life: "I am living, says the Lord Yahweh. . . . I
will make the effects of my oath fall upon his head" (Ezek. 17.19),
but also: "I am living, oracle of the Lord Yahweh, I have no
pleasure in the death of the wicked" (Ezek. 33.11).

Life is what differentiates Yahweh from other gods; before it is
expressed in a well formulated monotheism, the faith of Israel is
confident of the feebleness of the gods of the nations and contrasts
that weakness to the living God; the gods of the nations are stupid
and foolish while Yahweh is the true God and the living God (Jer.
10.9-10). Yahweh does not die: "Thou shalt not die" cries the
prophet Habakkuk[1] (1.12). The idea of God as living also implies
that Yahweh is the one who gives life: "As true as Yahweh lives,
who has given us this *nephesh*" (Jer. 38.16). It is because they
see in the Living One essentially the source of life that believers
regard as the supreme aspiration of piety the ability to approach the
living God (Ps. 42.3; 84.3); and finally it is belief in the living
God which will lead to the affirmation of victory over death.

From a literary point of view, faith in a living God attained its
best expression in anthropomorphic language; "the idea of a living
God," writes F. Michaeli, "gives to the anthropomorphism of the
Bible a significance quite other than that which applies to similar
expressions about pagan idols . . . it is because God is living that
one can speak of him as of a living man, but also in speaking of
him as of a human being one recalls continually that he is living."[2]
Anthropomorphism is found throughout the Old Testament; it
is by no means a "primitive" way of speaking of God and it easily
harmonizes with a highly spiritual theology, as, for example, in
Second Isaiah: God speaks (Gen. 1.3), hears (Ex. 16.12), sees
(Gen. 6.12), smells (1 Sam. 26.19), laughs (Ps. 2.4; 59.9), whistles
(Is. 7.18); he makes use of the organs suited to these functions:
he has eyes (Amos 9.4), hands (Ps. 139.5), arms (Is. 51.9; 52.10;
Jer. 27.5), ears (Is. 22.14), and feet (Nahum 1.3; Is. 63.3) which
he places on a footstool (Is. 66.1). His bearing is described with

---

[1] The actual form of the verse: "We shall not die" is due to a *tiqqun sopherim*
designed to correct the disrespect which the mere thought of the death of God
would involve.

[2] F. Michaeli, *Dieu à l'image de l'homme*, p. 147.

the help of the most realistic anthropomorphisms: he treads the wine-press like a grape-gatherer (Is. 63.1-6), he rides on the clouds (Dt. 33.26; Hab. 3.8), he comes down from heaven to see the tower of Babel and to scatter its builders with his own hands (Gen. 11.7), and he himself shuts the door of the ark behind Noah (Gen. 7.16). Figures of speech borrowed from military language are particularly frequent. Yahweh is a *gibbor* and an *'ish milchamah* (Ex. 15.3; Ps. 24.8; Zech. 9.13), because at the period which may coincide with the first age of settlement in Canaan war was the normal and even the only way for Yahweh to reveal himself.[1] Sometimes it is even the activity of animals which provides the term of comparison; when it is a matter of showing a terrifying aspect, the lion, the bear and the panther illustrate it in turn (Lam. 3.10; Hos. 5.14; 11.10; 13.7), and also the moth, which destroys more subtly but quite as surely (Hos. 5.12); yet the sacred character of animals in the majority of pagan religions was bound to hinder Israel from making too large a use of theriomorphism. Anthropomorphisms are accompanied by anthropopathisms: God feels all the emotions of human beings—joy (Zeph. 3.17), disgust (Lev. 20.23), repentance (Gen. 6.6) and above all jealousy (Ex. 20.5; Dt. 5.9).

There were mitigations of the anthropomorphism. Respect for divine transcendence led to the substituting for God of intermediaries for his communication with men, for example in the E editing of the J traditions, but it must be noted that these attenuations are attributable to ethical tendencies rather than to a spiritualizing for which the idea of a personal and present God was fundamentally unacceptable. Other limits to anthropomorphism are simply due to the fact that from the beginning Israel was aware that God was only partially the image of man. In the conception of God as a person Israel felt and expressed both the similarity and the separation, for such a person was felt not only as a different being but often indeed as a veritable obstacle; the " thou " who was God could say No! to the " I " of man, so that even while speaking of God in human terms account must be taken of the fact that one realized that between the two there was no common measure. God is not subject, like men, or at least not to the same extent as men, to changes of humour or feeling: " God

---

[1] G. von Rad, *Der Heilige Krieg im alten Israel*, 1951.

is not man, that he should lie, or a son of man, that he should repent. Has he said, and will he not do it? Or has he spoken, and will he not fulfil it? " (Num. 23.19). "I am God and not man" (Hos. 11.9); and then Isaiah summarizes the irreducible difference between God and man by the terms spirit and flesh (31.3), putting the opposition not between what is spiritual or corporeal, but between what is strong and what is feeble and ephemeral. Another limit to anthropomorphism is supplied by the very conception of man in Israel. According to the anthropology dominant in the Old Testament a man only exists as a member of a community, there is no isolated man, there are only *bene 'adam*, that is, participators in that great collective personality which is constituted by humanity and, more especially, Israel. But that idea of collective personality could not be applied to God: to exist and manifest his sovereignty, God has no need of the assistance of other beings; biblical anthropomorphism thus differentiates itself clearly from ancient anthropomorphism in general where the god is not only always associated with an attendant goddess, but where he is also surrounded by an entire court of equal or inferior personages like a human family. The Old Testament is unaware of any feminine partner to Yahweh, and Hebrew does not even possess any term for goddess and uses the ambiguous word *'elohim* (1 Kings 11.5, 33, Astarté *'elohe Sidonim*). Certainly it happened that, under the influence of the contemporary world and because of a very natural tendency of the human mind, the attempt was made to give a consort to Yahweh: Maacah, the mother of king Asa, made an idol which might serve as a feminine counterpart to Yahweh (1 Kings 15.13), and the Jews of the military colony of Elephantiné did not hesitate to associate with Yahweh the great Canaanite goddess under the name of Anat Yahu; but these are deviations which were never admitted within the framework of the orthodox faith which only knew a single consort of Yahweh, namely the people of Israel, but the union with the people is the result of an act of pure grace and in no way corresponds to a necessity of the natural order. Transcendence of sex is also shown in the absence of a son of God: the *bene ha'elohim* of Gen. 6.2 and of the prologue to Job are divine beings, but not sons in the proper sense. Finally, a last limit to anthropomorphism and one which clearly shows that anthropomorphism was unsuitable for expressing the divine personality in its fulness, is the prohibition of making a visual representation of Yahweh;[1] consistent anthropomorphism necessarily ends in plastic representations. Even if in the course of history the people of Israel sometimes had difficulty in keeping to the Mosaic order (Ex. 20.4, 22; Dt. 4.12, 15-18), it must be recognized that the prohibition on the making of images of the deity and adoring them (for an image of the divine is made to be adored) represents the main trend of Israelite religion. To make a representation of God means to desire to imprison him within certain limits and God was too great for anyone to be able for an instant to dream of setting a limit to what clearly never ceased, namely his life.

BIBLIOGRAPHY

EISSFELDT, O., "Mein Gott" im Alten Testament, ZAW, 1945-48, p. 3.
HEMPEL, JOH., "Jahwegleichnisse der isr. Propheten." ZAW, 1924, p. 74.
        "Die Grenzen des Anthropomorphismus Jahwes im Alten Testament", ZAW, 1939, p. 75.
MICHAELI, FR., Dieu à l'image de l'homme, Paris et Neuchâtel 1949.
OTTO, RUD., Aufsätze das Numinose betreffend, 2nd ed., p. 142.
VISCHER, W., "Words and the Word. The anthropomorphisms of the biblical revelation", Interpretation, 1949, pp. 1ff.

[1] As a God of nomadic origin and bound to a human society, Yahweh had no need like other gods of fashioned representations in animal or human form, though one must beware of equating nomadism with spirituality. But contact with the religion of Canaan, where the power of the image was very great, might have led the Israelites to use the same procedures sometimes to represent Yahweh, without there being necessarily in origin an act of infidelity. The fashioned image of a bull was not always an adoration of Baal; and the ephod itself, a human or closely human representation of Yahweh (cf. I Sam. 19.10ff.), could appear perfectly legitimate and even necessary for affirming the power of Yahweh. But as these attempts ultimately struck at the uniqueness of Yahweh and especially at his jealousy, a radical condemnation of all images and an insistent reminder of the Mosaic requirements was brought into operation.

II. THE DIVINE NAMES, AN EXPRESSION
OF THE LIVING GOD

A. EL-ELOHIM

THE Israelites form no exception to the general law of
primitive people in that they suppose that a person is concentrated in his name.[1] A man without a name lacks not
only significance but also existence (Gen. 2.18-23; 27.36). The
name is the bearer of a δύναμις which exercises a constraint upon
the one who bears it; in 1 Sam. 25.25 it is said of Nabal that he
is like his name, that is, he is a fool. But by virtue of this character
of δύναμις the name can also be separated from its bearer, be made
independent and even be employed against him. Since in the eyes
of the Israelites God was a power both dangerous and beneficent,
it was important to know his name. When the believer enters into
relationship with his god he starts by pronouncing his name, and
this ancient usage is continued in the liturgy of the Church under
the form of the invocation; similarly when God takes the initiative
of revealing himself he starts by uttering his name: Gen. 35.11;
Ex. 6.2; 33.18ff.

The generic name of God amongst all people of Semitic tongue,
except the Ethiopians, is expressed by the help of the root אֵל,
ilu, allah, etc. That root is interpreted in different ways, and the
time still appears remote when scholars will agree on its etymology.

(a) Some[2] attach to it a root expressing force, the root underlying
אָלָה and אֵלוֹן the oak, the typically strong tree and especially
the expression yesh be'el yadi = it is in the power of my hand, cf.
Gen. 31.29; Dt. 28.32; Mi. 2.1; Prov. 3.27; Neh. 5.5.

(b) Others[3] think the root to be אוּל = to be in front, to be the

---

[1] The fundamental study of the name remains that of O. Grether, *Name und Wort
Gottes im A.T.*, 1933, and more recently R. Criado, *Valor hipostatico del nombre
divine en el Antiguo Testamento*, Madrid 1953.

[2] Cf. amongst others E. Dhorme, *La religion des Hébreux nomades*.

[3] This is the etymology proposed by Noeldeke, "Elohim El", *Sitzungsber. der
preussischen Akademie der Wissenschaften*, 1882, pp. 1175ff., and more recently
by J. Starcky in *Archiv orientální*, "Melanges B. Hrozný", 1949, p. 383, and
"Abraham et l'histoire", *Cahiers sioniens*, 1951, p. 118.

first; the noun אַיִל = ram, would signify the one which goes at the head of a flock, and in the Temple at Jerusalem the front part of the structure bore the name of אוּלָם.

(c) אֵל might go back to the preposition אֶל = towards, and the two spring from a root אלי = to reach. Paul de Lagarde[1] thought that El was the one towards whom one moves, and Père Lagrange[2] saw there the one towards whom men's steps are directed in order to worship him.

(d) Procksch[3] associates El with the root אלל = to tie (cf. the Arabic *illun* = bond); according to him the meaning of El would be the one whose constraint cannot be thrown off. This last etymology is wrecked on the fact that the vowel of El (ilu) is always long; whilst that suggested by Lagarde seems far too fantastic and presumes a power of abstraction hardly conceivable for Semites.

It seems to us that the idea of power, involving also that of pre-eminence, most adequately expresses the reality designated by El: the mountains of El (Ps. 36.7), the cedars of El (Ps. 80.11), the stars of El (Is. 14.13), the army of Elohim (1 Chr. 12.22) and the wind of Elohim (Gen. 1.2) only express the idea of the divine as subordinate to that of power. What is powerful is divine; one of the most elementary experiences of the divine is that of a power on which, in varying degrees, man feels himself dependent.[4]

El designates any god, but alongside this use as a common noun we find the name El as the proper name of a particular deity. The existence of a particular god named El is not only important for the origins of the religion of Israel, but it raises the problem of a primitive Semitic monotheism. Formerly defended by Renan,[5] the thesis of an original monotheism has been upheld more recently and with more convincing arguments by scholars of such varied

---

[1] P. de Lagarde, *Übersicht über die Nominalbildung*, 1882, p. 170, defines El as " the goal of all human desire and all human striving ", a definition unfitting for the Semites and still more for the Israelites for whom it is always God who comes to encounter man.   [2] *Etudes sur les religions sémitiques*, p. 80.

[3] *NKZ* 1924, p. 20, and *Theologie des Alten Testaments*, p. 444.

[4] In his last (posthumous) work A. Bertholet defines the experience of God as that of a power which manifests itself in a dynamic material form or in a personal form (*Grundformen der Erscheinungswelt der Gottesverehrung*, 1953).

[5] *Histoire générale et système comparé des langues sémitiques* and *Nouvelles considérations sur le caractère général des peuples sémitiques et en particulier sur leur tendance au monothéisme*, 1859.

outlook as Andrew Lang, N. Söderblom,[1] R. Pettazzoni,[2] Father W. Schmidt[3] and Geo Widengren[4] and finally, and on the particular grounds of the religion of Israel, I. Engnell[5] believes that El, the supreme god of the Canaanites, was a "high god" who was worshipped in the whole of the west Semitic world under the names of El Shadday, El Elyon, Shalem and Hadad. According to this author, Yahweh would then be a parallel form of manifestation of this supreme god to whom Moses attributed a new activity. That would explain how the fusion of Yahweh with the different forms of Canaanite El took place so easily after the entrance of the Israelites into Canaan, since these gods had a common origin. In spite of the attractive appearance of this thesis, which would solve many problems, we do not think that it accurately corresponds to the historical process. Certainly the god El played a great part in Canaanite religion; in the Ugaritic texts we meet a definite tendency towards the supremacy of this god called *ab shnm*, father of years or father of mortals, *'ab 'adam*, father of humanity, *bny bnwt*, creator of creatures, and, the most significant title, *El bn el*, god of gods[6] (*ben* indicates here the category and not the relationship).

The god El is supreme, but the part played by El as a supreme god represents a terminus rather than a point of departure. Amongst west Semitic gods which had as their chief characteristic an attachment to a place (town, tree, mountain, spring), some, in virtue of their more privileged position, surpassed others to the point of temporarily eclipsing them or entirely absorbing them. That must have been the case of the local god of Jerusalem *El Elyon* = the very high god[7] who, as creator of the heavens and the

[1] *Das Werden des Gottesglaubens*, in French: *Dieu vivant dans l'histoire*, 1937.

[2] *Formazione e sviluppo del monoteismo nella storia delle religioni*, 3 vol. Rome 1922ff.; a summary in French of his principal contentions appeared in *RHR*, 1923, pp. 193ff.

[3] *Der Ursprung des Gottesidee*, 1926-1940.

[4] "Evolutionism and the problem of the origin of religion", *Ethnos*, 10, 1945, pp. 57-95, and *Hochgottglaube im alten Iran. Eine religionsphänomenologische Untersuchung*, Uppsala and Leipzig 1938.

[5] *Studies in Divine Kingship in the Ancient Near East*, p. 177 and *passim*.

[6] El bn el might also signify El the maker or creator of El. On the religion of El at Ugarit, cf. the very interesting monograph of O. Eissfeldt, *El im ugaritischen Pantheon* and the more recent work of M. Pope (cf. bibliography).

[7] The name Elyon can only describe one god as superior to others, which is still far from monotheism. As we knew from Philo of Byblos (Eusebius, *Praep. Evang.* I, 10) Ἐλιοῦν καλούμενος ὕψιστος had a very large diffusion, though it is almost

earth and master of the country to which he gives access only on condition that a tithe is offered, has collected in his own person all the functions elsewhere distributed among many deities. The evolution of polytheism towards monotheism, which we recognize in Canaanite religion from a very early period, must also have taken place *mutatis mutandis* among the ancient Israelites. The religion of the patriarchs was characterized, as in our opinion Albrecht Alt[1] and Julius Lewy[2] have decisively shown, by the cult of familiar gods associated with the individual or group of individuals who have chosen them for their protectors; that religion predisposed them to accept later on the cult of Yahweh who himself also had no local attachment and who was characterized by the covenant which he contracted with those faithful to him. The contact of the ancestral Israelite religion, at the head of whose pantheon was probably found Shadday,[3] with the Canaanite religion dominated by the figure of El, took place in many stages, of which the following outline only sets out to give the general lines:

(*a*) The first contact took place at the time of the patriarchs; between Shadday of the mountains and El the powerful there were so many points of contact that the fathers were able to feel relatively at home in the Canaanite environment.

(*b*) Yahweh, who became the God of the Israelites when they became a nation, quickly took the place of the gods of the fathers, who were far from being as demanding and jealous as he; but he was different, in the matter of nature and origin, from El and the Elim of the Canaanites, gods who were tied to nature. However, because of his jealousy he could not tolerate that creation and the maintenance of life should be reserved for other gods; so the settlement of the Israelites in Canaan leads to Yahweh's taking all the

certain that this term does not always apply to the same god; the Elyon which appears on an Aramaic stele of Sefiré (near Aleppo) in the eighth century is probably not identical with El Elyon of Jerusalem at the time of Melchizedek.

[1] *Der Gott der Väter*, 1929.

[2] "Les textes paléo-assyriens et l'Ancien Testament", *RHR*, 1934, pp. 1ff., J. Lewy insists, with reason, against A. Alt, on the tutelary character of the god El Shadday.

[3] The explanation of Shadday as "the mountain one" can be regarded as established (for the proof see Albright, "The names Shaddai and Abram", *JBL*, 1935, p. 173). Proofs supporting the antiquity of this name amongst the ancestors of the Israelites are supplied by its use in two ancient texts, Gen. 49.25 and Num. 24.4, 16, as well as by the names Shedeur, Zurishaddai, Ammishaddai in the list of proper names in Numbers 1; and so we think that the text of Exodus 6.3, where the priestly writer presents El Shadday as the first form of the appearance of Yahweh, rests on a very solid historical foundation.

functions retained until then by the god El or by Baal, his associate and then his successor.[1]

(c) In the third stage Yahweh, who has already taken the functions of El, will likewise take his name to show that there was no other god (el) besides himself. Yahweh will be called El or more often Elyon[2] which will link with the ancient title Shadday, a heritage of patriarchal religion; above all he will be called Elohim.[3] The substitution of this latter name for that of Yahweh, which took place systematically in the Pentateuch and the Psalter and occasionally elsewhere, carries an echo of this process of integration; integration could only have taken place at a time when the cult of El was sufficiently "Yahwistic" to present no danger of paganization and when the spiritual authority of Yahweh was strong enough for there to be no danger in his assuming a garb which was originally pagan or at least alien.[4] From the seventh century the name of El appears again frequently in the composition of proper names.[5] This process was natural, for at the time when Yahweh was established as being the only one with power it was necessary for him also to have the name El; the name Elohim which, out of the 2,550 occasions it is used in the Old Testament, designates sometimes the gods, sometimes one god amongst others, sometimes

[1] The prophet Hosea is the best witness of this change of prerogative of Yahweh (cf. Hos. 2.10). At that time El had recently yielded his place to Baal; but the substitution of Baal for El marked a downward step in religion by introducing a demoralizing mystical element, foreign to the cult of El.

[2] The title of Elyon given to Yahweh can sometimes have no other meaning than that of very high, but the fact that this appellation is chiefly met in the Psalms (46.5; 50.14; 73.11; 83.19; 87.5) seems to indicate some connection with the ancient local god of Jerusalem; it was a matter of proving that the god of Melchizedek was already identical with Yahweh, whence in the narrative in Genesis 14 the avowal put into the mouth of Abraham "Yahweh El Elyon" (v. 22), which seemed too bold to the authors of the Septuagint. It may be admitted that this is only one hypothesis, that certain rites of the cult of Elyon have penetrated into the cult of Yahweh in its Jerusalemite form, particularly rites associated with cosmic power, since this god was creator of the heavens and the earth.

[3] By giving to these gods the names ὕψιστος, παντοκράτωρ ἱκανός as a translation of she-day, he who is self-sufficient, translators have wished to obliterate their origin from secondary gods. The term Shadday is frequent in the book of Job, both out of a concern for archaism and also, it seems, through association with the root shadad, to destroy (cf. the same relation of Shadday with shadad in Is. 13.6; Joel 1.15), but this phenomenon of paronomasia cannot be invoked in favour of the etymology.

[4] One text which shows how Yahweh reunited in himself all the ancient deities is Ps. 91.1: "Dwelling under the shelter of Elyon, and abiding under the shadow of Shadday, I say to Yahweh: my refuge, my fortress, Elohay in whom I trust."

[5] Cf. M. Noth, Die israelitischen Personennamem, 1928.

the divine,[1] and lastly the sole legitimate God, expresses henceforward the totality of the divine reunited in one person. Nevertheless this name in its plural form, which is found as a term for one deity not only amongst the Israelites but also among the Phoenicians (elim)[2] and the Babylonians (ilani), seems to provide proof that the Semites experienced the divine as a plurality of forces and not as a unity which might later be broken up. So far as our knowledge goes, still very incomplete in spite of the mass of accumulated material, it seems the reunion of many gods into one belongs to a quite general tendency of which the supremacy of El at Ugarit and of El Elyon at Jerusalem are two expressions, but it seems just as probable that these superior—not to say unique—gods are again in their turn fragmented to satisfy the desire of piety to have gods at the disposal of man.[3]

B. YAHWEH

Yahweh is always a proper name and as such it carries a definite meaning. It is true that, according to one opinion, which invites serious consideration because of the authority of those who voice it, Yahweh in its primitive form *Yah* was only originally an interjection,[4] a kind of ejaculation uttered in moments of excitement and in connection with the moon cult; the complete name of Yahweh or Yahu would then be this interjection followed by the personal pronoun for the third person: O it is he . . .[5] This explanation, in support of which interesting parallels could be cited, makes it difficult, however, to account for the religious content which faith has always found in the name of God and of the revelatory value attached to the name. Could Yahweh be a foreign

---

[1] Elohim has the impersonal sense of divine in Ps. 36.2; 2 Chr. 20.29, *pachad Elohim*, a divine fear, i.e. a very strong fear.

[2] The word *elm* is only very rarely found in Ugaritic with a singular verb.

[3] Cf. Bertholet, *Götterspaltung und Göttervereinigung*, 1933. Even H. Ringgren, who defends original monotheism, recognizes the existence of a process of reunion of gods (*Word and Wisdom*).

[4] This opinion has been defended by G. R. Driver, *ZAW*, 1928, p. 24; by an analogous process the name of Bacchus came from Ιάκχειν, to cry ya, ya, cf. Movers, *Die Phönizier*, 1, 1841, p. 542.

[5] The connection of the personal pronoun *hu* with Yahweh in passages like 2 Kings 2.14 and Jer. 5.12 as well as the proper name Elihu could point us towards this etymology.

name borrowed by the Israelites? In spite of the attractiveness of many hypotheses, of which the one that attributes the name Yahweh to Kenites retains a certain measure of probability, it must be recognized that up to the present we have no attestation of Yahweh as a name for God outside Israel. Its occurrence in the Ugarit texts under the form *Yw'elt* which Dussaud interprets as Yahweh son of Elat, the wife of El, is far from certain.[1] As for the king of Hamath, Yaubidi, written in the same document as Ilubidi preceded by the ideogram for divine, he could well be a usurper of Israelite origin, the more so since we have from 2 Sam. 8.9ff. that from the time of David there were political connections between Israel and the kingdom of Hamath. But although the presence of Yahweh as a divine name is most doubtful outside Israel, the verbal form appears in the west Semitic name list from the time of Hammurabi;[2] names like *Yawi-ilu* and *Yawi-um* which figure in the Mari texts certainly show that the verb *hawah* was used to designate the existence of a god, and this information, although it does not settle the problem, indicates the direction which enquiry should take. Was the name Yahweh revealed to the children of Israel by Moses? Most certainly it was, according to the Elohistic narrative of Exodus 3; but we have several indications in the Old Testament according to which the name Yahweh may not have been an absolutely new revelation to Moses. Genesis relates that Enosh the son of Seth first invoked the name of Yahweh (4.26) and in the benediction of Noah upon his sons Yahweh is called the " god of Shem " (Gen. 9.26). It could then be that Yahweh was one of the gods worshipped by the Hebrew tribes, especially the Leah tribes, before their final settlement in Canaan; that would afford a solution of the problem of the name of Moses' mother *Yokebed* (Ex. 6.20; Num. 26.59) and perhaps that of Judah also, whose name could mean: Yahweh leads. The link between Yahweh and the gods of the patriarchs, upon which the narrative of Exodus insists, might not be entirely due then to the harmonizing attempts of redactors. All this leads us to assert that we do not have in the Exodus narrative the revelation of a

---

[1] In VI AB, col. 4, l.14 *sm bny yw elt* " the name of my son is Yw elt " (it is Ltpn who is speaking). Dussaud, *Les découvertes de Ras Shamra et l'A.T.*, 2nd ed., pp. 16ff., translates *Yw* son of Elat and uses this text to show the kinship of El and Yahweh. This single reference appears to us too slight to be able to lead to any positive conclusion.

[2] Dhorme, " Le nom du Dieu d'Israël ", *RHR* 1952, pp. 1ff.

new name but the explanation of a name already known to Moses which in that solemn hour is discovered to be charged with a content the richness of which he was far from suspecting.

The text of Exodus 3 attempts an explanation of the name Yahweh. Without claiming a scientific rigour which must never be expected in the etymologies of the Old Testament, it connects the divine name with the root *hawah* (Ar. *hawah*). According to what we now know by means of the proto-Aramaic names mentioned above, and by the example mentioned long ago by Wellhausen of the existence among the pre-Islamic Arabs of a god *Yaguth* = he helps,[1] the formation of a divine name by the help of the preformative " y " is by no means impossible. According to Albright,[2] basing his statements on Babylonian, Egyptian and Canaanite analogies, the name Yahweh could be a *hiphil* form of the verb *hawa*; more recently Obermann[3] believed he had found in the great Phoenician inscription of Karatepe a participial form with causative sense commencing in " y ", which would confirm the explanation of the form Yahweh as a *hiphil* and which would have the advantage of answering admirably to all that the Old Testament says of the function of Yahweh as creator of life and lord of history; but an important if not decisive objection is that the existence of the verb *hawah* in the *hiphil* is nowhere attested up to the present. At all events there seems to be growing unanimity in favour of abandoning the more fanciful explanations[4]

[1] Wellhausen, *Reste arab. Heidentums*, 1897, p. 22, mentions the existence of a god Yaghut and quotes the verse recorded by the chronicler Yaqut: " When will your help (*ghiyath*) come from the one who aids (*yaghut*)? " The Old Testament knows the proper name Ya'ush (Gen. 36.5, 14; 1 Chr. 7.10) which might be of Edomite origin.

[2] From the *Stone Age to Christianity*, p. 198 (cf. also *JBL*, 1924, p. 370), the name Yahweh may be the first part of a longer name: Yahweh asher yihweh or Yahweh zeh yihweh after the analogy of zeh sinai in Judges 5.5; he brings into existence what exists, *yahweh* having a causative sense. Albright reminds us that Dumuzi (Tammuz) is an abbreviated form of Dumu-zid-abzu, and Osiris of Osiris-onnophris.

[3] " The divine name Yhwh in the light of recent discoveries ", *JBL*, 1949, p. 301. The existence of the form *yqtl'nk* in a causative sense leads to the supposition that Yahweh was a mode of address before being a proper name and had significance as an epithet of the god of Israel: the one who establishes, who maintains; the words combined with Yahweh, as for example, *shalom, nissi* and particularly *tsebaoth*, could be understood simply as direct objects. But the use of the root *hawah* in a causative sense still remains problematical.

[4] Certain authors again seek the meaning of the name Yahweh outside the O.T. texts: H. Schrade, *Der verborgene Gott*, 1949, p. 37: " The interpretation varies between ' the almighty ', ' the one who descends (in fire) ', ' the destroyer '."

and to seek the origin of the name of the God of Israel in the root *hawah*. This demands a more careful examination of the text of Exodus (3.14). The construction employed, *'ehyeh 'asher 'ehyeh*, is not without parallel in the Old Testament. In several cases it expresses indetermination: 1 Sam. 23.13 *yithalleku be'asher yithallaku*: they will go wherever they are able to go; 2 Sam. 15.20 *'ani holek 'al 'asher 'ani holek*: I go I know not where; 2 Kings 8.1 *guri ba'asher taguri*: sojourn where you can; Ex. 4.13 *shelach na beyad tishlach*: send whom you will. At other times, particularly when it is God who is speaking, this form of expression is a way of giving additional intensity to the phrase: Zech. 10.8 *rabu kemo rabu*: they shall be as many as they were; Ex. 33.19 *chanoti 'et 'asher 'achon*: I will show mercy on whom I will show mercy, that is to say, I will indeed show mercy to the one who is its object; Ezek. 12.25 *'ani Yahweh 'adabber 'et 'asher 'adabber*: I. Yahweh, speak truly what I speak.

It is particularly in the light of these two last passages that we must understand the Exodus text: it is not a rebuff that Yahweh gives to Moses,[1] rather he wishes to insist on the fact that he is indeed what he is and that he truly accomplishes what he says. Doubtless God's refusal to entrust his name to a mere mortal, by saying to him: my name does not concern you, would be on the line of general teaching in the Old Testament on the subject of the hidden and transcendent God, but in the particular situation of our text Moses is not a mere mortal but the one who bears to the people the revelation which will make them the people of God, and for the accomplishment of this mission he needs precise information. What then is the new element which God reveals to Moses by reminding him of his name? Since the name is the expression of the living God it must make evident one of the aspects of that life; El expresses life in its power, Yahweh expresses life in its continuance and its actuality. Yahweh is indeed he who is. It must not be supposed from the

---

[1] Father Dubarle, *RScPhTh*, 1951, *art. cit.*, arrives at the conclusion that the text of Exod. 3.14 constitutes a refusal on the part of God, who cannot compromise his liberty to the extent of consenting to reveal his name at the request of a mere mortal; the same position, though with more subtlety, is held by G. Lambert, *NRTh*. 1952, pp. 897ff. We do not think that the revelation of the name abolishes the mystery, one might even say that it increases it, since in God's case the giving of his name does not place him at the disposal of man, but reveals a presence before which man can only tremble.

little grasp which the Israelites had of abstract ideas that they were incapable of understanding the reality of being and it is not attributing to them a metaphysics too highly developed when we imagine they could define God as "he who is" over against things which are temporary—the succession of days and seasons, the verdure of the desert which grows and withers, flocks which are born and die, the successive generations, men whose bodies return to the dust. The Old Testament is full of statements about the eternity of Yahweh as over against the ephemeral character of all created things (Ps. 90.1; 102.27-28), the God of Israel does not die (Hab. 1.12), the terms eternity and Yahweh are sometimes even synonymous, thus we read in Lev. 11.15; 18.5; 19.2; Num. 3.13 a certain number of exhortations which end with the words *ani Yahweh* and in Ex. 30.8; Lev. 3.17; 6.11 comparable exhortations are motivated by the fact that they are a perpetual law, *choq 'olam*, a parallelism which seems to us significant for the relation of Yahweh with *hawah*. However, it is not the idea of eternity which is primary when the Israelites pronounce the name Yahweh, but that of presence. Like all the other Israelite concepts, existence is a concept of relation, that is to say, it is only real in connection with another existence. God is he who is *with* someone; in the passage immediately preceding the revelation of the name, God says to Moses: *ki 'ehyeh 'immak* = for I will be with you (Ex. 3.12) and the same formula reappears in many other texts where the promise is presented as a revelation: Gen. 28.20; Jos. 3.7; Jg. 6.12, etc. The idea of relation is perhaps implied by the optative form of Yahweh, *Yahu*[1] which enters into the composition of numerous proper names in the sense of a wish: that it may be. It is evidently not being that is desired for Yahweh, whose existence was never discussed, but his effective presence near the individual or amongst his people. To make the people aware of the presence of Yahweh in their midst was exactly the task committed to Moses. Until then the tribes only maintained unity by the very loose bond of a common origin already a far distant memory, and opposing interests which show themselves in every Semitic society as soon as its clans become a little too numerous tended to dissociate them,

[1] Nothing authorizes us to see in *Yahu* the primitive form, since the tetragrammaton appears already in the ninth century in the inscription of Mesha (1.18). Use of the tetragrammaton in the *ostraca* of Tell ed Duweir (Lachish) at the beginning of the sixth century makes equally impossible the thesis which would oppose Yahu, used in common speech, to Yahweh, reserved for liturgical use.

the more so as the sojourn in Egypt tended to cause forgetfulness of the ancestral heritage. "To rally them a God was needed whose omnipotence they had experienced, who was for them as a rallying banner round which their unity might be effectively recovered. This is what Yahweh will henceforth be for Israel, and so Moses will give him the significant epithet: *Yahweh nissi* = Yahweh my banner (Ex. 17.15)."[1] Yahweh, because he is the God capable of being with someone,[2] and that in a more complete sense than the tutelary and family gods of the patriarchs, becomes the God of the people to which he is joined by a covenant. Israelite tradition is unanimous in affirming that Yahweh is the God of Israel, that he is only truly Yahweh from the time when that religious community called Israel was constituted, that is, since the Exodus from Egypt (Hos. 12.10). The priority of presence over existence gives a new and unexpected aspect to all the interventions of Yahweh; the presence of Yahweh corresponds each time to a new approach and the prophets stigmatize as a grave illusion the faith of those who interpreted the "God is with us" in the sense of a definite and inalienable possession. The approach of Yahweh always signifies punishment or blessing, usually both at once. Particularly with the prophet Ezekiel this double action of Yahweh is found expressly connected with his name. The statement "you shall know that I am Yahweh" is made in connection with judgment: 6.13; 7.27; 11.10; 12.16; and on the contrary, it marks a promise in 34.3; 37.13, 14, 27. It has been thought possible to trace back this double activity of Yahweh to the common denominator of the divine jealousy;[3] jealousy is in fact one of the specific marks of this God whose presence never leaves man in repose and who always supervenes either in moments of distress to save man or when man behaves as if there were no such presence.

There is, however, one moment when this double activity of Yahweh will manifest itself with unique clarity; that will be at the great dramatic finale.

[1] A. Vincent, *La religion des Judéo-Araméens d' Eléphantine*, p. 59.

[2] Just in the same way it is the idea of relation which is implied by the translation of Martin Buber: "*Ich werde da sein, als der ich da sein werde.*" Dhorme, *art. cit.*, in referring to the *to be or not to be* of Hamlet, seems to us to attach too much importance to existence, which for the Israelites was neither a problem nor a mystery.

[3] Cf. particularly J. Haenel, "Jahwe" in *NKZ*, 1929, p. 614: "One might expect that the conception of jealousy embraced by the name of Yahweh represents the most characteristic feature of the early Israelite idea of God."

It is not, in fact, too rash to assume a relation between the name Yahweh and the origin of eschatology,[1] for a God who defines himself as "I am" does not rest until that being and that presence are actualized in their perfection. Second Isaiah, who with Ezekiel is the theologian of the name Yahweh, shows its eschatological bearing by defining Yahweh as the first and the last: "I, Yahweh, am the first and I will yet be with the last!" (Is. 41.4). "I am the same, I am the first, I will also be the last" (Is. 48.12).   In these passages the expression: *'ani-hu,* I am he, is, it would appear, the best commentary on Exodus 3.14 where the revelation of a God is found who in speaking of himself says: I am (*'ehyeh*) and of whom men affirm: he is (*yihyeh*). With Second Isaiah, the most accomplished theologian amongst the writers of the Old Testament, we witness the full flowering of all the potentialities contained in the name of Yahweh: the only genuine existence as over against that of idols which are nothing, a complete presence since the ends of the earth shall see him, an eternal presence since it knows no end (Is. 49.6, 26).

Yahweh Tsebaoth

This name occurs 279 times in the Old Testament, though with a very variable frequency according to the various books. Totally absent from the Pentateuch, Joshua and Judges, the title appears only 11 times in the books of Samuel and 8 times in Kings; on the other hand, it is frequent in the prophets: we find it 54 times in Isaiah 1-39, 77 in Jeremiah, 10 in Amos, 14 in Haggai and 44 in Zechariah 1-8, 15 times in the Psalms and 6 times only in Second Isaiah. In addition to the usual expression Yahweh Tsebaoth, we meet the more complete form *Yahweh 'elohe hatsebaoth* (Hos. 12.6; Amos 3.13; 6.14) and *Yahweh 'elohe tsebaoth* (2 Sam. 5.10; 1 Kings 19.10; Jer. 5.14; Ps. 89.9). Naturally it must be asked what are these armies of which Yahweh is the head? Three equally possible interpretations share the favour of scholars: (*a*) they are the earthly armies of the Israelites; (*b*) they are the armies of the stars; (*c*) they are the celestial armies of spirits and angels. From the frequency and the context of the

[1] On the relation between the name Yahweh and eschatology, cf. amongst others L. Dürr, *Die isr. Heilandserwartung,* p. 52.

expression it is possible to extract the following conclusions: (*a*) in the historical books the expression is found in connection with the ark of the covenant (2 Sam. 6.2, 18; 7.2, 8, 26-27; 1 Chr. 17.7). Now originally at any rate the ark was a palladium of war, as the ancient invocation at the moment of the departure for battle shows: whenever the ark was lifted it was said, "Arise, Yahweh, and let thy enemies be scattered" (Num. 10.35). It therefore seems, in spite of the contrary opinion of B. N. Wambacq,[1] that the relation between Yahweh Tsebaoth and the ark must be upheld; the association of Yahweh Tsebaoth with the armies of Israel is moreover formally stated in 1 Sam. 17.45 *Yahweh 'elohe ma'arekoth Israel*; now the term *ma'arekoth* always denotes armies ranged for battle; (*b*) the term is found with maximum frequency among the prophets for whom Yahweh was definitely other than a national God and above all other than a warrior God. It might be concluded that the prophets have transposed the term from the terrestial to the celestial plane;[2] yet it is more exact to say that for the prophets the expression *Yahweh Tsebaoth* refers to the totality of forces over which Yahweh asserts his rule. The Assyrian title *sar kissati*, given to kings and gods, is an interesting analogy. Yahweh is lord of all, and this explains the use of the expression by men with a universal outlook; but the universalism of Yahweh is itself a result of the dynamism which could not be better expressed than by a term borrowed from the language of war, though faith had long abandoned a warrior ideal; (*c*) nevertheless it remains possible that alongside this essential aspect the prophets saw in the use of the expression a polemical point directed against the spread of the cult of the stars and of spirits which were thought to animate them, and in face of which it had to be affirmed that Yahweh was the only lord of the army of the heavens. But the best way of neutralizing these powers was to integrate them into the being of Yahweh, the only lord. According to one of the most recent explanations of the name, *Yahweh Tsebaoth* is meant to translate Yahweh the sebaothic, that is to say, he whose power is like that of the summation of all armies.[3]

[1] *L'épithète divine Jahvé sebaot, étude philologique, historique et exégétique*, 1947.
[2] Cf. G. von Rad, *Der heilige Krieg im alten Israel*.
[3] This thesis had been upheld by O. Eissfeldt who translates Yahweh *der Zebaothhafte* or *der Gott der Zebaotheit*, in *Miscellanea Academica Berolinensia*, 1950, pp. 128-150.

C. OTHER TITLES OF THE GOD OF ISRAEL:
BAAL — ADON — MELEK — AB

When these titles are met with as epithets of Yahweh they present no particular problem, but when they occur independently we have the right to ask whether under these names there is not hidden some primitive deity different from the God of Israel and assimilated by him.

Baal

In the root *ba'al* there are two correlative notions always mingled, that of ownership and that of lordship, and these two notions are common both to the profane and the religious usage of the term. Calling a husband the baal of his wife is to be understood as saying that he is her owner and her lord. A god called baal is essentially the owner and hence the master of such and such a place or man; thus the name baal is generally found compounded with the name of a city or mountain or spring; and so we have the baal of Lebanon, the baal Tsaphon, the baal and baalah of Gebal. Even if in these names baal refers to an obviously localized god whose power does not extend beyond the limits of a clearly defined place, there are cases where Baal is used as the proper name of a god whose local attachments were hard to define precisely. To see in the cult of Baal a multitude of local gods with certain features in common is no doubt true enough, but it only covers part of the reality contained in the name Baal. The existence of a supreme Baal is shown by numerous testimonies, the most ancient of which goes back at least to the twelfth century and concerns the Baal of the heavens,[1] *ba'al shamayim*, whose supremacy is comparable to that of El. This baal shamayim was widespread in the whole west Semitic area; it is probably also of him that the Ugarit texts speak. These, according to Dussaud, are the characteristics of this god Baal, who was probably identical with the Aramaean god Hadad whose sky aspect seems quite obvious: "Although sometimes he destroys crops, he also makes them fertile; he dispenses abundance and life. To these

---

[1] The earliest reference to Baal Shamayim is that of the inscription of Yechimilk of Byblos in which this god figures in the leading position before the Baal of Byblos and the other holy gods of the city. Cf. the study by O. Eissfeldt in *ZAW*, 1939, p. 1.

functions he adds those of a warrior god and of lord of the under-world. He has the power of divination, he judges and, with Shamash, he fixes destiny.''[1] Just as for El, Baal is met with as a qualification of certain gods and that throughout the Semitic world, and also as the proper name of a god whose prerogatives were those of a supreme god. Both in nature and function *Baal Shamayim* and *El Elyon* must have been quite similar; the local god of Shechem is sometimes called Baal berith (Jg. 8.33; 9.4), sometimes El berith (Jg. 9.46), which would not be possible if Baal and El represented two conflicting entities. We can therefore assume that the contact of Yahweh with Baal followed an analogous process to that of his encounter with El. The former took place without a clash; the title of Baal was very suitable for tutelary deities[2] of the patriarchal age and Yahweh as he appears in the Song of Deborah (Jg. 5.3-5) shares with the Baal of Ugarit the terrifying character of a storm god. Thus by giving to Yahweh the title of Baal, the ancient Israelites saw not only a way of expressing the realities of sovereignty and of the covenant, but an opportunity of integrating into the cult of Yahweh the positive values of the great Semitic deity. Genuine worshippers of Yahweh bear names compounded of Baal, for example Yerubaal, a name in which the theophoric element probably indicates the god wor-shipped by this person; and the theophoric element also figures in the names of descendants of Saul and David, Eshbaal, Meribaal Baalyada (Elyada in 2 Sam. 5.16) (1 Chr. 8.33; 9.39; 14.7). In general, the testimony of proper names, apart from that of Baalyah (1 Chr. 12.6) does not enable us to conclude whether in the first instance Yahweh is meant by Baal or the Canaanite god assimilated by him; but in any case the coexistence within the same family of names involving Yahweh and Baal proves that no serious con-tradiction was felt between Yahweh and Baal.[3] Through contact with Canaanite cults, with their mythology developed to a point which perhaps betokens degeneracy in relation to more ancient

[1] Dussaud, *Les découvertes de Ras Shamra-Ougarit et l'A.T.*, 2nd ed., p. 99.

[2] The name baal indicates a bond of parentage and is consequently not alien to a religion where the deity was regarded as a parent of the believer. By classifying gods into master-gods and parent-gods, Dhorme (*Rel. des Hébreux nomades*) has thrown much light upon a region which is yet far from fully explored.

[3] The gods El and Baal followed an inverse development; the former becomes depersonalized and little by little loses substantiality; at Ugarit, El is already on the way to becoming a *deus otiosus*; while Baal reaches his apogee towards the ninth century, at any rate in the geographical horizon of the Israelites.

forms, and with their immoral practices, the alliance of Yahweh and Baal appeared dangerous. In the coexistence of the two gods it was Yahweh who ran the risk of being vanquished, for in an agrarian civilization Baal enjoyed clear superiority and also the right of priority to Yahweh the desert God. The prophets proclaimed in vain that since Yahweh had given the children of Israel the land of Canaan, it was he also gave the rain and the harvests (cf. Hos. 2.10), they had difficulty in turning the people from the cult of the baals who answered so much better to the instincts of popular piety. Although a powerful god might tolerate the proximity of Baal, it is not the same with a jealous god, and by insisting on this aspect of Yahweh the prophets Elijah and Hosea, a century later, opposed all compromise. It will no more be said to Yahweh: "you are my baal, but you are my 'ish'', this latter term allowing no equivocation (Hos. 2.10, 15, 19; 13.1). Nevertheless the prophet Hosea, although violently opposing baalism, adopted the mystic note of the union of the god with the believer and applied it to Yahweh without, of course, leaving the ground of the historic covenant; and this element of divine tenderness is more a heritage of the Canaanite baals than a characteristic mark of the God of Sinai. The preaching of the prophets succeeded in making the name Baal disappear from the list of proper names, where it was henceforth replaced by that of Yahweh or of El, the Canaanite god of this name having long lost his active rôle and being no more a rival to Yahweh. The name Baal will even inspire such horror that it will be eradicated from the names in which it figured and will be replaced by the term boshet = shame (2 Sam. 11.21; 2.8; 4.4). This radicalism was salutary because it safeguarded the integrity of the religion of Israel and prevented the people from losing, through the disintegrating influence of the cults of Baal, the feeling of its cohesion; but that does not mean that popular piety did not retain a certain nostalgia for the name Baal; so the prophet of the exile is to remind those who regret the disappearance of Baal that "your Maker is your Baal: Yahweh Tsebaoth is his name" (Is. 54.5).

Adon

Contrary to Baal, the term *Adon* was used, at least in the biblical period, only as a divine epithet and its use, more restricted than that of Baal, is limited to the Canaanite and Israelite background. The etymology of the word remains uncertain, but the geographical area over which it is distributed seems to suggest a borrowing from some pre-Semitic population of Canaan. Wherever we meet it it has the meaning of lord. Rarely used absolutely (Mal. 3.1; Ps. 12.5; 114.7), it is on the other hand frequently in the vocative *'adoni*: it was thus that a subordinate addressed his superior, whether orally or in writing. Therefore this title speaks less of what the deity is in himself than of what he represents to someone who addresses him. Adon was destined to have a great future because under the form *'adonay* (literally, my lords or thy lordship, intensive plural) it replaced the now ineffable name of Yahweh. This substitution took place under the influence of the stress on divine transcendence and it found expression in the translation of the divine name by κύριος in the LXX version. But for those who remembered its original meaning the term *Adon* was a reminder that in spite of his transcendence God entered into relation with the faithful and heard their prayer.

Melek

The term *Mlk* is also met with as a title and as a proper name. The existence of a god Mlk is attested among both the eastern and western Semites. Among the latter the best known are Milkom, which is the name Mlk followed by a mem in place of the article, the national god of the Ammonites, and Melqart, the king of the city of Tyre. Applied to Yahweh this title served, in certain situations, to express the specific content of faith in Israel's God: many exegetes, following especially S. Mowinckel, have seen in the kingship of Yahweh the central theme of the Old Testament;[1] following a parallel line, Martin Buber has defined the religion of Israel as that of the kingship of Yahweh.[2] In fact, the ideas of power, presence and permanence contained in the name Yahweh are made concrete in the term *mlk* and in its various nominal and verbal derivatives. But as this term was employed as well and indeed chiefly for the earthly king, its religious use varied with the fluctuations undergone by the kingly office and by the ideology of kingship within Israel.

[1] *Psalmenstudien II.*
[2] *Das Königtum Gottes.*

(*a*) Originally the term *mlk* is used of a chief or counsellor; this meaning appears in Micah 4.9: "Is there no king in thee, and has thy counsellor (*yo'ets*) perished?" It is found amongst the early Arabs who did not know any royal régime and also in Assyria under the form *maliku,* when the royal office is expressed by the root *sharru.* The conclusion which logically follows is that the title of Melek given to Yahweh is not linked to the adoption by the Israelites of a monarchic régime; also certain texts where Yahweh is called king may very well be of earlier date than the time of the monarchy, for example Ex. 15.18; Num. 23.21; 24.7; Dt. 33.5.

(*b*) The adoption of the monarchy acted both as an accelerator and a brake upon the use of the title Melek for Yahweh. According to one tendency, the importance of which Buber has underlined, the kingship of Yahweh was thrown into relief by kingship on the human level, considered as an act of infidelity (Jg. 8.23; 1 Sam. 8.7). Just as for *Adon* the cult seems to have been the terrain preferred by the title Melek; the two principal attestations which are certainly pre-exilic and contemporary with the monarchy, Is. 6.5 and Ps. 24.7ff., are clearly placed in a cultic setting. Outside the cultic sphere, which always shows a greater power to conserve the past, the title of Melek was rather avoided. The prophets hardly use it, probably less because of a concern to avoid associating with the holy and unique name of Yahweh a title overmuch tainted by humanity, than to differentiate themselves from the false prophets who made a good deal of the God-King in their own announcement of salvation (Mic. 2.13; 4.7; Zeph. 3.15; Jer. 51.57). In addition, the existence of a god named Melek (LXX Moloch) to whom child sacrifices were made and whose cult found fervent devotees at the very gates of Jerusalem, must have aroused as much revulsion from the use of the term as in connection with Baal—a point already made.[1]

(*c*) After the disappearance of the kingdom the title of Melek

---

[1] The existence of this god Mlk has been contested by O. Eissfeldt who has thought it possible to prove, chiefly by means of certain Carthaginian inscriptions, that the expression *lmlk* did not mean "to Mlk" but "in votive offering"; we must probably interpret in the light of this discovery such texts as Lev. 20.2 and Jer. 32.25 in which Yahweh may be the object of human sacrifices, as is similarly suggested by other texts, e.g. Mic. 6; while on the other side, when it is a question of playing the harlot after Mlk (Lev. 20.5) it seems difficult not to see in mlk the proper name of a god.

applied to Yahweh saw a new lease of life. The theme of the kingship of Yahweh which had suffered an eclipse, so far as the name only was concerned, becomes dominant in Second Isaiah and in numerous Psalms which he influenced more or less directly (cf. Is. 52.7; Ps. 29.10; 93-99; 84.4, etc.). It is by the formula "Your God has become king",[1] modelled upon that used to announce the installation of a new sovereign, that the prophet announces the inauguration of Yahweh's reign. Henceforward the eschatological sense which had never been alien to the title becomes dominant: Yahweh will be king not only of his own people who will know the fulfilment of the revelation which has been entrusted to them, but also of other peoples whose gods will collapse before the splendour of his kingship. It is under this form that the idea was perpetuated in Judaism: the books of Daniel and Chronicles insist on the theme of God as king (1 Chr. 29.11; Dan. 3.33; 4.31, 34). That eschatological orientation gave all the more force to the affirmation of the present kingship of Yahweh as it was set forth in the various institutions of the Torah.

Ab

It is true that only Christianity has made the fatherhood of God the centre of religion, though that idea comes to it by direct descent from the Old Testament: Jer. 3.4: "Now thou callest me my father"; Jer. 31.9: "I am a father to Israel"; Is. 63.16: "It is thou, Yahweh, who art our father". In this passage divine fatherhood is put in contrast to that of the "fathers" of the nation. Is. 64.8: "Yahweh, thou art our father, we are the clay and thou art the potter who didst fashion us".

But whilst in Christianity the fatherhood of God is shown in his love, it is in the Old Testament an expression of his lordship. The relation of son to father is one of obedience: Ahab says to Tiglath Pileser, "I am thy servant and thy son" (2 Kings 16.7); or that of service, "A son honours his father, and a servant his

---

[1] The expression *Yahweh malak*, particularly frequent in Psalms 95-100, has no well marked temporal meaning: Yahweh has become king, or: Yahweh will be king (prophetic perfect); it can be understood of the past, present or future kingship of Yahweh and therefore affords too slender a basis for exact historical reconstructions. It is also important to notice that in that formula the accent lies upon Yahweh and not upon malak: it is Yahweh and none other who is king (cf. L. Koehler, *Syntactica V.T.*, 1953, p. 188).

master. If then I am a father, where is the honour due to me? "
(Mal. 1.6, cf. Mal. 3.17). The title of father given to one or more
gods is met with in the whole Semitic world, whether it concerns
a father of gods or a father of men. In the Old Testament, 'ab as
a theophoric element is found in proper names such as Abichayl,
Abiyah, Abram, Abner, Eliab, Yoab. As in the case of Baal it
can be asked whether under the element 'ab there is not sometimes
hidden another god, who belonged to the Israelite pantheon before
the exclusive adoption of the cult of Yahweh. Yet it is more
important theologically to know whether this divine paternity is
to be understood in a realistic or in a metaphorical sense. The use
in Hebrew of the word 'ab in a very wide sense, as a term for
priest, prophet or benefactor, might suggest that it should be
understood in an exclusively metaphorical sense, but it is the realist
interpretation which must be retained when the term is applied to
Yahweh: Yahweh is called father not because he has certain
qualities normally connected with this title but because he is the
sole genuine creator of his people and of the faithful who make up
the people; the figure of the clay and the potter well shows this
realist character. We must notice that the Israelites only rarely give
to Yahweh the title father when they address him and that only
rarely do they call themselves sons of Yahweh. It is rather
God who designates himself as father by calling the Israelites his
sons. That prevented any mysticism based upon a bond of physical
parentage between God and man.

Various titles

The other titles given to the God of Israel are figures of speech,
often very suggestive and interesting in the history of piety but
furnishing no new theological information. Amongst these various
titles, however, it is fitting to mention specially the designation of
God as the rock, *tsur*, which from simple metaphor tends to become
sometimes a genuine proper name: "Thou, O my Rock, hast
established him for correction" (Hab. 1.12) and: "The Rock, his
works are perfect . . . El is faithful and without iniquity" (Dt.
32.4, cf. verses 31 and 37). It is possible that we have here a survival of the worship of divine power enclosed within the sacred
stones, or, on a re-reading of these texts, in the Jerusalem temple.
Other titles, such as judge, witness, shepherd, physician, are to be

placed on the same level as the comparison of God with certain material objects or natural phenomena, like a sword, wall, fire, spring, etc. But the multiplicity of these designations is an illustration of the activity of the living God who is always so near to man that the latter is unable to think of God otherwise than in his own image.

BIBLIOGRAPHY

A. EL-ELOHIM

ALBRIGHT, W. F., "The names Shaddai and Abram", *JBL*, 1935, p. 173.
ALT, A., *Der Gott der Väter*, 1929.
BAUER, H., "Die Gottheiten von Ras Shamra", *ZAW*, 1933, p. 81 & 1935, p. 54.
EISSFELDT, O., *El im ugaritischen Pantheon, Berichte über die Verhandl. der sächs Akad. d. Wissensch. Phil.-hist. Kl.* 98, 4, Berlin 1950.
HEHN, J., *Die biblische und die babylonische Gottesidee*, Leipzig 1913.
KLEINERT, P., "El", *BZAW*, 1918, p. 59.
LAGRANGE, M. J., "El et Yahwé", *RB*, 1903, p. 362.
LEVI DELLA VIDA G., "El Elyon in Genesis 14.18-20", *JBL*, 1944, p. 1.
MAY, H. G., "The God of my Father. A study of patriarchal religion", *Journal of Bible and Religion*, 1941, p. 155.
MORGENSTERN, J., "The divine triad in biblical mythology", *JBL*, 1945, p. 13.
NIELSEN, D., *Ras Shamramythologie und biblische Theologie*, Leipzig 1936.
NÖLDEKE, TH., *Elohim, El*, 1882.
NYBERG, H. S., "Studien zum Religionskampf im A.T.", *ARW*, 1938, p. 329.
POPE, MARVIN H., *El in the Ugaritic Texts, Supplements to Vetus Testamentum* 2, Leiden 1955.
PROCKSCH, O., "El", *NKZ*, 1924, p. 20.
STARCKY, J., "Le nom divin El", *Archiv orientální Mélanges Hrozný*, 1949, p. 383.

B. YAHWEH

DHORME, ED., "Le nom du Dieu d'Israël", *RHR*, 1952, p. 5.
DRIVER, G. R., "The original form of the name Yahweh. Evidence and conclusion", *ZAW*, 1928, p. 7.

DUBARLE, A. M., "La signification du nom de Yahweh", *RScPhTh*, 1951, p. 3.

EISSFELDT, O., "Neue Zeugnisse für die Aussprache des Tetragramms als Jahweh", *ZAW*, 1935, p. 59.

FREDRIKSSON, H., *Jahwe als Krieger*, Lund 1945.

HÄNEL, J., "Jahwe", *NKZ*, 1929, p. 610.

KÖNIG, ED., "Die formell genetische Wechselbeziehung der beiden Worte Jahwe und Jahu", *ZAW*, 1897, p. 172.

KUHN, K. G., "Über die Enstehung des Namens Jahwe", *Orient Studien Enno Littmann*, Leiden 1935, p. 25.

LAMBERT, G., "Que signifie le nom divin YHWH?" *NRTh*, 1952, p. 897.

LANGHE, DE R., "Un dieu Yahweh à Ras Shamra?" *Bulletin d'histoire et d'exégèse de l'A.T.* No. 14, p. 91, Louvain 1942.

MAAG, V., "Jahwes Heersharen", *Festschrift L. Köhler*, Berne 1950, p. 27.

MURTONEN, A., "The appearance of the name YHWH outside Israel", *Studia orient. soc. or. Fennica XVI* 3, Helsinki 1951.

OBERMANN, J., "The divine name YHWH in the light of recent discoveries", *JBL*, 1949, p. 301.

NYSTRÖM, S., *Beduinentum und Jahwismus*, Lund 1946.

VRIEZEN, TH. C., "Ehyeh asher ehyeh", *Festschrift A. Bertholet*, 1950, p. 498.

WAMBACQ, B. N., *L'épithète divine Yahweh sebaoth*, Paris-Bruges, 1947.

C. OTHER TITLES OF THE GOD OF ISRAEL

CERFAUX, L., "Le nom divin Kyrios dans la Bible grecque", *RScPhTh*, 1931, p. 27.

EISSFELDT, O., "Jahwe als König", *ZAW*, 1928, p. 81.
    "Baalshamem und Jahwe", *ZAW*, 1939, p. 1.
    Molk als Opferbegriff im punischen und hebräischen und das Ende des Gottes Moloch, Halle 1935.

GALL, A. VON, "Über die Herkunft der Bezeichnung Jahwes als König", *Studien zur sem Relig.* (Wellhausenfestschrift), 1914, p. 145.

GRESSMANN, H., "Hadad and Baal" *BZAW*, 1918, p. 213.

KAPELRUD, A. S., *Baal in the Ras Shamra Texts*, Copenhagen 1952.

LAGRANGE, M. J., "La paternité divine dans l'A.T.", *RB*, 1908, p. 481.

RAD, G. VON, "Erwägungen zu den Königspsalmen", *ZAW*, 1940, p. 216.

III. YAHWEH AND OTHER GODS

THE important place held by the god El in Semitic religion has led some historians to consider favourably the possibility of a primitive monotheism and thereby to arrive back by a more scientific method at the position of those who supported their thesis by the presence of an *All-father* in African religions or merely upon an *a priori* anti-evolutionism. Although the frequent occurrence of the god El is a certainty it is nearly as certain that this name bears a number of senses. Sometimes it does not refer to one definite god, but to the group of gods who, even in the most developed polytheism, have in common certain qualities and attributes such as benevolence towards their worshippers and the protection of justice, particularly defence of the feeble and the oppressed, in such a way that one could talk of god without thinking of any definite god or thinking of all the gods at once. The unity of the divine was likewise equally imposed by the power which a god could have of pushing all the other gods into the background on some definite occasion, a phenomenon well known under the name of henotheism. As for the use of the term El as a proper name, which is only met in West Semitic circles, it is fitting to see here belief in a supreme god who, however, is always merely the head of a pantheon in the midst of which he does not always play the most active part, as is the case at Ugarit. In spite of the interest of these facts judgment must be reserved about the assimilation of belief in higher gods to monotheism. There are here two different realities whose co-existence never presented any problem to believers in those gods. To see in polytheistic pantheons the division into hypostases of functions originally belonging to one god is to introduce into the history of religion a schematism as dangerous as the radical evolutionary view which it claims to combat.

On the particular terrain of Israel's religion, monotheism takes shape at the moment when Moses has the revelation of a god infinitely superior in power to the gods of the fathers and to all variety of Palestinian *'elim*.[1] By the mediation of Moses the people have the experience that a single God can be so powerful as to impose himself alone for the worship of the faithful. Yahweh does not present himself to Moses as the only God but as the jealous God, which leaves the door open for the existence of other gods but carries for the covenant people the absolute prohibition against believing that these gods have any power over them. The witness of the texts makes it difficult to deny that for a very long time Yahweh had been the God peculiar to Israel: the Israelites depend on Yahweh whilst the Moabites are under the power of Chemosh (Jg. 11.23-24); even in David's time it was thought that Yahweh's power ended at the frontiers of Israel (1 Sam. 26.19) and Ahaz offers sacrifices to the gods of Damascus which are deemed by him to bear sway outside his territory (2 Chr. 28.23). But even if Yahweh is originally one God amongst others he is not a God like others. The history of Israel is, from its origin and throughout its development, a succession of manifestations of the superiority of Yahweh over other gods: Moses confounds the gods of Egypt, and the prophet Elijah, one of the most zealous champions of the Mosaic spirit, pours scorn upon the worshippers of Baal and Baal himself. Face to face with Yahweh other gods not only become aware of their inferiority but they undergo a veritable defeat from which they never recover. This progressive dethronement of gods for which the history of Israel is the theatre, faith transposes into primordial times, those of myth, by relating how at the beginning of the world Yahweh triumphed over rival deities by way of combat (Is. 51.9; Ps. 74.2ff.) or by that of a trial; and in this respect Psalm 82 is particularly interesting: there Yahweh is represented as exercising judgment in the assembly of the gods and reducing the latter to the rank of angels or princes for not having exercised justice. Affirmation of Yahweh's victory over other gods led logically to the denial of all power to these gods both in the development of history and in the ordering of the world. In the thought of the Yahwist and of that of the earliest prophets,

---

[1] One cannot speak of evolution within the faith of Israel towards monotheism, for from the moment when Israel becomes conscious of being the people chosen by *one* God it is in practice a monotheistic people; and so one can speak with Albright, to name only one of the most recent and illustrious historians, of the monotheism of Moses (*From the Stone Age to Christianity*), on condition however that by this term there is understood a conviction of faith and not a result of reflection.

universal history is directed by Yahweh, even when that history has no direct connection with that of Israel (cf. Amos 1.3-2.3; 9.7; Is. 7.18; 8.7-10; 10.4ff.). The invective of the prophets against the gods of the nations are not motivated by hate or arrogance, but by the convictions that these gods are powerless to grant to the nations the place to which they have a right in the order of creation; with still more reason these gods could not be of any help to members of the people of Israel who committed the folly of forsaking Yahweh to put themselves under their protection. The Deuteronomist by the repetition of the classic formula: "Yahweh is God and there is no other God than he" (Dt. 4.35; 6.4; 32.39), insists on the need for a unique religious object, and in an analogous spirit Jeremiah speaks of foreign gods as gods "who are no gods" (Jer. 2.11; 5.7, 10). After that it was easy for Second Isaiah to draw the ultimate consequences of faith in the all-mightiness of Yahweh by proclaiming that gods other than Yahweh not only had no power but were even non-existent; he says they are *'elilim*, non-entities, *habalim*, empty breath, *ma'aseh*, *yadayim*, human creations which have no reality other than the matter of which their idols are made (Is. 41.1; 43.9; 44.6; 45.22) and where these were truly worshipped—for the Israelites were not so narrow as to deny all sincere religious life outside their own religion—the prophets regarded it as the unwitting worship of Yahweh (Mal. 1.11).

IV. ANGELS AND OTHER POWERS
DIVINE OR DEMONIC

THE beings denoted by the terms "sons of God" (*bene 'El* or *bene ha'elohim*) or "heavenly host" formed the celestial court of Yahweh. What we know about their origin is confined to fragmentary references to a myth in chapter 6 of Genesis, no doubt formerly more fully developed, whose impact the Yahwist tradition was forced to mitigate by setting this fall of the angels in harmony with that of men.[1] Their creation is nowhere mentioned, for the heavenly host in Gen. 2.1 must be understood in a very wide sense. Job (38.7) speaks of the "sons of God" as existing prior to the creation proper and Psalm 148 (vv. 1-6) mentions angels at the head of the works of creation which must praise God. The nature of angels is expressed by the title *ben ha'elohim*, that is to say one who belongs to the category of the divine. There is no Adamic element in them although they are almost always represented in human form when they enter into contact with men (Gen. 18.2; 19.1; Jos. 5.13; Jg. 13.3ff.; 6.11; Ez. 9.2; Dan. 9.21); they behave in a very human way, sharing meals, for instance (Gen. 18.19), but from an early time these texts have been emended in order to safeguard the spiritual nature of the angels (in Jg. 13.15, 16 the angel does not eat).[2] The function of angels is expressed by the term *mal'ak*, messenger; they are in fact sent by God to carry a message which, in the form of an order or a promise, is always a revelation on his part. Questions of personality and precedence are unimportant in the early days; it is only from the time of Daniel, and probably under the influence of Persian angelology, that a hierarchy is established in the angel world and it is Michael and Gabriel who henceforward play the leading rôle (Dan. 9.21; 10.13). The Seraphim and Cherubim[3] do not include all the angels, only those whom Yahweh attaches most especially to the service

[1] In Gen. 6.3, 5 it is a matter of the punishment of men who, however, had no part in the angels' misdemeanour.

[2] In Tobit 12.19 the angel pretends to eat, and Josephus introduces the same suggestion into his exegesis of Genesis 18 (Ant. 1.11, 2).

[3] Cf. for Cherubim the study of Dhorme and Vincent *RB*, 1926, pp. 328ff.

of his own person. The root *srph*, to burn, to be warm, does not necessarily imply that the seraphim were represented in the form of serpents, although in two passages the two terms are associated (Num. 21.6; Dt. 8.15); we might be more tempted—with the support of Is. 14.29 and 30.6 where it is a matter of a *saraph* flying, and particularly of the inaugural vision in chapter 6—to consider a solar or at least astral origin for these beings. The *kerubim* must be linked with the *karibu* or *kuribu*, terms which in Assyro-Babylonian religion mean either the believer worshipping his god or the divine intercessor presenting the prayer of the believer to a principal god, and which we often find represented in the form of monsters with human faces on the monuments which guarded the entrances of temples and palaces. It is just this function of guardian of a sacred area which is exercised by the *kerub* in Genesis. The cherubim are directly connected with the presence of Yahweh whether that presence is made evident over the distance which separates it from the human sphere, as in the case of the Ark (Ex. 25.17-22), or communicates itself to men (Ps. 18.11; 2 Sam. 21.11), this double aspect being illustrated by the fixity and the mobility of the cherubim (cf. Ez. 1.4ff.). It would be wrong to contrast the *Seraphim* with the *Cherubim* in so far as both groups are messengers of grace; both alike serve the purpose of safeguarding divine holiness and of making possible without danger its communication to man. Are we to regard these angelic powers as distant echoes of a pre-Israelite tradition, as might be suggested by the mention of Kerub in Ez. 28.13, or only as imperfect sketches of a theology of the communication of God with man? The second solution appears to us preferable, though it does not preclude Israel from having borrowed material from alien mythologies.

Sometimes the demons are ancient Canaanite deities, sometimes they are reminders of the desert period when Yahwism had not yet received dogmatic formulation and as a consequence easily tolerated the presence of beliefs which are spoken of very vaguely as popular religion. At other periods of syncretism certain of these demons received sacrifices, like the *se'irim*, the hairy ones, goat-faced demons (Lev. 17.7; 2 Kings 23.8; 2 Chr. 11.15); there were also the *shedim* (the black ones?) to whom occasionally children were sacrificed (Ps. 106.37; Dt. 32.17); a single passage mentions the goddess Lilith (Is. 34.14), a nocturnal monster which lurks amongst ruins. At least one of these demons was integrated into Israelite ritual: at the time of the great atonement festival the high priest sent away one goat for Yahweh and another for Azazel; this Azazel whose mysterious name suggests some connection with the goat (the root *'azaz* means to be strong and to be proud) was a desert demon (Lev. 16.22), the desert always being regarded as the places where forces hostile to Yahweh might operate (Is. 34.11; 13.21; Lk. 11.24). Since generally man remained outside that dangerous area, demons played no vital part in his life; for Israelite faith it is Yahweh who is the author of good and ill (Amos 3.6; Lam. 3.37-38; Job. 9.24) and it is only at a late period, when that belief became increasingly difficult to sustain, that demonology took an important place in theology.[1]

Satan

This personage has a history in the Old Testament, and we can say of him that he does not exist but he comes into being. The focal point of that history appears in the book of Chronicles (1 Chr. 21) where, used for the first time as a proper name, Satan plays the part of a kind of anti-god. The root *stn (stm)* expresses the act of putting oneself crosswise, which in the realm of justice can show itself as accusation and calumny. On occasion human beings can exercise that satanic function: David (1 Sam. 29.4), the sons of Zeruiah (2 Sam. 19.23), any adversary (1 Kings 5.18), Hadad the adversary of Solomon (1 Kings 11.14, 23); divine beings like the angel of Yahweh in the Balaam story (Num. 22.22, 32) can also bar the way to a man's purposes. In all these passages "satan" is never identified as a distinct person, but the example of men or spirits opposing another's plans, especially in the military or judicial spheres, largely supplied the material for that figure of the adversary *par excellence*. The earliest text in which Satan figures as an individual (Zech. 3) shows him in process of accusing the High Priest Joshua before the divine tribunal. According to that scene the *Sitz im Leben* of Satan might be found in the lawsuit where, as we know from the story of Naboth and by certain allusions in the Psalms (71.11, 13; 109.6, 20), the accusers were the determining factor in the condemnation of the guilty and still more in that of the innocent. According to an hypothesis put for-

[1] In Psalm 91.5 pestilence and destruction are not demons but personifications natural to a poetic style.

ward by Torczyner and taken up by Ad. Lods[1] the origin of the figure of Satan should be sought in connection with police. There were in Egypt and at the court of the Persian kings officials called the "eye" and "ear" of the king. According to the description which Xenophon gives,[2] each year they travelled through the provinces of the kingdom accompanied by a body of soldiers; they presented reproofs to the satrap when they found him abusing his power, and if they did not obtain satisfaction they referred the matter to the king who, on their report, took irrevocable decisions, deposing the governor without trial or defence, sometimes having him put to death by his own guards. It is possible that the figure of Satan was inspired both by the customs of Israelite lawsuits and by the police methods of the Persian kings. By nature Satan belongs to the general category of *bene ha'elohim* and the use of the preposition *betok*, in the midst of, in Job 1.6 (cf. Gen. 23.10 and 1 Sam. 10.10) indicated a relation of similitude and kinship. Satan is not an intruder into Yahweh's celestial court, he enjoys a privileged position even among the angels for, while these have a limited mission such as that of executing an order or of watching over a kingdom, Satan has at disposal a greater liberty which allows him to go to and fro on the earth and to walk therein, for his mission, wider than that of all the other angels, consists in discovering on the whole earth the faults or infidelities of men and reporting them to God. This police function leads him to be the adversary *par excellence*. In virtue of his office he regards all human beings with suspicion, spying upon their slightest actions, in order to find some occasion of accusing them. His office obliges him, in Lindblom's phrase, to "have the poison of suspicion in his heart and the spy-glass of malice before his eye"[3] and his suspicion ends by making him malicious and unjust: from accuser he becomes destroyer, for the opposition which he shows towards men leads him to a like opposition to God, whose office certainly involves

---

[1] In an article which appeared in the *Bulletin de l'Université hébraïque de Jérusalem*, 1938, pp. 15-21: "Comment Satan a fait son entrée dans le monde" and in the *Expository Times* 1936-37, p. 563. Ad. Lods' study appeared in *Mélanges syriens* presented to M. René Dussaud, p. 649. *Les origines de la figure de Satan.* A closely similar point of view has been defended by A. Brock-Utne, *Der Feind. Die alttestamentliche Satansgestalt im Lichte der sozialen Verhältnisse des nahen Orients*, Klio, 1935, pp. 219ff.

[2] Cyropaedia VIII, chap. 6; the same title is also found in Egypt (cf. A. Moret, *Histoire de l'Orient*, t. 2, p. 760).

[3] *Composition du livre de Job*, Lund 1945, p. 23.

judging men, but whose *chesed* is always disposed to love them. Once set over against God—and in 1 Chr. 21 there is attributed to Satan what in the parallel narrative of 2 Sam. 24 is Yahweh's work—Satan soon unites in his person all the functions of the evil powers previously divided amongst a multitude of demons and evil spirits or he becomes the head of the army of demons who are opposed to the celestial hosts of Yahweh.[1]

BIBLIOGRAPHY

CANAAN, T., *Dämonenglaube im Lande der Bibel*, Leipzig 1929.
DHORME-VINCENT, "Les chérubins", *RB*, 1926, p. 328 and 481ff.
DUHM, H., *Die bösen Geister im A.T.*, Tübingen 1904.
JIRKU, A., *Die Dämonen und ihre Abwehr im A.T.*, Leipzig 1912.
Satan, Etudes carmélitaines, recrueil collectif, Desclée de Brouwer 1950.

[1] Here we keep strictly to the testimony of the canonical books of the O.T. In the Apocrypha the figure of Satan takes such an amplitude that he becomes a real anti-god; through the identification of the serpent of Genesis with Satan and his being associated with death (Wisdom 2.24) he becomes a reality no one can escape. It must, however, be stressed that the "dualism" we find in certain texts of the apocrypha or New Testament (John 12.31; 2 Cor. 4.4) is only moral and religious and never metaphysical; the demons and Satan remain dependent on the one God who has created everything.

V. MANIFESTATIONS OF GOD

A LIVING and sovereign God like Israel's can choose all sorts of ways of manifesting his presence, but since his true nature is spiritual and therefore invisible, no means will be sufficient to give adequate expression to that presence. The God of the Old Testament will always remain the hidden God whom Moses saw only from behind and the skirts of whose robe alone Isaiah perceived. But this hidden God had the strong intention of manifesting his presence and chooses for that the normal phenomena of creation and certain forms which he creates specially for the purpose.

The first are three in number:

(a) God appears in nature. In the majority of ancient religions the gods are originally personifications of natural forces; thus in Babylon the chief divine triad is composed of the sun (Shamash), the moon (Ishtar) and water (Ea). Quite often Yahweh is also found associated with the forces of nature, but he manifests himself less in those which secure the regular course of the times and seasons than in catastrophic forces, fire, lightning, earthquake. These catastrophic aspects are found together in a text which is one of the most important for the Old Testament idea of revelation: the prophet Elijah at Mount Horeb sees wind, earthquake and fire follow one another only to learn that these means by which the deity was accustomed to reveal himself were only the prelude to a more effective manifestation, that of the word (1 Kings 19). Nevertheless there is a very large number of passages which show God linked with these natural forces,[1] particularly the historical

[1] Amongst the phenomena of nature fire, storm and earthquake are the ones which appear most often in connection with Yahweh, but that does not allow us to make him a storm god or volcano god; but these manifestations were peculiarly appropriate for his power and his mysteriousness. Theological reflection seized upon these natural phenomena in the formulation of concepts which were intended to resolve the problem of the divine presence; this is particularly clear in the case of the pillar of cloud which became luminous at night, a theme the history of which in biblical tradition is an attempt to make a permanent presence out of an occasional presence. The combination of this theme with that of the ark, the tent and the glory illustrates the subordination of nature to history (cf. A. Dupont-Sommer: "Nubes tenebrosa et illuminans noctem. Esquisse d'une histoire du concept de la nuée divine dans l'A.T.", *RHR*, 1943, pp. 1f.).

and poetic accounts of the theophany at Sinai (Ex. 19.19; 20.18; Ps. 29.3; Job 37.5); in these manifestations Israel had the conviction of really seeing God, beholding however in nature his vestment rather than his body.[1]

(b) God appears in a human form. This type of appearance is common to the whole of antiquity. In Israel we find it only sporadically, but such passages as Genesis 18 and 32 closely approach in their realism certain pagan narratives about the visit to earth of a deity clothed in human form. A less crude realism appears in the prophetic visions of God (1 Kings 22.19; Amos 9.1; Is. 6.1ff.) where God always appears in a human form, whilst the way in which these visions are recounted serves to underline that anthropomorphism did not begin to grasp the full implications of the divine. The phrase characteristic of the prophet Ezekiel, *demut kemar'eh 'adam* (1.12ff.) shows clearly that man, as an expression of the deity, goes no further than appearance or resemblance.

(c) The gods appear in animal form. Such appearance is rarely met with in Israel, although it was widely current amongst their Egyptian neighbours. Nevertheless it could be admitted that certain animals might be charged with divine mana and therefore be capable of representing the deity, just as the bull and perhaps also the serpent were sometimes in Israel representations of the legitimate divinity; far more frequently, however, an animal was the expression of demonic forces hostile to Yahweh (cf. the book of Daniel).

Alongside this naïve view, which admits in short the possibility of seeing God, we find from a very early time the belief that God could not be seen and that, as a way of revealing himself, he chooses means which at the same time respect his transcendence and his desire to be present. In this theological reflection Israel had to take into account three considerations of principle:

(a) God is invisible and therefore essentially spiritual.

(b) God is present, and that presence is not a remote reality, but must be shown through God's dwelling in the midst of his people.

(c) God is unique; there is only one God and there is no one who could be like him.

---

[1] The comparison of Psalm 104 with the Egyptian hymn to Aton shows clearly two conceptions of nature; the Egyptian hymn is addressed to Aton, that is to say to the solar disc: " You rise at the horizon, you illumine the earth ", etc., the Psalm on the contrary says: " Thou coverest thyself with light as with a garment."

These three principles were not always easy to reconcile and even had a tendency to exclude each other, as with the principles of the invisibility of God and his nearness. But Israel attempted to resolve the difficulty; the solutions could only be tentative, but in the light of their fulfilment we must regard them not as vain speculations but as approaches to the biblical solution of the divine presence, that of God become man in Jesus Christ.

A. THE ANGEL OF YAHWEH

The figure of this personage has been spoken of as elusive and perplexing;[1] in fact by this name there is meant either a form of appearance of Yahweh in the nature of a double or outward soul, or a being enjoying a personal existence clearly differentiated from that of Yahweh. The noun *mal'ak* comes from the root *la'ak*, which in Arabic, Ugaritic and Ethiopic has the meaning of "to send with a message that is to be conveyed"; so although etymologically the term can have no other meaning than that of "messenger",[2] the scope and attributes of the messenger can be subject to variation. On occasion the messenger could become a genuine representative of God, playing a part comparable to that of a divine or royal statue whose presence had the same import as that of the sovereign himself; according as the angel was envisaged as a messenger in the narrow sense of the word or as a representative, the stress was laid on what distinguishes him from Yahweh or on the bond which unites him to Yahweh. In the Old Testament the angel of Yahweh varies between a representative and a messenger.

The most ancient text in which the angel is mentioned may be the blessing of Jacob, Gen. 48.15-16, over the sons of Joseph: "The God before whom my fathers Abraham and Isaac did walk, the God who has been my shepherd all my life long unto this day, the angel (*hammal'ak*) who has redeemed me from all evil, bless the lads." The angel in this passage is not distinguished from the God of the fathers and his attributes are those of God: protector of

---

[1] Ad. Lods, "L'ange de Yahweh et l' 'ame extérieure'" in *Studien zur semitischen Philologie* presented to J. Wellhausen, p. 265.

[2] P. Lagrange, *art. cit.*, and Stade, *Biblische Theol. des A.T.*, 1905, p. 96, insist on the rôle of messenger.

the people or more exactly of the clan to which he is united by a bond of kinship, he directly participates in the life of this people and therefore he shows strongly human features which he will also retain throughout the evolution that he undergoes.

The kinsman God becomes the transcendent God on the one hand through contact with the gods of Canaan, on the other hand through the Mosaic revelation; henceforth the simple identification of the *mal'ak* with God is impossible and the *mal'ak* is subordinated to Yahweh by becoming either a form of manifestation or a messenger. This idea of the *mal'ak* not only allowed Israel to declare a continuity, even an identity, between the religion of the fathers and that of Moses, it also made it possible to speak of the presence of Yahweh in many places without calling in question his unity, and his intervention amongst men without challenging his transcendence. In many texts the functions of Yahweh and the angel are to some extent interchangeable: one who sees the angel can say he has seen God (cf. Gen. 16.13; Jg. 6.22; 13.22). It is indeed important to notice that the rôle of the angel, in the various aspects which that figure assumes, is always beneficent (Gen. 24.7-10; Ex. 33.2); even when he appears sword in hand it is to warn the people of the dangers into which they are running (Num. 22); in one solitary passage the angel of Yahweh comes to punish (2 Sam. 24.16; 1 Chr. 21.16). To explain the coexistence within one single passage of the angel and Yahweh, Adolphe Lods had recourse to the concept of an outward soul which is found amongst primitive peoples and also amongst others more developed, such as the Egyptians. "According to that way of thinking certain parts of the personality can be detached without ceasing for that reason to belong to it, and without the personality on its side ceasing to exist; these detached elements are the property of the person himself and yet distinct from him."[1] This external soul can be housed in a material object and it dies when that object comes to be destroyed. This is perhaps not unknown to the Old Testament, for when Gehazi runs after Naaman to try to obtain a gift, the "heart" of Elisha "went" with his unscrupulous servant while the prophet had stayed in his house (2 Kings 5.26). But nothing allows us to state with certainty that the same psychology applies to God. Besides, careful study of all the texts concerning the angel of Yahweh shows that one can only give partial assent

[1] Lods, *art. cit.*, p. 270.

to that explanation.[1] Even in texts where Yahweh and the angel act side by side their functions are distinguished; thus in Gen. 16.7-14 it is the angel of Yahweh who speaks to Hagar and who says to her, "Yahweh has heard thy cries". The angel is therefore the messenger who appears and who speaks in place of Yahweh, but the prayer can only be granted by Yahweh himself. Similarly in Genesis 22 the angel of Elohim calls to Abraham from the height of heaven and proclaims to him Yahweh's oath (vv. 15-16). The function of the angel is comparable to that of a prophet who, though identifying himself for the time being with the one who has sent him, nevertheless remains a fundamentally distinct personality. It is not without interest to observe that the angel of Yahweh is never mentioned by the great prophets, so that it can be asked whether it is not the prophet who has taken the place elsewhere held by the angel; and the title of *mal'ak Yahweh* given to one prophet (Haggai 1.13) could point in this direction.[2]

Whether as a double of Yahweh or a messenger, the angel only exists and functions by virtue of Yahweh's free decision; he is so little a person in his own right that it cannot be said from one narrative to the next whether the same personage is being referred to, the more so because grammatically the expression can be translated "the angel of Yahweh" or "an angel of Yahweh". The angel exists when Yahweh has need of him, just as the host of angels, amongst which the angel of Yahweh ultimately belongs, and which constitute the heavenly court, only truly exist when the lord of angels gives them a definite and temporary mission to execute.

B. THE FACE OF GOD

Of all the parts of the body the face is the one which expresses the greatest variety of feelings and attitudes: joy lights up the face (Ps. 104.15; Prov. 15.13), anger makes it fall and turns it evil (Gen. 4.5; Neh. 2.2). Hence it is quite normal for the face of God to hold a very important place in the Old Testament as a manifestation of his feelings. The whole personality of Yahweh

[1] Comparison with the *fravashis* of Zoroastrianism and the *genii* of the Latin gods is not conclusive, because with these powers pre-existent to a being are concerned, while the *mal'ak* only intervenes when God wants to enter into relation with man.

[2] The angel states the orders of God adding to them *ne'um Yahweh* just as the prophets do (cf. Gen. 22.16).

is concentrated in his face, his love as well as his anger, although the latter is expressed rather by the turning away or the absence of the countenance. The face of God is thus the presence of God without any reservation. In the passage which is the clearest for studying this conception, Exodus 33, where Yahweh promises Moses that his face will go with the Israelites, it is entirely a question of the personal presence of Yahweh in the midst of his people; but this passage is located in a context which leads us to suspect that there is theological exploitation of the idea, because the face seems to be a substitute for Yahweh himself, who clearly states his refusal to accompany the people across the desert (33.3-5) and his intention to use an angel as a substitute. By distinguishing between Yahweh and his face this chapter places the conception of the face in a perspective which does not completely correspond to the Israelite picture. That God reveals himself and that man can see him is a statement which in ancient Israel was hardly doubted. In Dt. 4.37, "He brought you out of Egypt by his face and by his great power", the expression denotes the person, that is to say, God himself and not one of his representatives. The sense is still more clear in Isaiah 63.9 (adopting the reading of the LXX in preference to the M.T.), "Not a messenger nor an angel, but his face saved them", and in Psalm 21.10 the "time of his face" is the moment of Yahweh's personal appearance. The name of Penuel, attesting that Jacob the ancestor of the nation had seen God face to face, and the example of Moses speaking to God face to face, shows us that the face did not constitute any problem (Ex. 33.11; Num. 12.8; 14.14). Nevertheless the dogma was affirmed in Israel from very early times—a development belonging no doubt to the current which issued in the Elohist editings of the Yahwist source—that the face of God could not be seen (Ex. 33.20-23; 1 Kings 19.13). The narratives relating the visions of Jacob and Moses were edited in such a way as to show that the phenomenon was most exceptional and that Jacob had seen it only at the price of an injury and Moses had seen it only from behind. In their concern to support this dogma the Massoretes much later on replaced the Qal *ra'ah* by the Niphal *yera'eh* when the face of God was the direct object (e.g. Ex. 23.15-17; 24.11; Ps. 42.3).

These developments were in accord with the general weakening of anthropomorphism, but we are not of the opinion that the same tendency gave any suggestion of making a distinction between the face and Yahweh himself, making it a kind of double or even hypostasis. It is, in fact, difficult to think that a term which expressed so strongly and in every age the essential nature and presence of a person could have been chosen to express his separateness. What happened in Phoenician religion, where a secondary deity could be called the face of the principal deity, as with *Tanit pen Baal*, provides no analogy, the face being vital for the manifestation of a person and in the religion of Israel this person can only be Yahweh.

For the purpose of reconciling the presence of God with his invisibility and his unity, the conceptions of angel and of glory, both of which had a material basis, the one in humanity and the other in nature, eclipsed that of the face as a form of God's appearance. Yet it must be observed that the face never ceased to be considered as a revelation of God; seeking the face of Yahweh, that is to say his personal presence, sums up both the temple cult and communion with God by the way of private prayer (Ps. 63.2-3; 100.2; 17.15 etc.) and believers had the certainty that this seeking of the face had as its counterpart Yahweh's blessing which consisted precisely in his countenance looking upon them (Num. 6.25; Ps. 80.4, 8, 20).

C. THE GLORY OF GOD

The fundamental idea expressed by the root *kbd* is that of weightiness. *Kabod* designates whatever had weight—it is used of riches: Gen. 31.1; Is. 10.3; Hag. 2.7; Ps. 49.17; of success: Gen. 45.13; 1 Kings 3.13 and of beauty: Is. 35.2. Since anything weighty inspires respect and honour, *kabod* not only denotes the obvious objective reality but the feeling which is experienced towards what inspires respect. This double meaning is particularly evoked where the glory of God is concerned. God reveals his glory, but his creatures must also give glory to him, as in Ps. 29.1; Jos. 7.19; Is. 42.8; 48.11. This glory is what God possesses in his own right, it is a kind of totality of qualities which make up his divine power; it has close affinity with the holiness which is of the nature of deity and it is a visible extension for the purpose of manifesting holiness to men. Whether it be manifest in the sphere of creation, history or the cultus, it is always, to use Bengel's particularly happy expression, uncovered holiness (*die aufgedeckte Heiligkeit*) or, to express it in more picturesque language which takes account of the concrete aspect of *kabod,* "the incandescent ectoplasm of his invisible spirit".[1] *Kabod* is always conceived as something concrete and we prefer for the usual distinction between abstract and concrete *kabod* that of general and special *kabod*. *Kabod* is always intended to be seen, witness its constant association with phenomena connected with light. In one early text belonging to the JE source, naïvely anthropomorphic but rich in meaning, the glory is represented as a luminous reality, less directly divine than the face, but nevertheless sufficient to annihilate the man who may look directly at it and the reflection of which, left after its passage, is perceptible to human eyes (Ex. 33.18ff.). This more special concrete sense is most in evidence in the Priestly source P. Even while using the term to denote the divine power in general (e.g. Ex. 14.4-17) it envisages the glory primarily as a concrete form of Yahweh's appearance, as a veritable *theologoumenon* of the divine presence. The description· given of it is that of fire which appears at certain times through the cloud which normally hides it (Ex. 16.10; Num. 17.7), although the part played by the cloud as a manifestation of Yahweh is greater in scope than that played by the glory (cf. Ex. 33.7f.; 40.36-38). The origin of this conception is probably multiple: phenomena of the natural order such as a volcanic eruption (Ex. 24.16ff.) or a storm (Num. 16.19-35) but also cultic rites like the fire of the altar (Lev. 9.23ff.) and light in general,[2] first of all the works of creation and their essential condition (Gen. 1), lie at the base of this concept which, having its origin in the events of Sinai, seeks each time it is used to confront the people with the divine presence in its overwhelming yet saving solemnity: Ex. 24.17. The glory appeared to the children of Israel in the form of devouring fire at the top of the mount. Ex. 29.43: God meets with the children of Israel in the tent and he will be sanctified by his glory.

Ex. 40.34ff.: When Moses had completed the construction of

---

[1] Paul Humbert, "Les prophètes d'Israël ou les tragiques de la Bible", *RThPh*, 1926, p. 229.

[2] The perpetual lamp of the sanctuary must likewise be regarded as a representation of *kabod*; when Eli cries: *I-kabod*, the glory is departed from Israel, he is thinking of the end of the cult and the extinguishing of that lamp brought about by the capture of the ark (cf. 1 Sam. 3.3; 4.21).

the tent, the cloud covered the tent and the glory of Yahweh filled the place.

The important position occupied for the prophet Ezekiel by the idea of glory is the result of a current which developed independently of that which led to P. Ezekiel moves along the line which starts from Isaiah chapter 6 where the glory appears as the normal expression of the divine presence. Moreover there are undeniable analogies between the inaugural visions of the two prophets: the four animals of Ezekiel are reminiscent of the seraphim; the burning coals of fire, of the altar. According to Ezekiel the *kabod* is not merely the manifestation of God in concrete form, it is identical with him; that is why, as in certain passages of Genesis where the angel of Yahweh and Yahweh are almost confused, God and the *kabod* are interchangeable, e.g. Ez. 9, where in verse 3 *kabod* is the subject, but in verse 4 the subject is Yahweh. Since the *kabod* is identical with Yahweh it is natural that the prophet insists on the fact that he cannot be seen in his essence but only in his image: *mar'eh demuth Yahweh kebod Yahweh* (1.26-28). The *kabod* is very closely linked with the Temple; by it God consecrates the temple as the place of his presence. While the temple is the normal place of his residence, as is brought out by 43.2ff. where the *kabod* returns to indwell the temple, Ezekiel nevertheless implies that this association is not automatic and absolute but that it is due to the free choice of Yahweh. The *kabod* appears as a kind of celestial temple stationed above the world and able to move very swiftly from one extremity to the other of the universe; this mobility of the *kabod* is the mobility of Yahweh himself, of the God who has a history and who directs world history. It is interesting to note that right above the *kabod* a human form appears, so that the glory is the image of God just as man is, and this association of image and glory reunited in one man will be developed along Ezekiel's lines by the apostle Paul (2 Cor. 3.18). Comparing the concept of glory in P and in Ezekiel, we can say that for the latter it is a permanent presence intended to express the freedom of Yahweh, master of the world and of history, whilst the former wishes to bring to light the reality of Yahweh's approach, whether for salvation or more often to announce the punishment of those who have rebelled against his will, e.g. Num. 16.42; Lev. 10.1-3. These differences, moreover, are by no means irreducible, for the God who comes and the God who directs history are only two aspects, or better still two anticipations, of God's kingdom which will be made manifest at the end of time.[1] The eschatological significance of the *kabod* of Yahweh is already implied in the vision of Isaiah 6 where the prophet contemplates in advance what will happen when the kingdom of Yahweh is made real in its perfection. In support of this meaning we can appeal to the following passages: Is. 40.5: The glory of Yahweh will be revealed and all flesh shall see it together—Is. 58.8: Then . . . the glory of Yahweh shall follow after thee—Is. 59.19: His glory shall be feared from the rising of the sun—Is. 60.1: Arise, for the light is come and the glory of Yahweh shines brightly upon thee—Hab. 2.14: The earth shall be full of the knowledge of the glory of Yahweh—Num. 14.21: The glory shall fill the earth—Ps. 57.6-12: Let thy glory cover the earth—Ps. 72.19: Let the name of his glory be blessed for ever. Lastly, if the text is not to be emended, the hope of the author of Psalm 73 must be understood as a reference to the glory to come, when he affirms that God will receive him after all his misfortunes in his kingdom of light. Israelites believed that a time would come when the glory would rise up for all peoples and they saw the preliminary signs of this in the cultus and in prophecy.

D. THE NAME OF GOD

We shall not deal within the limits of this chapter with the numerous passages in which the name is synonymous with Yahweh, a usage which became more and more frequent in post-exilic times,[2] but merely with those in which the *shem-Yahweh* operates with the force of an appearance of Yahweh. At the origin of this use there is to a large extent, as for *mal'ak*, the desire to procure some weakening of a too vivid anthropomorphism: thus in Ex. 23.19ff. the *shem Yahweh* is on the one hand Yahweh himself, and on the other his substitute in which he shows his reality and by which he is able to accompany the people without abandoning his transcendence. The prophet Isaiah speaks of the "name of Yahweh which comes from far, burning with his anger, his lips are full of indigna-

---

[1] The theology of the Chronicler, which moves in the wake of Deuteronomy, insists on the beneficent function of the glory (e.g. 2 Chr. 7.1-3), whilst P more often sees in it the divine presence which comes to admonish and to punish.

[2] Amongst the passages where the name of Yahweh and Yahweh are interchangeable we may mention: Job 1.21; Dt. 28.58; Is. 48.9; Ez. 20.44; Amos 2.7.

tion and his tongue as a devouring fire" (30.27). Here what is normally only said of Yahweh himself is said of the name; therefore Yahweh can act by his name in as comprehensive a fashion as by angel or *kabod*. In the Deuteronomic writings particularly we witness the theological development of the name of Yahweh. According to Deuteronomy Yahweh has chosen a place as a dwelling for his name; characteristic passages of this type are: Dt. 12.5: Yahweh has placed his name in the Temple to make it dwell there—1 Kings 11.36: The name of Yahweh inhabits Jerusalem —1 Kings 9.3: The name of Yahweh dwells in the Temple for ever—2 Sam. 7.13: The Temple will be built for the *shem*—2 Chr. 20.8; Ps. 74.7: The sanctuary is called the dwelling place of the name. Certain writers, for example Smend[1] and Heitmüller,[2] have minimized the importance of this affirmation by saying that the Temple was simply the place where the name of Yahweh was invoked; nevertheless it seems difficult not to see in these texts the affirmation of a real habitation of Yahweh in the sanctuary. By that, Deuteronomy is saying "Yahweh does not dwell in the Temple in person, but is represented there by his name". Already in the dedicatory prayer 1 Kings 8.12, where the Massoretic text must be corrected by the LXX, it is said that Yahweh dwells in darkness, that is to say in the sky, and that the Temple is his lodging-place; not long afterwards Deuteronomy resolves this antinomy by speaking repeatedly of the dwelling in the Temple of the name, which, moreover, makes it possible to throw into greater relief the heavenly dwelling place of Yahweh, cf. 1 Kings 8.27-30. The theology of Deuteronomy is in the line of the preaching of the prophets, who admitted a particular association of Yahweh with the Temple, not in the sense of the deity's dwelling-place but in that of God's particular property. However, Deuteronomy makes a concession to popular religion since it retains the view of the Temple as a dwelling-place, but spiritualizes it through the concept of the name.

With Deuteronomy we are on the road to the hypostatizing of the name of Yahweh. In early texts the *shem* has only a limited existence; when the Exodus is over the *mal'ak,* with whom the *shem* is closely associated, returns to Yahweh until such time as he uses it for a new revelation. The *shem*, in Deuteronomic theology,

[1] *Alttestamentliche Religionsgeschichte*, 1893, p. 281, note.
[2] *Im Namen Jesu*, 1903.

is an attempt to give permanent expression to faith in a *deus revelatus*: by his name Yahweh dwells in the Temple and will only leave it at its destruction (cf. Jer. 7.12). The *shem* becomes in that case a veritable hypostasis within the meaning of the definition given by Mowinckel:[1] "a divine entity partly independent, partly a manifestation of a superior divinity; it represents the personification of a quality or an activity or of a component part of the superior deity. The personification of abstract concepts is often spoken of, but even if for us the name, the power, or the qualities of a person are abstractions it is not so to the primitive mind, for which qualities and actions are entities relatively independent of the subject."

The period following Deuteronomy strengthens the tendency to make the name an hypostasis; although we still find numerous passages where the name is only a synonym for Yahweh himself (Is. 56.6; Ps. 103.1, etc.), those in which the name is found endowed with full independence became more and more numerous; these are, in particular, passages where the *shem* forms the grammatical subject of the phrase, whilst in the others it is only the direct object: Zech. 14.9: Yahweh will be one, his name will be one—Ps. 8.2-10: the name of Yahweh is glorious over the earth. Since the Psalm deals with manifestations of God in nature, the use of the name is intended to show that Yahweh himself does not dwell in nature. In an analogous manner the author of Psalm 19 will say that the heavens proclaim the *kabod* of God in order to show the revelation of God in nature.

The expression "in the name of Yahweh" (*beshem Yahweh*) sometimes has the almost instrumental suggestion as of an actual power which man calls to his aid, as Ps. 54.3: "O God, help me by thy name and save me by thy power." In this passage the name is a means which Yahweh has available for action and not simply a formula of invocation, and in Psalm 89.25 the name of Yahweh is the means by which the prosperity of David is assured. Comparable speculations on the subject of the name are to be met with outside Israel where, however, the problem is more easily solved because of a plurality of gods: the inscription of Eshmunazar mentions *Astarte shem baal*,[2] which might be a

---

[1] *RGG*, 2nd ed., col. 2065.

[2] Line 18, unless the heavenly (sheme) Astarte of Baal is to be read (cf. Gressmann, *AOTB*, p. 445).

parallel to *Tanit pen baal*. In conclusion, we may say that the name, which we know always expresses the essential nature of a being, manifests the totality of the divine presence even more than the angel, the face or the glory; and at the same time this concept of the name safeguards the unity of God because name and person are identical. To make God known to men is to make his name known (cf. Jn. 17.6-26). The name associated with a person in history will mark the consummation of all the gropings of ancient Israel to resolve the problem so vital to it of the presence of God.[1]

BIBLIOGRAPHY

BAUDISSIN, W. W. VON, "'Gott schauen' in der altt. Religion", *ARW*, 1915, p. 173.

BOEHMER, J., *Das biblische "Im Namen", eine sprachwissenschaftliche Untersuchung*, 1898.
                             Gottes Angesicht, 1908.

BROCKINGTON, L. H., "The presence of God, a study of the term glory of Yahweh", *Expository Times*, 1945, October, p. 21.

DÜRR, L., *Ezechiels Vision von der Erscheinung Gottes*, Münster 1917.

GALL, A. VON, *Die Herrlichkeit Gottes*, Giessen 1900.

GIESEBRECHT, FR., *Die altt. Schätzung des Gottesnamens*, Königsberg 1901.

GRETHER, O., "Name und Wort Gottes", *BZAW* 64, 1934.

GULIN, F., "Das Antlitz Gottes im A.T.", *An. Ac. Fennicae*, 1923, p. 21.

JOHNSON, A. R., "The use of panim in the O.T.", *Festschrift O. Eissfeldt*, 1947.

KITTEL, HELMUT, *Die Herrlichkeit Gottes*, Giessen 1934.

LAGRANGE, M. J., "L'ange de Yahwé", *RB*, 1903, p. 212.

LODS, AD., "L'ange de Yahweh et l'âme extérieure", *Studien zur semit. Philologie presented to J. Wellhausen*, 1914.

NOETSCHER, FR., *Angesicht Gottes schauen nach biblischer und babylonischer Auffassung*, 1924.

RAD, VON G., *Deuteronomiumstudien* (devotes one chapter to *shem* and *kabod*), 1948.

RAMSEY, A. M., *The Glory of God and the transfiguration of Christ*, London 1948.

RYBINSKI, *Der Mal'akh Jahwe*, Paderborn 1930.

STEIN, B., *Der Begriff Kebod Yahweh und seine Bedeutung für die altt. Gotteserkenntnis*, Emsdetten 1939.

STIER, F., *Gott und sein Engel im A.T.*, Münster 1934.

[1] On the utilization of the name Yahweh in the form 'Ιάω in the magical papyri, cf. Baudissin-Eissfeldt, *Kyrios* II, pp. 206ff., though the identification of 'Ιάω with Yahweh is debatable.

VI. THE HOLINESS OF GOD

FROM the phenomenological point of view, holiness is a supernatural and mysterious force which confers a special quality upon particular persons and things. This definition best gives the idea of what the Old Testament understands by the term holiness. "Holiness," wrote Johs. Pedersen, "never lost its true nature as the force on which life depended and from which it was renewed."[1] Varied as its aspects may be it is always a manifestation of power; but for the Old Testament all power is concentrated in the person of Yahweh, apart from whom no life is possible in nature or mankind. Holiness is not one divine quality among others, even the chiefest, for it expresses what is characteristic of God and corresponds precisely to his deity, that is, by taking into account the representation of the divine among the Semites, to the fullness of power and life.

Yahweh is the holy one *par excellence*, but the concept of holiness exists independently of him. The root *qdsh*[2] which is encountered in the majority of Semitic languages very probably expresses a cut, a separation; locations which bear the name *Qadesh* are sacred places, that is to say they are separated from and forbidden to ordinary mortals; the sacred prostitutes, the *qedeshim* and *qedeshot* are separated from the sphere of ordinary life. The idea of power is found associated with that of separation: the person or object taken away from normal life and usage are under the dominion of a power which, like that of *mana* and *tabu*, can be either dangerous or beneficent. Any moral conception is foreign to this primitive notion of holiness: the man who falls smitten for

---

[1] *Israel, its life and culture*, III-IV, p. 295.

[2] The explanation from the root *qd(d)*, to cut, has been upheld by W. Baudissin, *Studien zur semit. Religiongeschichte* II, among others, and has been adopted by the majority of critics. Others such as U. Bunzel have suggested the root *quddushu*, to be brilliant (in a physical sense) and to be pure (moral sense). Others again derive *qdsh* from *dsh* which expresses the idea of youthfulness and freshness: *qdsh* would be an intensive form of *chdsh*; but *chdsh* designates what is new and brilliant, in particular the pure and soft light of the new moon. In any case, it must be stressed that the content of holiness is not exhausted by referring to its etymological meaning.

86

having attempted to steady the holy ark which threatened to over-turn (2 Sam. 6) shows us that the Old Testament was not un-acquainted with this impersonal and material aspect of a holiness which acted automatically.

Old Testament religion gives to holiness an aspect which goes well beyond the etymological meaning and the materialistic phase. In Hebrew the root *qdsh* undergoes a development without parallel elsewhere: "the root *qdsh* reappears in the majority of forms of the Hebrew language. In turn a regular verb, having its transitive and intransitive forms and seven complete conjugations, participle, abstract noun, adjective, concrete noun, proper noun, it might almost be said that it is the grammatical centre of the Old Testa-ment just as the idea which it expresses is the theological centre. Thanks to the marvellous flexibility of the Hebrew language the same root successively denotes a state and an action, the action suffered or produced, and the subject or object of that action. The richness of expression is in no way inferior to the richness of the idea, and the modifications of the one correspond exactly to the multiple aspects of the other".[1] It must therefore be recognized that holiness in the Old Testament has a character *sui generis* which is only very partially explained by etymology and by extra-Israelite analogies. The essential aspect of holiness is that of power, but of power in the service of a God who uses all things to make his kingdom triumph. As soon as Yahweh takes possession of holiness —holiness does not take possession of Yahweh—the power of holi-ness no more consists in prohibition, in the limitation of the sacred sphere, but in the power which communicates itself in order to bestow life. This subjection of holiness to Yahweh was so complete that very often Yahweh is defined as the holy one, the term holy being synonymous with the divine (Is. 40.25; Hos. 11.9); in other instances the terms God and holy are put in parallel[2] (Is. 5.24; Hab. 3.3; Ps. 71.22). When it is said that Yahweh swears by his holiness that means that he swears by himself, as the parallelism

[1] Alfred Boegner, *La sainteté de Dieu dans l'Ancien Testament*, 1876, p. 131. This work, although old, includes very interesting theological comments, particularly on the subject of the relation between the holiness and the name of Yahweh.

[2] Outside Israel the appellation "holy gods" appears for the first time in the inscription of Yechimilk of Byblos (twelfth century); and it is found in the inscription of Eshmunazar (fifth century, lines 9 and 22). It is possible that *qedoshim* in Ps. 16.3 means pagan gods. But nowhere is this term charged with a religious content comparable to what we discover in the O.T.

between holiness and *nephesh* shows (Amos 4.2 and 6.8; Ps. 89.36; 108.8). Likewise the relation between holiness and the name reveals the identity of holiness with deity (Lev. 20.3; 22.2, 32; Amos 2.7). It is possible, moreover, that the specifically Israelite notion of holiness is associated with the revelation of the name of Yahweh, for nowhere do the essential characteristics of holiness present themselves to us with such precision as in the scene of the burning bush, where both name and holiness are the most adequate expressions for the divine life. This text teaches us that, even in connection with Yahweh, the first effect of holiness is to keep man at a distance: " Who can survive before Yahweh, the holy God? " the inhabitants of Beth-Shemesh will say some centuries later (1 Sam. 6.20). In face of the revelation of holiness man feels his nothingness; not only is his creaturehood unveiled to him (Gen. 18.27; Job 42.6), but he recognizes that he is a creature tainted by sin and that sin separates him from God—a separation which can only be broken down by an initiative from God himself (Is. 6). So the first result of the manifestation of holiness upon man can only be fear; to recognize the holiness of God, which is the basic form of sanctification, since it is expressed by the causative form of the root *qdsh*, is above all to fear him (Is. 8.13; 29.23) and Psalm 99 gives three times as refrain a solemn *qadosh hu* in order to justify the invitation to the peoples to tremble and prostrate themselves before Yahweh. This overwhelming aspect of holiness also appears when it is related to glory. *Kabod* is what gives a person this weight, or, we could say, his soul. Each individual has his *kabod* (Ps. 16.9; 30.13), but Yahweh has a quality of soul superior to any that can be imagined and it is this quality which in his case is called holiness. Thus there is no clear distinction between holiness and glory. One cannot distinguish them by saying, for example, that holiness is the glory of God in itself, and glory is his holiness in relation to the world; no doubt the glory can be seen whilst holiness remains invisible, but God communicates both his holiness as well as his glory. If there is a difference we should see it in the fact that *kabod* has a rather negative aspect, it is a power which overwhelms, it is sometimes connected with terrifying manifestations in nature (Ps. 29), whilst holiness is a life-giving power; the *kabod* presents itself and, as such, it is a manifestation of the divine presence; holiness not only presents but gives itself.

The specific character of holiness according to the Old Testament is not, however, exhausted by its negative aspect; holiness receives its particular orientation from its relationship with the God of the covenant. Because he is the God of the covenant, Yahweh does not jealously keep his holiness for himself, shielding it from all contamination by making it the barrier between the spheres of the divine and human. His jealousy impels him, on the contrary, to manifest his holiness: thus the holiness revealed to Isaiah is not only a power which annihilates him but one which raises him up and makes him a prophet full of the power of Yahweh and charged with displaying it before the eyes of the peoples. Yahweh sanctifies himself, *niqdash*, he sanctifies himself in the destruction of Gog (Ez. 38.16) or in Sidon against which he carries out his judgments (Ez. 28.22). This sanctification should make it possible to maintain the covenant with Israel, just as the people of Israel at Meribah are the object of a manifestation of holiness on Yahweh's part when they receive water from him, in spite of the strife by which they oppose him (Num. 20.13). All the acts of deliverance for Israel's sake are manifestations of his holiness. The great deliverance by which the people of Israel will be re-established in their land (Ez. 20.41; 28.25; 36.20-24; 39.27) will be in the eyes of the nations a demonstration of the vanity of their attacks and a source of confusion, though not of utter annihilation. The link between holiness and the covenant appears in its full paradox in the title the "holy one of Israel" which the prophet Isaiah gives to Yahweh, without doubt for the first time. It is found 14 times in the first part and 16 times in the second part of the book. Because Isaiah's oracles were so widely known the expression has passed into three Psalms (71.22; 78.41; 89.19), into Jeremiah (50.29; 51.6) and into Ezekiel (39.7); but the germ of this title is probably to be found already in Hosea, who thinks of Yahweh's dwelling in the midst of his people as characteristic of his holiness (Hos. 11.9). The appellation "holy one of Israel" does not mean that the holy one belongs to Israel, though strict grammar would permit such a translation. Yahweh is the holy one of Israel not because he is consecrated to Israel but because he has consecrated Israel to himself, and Israel itself is holy only because of this consecration to Yahweh.

In some of the passages referred to the expression occurs, moreover, with a slight variation which excludes any relationship of possession. Hosea calls Yahweh: the holy one in the midst of thee, *qadosh beqirbeka* (11.9), and Ezekiel: the holy one in Israel, *qadosh be Israel* (39.7). This association, which rests upon election, implies that the holiness of which Israel is the object can turn against them and in certain circumstances in the course of history the divine holiness was for Israel an effective manifestation of judgment. "The light of Israel shall become a fire and his holy one a flame consuming and devouring his thorns and his briers in one day" (Is. 10.17). But the term holy one of Israel means above all else that Yahweh keeps close to Israel, that he could not abandon them without denying himself. The holy one dwells in the high places, yet comes down to the contrite and humble (Is. 57.15), for although holiness is that which qualifies God as god it is also that in him which is most human. The holy one of Israel is he who gives his word (Is. 5.24; 30.12, 15), the one who is always near to help (Is. 31.1; 37.23), whose blessings are so evident that the peoples will exclaim: "Yahweh is only found in thee" (Is. 45.11, 14). The association of the term holy with *yoshea'* (Is. 43.3) and particularly with *go'el* (43.14; 47.4; 48.17; 49.7) equally well illustrates the communicative nature of holiness. If God is the *go'el,* that is to say the near relative who exercises the right of redemption, that means that the holy one, in spite of his distance yet because of his vivifying power, is the near relative of his people with whom he enters into a relationship intimate to the point of jealousy: holiness and jealousy make up the contents of the name Yahweh (Jos. 24.19). The entire history of Israel is the work of holiness; it is not without reason that the prophet who forged the title holy one of Israel is also the one who best showed the realization of God's plan in history, illustrating the exclamation of the Psalmist: "Thy way, O God, is in holiness" (Ps. 77.14; 68.25). Whilst subordinating holiness to the covenant, Yahweh remains free to manifest his holiness outside the covenant, and the breaking of the covenant by men does no injury to divine holiness. God is holy and that is why he chooses to enter into the covenant; man, on the contrary, can become holy only by entering into the covenant.

In a general way the people in their entirety are the recipients of the holiness of Yahweh, but within the nation there are individuals and objects which more than others are charged with divine holiness. Whatever may be the vestiges of a primitive and materialistic conception of holiness, in its theological reflection the Old Testament always regards the holiness of objects as a property conferred upon them by Yahweh, that is, as a holiness by relation-ship. In chronological order, the first object charged with holiness is the ark in which the *kabod* of Yahweh is concentrated: *Ikabod* the daughter-in-law of the priest Eli will say "the *kabod* has departed from Israel, for the ark of God has been taken" (1 Sam. 4.19-22). The holiness of the ark was never able to get rid of its material and magical aspect, so under the influence of prophetic Yahwism it was pushed into the background by the Jerusalem temple which, since it was henceforward the place of revelation rather than the habitation of the deity, answered better the spiritual requirements of the religion of Israel. "Holiness belongeth to thy house" (Ps. 93.5), such is the affirmation of piety from the time of Solomon to that of Zerubbabel (cf. Dt. 12.5; 16.6; Ps. 5.8; 79.1; Is. 16.12; Jer. 17.12; Ez. 5.21; 42.14; Jonah 2.5). The holiness of the temple is shed upon all objects connected with the cult: the sacred utensils are holy, water poured into a vessel belonging to the furnishings of the Temple becomes holy (Ex. 30.18; Num. 5.17), the vestments of the priests are holy (Ex. 28.2; Ps. 29.2; 96.9; 110.3). Holiness by consecration does not differ essentially from the holiness conferred by election, for man offers only what he has been expressly commanded by Yahweh. The aim of sacrifice is to communicate some of the power of life which is the divine holiness, and so the absence of the sacrificial cult can often be regarded as a refusal of God to communicate his holiness to those who are unworthy of it (Ex. 28.38; 29.33; Dt. 12.26; Jer. 11.15). Consecration by sacrifice is different from that produced by the *cherem*; this latter consists in vowing a thing or person (or persons) to the deity without concern for the consequences of the action, whilst one who offers a sacrifice expects the revelation and the setting free of a vitalizing power. The "materialization" of holiness did not exist without introducing a great danger which Israel was not always able to resist. Holiness risked being looked upon as linked in a permanent way with certain objects and of causing the essential aspect of relationship to be forgotten; in this way the holiness of the temple and later that of the *torah* took on the appearance of veritable idolatry. Besides the ark and the temple, holiness is conferred upon the sky, which never ceases to be the actual residence of Yahweh (Dt. 26.15; Is. 63.15; Mic. 1.2; Ps. 11.40; 18.17; 20.7; 102.20) and on the land of Israel, although the first mention of this is made only in Zech. 2.16 (cf., however,

Ex. 15.13; Ps. 78.54; Is. 63.18; 2 Macc. 1.7). In this evolution of the idea of holiness stress is laid principally upon two aspects: there reappears the character of tabu which had been supplanted by that of relationship, and the distinction between the sacred world and the secular world is found amongst all those in Judaism who are the heirs of the thought of Ezekiel. Within the sphere of the sacred itself there are various degrees of holiness, there is a distinction between what is holy and what is very holy, which would possess no meaning when holiness was regarded solely as a relationship (Ex. 26.33; 29.37; 30.10; Lev. 2.3, 10; 6.10, 18, 22; 14.13; 1 Kings 6.16; 7.50; 8.6; Ez. 41.4; 42.13; 43.12; 44.13). In addition, the materialization of holiness led to its being regarded less as an attribute than as a state and to its identification with purity. The narrative about the revolt of the sons of Korah (Num. 16) is an example of speculations about the diverse degrees of holiness: the sons of Korah revolt against Moses and Aaron in the name of the principle of the holiness of the people in its entirety and they contest the right of Moses and Aaron to elevate themselves above the assembly of the people, the sole depository of holiness. Decision is given in favour of a specifically sacerdotal holiness: only men detached from the sphere of the secular and consecrated by special rites can approach God.[1] As for purity, which becomes the principal content of holiness, this is shown sometimes in the realm of morals and sometimes in that of ritual, most often in both at once (ritual aspect: 1 Sam. 21.6; Lev. 21.6; Num. 6.5; ethical aspect: Lev. 19.3, 11, 15; 20.7, 10). Man's obligation to be holy following the example of divine holiness (Lev. 19.2; 20.7; 21.8; 22.9, 31) implies cultic duties as well as a personal attitude; in this setting, however, stress is laid less upon separation than upon the necessity of man to realize the fullness of his life, which he will not do without a struggle against the destructive powers which are opposed to the fulfilment of his vocation.[2]

---

[1] It is in the same circles that there is a preoccupation with the problem of the contagion of holiness; the priestly torah related by Haggai (2.10ff.) reconciles, however, moral requirements with the ritual aspect by showing that the contagion of holiness is not automatic like that of impurity.

[2] The relationship of all holiness with Yahweh makes us very sceptical about attempts to classify holiness. J. Haenel (cf. bibliogr.), who regards holiness chiefly from the viewpoint of distance, distinguishes the five following aspects: (a) inaccessible holiness; (b) holiness of majesty; (c) holiness of jealousy; (d) holiness of perfection;

BIBLIOGRAPHY

ASTING, R., *Die Heiligkeit im Urchristentum*, Göttingen 1930.
BAUDISSIN, W., *Studien zur semitischen Religionsgeschichte* II, Berlin 1878.
BOEGNER, A., *La notion de sainteté dans l'A.T.*, 1876.
BUNZEL, U., *Der Begriff der Heiligkeit im A.T.*, Lauban 1914.
DIESTEL, L., " Die Heiligkeit Gottes ", *Jahrb f. prot. Theol.*, 1859, p. 3.
FRIDRICHSEN, A., *Hagios-Qadosh*, Oslo 1916.
HAENEL, J., *Die Religion der Heiligkeit*, Gütersloh 1931.
KÜCHLER, F., " Der Gedanke des Eifers Jahwes im A.T.", *ZAW*, 1908,
    p. 42.
LEENHARDT, FR. J., *La notion de sainteté dans l'A.T.*, Paris, 1929.
RINGGREN, H., *The Prophetical Consciousness of Holiness*, Uppsala 1948.

(*e*) holiness of transcendence (Jenseitsheiligkeit). The " sociological " classification proposed by F. J. Leenhardt (cf. bibliogr.) seems more subtle and therefore preferable : (*a*) in popular circles holiness evolved from the simple tabu to become the expression of the covenant; (*b*) priestly circles regarded holiness as the setting apart of priests for the correct approach to sacred things; (*c*) to the prophets God is holy towards men and holy in himself.

VII. THE RIGHTEOUSNESS OF GOD

"A TWENTIETH-CENTURY reader encountering the word *justice*[1] in Semitic texts must always be careful to adjust his thought and not to place this term in the categories to which our word justice has accustomed us."[2] This wise warning cannot be pondered too much; righteousness in the Old Testament is in fact far more than a simple juridical concept, but we must not allow an unbalanced reaction to send us to the opposite extreme and think of righteousness as something fundamentally different from what we understand by this term.

The peculiarity of the Israelite concept of righteousness appears in connection with the exact meaning to be given to one of the principal terms used for it. The root *tsdq* appears in Arabic with a concrete and material meaning, but one which already has acquired several facets: *tsdq* denotes what is right, stable and substantial, in such a way that it may be asked whether these three senses are not variants of a single more general notion which might be conformity to a norm. When in Arabic a date is called *tsdq* that can refer neither to its form nor to its taste, but can simply mean that it conforms to what it should normally be. It is, therefore, suitable, in spite of some contrary opinions which have been expressed, to adopt the opinion of Kautzsch, who concludes his important analysis[3] of the root *tsdq* with these words: "The fundamental idea of *tsdq* which is available to us is the state corresponding to a norm, a norm which remains to be defined in each particular case." Righteousness is therefore conformity to a norm; in origin it is neither punitive, nor distributive, nor justificatory, but in a general way fidelity to a state or to a way of acting or thinking; many instances of the root *tsdq* in the Old Testament support this interpretation.

---

[1] (In the translation justice and righteousness have been variously used to render the French *justice*, which covers both, as did the Hebrew *tsdq* it represents.—Trans.)

[2] H. Cazelles, " A propos de quelques textes difficiles relatifs à la justice de Dieu dans l'A.T.", *RB*, 1951, pp. 169ff.

[3] *Die Derivate des Stammes tsdq im alttestamentlichen Sprachgebrauch*, Tübingen 1881.

(*a*) Objects which conform to a certain type are called *tsdq*: just balances, just weights, just measures are objects in conformity with what they ought to be (Lev. 19.36; Ez. 45.10); *zibche tsedeq* (Dt. 33.19; Ps. 4.6; 51.21) are sacrifices offered according to the accustomed rite; *'ele hatsedeq* (Is. 61.3) are trees that are always green and not "terebinths of justice"; just paths (Ps. 23.3) are paths which one can walk along. The opposite of *tsdq* is *rasha'*, that is to say something not as it should be.

(*b*) Conformity to the norm can also apply to the inward dispositions of men and the way they act. Samaria and Sodom are called more righteous than Jerusalem simply because they have committed lesser sins (Ez. 16.52). When Judah cries that Tamar is more righteous than himself he is saying that in the particular circumstances which are being narrated she has acted according to the rules and customs of prostitution whilst he himself has not respected them (Gen. 38.26), and when Ecclesiastes presents excess of righteousness as a thing to be avoided it is because, according to the general spirit of his book, too rigid a conformity to any kind of norm runs the risk of being injurious (Eccl. 7.15).

(*c*) The relative and temporary conception of justice in human relationships tends to take on a more unconditional meaning when humanity is divided into the just and the wicked, the former being exclusively the object of divine favour.

Conformity to a rule is, of course, very different according to the subjects who practise it; but whether contacts between men themselves or between God and men are concerned, righteousness is always a concept of relationship, fashioned upon the everyday dealings between two people and variable according to the requirements which devolve from these various contacts. That is why righteousness is an action much more than a state: a person is righteous because he acts justly; he does not act justly because he is righteous. The prophets never exhort men to acquire righteousness as a quality or state, but they constantly ask that justice be practised. When it comes from God righteousness is a transitive action and a visible manifestation of the being of Yahweh in his relations with man; thus the manifestations of righteousness are always placed in a temporal sequence: the Old Testament speaks of the righteousness of Yahweh when he shows his action in history; righteousness is exercised within the framework of the covenant and is only rarely made relative to the creation. Since the term righteousness in itself has no religious or moral connotation it is quite difficult to define the righteousness of God; the latter is essentially variable according to the diverse situations in which it is manifested. These different aspects have been defined in the following way : " Righteousness is attributed to the holy God who commits no iniquity; it is attributed to the holy God who cannot leave wickedness unpunished nor the good unrecognized; it is attributed to the God who is merciful and slow to anger who, according to Ezekiel's phrase, does not desire the death of a sinner but that he should repent and live. It is attributed to the God of love who pursues after the salvation of his people; and finally it is attributed to the God of love who communicates his righteousness to the sinner and justifies him.''[1]   Many aspects—because conformity to the norm represents for God, in the course of history, realities which are sometimes different and that for the important reason that the God of the Old Testament is not an idea which imposes itself with the immutability inherent in ideas but a living person, and that his norm can only be this personal being in his totality; this personal being is the sovereign Lord and all he does conforms to that fundamental attitude. " Righteousness is found under the sign of power ''[2] and shares in the diverse expressions of that power which assumes sometimes a terrible aspect, sometimes a bountiful one. Nevertheless, when the Old Testament states that God is just it is generally speaking of his power in a somewhat less vague way. The righteousness of God cannot be separated from the figure of God the judge. It is in fact this image which is always implied by the use of the root *shpht*[3] which in the form of *mishpat* is often found

---

[1] G. Martin, *La notion de la justice de Dieu dans l'A.T.*

[2] *DBS*, col. 1448, article " justice " by A. Descamps.

[3] The root *shpht* always has the meaning of to judge; we follow the view of van der Ploeg (Shpht and mishpat in *Oudtestamentische Studien* II, Leiden 1943); a different opinion has been sustained by H. W. Hertzberg amongst others, " Die Entwicklung des Begriffes mishpat im A.T." in *ZAW*, 1922, pp. 256ff., according to which the primitive meaning of *shpht* would have been " to rule " (herrschen). This latter contention relies notably on the title *shophetim* given to the heroes in the book of Judges who were military leaders and not judges; but that appellation is probably not primitive; the term *shophetim* was originally kept for the " minor " judges (Jg. 10.1-5; 12.8-15) who were not warrior leaders but guardians of the right and of the traditions of the Israelite amphictyony, comparable with the judges of ancient Iceland (according to A. Klostermann, *Der Pentateuch* 1907, pp. 348f., and Alt, *Die Ursprünge des israelitischen Rechts*, 1934); these judges formed a fixed order; the chief judges were originally called *moshi'im*, saviours; the extension of the title *shophetim* to these charismatic personalities was made under the influence of the royal régime, the king being the supreme judge of the nation, and it marked

associated with *tsedaqah*. Although it too underwent development, the root *shaphat* never lost its fundamental meaning of to judge, but to judge is not only to give a verdict so the word covers all the phases of a trial from the moment when the parties come before the judge, to plead their case, up to the final decision. The outcome of the judgment is a veritable liberation for the one who has been the object of a declaration of innocence, since he is not only reinstated in his right, but by the operation of the power of which he has been a beneficiary his life-potential is in some way augmented; the *mishpat* of the judge "establishes the one in the reality of his right, the other on the contrary in the reality of his wrong".[1] This dynamic nature of justice is still clearer when the function of *shophet* is exercised by God. Like the chief of the clan and in the manner of the gods of the fathers, Yahweh had to resolve the inevitable conflicts which arose between members of the clan. Expressions such as "May Yahweh be judge (*shaphat*) between me and thee" (Gen. 16.5; 1 Sam. 24.13) as well as the numerous proper names in which the theophoric element denotes a judiciary function: Elisaphat, Yehoshaphat, Shaphatyahu, Shaphat, Shiphtan, Abidan, Dan, Danel, Peliliyah, Eliphal, Phalal, show that in Israel the idea of God as judge perhaps held an even greater place than in other religions. The reality of the covenant found one of its most characteristic expressions in the figure of a lawsuit of Yahweh with his people (Is. 1; Mic. 6 and Jer. 2). Here Yahweh and the people appear as two parties pleading their respective rights, but since Yahweh is at the same time litigant and judge the result is an affirmation of his sovereignty to which the people can only submit. The judgment of Yahweh is always made with *tsedeq* (cf. Ps. 98.9: He will judge the earth with *tsedeq*) that is to say, according to his sovereignty which is the norm; very often this norm is exercised within a judicial framework, but it can also shatter this framework since the institutions of the law depend only on his own freedom. The conception of *mishpat*, evolving in the direction of custom, rule, law, into the character of what is obligatory and constraining, became incapable of

a victory of the constitution over events (cf. O. Grether, "Die Bezeichnung 'Richter' für die charismatischen Helden der vorstaatlichen Zeit" in *ZAW*, 1939, pp. 110ff.) In a recent study (*RThPh*, 1954, p. 283) G. Pidoux shows that the cosmic aspect of justice was not entirely unknown, and he appeals to passages like Ps. 72.2-3; 85.12; Joel 2.23.

[1] A. Neher, *Amos*, p. 262.

expressing all that was meant by the righteousness of Yahweh; therefore in speaking of God the judge stress had to be laid on the norm of his action (*tsedeq*) and on the visible manifestation of that norm (*tsedaqah*). The *tsedaqah* is not contradictory to the view of God as judge, it is indeed its essential condition.[1] Moreover, this term appeared to be so apt for expressing the idea of the divine that it became a proper name for one or more gods; the Old Testament figures of Melkitsedeq (Gen. 14.18) and Adonitsedeq (Jos. 10.1; Jg. 1.5-7), the Rabtsidqi of the El Amarna letters a Tsdqel and Tsdqshlm at Ugarit seem to attest the existence of a god of this name who, in the form he had taken in the religion of Israel, had a particular connection with Jerusalem, which Isaiah calls the '*ir hatsedeq* (1.26) and whose priesthood belonged to the dynasty of the descendant of Tsadoq. The active and personal rôle of Tsedeq in certain Psalms must also be mentioned: tsedeq goes before Yahweh (Ps. 85.14), it looks down from the height of heaven (Ps. 85.12), along with mishpat it is the foundation of Yahweh's throne (Ps. 89.15; 97.2), Tsedeq and Shalom, another Jerusalemite deity, embrace each other (Ps. 85.11). Whether this refers to primitive gods become servants of Yahweh or to the hypostatization of the attributes of one great god, it shows that righteousness was always regarded in the Old Testament and in the surrounding world as one of the principal attributes of deity. One would almost be tempted to regard it as the essential quality and to put it alongside holiness; perhaps it could be said that it is righteousness which characterizes El (Elohim), cf. Ps. 50.6, whilst holiness is the particular attribute of Yahweh.[2] Tsedeq is also one

---

[1] According to Th. Gaster, *Thespis*, Tsdq and Yshr figured as the names of divine beings in one Ugaritic text (1 K II, 12), but that very hypothetical reading seems rather to have been inspired by what Philo of Byblos says about the divine pair Misor and Sydyk, names signifying εὔλυτος & δίκαιος to whom tradition ascribed the discovery of the use of salt (cf. Eusebius, *Praep. evang.* 1, 10, 13, Migne *Patr. Gr* XXI, col. 80 b).

[2] In Psalms 50.6 and 75.8, Elohim is called Shophet; and in this context we can also remember the passage in the Book of the Covenant dealing with the rite of emancipation of a slave (Ex. 21.6): "His master shall bring him before Elohim"; the Syriac version, depending upon Ps. 82.1 translates "to the judges"; whilst recognizing that the term Elohim sometimes means the divine rather than the deity, we do not think that it was ever applied to human beings (except to the king in one solitary text in the O.T., Ps. 45). What we can say, however, is that justice is less an attribute peculiar to Yahweh than is holiness. Justice was characteristic of gods by and large (cf. the goddess Ma'at in Egypt, Shamash and his associates Kettu and Mesharu in Babylon, Mitra and Varuna amongst the Mitanni), but Yahweh alone is the Holy One.

of the principal attributes of those who on the earth are the most highly qualified representatives of God, the king and the Messiah. In the prayer at Gibeon Solomon asks Yahweh to give him discernment in judging (1 Kings 3.11) and the title *shophetim* given by tradition to those who were—before the title was actually used—the first kings of Israel, shows to what extent the qualities and functions of the judge served as a model for the king (cf. the importance of righteousness in the prayer of intercession for the king: Ps. 72). The Messiah will only take up on a wider and more perfect plane the activity of a king. The terms *tsedeq, mishpat, tsadiq* form part of the typical style of all Messianic oracles (Is. 9; 11; Zech. 9) and Jeremiah will invent for the Messiah the name of Yahweh *tsidqenu*, which is not only in opposition to the name of the reigning king *Tsidqiyahu* but which summarizes for him the whole work of the Messiah (Jer. 23.5).

When performed by Yahweh judgments always conform to the rule; they are right and they attain their end, which is the establishment of his kingship; yet along the right way of Yahweh's deliverances (*tsidqot*) there is a place for salvation and for the punishment of sin, which is not an accident of no importance for the realization of God's plan but a reality able to oppose his designs which he has to take seriously. Doubtless the decisions constantly repeated by Yahweh towards his people represent the line of action of divine righteousness, but that does not necessarily imply that we must speak of the unilateral character of that righteousness by seeing in it only the manifestation of benevolence. Diestel,[1] Ritschl[2] and others following them[3] have seen in righteousness the sequence of God's plans for the salvation of believers, the punishment of the wicked being the work of his wrath, which some texts indeed contrast with his righteousness (*v. infra.*). It is certain that never in the Old Testament does justice appear as distributive in the strict meaning of the term. The justice of Yahweh is not of the type of the blindfolded maiden holding a balance in her hand, the justice of Yahweh extends one arm to the wretch stretched out on the ground whilst the other pushes away the one who causes the misfortunes, and so its saving aspect does not exclude every

---

[1] *Die Idee der Gerechtigkeit.*
[2] *Die christliche Lehre von der Rechtfertigung und Versöhnung* II, *Der biblische Stoff der Lehre*, Bonn 1874, pp. 101ff.
[3] Amongst recent writers, H. Cazelles, *art. cit.*

distributive element. One of the earliest old Testament texts, the song of Deborah, speaks of the *tsideqot* Yahweh when celebrating the great military victories won by Israel, but these *tsideqot* are the decisions of the just judge, that is to say the victory for Israel and the defeat for the Canaanites who in their wickedness have dared to stand in the way of the chosen people (Jg. 5.11); at other times the division between the righteous and the wicked cuts across the chosen people themselves. Psalm 7 clearly says that the activity of a righteous God must be exercised simultaneously in favour of the righteous and for the punishment of the wicked. "Yahweh judges the peoples (*yadin*). Judge me (*shophteni*), O Yahweh, according to thy righteousness (*ketsidqu*) and my innocence. Oh let the wickedness of the wicked (*resha'im*) come to an end, and establish the just (*tsadiq*)" (vv. 9-10). Solomon's dedicatory prayer asks Yahweh to judge between his servants, to condemn the guilty, making the consequences of his action fall on his own head, and to pardon (justify) the just by treating him according to his righteousness (1 Kings 8.32). The *mishpat* and *tsedaqah* with which Zion will be redeemed mean for Isaiah (1.27) the judgment she must pass through and which alone will remove from her the sin which draws Yahweh's wrath upon her. The right and the righteousness which Yahweh will use as a measure are an allusion to the structure which is to be erected, but this will take place only through judgment (Is. 28.17). The negative and positive aspects of righteousness are also present in the text of Isaiah 10.22 : "The destruction is fixed which will make righteousness (*tsedaqah*) overflow." It is not a question here of a life-bringing stream but of the severity of Yahweh which destroys those who lack faith in him, and the manifestation of his holiness by righteousness does not appear in the context in which it is mentioned as an intervention of a particularly saving kind (Is. 5.16).

The righteousness of Yahweh who is an *'elohe mishpat* (Is. 30.18) implies that the faithful man will be truly declared righteous only after submitting to the discriminatory judgment of Yahweh. On this point all the prophets follow the thought of Isaiah (cf. Jer. 12.1; Zeph. 3.5, 8) and one Psalmist echoes current belief: "With the faithful thou showest thyself faithful, upright with the upright, pure with the pure, but wily with the perverse" (Ps. 18.26-28). But even in cases where righteousness implies a punitive aspect it never exhausts itself in judgment; wrath leads on to punishment, whilst *mishpat*, remaining purely educative (*ysr*), opens the door to grace (Jer. 10.24). The idea of grace and deliverance never ceased to underlie the concept of righteousness looked at in the light of election and covenant. The prophet Hosea speaks of *tsedeq* and *mishpat* as gifts which the husband makes to his wife after her return to grace (2.21). If from the time of Jeremiah the punitive aspect of righteousness passes more and more into the background it is doubtless because the just judgment of Yahweh was thought to have been accomplished by the exile. It is above all with Second Isaiah that righteousness becomes synonymous with grace and salvation; except for certain passages in which the word is used forensically (41.26; 43.9, 26; 50.8) righteousness is not only for him the deliverance of the oppressed and the restoration of their normal state, but the gift of a new reality superior to what previously existed. This fresh aspect of righteousness is due less to the experience of exile (cf. Is. 40.2) than to the eschatological and messianic perspective which dominates his whole message: righteousness is a communication of grace and glory; its beneficiary will not be the innocent and the oppressed but the people who have no other merits than being the elect of Yahweh. The framework of the covenant is widened because righteousness will extend not only to the Israelites but to all peoples. The salvation of Israel will no longer have, as in the time of Deborah, judgment upon the Gentiles as its counterpart, it will extend to them as well, the more so as the salvation of Israel itself is wrought through the intermediary of the Gentile king Cyrus (cf. 42.6 and especially 45.20ff.). Whilst in pre-exilic texts the announcement of messianic righteousness is still veiled and conditioned by the judgment upon sin, now these new things are on the point of appearing.

Righteousness as the free and saving favour of God has many echoes in the Old Testament, particularly in the Psalms where the righteousness of God is presented as the refuge of the faithful and as the source of pardon. In a text, probably post-exilic, in the book of Micah (7.9ff.) the believer awaits the manifestation of Yahweh's righteousness, not as the sanction for his sin but as the grace which will put an end to it (cf. also Ps. 51.16; 143.1-2; Zech. 9.9; Joel 2.23; Ps. 85.10-11). Does this new meaning of the word contradict the picture of God as judge or is it perhaps its final consequence? This evolution must be linked with the new meaning of the words for poor and unfortunate; following a line of thought whose origin is found with Jeremiah and Zephaniah, the poor is no longer, or not merely, the unfortunate one, the victim of an injustice, awaiting the re-establishment of his rights, but every believer has before God the attitude of a suppliant, of an *'ebyon*[1] who begs for a decision in his favour, not in order to be justified against an adversary but in an absolute manner. By virtue of the constant tendency for ideas to develop into actions, righteousness tends, in post-biblical Judaism and especially in Aramaic, to take the meaning of mercy and particularly alms-giving.[2] "Compensate thy sin by *tsedaqah* [that is to say, by good works] and thine iniquity by showing mercy to the poor," Daniel counsels Nebuchadrezzar (Dan. 4.24). As for the righteousness of God, this remains an act of his mercy so much the more real because the one who expects it will not rely upon his own righteousness (Dan. 9.18), yet in face of the righteousness of God the practice of righteousness by man is the best way of knowing all its richness (cf. Is. 56.1).

BIBLIOGRAPHY

BAUDISSIN, W. W. VON, "Der gerechte Gott in altsemitischer Religion", *Festgabe A. Harnack*, Tübingen 1921, p. 1.

DALMAN, G., *Die richterliche Gerechtigkeit im A.T.*, Berlin 1897.

DIESTEL, L., "Die Idee der Gerechtigkeit, vorzüglich im A.T.", *Jahrb. f. deutsche Theol.*, 1860, p. 173.

FAHLGREN, K. H., *Sedaka. Nahestehende und entgegengesetzte Begriffe im A.T.*, Uppsala 1932.

KAUTZSCH, E., *Die Derivate des Stammes tsdq im alttest. Sprachgebrauch*, Tübingen 1881.

KOCH KLAUS, *Sdq im A.T.*, 1954.

MARTIN, G., *La notion de la justice de Dieu dans l'A.T.*, Montauban 1892.

MONNIER, J., *La justice de Dieu d'après la Bible*. Paris 1878.

NOETSCHER, F., *Die Gerechtigkeit Gottes bei den vorexilischen Propheten*, Münster 1915.

[1] On the meanings of the word *'ebyon* in the O.T., cf. the article by P. Humbert in *RHPR*, 1952, pp. 1ff.

[2] In Rabbinic literature *tsedaqah* differs still more from anything juristic; the Tosephta Sanhedrin 1, 5 says: "In the place where there is *din* (righteousness in the sense of judicial action), there is no tsedaqah, and where there is tsedaqah there is no *din*" and in Matthew 6.1 certain manuscripts read ἐλεημοσύνη in place of δικαιοσύνη. This sense of *tsedaqah* is not absolutely new: it is only the crystallizing out of the idea of salvation contained in the term since Deutero-Isaiah and no doubt even since Amos.

VIII. THE FAITHFULNESS OF GOD

THE word *chesed*, which is the term most frequently used for divine fidelity, has no exact equivalent in our modern languages; the LXX renders it usually by ἔλεος, mercy, but as this sense applies only in a relatively limited number of cases modern versions translate it by kindness, grace, fidelity. Etymology, without supplying us with an absolutely satisfactory answer to the problem, at least directs us to the primitive signification, which is that of strength.[1] This fundamental sense appears again in many passages, as: "All flesh is as the grass and all its strength as the flower of the field" (Is. 40.6); in 2 Chr. 32.32 and 35.26 the actions of a king of Judah are qualified by the term *chesed*; but the parallel text in Kings has the word *geburah*, strong and effective action (2 Kings 20.20); in one other instance *chesed* is placed parallel to *'oz*, strength: "Strength belongs to Elohim, *chesed* to thee, O Lord" (Ps. 62.12-13). Yahweh is called *chesed*, fortress and shield (Ps. 144.2) and the Psalm of Jonah contrasts *chesed* with vain and transitory things (Jonah 2.9). The idea of strength likewise appears in the association of *chesed* with *'emet*, the fundamental meaning of which is firmness, stability, and thus, derivatively, of security and truth (Ps. 25.10; 40.11; 61.8; 138.2, etc.). Since the idea of strength has in itself no moral content it is not surprising that alongside the use of the term *chesed* in a clearly positive sense we can meet the same word with the sense of shame and infamy: Prov. 14.34; 25.10; Lev. 20.17, that is to say of a strength which, instead of uniting, erects barriers and sets men in opposition to each other.[2]

In Israel the term was associated early with a clearly delimited strength, namely that which binds together two individuals or a

---

[1] The meaning strength has been stressed by F. Perles, *Analekten zur Textkritik des A.T.*; he sees in it the common denominator to the threefold use of the root *chsd* in Arabic and in Hebrew: (a) to assemble; (b) to envy; (c) to be hard.

[2] Instead of getting rid of the difficulty by emending the text, we must rather see here the form which is retained in Aramaic and which means to be ashamed, often assimilated to *cherpah* (cf. Nöldeke, *Neue Beiträge zur semitischen Sprachwissenschaft*, 13, p. 93).

group and which, in the religious sphere, means the bond uniting God to man and vice versa. When it is used for the attitudes of man, the term religion, understood as that which binds, would very well render the multiple senses of *chesed* which corresponded closely to the Latin *pietas* and described not only the attitude of the believer towards God or of the son towards his father (filial piety), but also that of God or of the chief towards his subordinates, and in general the natural sentiment which without legal constraint causes one to show benevolence and indulgence towards the members of one's family or tribe.[1] It is to the credit of Nelson Glueck, following a way opened earlier by I. Elbogen,[2] that he showed the link between *chesed* and the covenant, an interpretation which has seemed so convincing that L. Koehler, in his Lexicon, replaces the usual translations of mercy, benevolence and fidelity by those of social obligation, association, solidarity (Gemeinschaftspflicht, Verbundenheit, Solidarität). The use of the term *chesed* for human relationships shows clearly that the meaning of benevolence and mercy is secondary to that of solidarity or simply of loyalty : in the book of Genesis (19.19) Lot says to one of his three visitors : " You have shown great *chesed* towards me ", and he means respect for the sacred rights of hospitality. When David says : " I want to show *chesed* to the king of the Ammonites as his father showed *chesed* to me " (2 Sam. 10.2), there is no question of an act of friendliness, still less of compassion, but of the maintenance of loyal relations between two peoples; in this last case *chesed* is the equivalent of *berith*, and the two terms are moreover found together in Dt. 7.2, 9, 12; 1 Kings 8.23; 2 Chr. 6.14; Neh. 1.5; 9.32; Dan. 9.4; Ps. 50.5, 36; 89.29, 34, so we can define *chesed* as the power which guarantees a covenant and makes it strong and durable. The expression " keep covenant and *chesed* ", which probably originated in Deuteronomic circles, penetrated into the liturgy; it is not without significance that the term is most used in the Psalms and that it has passed into the liturgical tradition of Judaism.

The *chesed* of God is revealed in and through the covenant; it is because God has concluded a covenant that he has shown *chesed*; this is therefore less a quality or attribute of God than a proof which he intends to give, and the multiplicity of meanings

---

[1] Lods, *Les prophètes d'Israël* . . . , p. 100.
[2] In " Chesed, Verpflichtung, Verheissung, Bekräftigung ", *Oriental Studies dedicated to Paul Haupt*, Baltimore-Leipzig 1926, pp. 43-46.

the term can assume is better understood with that in mind. *Chesed* is always connected with somebody (Ex. 20.6; Dt. 5.10; 2 Sam. 22.51; Ps. 18.51; Jer. 32.18), but since relationship is one of the essential aspects of God himself, it is quite normal that we should find *chesed* mentioned on certain particularly solemn occasions in which God presents himself; thus when he manifests himself to Moses, Yahweh passed before Moses saying: "Yahweh, Yahweh, a compassionate (*rachum*) and merciful (*chanum*) God, slow to anger and rich in *chesed* and *'emet*, keeping *chesed* for thousands . . ." (Ex. 34.5). In the midst of the changes inherent in a revelation of God in history *chesed* represents the permanent element which allows Yahweh to be always faithful to himself. It is to this *chesed* that every member of the covenant can appeal when he wishes to see the covenant maintained and confirmed. Eliezer the servant of Abraham asks Yahweh to prove his *chesed* towards him at the time when he is entrusted with a particularly delicate mission (Gen. 24.12). Solomon asks that Yahweh will show him the same *chesed* which he has shown towards David (1 Kings 3.6); one who finds himself in a dangerous situation is recommended to the *chesed* of Yahweh (2 Sam. 15.20; Jer. 33.11ff.; Ps. 100.5; 106.1; 107.1-8, 15). The initiator of the covenant cannot abandon those who are his partners: the majority of the metaphors by which the Old Testament illustrated the reality of the covenant bring to light the aspect of firmness and fidelity contained in the term *chesed*, whether the metaphor be that of father and son, of the shepherd and the flock, or of conjugal union. Marriage is the realm *par excellence* for the exercise of *chesed* and it is not surprising that it is with the prophet Hosea that the term reaches its greatest significance, designating in turn the relation of Yahweh with the people, the obligations of the people towards Yahweh and the reciprocal obligations of the members of the nation between themselves, for in the teaching of the prophets about human relations *chesed* is conceived after the pattern of the divine *chesed* and a summary of obligations like that of Micah 6.8 shows that the imitation of God is the mainspring of all the religion and ethics of the Old Testament.

The deepening of the idea by the prophets sometimes places *chesed* beyond the covenant: this is why the breaking of the covenant by the human partners in it does not entail of necessity the suppression of *chesed*. To faithless Israel Yahweh says: "I will betroth thee unto me for ever by means of righteousness and judgment, *chesed*, and mercy" (Hosea 2.21) and again: "Return, rebellious Israel, saith Yahweh, I will no longer show thee an angry face for I am *chasid*, I do not keep my anger for ever" (Jer. 3.12) and again: "For a brief instant I have abandoned thee, but with great compassion (*rachamim*) I will gather thee. In the unleashing of my wrath I had hidden my face from thee for a moment, but with eternal *chesed* I will have compassion upon thee" (Is. 54.7-8). In such passages *chesed* is no longer the bond upholding the covenant, it is the very source of the attitude which impels God to enter into relation with his people, therefore in reading them we must remove the strictly legal conception as N. Glueck has defined it and translate by love or grace.[1] The terms *chen* and *rachamim* which replace that of *berith* in making the meaning of *chesed* explicit (Ex. 34.7; Num. 14.19; Is. 63.7; Jer. 32.18; Lam. 3.32; Neh. 13.22; Ps. 86.5; 106.7-45; 145.8) do not belong to the language of covenant and are only used in a unilateral sense which excludes reciprocity. *Chesed* is to such a degree an unexpected act that several texts celebrate it as a miracle: "Yahweh has made marvellous his *chesed*" (Ps. 4.4). "Make marvellous thy *chesed*" (Ps. 17.7). "Blessed be Yahweh for he has made his *chesed* wonderful for me" (Ps. 31.22). "O that he would give thanks to Yahweh for his *chesed* and for his wonderful works" (Ps. 107.8, 15, 21, 31); nevertheless in keeping the term *chesed* the prophets wanted to insist upon the firm nature which always characterizes the action of God; according to them what is rightly astonishing is not that God is loving and merciful, for other gods were equally so, but that this love is firm and true. Parallel with the deepening of the idea of *chesed* we witness the extension of its temporal significance. The *chesed* of Yahweh belongs to the future as well as to the past, it is an undertaking by which God stands as surety for the future; the *chesed 'olam* (Ps. 89, *passim* and Is. 55.3) is not only the manifestation of divine faithfulness in the past, but "the grace irrevocably promised" of which king David was only the first sign

---

[1] N. Glueck's thesis has recently been criticized by H. J. Stoebe (*V.T.* 1952, pp. 224ff.) who contests the legal meaning and comes to the following conclusion: "The special feature of the theological assertion of God's *chesed* is to be seen in God turning to man in unconditional friendliness and magnanimity. He surrenders his divine right in order to have fellowship with man." Concerning this thesis we hold that certain modifications must be made in Glueck's one-sided interpretation, but we do not think his initial viewpoint should be abandoned.

and whose fulfilment the people await. This widening of the concept is similarly shown in the realm of space: the attitude of Yahweh towards all creation is characterized by *chesed* (cf. Ps. 33.5; 36.7; 119.64 and the great liturgy of Ps. 136 which views not only history but creation as a result of *chesed*: vv. 5-9).

It may appear paradoxical that a term denoting an action and clearly legal in appearance should have been preferred to others which expressed profound qualities and feelings of God;[1] but that demonstrates yet again that the Old Testament is interested less in the nature of God than in his work, less in his existence than in his presence. Now the term *chesed* is particularly suitable for expressing that Yahweh was an active power in the midst of men, a power from which they could not escape.[2]

BIBLIOGRAPHY

GLUECK, N., *Das Wort Hesed im alttestamentlichen Sprachgebrauch*, *BZAW*, 47, Glessen 1927.

GULKOWITSCH, L., *Das Wort hasid*, Tartu 1934.

STOEBE, H. J., "Die Bedeutung des Wortes häsäd im A.T.", *VT*, 1952, p. 244.

[1] T. F. Torrance, *Scottish Journal of Theology*, 1948, p. 60, calls *chesed* the "great sacramental word of the Old Testament faith".

[2] The theme of *chesed* in the O.T. became the pattern by which the life of the believer called to be an chasid had to be directed; together with *tsedeq* = *tsadiq*, it is the only term which gave birth to a style of life. The chasid is, in general terms—and before the word is used with a more limited meaning—one who fears God and who shows "piety" towards those who are within the covenant like himself.

IX. THE LOVE OF GOD

THE covenant by which God binds himself to his people
—and through his people to humanity as a whole—has
profound roots which cannot be defined otherwise than by
the mystery of election; but the origin of election is found in love,
that is to say in the spontaneous movement which carries one being
towards another being with the desire to possess it and to find
some satisfaction in that possession. The prophet Jeremiah in a
familiar verse expresses the relation between love and *chesed*: "I
love thee with an everlasting love, therefore with *chesed* do I draw
thee" (31.3). The Hebrew root which serves to express the reality
of love under the double form of eros and agapē is *'ahab*, which
itself derives from a biliteral root *hab*, in Arabic *habba* = to blow;
this etymology was first proposed by Schultens:[1] "*thema ahab
amare, diligere, vim istam secundariam induit a primaria spirandi,
anhelandique; prout anhelare aliquit est vehementius petere, et
adamare*". The root *'abah* = to desire is itself a variant of this same
fundamental meaning so that love can be defined as a desire at
once violent and voluntary.[2] The term *'ahab* (substantive *'ahabah*)
is used chiefly with a personal object,[3] yet it is only once met with
for expressing the love of a woman for her husband (1 Sam. 18.20:
Michal loved David) and once for the love of a subordinate for his
superior (Dt. 15.16).

Since love is the attitude of a superior towards an inferior, the
term *'ahab* is not used for the attitude of a wife to her husband
nor for that of children to their parents. As for the love of man
for God, which often arises, it must not be understood in the sense
of abolishing the distance between God and man and it is moreover

---

[1] In "Proverbia Salomonis" (1748) at the end of the work *Index hebraeorum
vocum sub "habab"*; cf. also D. Winton Thomas: "The root *ahab* 'love' in
Hebrew" in *ZAW*, 1939, pp. 57ff. This form *habab* is met in Prov. 30.15; Ps. 55.23;
Hos. 8.13 where the translation "love" is adopted by the majority of versions.

[2] This is the opinion of Eichrodt, *Theol. A.T.* I, p. 127, who dealing with
ahab speaks of "Willenseinsatz" and the "starkes Gefühl".

[3] The root *'ahab* is never met in proper names, which express the whole gamut
of divine attributes; on the other hand the root *yadad* is quite frequent.

formulated as an order, which considerably weakens the idea of desire and possession contained in the root *'ahab*. As the subject of love God can have several objects, but in the great majority of cases that object is the nation as a whole. The two passages where Jerusalem is given as the object of God's love (Ps. 78.68 and 87.2) are only a variant of that basic idea. Three times only are we told that God loves individuals (2 Sam. 12.24 of Solomon, Neh. 13.26 of Solomon, Is. 48.14 of Cyrus). But in these three passages royal personages are concerned, which gives the use of the verb to love a significance it is impossible to extend to all men. The sense of ardent and voluntary desire contained in the root *'ahab* is found to be confirmed by the other terms by means of which the Old Testament designates the love of God: *chashaq* = to attach oneself to (Dt. 7.7; Ps. 91.14), *chaphets* and *ratsah* = to take pleasure in (Gen. 34.19 and 2 Sam. 24.23) and especially *yada'* = to know; that knowledge is in no degree theoretical knowledge, but its primitive sense is that which we find expressed in Gen. 4.2: Adam knew Eve; the opposite of *yada'* is expressed by the prophets with the root *zanah* = to prostitute oneself, thereby marking the breaking of the marriage bond. The frequency of the figure of marriage to describe the relationship of God with his people confirms the connection we have pointed out between love and *chesed*: underlying marriage is a spontaneous feeling which leads to the making of a choice, but this feeling must be exercised according to rule and be subject to certain laws, in a word it becomes a *berith* which needs to be established by *chesed*. The idea of desire, of choice and of election is again confirmed by the term which expresses the contrary to love. With the root *'ahab* is contrasted the root *sana'* = to hate; but that root does not always have, and in particular did not have originally, the active and violent sense which we usually attribute to it. If *'ahabah* denotes election, hate indicates non-election. That comes out very clearly from the following passages: Gen. 29.31, Leah is called *senuah*, that is to say she who has not been chosen. The same antithesis is found again in Dt. 21.15-17; 1 Sam. 1.5 and Prov. 30.23 and similarly it is in the light of this relativity that we must understand the apparently very harsh words of Jesus about the hatred which his disciples must have for their kith and kin (Lk. 14.26). The election of the one does not *ipso facto* involve the disapproval of the other, although we have in the Old Testament itself proofs of the twist towards the understanding of God's love in an exclusive sense, for example in some oracles upon the nations.

These preliminary considerations lead to two conclusions which will allow us to define the love of God in the Old Testament: (*a*) as grace; (*b*) as education.

(*a*) The love of God is not conditioned but it springs forth spontaneously through the free decision of God and thus appears as a manifestation of his sovereignty: "You only do I know amongst all the families of the earth" (Amos 3.2) and the entire book of Hosea is a development of the theme of God's love. It is chiefly in Deuteronomy that we find numerous affirmations about the gratuitous nature of love, but here the tone of the prophet's living experience gives place to the theologian's reflection and to the exhortations of the legislator: "Although the heaven and the heaven of heavens, the earth and all that is found therein, belong to Yahweh, it is to thy fathers that Yahweh has attached his affection (*chashaq*), and after them he has chosen only you, their posterity, among all peoples" (Dt. 10.14-15). "Know that it is not because of thy righteousness that Yahweh thy God hath given thee the possession of this good land" (Dt. 9.6ff.). "He found him in a desert land, in the waste, he watched over him, he guarded him as the apple of his eye, as an eagle which drives its brood from the nest, hovers above them, then spreading its wings takes them and bears them upon its feathers" (Dt. 32.10-11).

Had Israel anything attractive to become in this way the object of God's love? One passage of the prophet Hosea might lead us to an affirmative answer: "Like grapes (that might be discovered) in the wilderness, I found Israel. Like an early-ripe fig on a fig tree, I saw your fathers" (9.10). The prophet compares Yahweh to a traveller pleasantly surprised by finding grapes in an arid wilderness. Israel must therefore have had some trait to arouse Yahweh's interest, but this passage, unique of its kind, might also mean that the impossible has become true, and so put in relief the extraordinary and miraculous character of election. In the very realistic allegory by means of which the prophet Ezekiel represents the election of Israel, Israel had nothing attractive and God's initiative is aroused only by his pity (Ez. 16.1-52).

Israel always felt that in its election there was a mystery beyond its understanding; nevertheless it attempted to give a rational explanation of that election:

1. God loves and chooses Israel because he is bound to the fathers by an oath: "He loves you and wishes to keep the oath which he made to your fathers" (Dt. 7.7-8, cf. also Dt. 4.37 and 10.15).

2. God loves Israel because he made a promise to David: "I will protect this city, I will save it out of love for myself and of David my servant" (2 Kings 19.34; Is. 37.35).

3. God loves Israel for his own sake and particularly for his name's sake; perhaps there is implicitly present the idea that God chose his people in order to set himself up in opposition to other gods (Ps. 79.9; 106.8; Is. 41.21; Jer. 14.21).

4. God loves Israel in order to punish the wickedness of the nations: "It is because of the wickedness of these nations that Yahweh thy God dispossessed them before thee" (Dt. 9.4-5), a motive which is found combined with that of the promise made to the fathers.

From these explanations Israel often drew consequences which ran contrary to the true nature of God's love. They stiffened into rigid exclusivism, interpreting their election, which had become a hardened conception, as a duty to hate and a matter for pride. With the prophet Malachi, who gives us a most authentic echo of Jewish exclusiveness, the affirmation of God's love: "I love you" (1.2) is no longer the certainty by which the people live and in which they believe, but a collection of proofs which the people turn to their profit as a source of pride and glory. Happily the prophetic message of God's love had in itself too much power for such deviations to be decisive.

(b) It was also the prophets who best showed the educative element of the love of God. They were all firmly persuaded that the motives of the divine action were inspired by its ultimate purpose. God loves his people in order to achieve his aim with them, that is to say the establishment of his kingship over the world; that eschatological orientation preserved the love of God from any form of mysticism, for mysticism implies a suppression of time, whilst love according to the Old Testament is a slow but certain education of his people. It is because Yahweh has a purpose for his people that his love is not opposed to his justice and his wrath. The idea of education as the Israelite conceived it is inseparable from punishment and he who abstains from punishment would be a bad pedagogue (Prov. 3.12 and in certain passages of the book of Job), which does not eliminate the fact that the punishment is accompanied for God by genuine suffering and that he never gladly resorts to it (Hos. 11.7-9; Jer. 12.7-9). The figure of the marriage union, so rich in suggestiveness, illustrates this educative function of love. The essentially contractual and even commercial aspect of marriage in ancient Israel did not exclude the idea of mutual education of the partners and specially that of the wife by the husband; that education will cease when God the spouse of his people has attained his ends, that is to say when history is completed. It is interesting to observe that the figure of conjugal union is never encountered in the pictures of messianic bliss;[1] in the same way the future aeon will be characterized by the suppression of marriage, the bond between God and the people will be replaced by something more profound and more real than that of marriage. To attain his purposes God places at the disposal of his people certain means which will preserve them in the love of God. The prophets and most distinctly Deuteronomy stress the rôle of the law as the most efficacious means of education for assuring the permanence of the election (Dt. 4.5-6, 32, 36; 28.63; 30.9, 11-14), though confusion between the end and the means often led to a caricature of the love of God.

The love of God is addressed in a general way to the people as a nation and this gives the love a different tone from that which appears in the New Testament; yet there is every reason for supposing that the thought of isolated individuals being the objects of God's love was not entirely strange to Israel : there is a proof, it seems, in the invocation "my God",[2] frequent in hymns and lamentations, by which individuals committed their fate into the hands of a God with whom they knew themselves to be in personal contact and by whom they knew themselves to be loved.

---

[1] At least under the form of the *berit*; knowledge will continue and even attain to its fullness, once it is freed from all juridical attachment. It is interesting to observe that Jesus when he speaks of the life of the age to come shows it as passing beyond the condition of marriage (Matt. 22.30).

[2] See O. Eissfeldt, "'Mein Gott' im Alten Testament", *ZAW*, 1945-48, pp. 3ff.

BIBLIOGRAPHY

DEAK, J., *Die Gottesliebe in den alten semitischen Religionen*, Eperjes 1914.
FEUILLET, A., *Le Cantique des Cantiques*, coll., "Lectio divina", Paris 1953.
BUCK, F., *Die Liebe Gottes beim Propheten Hosea*, Rome 1953.
WINTON THOMAS, D., "The root ahab, love, in Hebrew", *ZAW* 1939, p. 57.
ZIEGLER, J., *Die Liebe Gottes bei den Propheten*, Münster 1930.

X. THE WRATH OF GOD

WRATH is one of the most frequently mentioned of the feelings of God and the expression "slow to anger" is far from meaning that it was foreign to his nature. The numerous terms which serve to denote it are all borrowed from the concrete language of the physiological expressions of anger: it is called *'ap* nose, from the root *'anap* to blow violently, *chemah* heat, from *yacham* to be warm, *qetsep* outburst, *'ebrah* overflowing. It is interesting to note that these terms are met with more often in connection with God than with men. Some even like *za'am* and *charon 'ap*, are used only of the divine anger; thus it is fitting to preserve for these terms their exact meaning: the Israelite really believed in the wrath of Yahweh and did not project it upon God from the testings and punishments which he himself had passed through.[1] It would be just as false to run to the opposite extreme and to see in wrath an element which the God of Israel had inherited from foreign deities or demons. It is always connected with Yahweh and the few passages where it seems to act as an independent power are to be attributed to the theological tendency to eliminate anthropomorphisms. Rather let us say that wrath is part of the divine πάθος and that it fits very well into the framework of this covenant religion, at the base of which there is the affirmation of Yahweh's sovereignty. Like the majority of the sentiments, wrath is primarily an action: God pours it out (Ez. 20.33; Lam. 4.11), he makes it rise up (2 Chr. 36.16), he sends it out (Job 20.23; Ps. 78.49), he performs it (1 Sam. 28.18; Hos. 11.9). Wrath is so much part of the figure of God in the Old Testament that the ancient Israelites saw no problem in it, but they accepted this reality as being a normal part of the irrational and mysterious in God. What Paul Volz[2] has called the demonic element in

---

[1] According to statistics given by J. Fichtner, *Theol. Literaturzeitung*, 1950, 4-5, *'ap* is used 170 times of God and 40 times of man, *chemah* 90 times of God and 25 times of man, *'ebrah* 24 times of God and 6 times of man, *qetsep* 26 times of God and twice only of man.

[2] *Das Dämonische in Jahve*, 1924.

Yahweh is not a foreign element attributed to the God of Israel, but is linked with the profound and intimate being of this God and of his religion. Many texts show this destructive and terrible power at work, and even when they do not always mention wrath in this connection they express its essential content, namely the threat which a mysterious and powerful God imposes upon all that exists. This aspect appears, for instance, in the wrestling of Jacob with the angel (Gen. 32), in the nocturnal attack upon Moses (Ex. 4.29) or in the numerous passages which speak of the face of God which is unwilling to be seen, and of the holiness too direct contact with which produces death (Ex. 33.20; 19.9-25; Jg. 13.22; 1 Sam. 6.19; 2 Sam. 6.7; Is. 6.5). Although in some cases wrath can be evoked by the transgression of a given command, there are others, few in number, in which it is kindled without anything to provoke it. In the account of the David story we read that the anger of Yahweh was kindled against Israel (2 Sam. 24.1) when according to 2 Sam. 21.14 it had just been appeased and when in the meantime no event had taken place likely to rekindle it. As an expression of his power, Yahweh puts his wrath at the service of his purposes, for all that Yahweh does has an aim, which is the establishment of his kingship and of which the great judgment will be the decisive act. The day of Yahweh will in fact be a day of wrath: in the earliest pictures of it given us the nations are threatened with his wrath simply because their existence is an obstacle to the establishment of the sovereignty of Yahweh, and according to some traditions the same viewpoint also prevailed at the conquest of Canaan (Ex. 23.27-30; Num. 24.18; Jos. 24.12). This unmotivated character of the divine wrath appears again in those texts which connect it with the ephemeral nature of human life. As a human being man is threatened with God's wrath (Job 14.1-4); this may not even have been foreign to his creation and God might have made man mortal the better to control him.[1]

However, stress upon the covenant and the moral aspect inherent in it led to the belief that transgression of that covenant was the cause of wrath. Wrath then appears as a particular aspect of the divine jealousy, of that jealousy which is an exclusive love when

[1] In certain laments of Job the anger of God seems to be his normal activity, so that it could disappear only by a change in his nature; but in the book of Job allowance must be made for the readily exaggerated style of poetry (cf. Job 16.9, 20; 19.11).

the people are faithful, but which turns to wrath when the people respond to that love with ingratitude by going after other gods. The Pentateuch, particularly the exhortations in Deuteronomy, as well as the prophets, relate the outburst of wrath to the transgression of the covenant (Dt. 6.15; 11.16ff.; 12.23; 13.19; 29.15-19; Jos. 23.16; Ez. 5.13; 16.38; 36.6; Nahum 1.2; Zeph. 3.8; Ps. 79.5). In a parallel way, wrath against the nations answers to motives of a moral order; they will be punished either for pride or for contempt for the elementary rules of humanity; the day of wrath becomes the day when quite definite sins are judged (Amos 1 and 2). Always there is correlation between the intensity of sin and of wrath: the graver the sin the fiercer will be the wrath; but the diminution of sin will weaken the wrath. The history of Israel is presented by the prophets as a series of manifestations of Yahweh's wrath: Isaiah punctuates his great discourses of threats with the refrain: "His wrath does not return and his hand is stretched out still"[1] (5.25; 9.11; 16.20; 10.4). Yahweh will deliver his own people to the Assyrian, the executive rod of his anger (Is. 9.10ff.; 10.5), taken for the moment out of his armoury as the prophet Jeremiah metaphorically expresses it when speaking of Babylon (50.25); and in face of the display of this wrath the people can only make the confession: "I must bear with the wrath of Yahweh, for I have sinned against him" (Mic. 7.9). But the wrath only lasts for a time; Second Isaiah finds that the sufferings of the exile have even exceeded the just punishment (Is. 40.1ff.) and the metaphor of the cup sometimes used for the wrath (e.g. Jer. 25.18) reveals its temporary and essentially restricted nature, while the *chesed* of God can be compared with an inexhaustible spring. It is precisely the divine *chesed* which ensures that holiness builds up more than it overthrows: "I am the holy One, saith Yahweh, I will not come with wrath" (Hos. 11.9); for with a living God and one who bestows life, wrath could not be the last word. Thus the Old Testament teaching about God's wrath finds its logical expression in the statement of the Psalmist: "His wrath is for a moment, his faithfulness (*chesed*) life-long" (Ps. 30.6).

[1] Merely out of curiosity we may notice Boehmer's thesis, "Zorn", *ZAW*, 1926, p. 320, who, observing that the wrath is sometimes mentioned independently of Yahweh (Dt. 29.27; 2 Kings 3.27; Jer. 21.5; 32.37), regards it as a demon, "the great Demon *qetseph*". Our view, rather, is that in these personifications there is an attempt to separate the wrath from Yahweh because of a moralistic and anti-anthropomorphic reaction.

BIBLIOGRAPHY

BOEHMER, J., "Zorn", *ZAW*, 1926, p. 320.

GRAY, J., "The Wrath of God in Canaanite and Hebrew Literature", *Journal of the Manchester University Egyptian and Oriental Society*, No. 25, 1954, p. 38.

POHLENZ, M., *Vom Zorne Gottes, FRL* 12, 1909.

TASKER, R. V. J., *The Biblical Doctrine of the Wrath of God*, London 1951.

VOLZ, P., *Das Dämonische in Jahwe*, 1924.

XI. THE WISDOM OF GOD

B Y saying that God is wise (Is. 31.2; Job 12.13) or that he possesses wisdom (2 Sam. 14.20; Job. 15.8; 28; Dan. 2.20-23) the Old Testament is expressing the universality of his knowledge and the omnipotence of his deeds; so wisdom is often mentioned along with knowledge and power. The fine twenty-eighth chapter of the book of Job shows how that divine wisdom plumbs the ultimate secrets of creation and the Yahwist is also dealing with the divine wisdom in his theme of the knowledge of good and evil. To his mind it is a complete knowledge which can only be the privilege of Yahweh or at least of the Elohim and whose acquisition by man, through disobedience or trickery (cf. Job 15.8) infallibly turns to his ruin. God alone is πανσόφος as a late author expresses it (4 Macc. 1.12; 13.19) and everything which plunges man into mystery—the nature of Sheol, the birth and growth of living beings, knowledge of the future—is naked before God (Job 26.6). In the canonical literature of the Old Testament stress is laid less upon theoretical wisdom than upon its active manifestations: the wisdom of God shines in his works and mainly in the creation whose order and harmony are a clear witness to it. Certain texts even suggest that wisdom was represented as a personal being, either a foreign deity[1] whom Yahweh married, or as a being created by Yahweh before the world itself, perhaps serving as the prototype of the whole creation. The book of Proverbs, in a much-discussed passage (8.22ff.) represents wisdom as a child playing in front of its father and lord; we are not in the presence of a pre-existent wisdom figure, although the personification reaches such a degree that we can think of it as a kind of hypostasis;[2] in every case it is from this text that the apocryphal

[1] Boström, *Proverbiastudien*, 1936, sees in the figure of wisdom a substitute for the goddess Astarte; in short, speculations about wisdom may have arisen from the desire to give Yahweh a consort, but the passages called upon such as Prov. 4.8ff. and 7.4 simply seek to contrast wisdom with folly which might occasionally show itself through the allurements of foreign women.

[2] The personal nature of wisdom is more developed in Job 28.27 and in Prov. 8.22ff.; in this latter passage the words *qanani* (v. 22) and *'amon* (v. 30) present some difficulty; if, as there is plenty of reason for supposing, *qanah* means to create, we do not have in this text the statement of a mythical origin of wisdom, but it is

writings such as Baruch and the Wisdom of Solomon will develop their speculations about the hypostatization of wisdom. By presenting her credentials of nobility, as ancient as they are weighty, wisdom seeks to invite men to follow her and to attain once again by her help that original state when sin had not yet corrupted the work of creation. Wisdom which reigns in nature should also preside over God's directing of human life. But in this realm wisdom is accompanied by the power of discernment between good and evil: *binah*, discrimination, is often mentioned along with *chokmah*, the art of success. The punishment of evil and the reward of goodness are one of the dominant themes of wisdom literature, but in distinction from the historical and prophetic books which base retribution upon the covenant, the wisdom books connect it with the creation. By regarding man independently of all national attachment, as a creature governed by certain elementary laws quite well summarized by the term righteousness,[1] the wisdom movement affirms the universality of God in opposition to the restrictions which the covenant and the law, manifestations of a jealous God, ran the risk of introducing. However, in the course of history it is the legalist current which ended by absorbing the wisdom current; and already within the Old Testament certain texts see the ideal of wisdom in a scrupulous study of the torah (Ps. 1 and 119) and the Wisdom of Solomon and Ecclesiasticus sturdily identify wisdom with the law when they make it the instrument of divine direction for the people of Israel (cf. particularly Ecclus. 24.8ff.). This narrowing of wisdom also marks the beginning of its decline. Nevertheless it must be observed that the ideal of a wise and universal God had sufficiently penetrated Jewish religion so that even in the midst of the strictest legalism it never lost the vision of humanity.[2]

not impossible that the wise man of the Proverbs thought of wisdom as the first thing created by God and as a thing which was intended to serve as a model for all the others; the apocryphal texts like Wisd. 7.22ff.; 9.9; Enoch 42.1-2 and Philo, *De Cherubim*, 48-50, Baruch 3.29 are very probably inspired by this text in Proverbs.

[1] The idea of justice on which the prophets insist so strongly is more a part of the wisdom tradition than of the specifically prophetic tradition which is dominated by concepts of election and covenant; but the contacts of the two traditions show the place of honour occupied by wisdom and by the wise men among the people of Israel.

[2] Cf. A. Causse, " L'humanisme juif et le conflit du judaïsme et de l'hellénisme " in *Mélanges Franz Cumont*. *Annuaire de l'Institut de philologie et d'histoire orientales et slaves*. t. 4, 1936, p. 525.

Sometimes God gives this wisdom to men; mainly to the sages, in its fulness to the Messiah (cf. Is. 11); but for common men the greatest wisdom will consist in recognizing the wisdom of God by an attitude of awe and humility (Prov. 1.7; 9.10; Ps. 111.10; Job 28.28).

BIBLIOGRAPHY

BOSTRÖM, G., *Proverbiastudien. Die Weisheit und das fremde Weib*, Lund 1935.
HEINISCH, P., *Personifikationen und Hypostasen im A.T. und im Alten Orient*, Münster 1921.
    Die persönliche Weisheit des A.T. in religionsgeschichtlicher Beleuchtung, 1923.
KNOX, W. L., "The divine Wisdom", *JTS*, 1937, p. 230.
RINGGREN, H., *Word and Wisdom. Studies in the hypostatization of divine qualities*, Lund 1947.
SCHENKE, W., *Die Chokma in der jüdischen Hypostasenspekulation*, Oslo 1912.

PART TWO

THE ACTION OF GOD ACCORDING
TO THE OLD TESTAMENT

I. THE INSTRUMENTS OF GOD'S
ACTION

A. THE SPIRIT

THE goal of divine action is to maintain and to create life; to achieve this aim Yahweh chiefly avails himself of two means which we encounter in varying intensities in all the realms of his manifestation: the Spirit and the Word. The striking resemblance between these two realities goes back to their common origin: the term *ruach* means originally and etymologically the air, which manifests itself in two forms—that of the wind in nature and of breath in living beings. Once it became the prerogative of God *ruach* threw off its material attachments though it never ceased to be an active power. Spirit and Word belong to anthropomorphic language; but since they continue to operate even apart from bodies they can be regarded as independent realities more easily than the hand or face of God.

Apart from some passages where it is the symbol of inconstancy and nothingness: Is. 26.18; 41.29; Mic. 2.11; Job 16.3; Jer. 5.13, wind as a physical reality is always closely associated with God, it is one of his best servants (Ps. 104.4) and is personified as the breath of his nostrils (Ps. 18.16). The Exodus, that liberating event which became the type of salvation, was due to the intervention of Yahweh in the form of a strong wind which dried up the sea and gave the Israelites passage (Ex. 14.21; 15.8). The wind fulfils a double function exactly corresponding to that of God; it is the destructive power which dries up the springs (Hos. 13.15), but at the same time and more importantly the force which by piling up the clouds brings fertilizing rain to the parched earth (cf. 1 Kings 18.45). Another aspect of the wind, less spectacular but not less suggestive, connects it with God, namely its light and intangible nature; it knows no limits and is capable of bearing the deity on its wings to the extremities of the earth (Ps. 68.4; 104.3) and no one can grasp its whence and whither. Power and mystery, such are the two characteristics of wind, and it is because the God of the Old Testament is both power and mystery that the wind is able to express so adequately the whole nature of the divine.

Although the wind accounts for life in nature and can be regarded without difficulty as the breath which gives life, the life of living beings should not be considered as an effect of the wind. The term *ruach* denotes the breath of life which is an effect of the breath of God. J. Hehn[1] has shown with numerous examples that this idea was to be found amongst the Egyptians, Babylonians, Assyrians, Canaanites, Phœnicians and Hebrews. It must have offered itself spontaneously to different peoples through the simple observation that life and breath ceased together, and because of the anthropomorphic picture of the deity the origin of this breath was attributed to his breath. Numerous texts in the Old Testament affirm that the breath of God is life-giving: Gen. 6.17; 7.15; Num. 16.22; Jg. 15.19; Ps. 104.29; Eccl. 3.1; 9.21; 12.7; Is. 37.6, 8; Zech. 12.1. Not only the origin of human life but its span is conditioned by the breath of Yahweh: "Thou hast granted me life and thy care has watched over my *ruach*" Job cries (10.12). This breath rarely, and only as a result of the systematization of language, becomes a merely anthropological reality; on the whole it always remains the property of God who is free at any instant to take it back to himself.

For the ancient Israelites the mystery which fills the world was not limited to certain natural happenings; even before the unique God Yahweh had assumed all aspects of power and mystery there was belief in the existence of powers more or less invisible, for the most part maleficent, and they were spoken of by the same term

---

[1] "Zum Problem des Geistes im Alten Orient und im Alten Testament", *ZAW*, 1925, p. 210.

ruach[1] in order to indicate their violent and mysterious character. In the present state of the texts, these evil spirits appear as subject to Yahweh, but their aspect as originally independent powers is shown by certain verbs which are used of their mode of action. Thus it is said of *ruach* that it clothes itself (*labash*), Jg. 6.34; 1 Chr. 12.18; that it falls upon an individual (*naphal*), Ez. 11.5; that it comes forth mightily (*tsalach*), Jg. 14.6; 1 Sam. 10.6, 10; 18.16; that it passes or traverses (*'abar*), Num. 5.14. If in these passages the term used had from the beginning referred to the spirit of Yahweh one cannot see why these early texts, which do not give ground before the most daring anthropomorphisms, did not simply say: Yahweh falls, Yahweh bursts in upon. Account must be taken of this sense of *ruach*. To get out of the difficulty by saying that the spirit is only the vivid personification of an evil power or passion,[2] is to by-pass the problem; in fact there is a notable difference between passages like Num. 5.14, 30; Hos. 4.12; 5.4; Zech. 13.2, where we have a rhetorical style, and the very concrete description of spirits in 1 Kings 22[3] where they play the part of individuals subordinate to Yahweh but acting independently of him.[4]

Physical, biological and demonic reality, the spirit is yet primarily in the Old Testament the prerogative κατ᾽ ἐξοχήν of God and his instrument of revelation and action *par excellence*. It is probable that this identification of Yahweh with the *ruach* was not made at the outset.[5] ·The quite frequent combination of the term with *'elohim* might suggest that the divine spirit was thought of as a force able to act without Yahweh and even to escape his control; thus the transmission of Elijah's spirit to his successor seems to imply no participation by Yahweh (2 Kings 2.9-15). However, from

---

[1] P. Volz in his work *Der Geist Gottes im A.T. und im Spätjudentum* has insisted on this aspect of *ruach*. Cf. the same author: "Der Heilige Geist in den Gathas des Sarathuschtra", in *Eucharisterion* (Gunkel Festschrift), 1925, p. 323.

[2] R. Koch, *Gottesgeist und Messias*; otherwise this work gives an excellent summary of the subject of the spirit in the O.T.

[3] The spirit (*haruach*) which comes before Yahweh in 1 Kings 22.21 plays a part comparable to that of Satan in the prologue of Job; Kittel, *Biblia hebraica* (3rd ed.) even proposes to alter *ruach* into *satan*, a purely gratuitous emendation.

[4] In 1 Kings 22.21 spirit is masculine, which indicates a more definite individualizing, though examination of all the texts does not allow any conclusions to be drawn from variations in gender of the word *ruach*.

[5] According to Ed. Koenig, *Hebr.-aram. Wörterbuch zum A.T.*, the primitive sense may have been that of spirit, and the material sense of wind and breath derivative; that seems difficult to reconcile with Hebrew semantic principles about the priority of concrete meanings.

the first traces of theological reflection about *ruach* as a divine power it was connected with Yahweh; a celebrated passage in the book of Isaiah shows that in the eighth century the spirit and Yahweh denote the same reality. The prophet reproaches the king and the people of Judah for the projected alliance with Egypt, for to seek salvation by military means is to reject Yahweh: "Egypt is man and not god (*'el*), his horses are flesh (*basar*) and not spirit (*ruach*). Yahweh will stretch out his hand and the protector will stumble and his protégé will fall and all will perish together" (Is. 31.3). The terms *'el* and *ruach* placed here in parallel signify that God alone has on his side power and immortality. The prophet does not go so far as the New Testament affirmation that God is spirit, but he implies—and everything suggests that he is not the first to do so—that spirit characterizes all that is contained in the word "god" and that Yahweh, once he has become the only God, is alone capable of giving it perfect fulfilment. It can therefore be said that the spirit is God himself in creative and saving activity; the spirit of God lies at the origin of creation (cf. Gen. 1.2), it is ceaselessly present in the form of wind, but because of the uniqueness of Israelite religion it is chiefly history which is the place of his manifestation. The action of the spirit in history has not been experienced with equal intensity in the course of the ages, but it can be said without risk of hasty generalization that throughout history it is the spirit who directs events. In the early ages the spirit acts intermittently; he falls unexpectedly upon certain persons and makes them capable of extraordinary acts. Thus, it is through a momentary gift of the spirit that Samson is able to tear in pieces a lion and a kid (Jg. 14.6); by this act Samson is able to ward off the Philistine danger and to restore the confidence of the people in Yahweh's power; through the gift of the spirit all these charismatic leaders are saviours (*moshi'im*) of the theocratic state and maintain the reality of the covenant. It has been very soundly written, "These acts are not merely marvellous exploits, they are acts of liberation. Though isolated deeds of local heroes they belong to the one historical process, they mark the stages of the forward march which leads Israel to independence. It is this movement of liberation which gives them unity. The intervention of Yahweh's spirit at these different stages gives prominence to one of the directions of divine action in the Old Testament. The spirit of God is the source of the national community of

Israel."[1] The prophets are animated by the spirit. The *nebi'im* of the time of Samuel are possessed by the *ruach* and he who comes into contact with them is willy-nilly so infected as to become "another man" (1 Sam. 6.10). The spirit could have effects upon men of God as violent as they were unexpected; it was commonly accepted that it could seize them and carry them to another place, even destroy them (1 Kings 18.12; 2 Kings 2.16). Nor is the spirit foreign to the activity of the great prophets; it is true that the pre-exilic prophets from Amos onwards never speak of the possession of the spirit in order to justify or authenticate their work. Opposition to the old nabiism and to its ecstatic manifestations produced by the *ruach* might explain this new attitude. According to Mowinckel[2] the prophets' reserve about the spirit may have been due to conflicts which some of them—Jeremiah in particular—had to suffer with the false prophets who boasted their possession of *ruach*, but which was really only "wind" (cf. Jer. 5.13). It is clear that for all the prophets it is not the spirit but the word which qualifies them for their ministry, because only the word creates between the prophet and God a relationship of person with person. But the word presupposes the spirit, the creative breath of life, and for the prophets there was such evidence of this that they thought it unnecessary to state it explicitly. There are in addition a few passages which show that the true prophets were also conscious of being clothed with the spirit and of being thereby the heirs of the ancient *nebi'im* as an instrument of divine revelation in history. Hosea, after having announced punishment, elicits from his adversaries the sarcasm: "The prophet is a fool, the man of the spirit (*'ish haruach*) is mad" (9.7), a passage which clearly does not prove that the prophet attributes his inspiration to the spirit, but which shows that the prophets did not refuse to be called men of the spirit among the people. Micah puts the spirit into more direct relation with prophetic inspiration: "As for me, I am full of power, of the *ruach* of Yahweh" (3.8),[3] and Isaiah

---

[1] J. Guillet, *Thèmes bibliques*, p. 233.

[2] Mowinckel, "The spirit and the word", *JBL*, 1934, pp. 199ff.

[3] This Micah passage, because of its unusual construction (*'et ruach Yahweh*), might be regarded as an addition to the text inspired by analogy with Is. 11.2; break in the rhythm has also been appealed to in support of its lack of authenticity; but instead of suppressing *ruach* we could just as well take *koach* as a gloss uselessly repeating *geburah* (cf. Giesebrecht, *Die Berufsbegabung der altt. Propheten*, 1897, pp. 123, 137).

says that to act without the spirit of Yahweh is to set oneself up against him and that to oppose the words of the prophet who is the mouthpiece of God is to reject God himself (Is. 30.1-2). Elsewhere the hand of Yahweh which seizes the prophet (Is. 8.11; 1 Kings 18.12, 46; Ez. 1.3; 3.12; 37.1; 40.1) acts exactly like the spirit, so that in spite of the infrequent reference to the spirit the upheaval which takes place in the great prophets through their calling is placed on the same plane as the marvellous acts attributed to the spirit when it fell upon the judges and the first *nebi'im*. From the Exile the spirit becomes an essential element in the inspiration of the prophets. Ezekiel speaks and acts under the inspiration of the *ruach* (2.2; 3.24; 11.5, etc.), and it is to the spirit that he attributes both the reception of the divine word and the superhuman power which makes him capable of announcing it. Many of the post-exilic texts in which we have a kind of résumé of the history of salvation present that history as a result of the spirit manifesting itself through the prophets. Speaking of Israel's past, the great prayer of repentance of Nehemiah (chap. 9) recalls that activity: "Thou warnedst them by thy spirit through the medium of thy prophets, but they did not listen" (v. 30) and in an analogous context of thought the prophet Zechariah speaks in the same way: "They made their hearts adamant for fear of hearing the instruction and the words which Yahweh Tsebaoth had sent—by his spirit—through the medium of the prophets of the past" (7.12).

In a similar presentation of history, Moses becomes the man of the spirit, with which he is so richly endowed that he can without loss transmit some of it to others (Num. 11.17, 25, 29). But it is not only past history which is a manifestation of the spirit; an even more splendid outpouring of the spirit is reserved for the future: the new age will be marked by abundance of vegetation, by prosperity and peace, all of which will be produced by the spirit of Yahweh "come from on high" (Is. 32.15ff.); the shoot of the stem of Jesse will be clothed with the spirit in a more complete and spiritual way than the leaders of the heroic age (11.2ff.); the spirit will also rest permanently on the servant of Yahweh (42.1ff.) but at the same time all the people will receive the benefit of this extraordinary gift: "I will pour forth my spirit upon thy race and my blessing upon thy posterity" (Is. 44.3) and since it will be shed in their hearts it will produce not a transient manifestation of power but a regeneration which will be the counterpart of the creative function of the spirit in nature (Ez. 36.22-28). With stress laid upon its creative function, the spirit's sphere of action is enlarged. Each individual life is directed by the spirit in the moral realm (the request is made for the spirit to lead in the path of uprightness, Ps. 143.10) as well as in that of intelligence (wisdom and artistic abilities are gifts of the spirit, Ex. 28.3; 31.3ff.) and the Wisdom of Solomon will draw the consequences of that evolution by identifying the spirit with wisdom. The spirit being of the very essence of God was brought into relation with the holiness which constituted his principal attribute, but it is only in two passages that this relationship is explicitly stated. One post-exilic prophet represents the holy spirit as the means *par excellence* by which God asserts his presence in the midst of his people, a presence as personal as that of the angel or the face against whom one can revolt and who can be grieved (Is. 63.10-11). The author of Psalm 51 has the very strong feeling that his faults deserve his removal far from God; so he begs that God, after having pardoned him, will not remove his holy spirit (v. 13), that is to say that he will not deprive him of his presence. Without the spirit—and on this point the testimony of the Old Testament is unanimous—it is not possible to have communion between God and man; but this theology of the spirit never took the form of an indefinite spiritism which would have undermined the personality of God.

B. THE WORD

That God reveals himself by his word is a truth confirmed by every one of the Old Testament books. It is by his word that he reveals himself as the living God and Second Isaiah, drawing the full consequences of anthropomorphism, will contrast Yahweh with pagan gods by the word of the one and the silence of the others. Of the false god made by human hands he says, "It is vain to cry unto him, he does not reply, he does not deliver from distress" (46.7; cf. also 41.21; 43.9; 45.20ff.). To understand the importance of the word of Yahweh it is necessary to remember the common belief throughout antiquity in the value and efficacy of a word. A spoken word is never an empty sound but an operative reality whose action cannot be hindered once it has been pronounced, and which attained its maximum effectiveness in formulae of blessing and cursing. This dynamic quality of the word already appears in the names by which it is denoted. The most usual term and the one which has become classical for the word is *dabar*, which must probably be associated with a root which in Hebrew has the meaning of: to be behind and to push; *dabar* could then be defined as the projection forward of what lies behind, that is to say, the transition into the act of what is at first in the heart. The realistic character of *dabar* is always strongly stressed, so that the term will denote thing as well as word (Gen. 20.10; 22.1, 20; 40.1; 48.1 etc.) and no term throws into clearer relief the fact that the Hebrew mind did not distinguish between thought and action. Realism and dynamism are features equally characteristic of the root *'amar*; derived from a root having the sense to be raised up or to be clear, the word would be the visible manifestation of the thought and of the will. In distinction from *dabar*, the stress with *'amar* is chiefly upon the spoken word; the expression *lemor* which introduces speeches is generally preceded by *dabar* (*wayedabber lemor*) which alone possesses creative dynamism.

The power of the word of God is similarly met outside the Old Testament.[1] Sumerian hymns very often celebrate the greatness of the word; the believer in Enlil-Marduk addresses his god thus:

" thy word, a sublime net, stretches over heaven and earth, it falls on the sea, and the sea is rough, it falls on the cane plantation and the cane sprouts, it falls on the waves of the Euphrates, the word of Marduk stirs up vast waves."

Belief in the creative power of the word appears in many proper names, with constructions such as " *Sin* gives the name " or " *Nabu* is lord of the name ", showing that existence and life was attributed to the all-powerful word of the god. In Egypt we meet the same theme of the creative word with the stress laid more on the efficacious word of the king who, as the image and son of the god, shares his power.

The idea of the divine word is, therefore, by no means peculiar to Israel, but the God of Israel, being essentially different from the nature gods and the national gods of other nations, stamps his particular mark upon the theology of the word, so that under

---

[1] The most abundant documentation is given in the work of L. Dürr and for the most recently discovered texts in that of Ringgren (cf. bibliogr.).

analogous terms very different realities are expressed. It is impossible to study the theology of the word without relating it to the revelation of God in history. Whilst in Babylon and Egypt the divine word intervenes in isolated events which have no connection with one another, the word of God in the Old Testament directs and inspires a single history which begins with the word of God pronounced at the creation and which is completed by the word made flesh (Jn. 1.14). Therefore it is in history that the word is revealed and its action in nature is only a pale reflection of its work in history. The laws and the oracles of the prophets are the two principal forms which that word assumes. Law belongs to the origins of Israelite history, not in its casuistical form but in that of brief apodictic declarations, to which just the name *debarim* was given and of which the various decalogues give us the best known instances (Ex. 24.3, 4, 8; 20.1; 34.1, 27, 28). These *debarim* constitute a revelation of God; in them Yahweh affirms that he is the Lord, but since God's affirmation is at the same time the manifestation of a power before which man can only bow, and therefore of an order which he can only obey, the word takes on the aspect of a law. The circumstances in which these *debarim* are uttered, their link with the establishment of the covenant, have conferred upon them an authority which in Judaism became merged with that of God himself.

The prophets never dream of questioning the authority of the ancient *debarim*; they were even to a large extent commentators upon the law, but with them the rôle of guardians of tradition is subordinate to the direct link which united them to God who places his words in their mouth, thereby affirming his presence not above but within the events of history.[1] The prophet is a man of the word; the wife of Jeroboam asks a *dabar* of Ahijah of Shiloh (1 Kings 14.5); king Ahab asks a *dabar* of his prophets and of Micaiah ben Imlah (1 Kings 22.5-13), and Jeremiah, in characterizing the various ministries, defines the prophet by the *dabar* (Jer. 18.18). There is an important difference between the legal and the prophetic

---

[1] Two practices inspired the formulation of the prophetic oracles: on the one hand the proclamation of royal edicts and orders, and on the other the forms of communication oral or written (letters). Cf. the conclusive comments of L. Koehler, *Deuterojesaja, stilkritisch untersucht*, pp. 102f., and of W. Baumgartner in *Eucharisterion* (Gunkel Festschrift), pp. 145ff. This dual origin well illustrates the double rôle of the prophet as the representative of God and as the servant of his people.

word: *debarim* have a lasting value for all generations, whilst the word of the prophet, spoken in quite definite circumstances, has no bearing after its fulfilment. Thus the *dabar* which the prophet Elijah announced to king Ahazaiah: "Thou shalt die" only exists for the king and loses its dynamic when it is fulfilled. The word of Micah about the ruin of Jerusalem and of the Temple (Mic. 3.12) weighed like a heavy threat over the people until the time of Jeremiah (Jer. 26.17ff.), but after the events of 587 B.C. it had no further significance. However, even in definite and individual cases, the prophets do not announce *a* word but *the* word of Yahweh. This means that each time the prophet speaks he reveals Yahweh in his totality under one of his essential aspects as judge or as saviour, and that revelation made to an individual has value as an example for all the people.

What is striking in a study of the word in the prophets is its objective and dynamic character. Jeremiah, who is the most explicit of all the prophets on the subject of prophetic experience, shows to what extent the prophet, in receiving the word, is seized by a mysterious power which sometimes crushes and tortures him (20.9), sometimes fills him with joy (15.16). The prophet is literally disturbed through and through by the *dabar* he receives, and which creates a new life within him. It is by this constraining power of the word which weighs upon him that Jeremiah authenticates his own ministry against that of the false prophets who also claimed to have received the words of Yahweh, but in whom no change in personal bearing was shown (23.11ff.) and Amos compares the situation of the prophet who has received the word to the terror which spontaneously seizes a man who hears the roaring of a lion (3.8).

The word is always far greater than the person of the prophet; he only receives it in order to transmit it, his function is that of a messenger. Even the form of prophetic discourses shows the nature of the prophets as men called and sent. The prophets in fact formulate their oracles in just the same way as a messenger transmits a message that has been entrusted to him; passages such as Num. 22.16; Jg. 11.12; 14.22; 1 Kings 20.3; 22.27; 2 Kings 18.28, which relate secular messages, have the same form as prophetic oracles. When the prophets introduce their discourses by the words: "Thus saith Yahweh", they imply the transmission of a message received without any addition of their own; and in other respects they take care to distinguish the word of Yahweh from their own words; so in Amos 5.1-2 it is the prophet who speaks, in verse 3 Yahweh, in Is. 18.1-3 it is the word of the prophet, in verses 4-6 the word of Yahweh. Once handed on, this word acts independently of the person of the prophet: "The Lord sends a word against Jacob and it falls on Israel" (Is. 9.7). It is like a projectile shot into the enemy camp whose explosion must sometimes be awaited but which is always inevitable, and these explosions are the events of history. It cannot be more explicitly stated that Yahweh is the sole author of history; human beings are the instruments of his word; even the Assyrian king Sennacherib represents his intervention as an order from Yahweh: "Yahweh told me: go up against this country and destroy it" (Is. 36.10; 2 Kings 18.20). It is particularly in Deuteronomy, and in the great work of historical synthesis created under its inspiration, that the idea of the word in relation to history is systematized. The permanence of the word is assured by the prophetic succession;[1] according to the word put into Moses' mouth by Deuteronomy, Yahweh promises an uninterrupted succession of prophets (Dt. 18.15-18). That prophetic succession was an historical reality, even though there were periods when the word of God was rare, that is to say practically non-existent and though the link connecting a prophet with his predecessors is less important than the direct and personal relationship which links him with God. After Deuteronomy the theology of the creative word in history found still greater expression in the work of Second Isaiah, whose book opens with the affirmation that in face of the succession of the generations the word of God abides eternally, and closes with the proclamation of that word's efficacy (40.8 and 55.11). This word is more to him than "the promises of the old prophets recorded in Scripture",[2] it is the entire action and revelation of God; with great power he shows its double aspect; noetic and dynamic. By his word God makes known the meaning of events; he makes them known in advance, for he who is the first and the last knows what will happen at the end of time (41.4; 43.10; 44.6;

---

[1] Five stages of that succession can be distinguished, with R. B. Y. Scott, *The Relevance of the Prophets*, New York 1944: (*a*) Moses; (*b*) the prophets of the time of the Judges and of the first period of the kingdom: Samuel, Nathan, Gad, Shemaiah, Ahijah, Jehu ben Hanani; (*c*) Elijah and Elisha and their disciples; (*d*) the golden age of pre-exilic prophecy inaugurated by Amos; (*e*) the post-exilic prophets, often anonymous and hence difficult to date.

[2] A. Robert, article "Logos" in *DBS*, col. 453.

48.12).[1] Above all it is the dynamic aspect of the word which he is interested in stressing, though with him the dynamism which had ended in catastrophe, as the majority of his predecessors had announced, blossomed forth into salvation. This function of the word in producing salvation can be compared with that of the servant of Yahweh and it can be asked whether the intuition of the prophet did not already discern one and the same reality in the word which remains eternally and in the figure of the servant fulfilling his mission right to the end. The word which creates and interprets history appears also in several Psalms where the *dabar* is sometimes above history and thus gives confidence and security to the Psalmist (Ps. 105.8, 42) and sometimes the action of God in history whose revelation is awaited. It is this that the believer awaits (Ps. 130.5) because it brings healing (Ps. 107.20) and for the author of Psalm 119 the word is both God's promise and the concrete reality of the written *torah*. Wisdom literature uses the term *dabar* and more often *'imrah* to refer to the teaching which the wise men dispense in the family circles or in schools: the word is here identified with wisdom. But as the master of Wisdom is God, the words of the wise were also a word of God, and the association of *dabar* with *mitswah*, found, for instance, in Prov. 13.13 and 16.20, shows that the same authority was attributed to them as to the *debarim* of the law.

The creative function of the word in nature is stressed less in Israel than amongst neighbouring peoples, but since the world is viewed from an historical angle, that is to say as the stage on which history will be unfolded, the action of God with respect to nature will be exercised through the same means. In Gen. 1 the word is the creative instrument of God, as in one of the most expressive Psalms dealing with the creation: "By the word of Yahweh the heavens were made, by the breath of his mouth all their host. . . . He speaks and it is done, he commands and it takes place" (Ps. 33.6, 9). The world is also maintained by the word; and what God utters by his mouth is concretely revealed in the form of natural phenomena, unusual like the manna (Dt. 8.3) or familiar like wind and snow, rain and thunder.

---

[1] There was no organic association between the prophet and the word. The word could fall upon the prophet at a moment when he was not expecting it, just as it could be refused him when he asked for it. Cf. the example of Jeremiah who had to wait ten days for the manifestation of a word (Jer. 42.7ff.).

"He sendeth out his *'imrah* upon the earth, his *dabar* runneth very swiftly. He giveth snow like wool, he scattereth the hoar frost like ashes. . . . He sendeth out his word, and melteth them, he causeth his wind to blow, and the waters flow " (Ps. 147.15-18).

"The voice of Yahweh (i.e. thunder) rumbles over the waters, the voice of Yahweh breaketh the cedars, the voice of Yahweh cleaveth the flames of fire " (Ps. 29.2ff.; cf. Ps. 46.7).

Natural phenomena are sometimes even regarded as continuations of Yahweh's word; thus the Psalmist speaks of the "stormy wind which fulfils his word " (Ps. 148.8).

Second Isaiah attributes to the word a power in the cosmos as great as in history and he seems to envisage both aspects in the celebrated picture in chapter 55 (cf. Is. 44.27).

The theology of the word resulted in two kinds of crystallizations; the first started with the fixation of the word in writing. While the *debarim* were from the start put into writing, which would ensure their permanence, the prophets had originally no other concern than that of transmitting the word orally to those for whom it was destined. Before Jeremiah only occasionally does the question arise of writing certain words down, as in Is. 8 with the purpose of reinforcing a symbolic action. The definite order which Jeremiah receives to write down his prophecies is probably not unrelated to the Deuteronomic reform. In the history of Israel Deuteronomy marks an attempt to reconcile and to identify the prophetic word with the legal word by presenting a book as the normative authority; in this book, which can always be consulted (Dt. 30.11-14), life is truly found (Dt. 32.47), so that any new revelation is superfluous. The *dabar* is, therefore, no more the hoped for reality whose manifestation was often awaited with anxiety, even by the prophets, it is given once for all and the Israelite will find there all that is necessary for his salvation. Only the backward glance matters, and every new revelation will have to assume an antique garb to avoid appearing new.[1] The part which this orientation towards the *dabar* has played in the destiny of Judaism cannot be disregarded. If we consider that because of it Judaism survived during the Exile, and if we measure the intensity of the piety aroused by the written word, then we appreciate all that was fruitful in that evolution. Nevertheless we are not prevented from regretting that, by opening the door to the idea of

[1] This is why so many apocalypses are attributed to men of the past.

complete and literal inspiration, it hampered an understanding of the dynamic of the word of God such as we find in the prophets. The other attempt at crystallization appears in the tendencies towards making an hypostasis of the word. Although it is impossible to speak of an hypostasis of the word in the canonical books of the Old Testament,[1] it must be recognized that many of the affirmations point in that direction. To speak of the word as a reality which falls and which unlooses catastrophe (Is. 9.7), or as a devouring fire (Jer. 5.14; 20.8; 23.29), or as a reality which is present with someone like one person with another (2 Kings 3.12), is to look upon it less as an effect than as an active subject akin to the angel or the face of Yahweh. The same hypostatic function of the word, which receives its full development in the pseudepigrapha, has its roots in the Old Testament without any need to admit foreign influences. The tendency to hypostatize was more obvious in the case of wisdom than of the word, but it is the latter which provided a foundation for the theology of wisdom.[2]

BIBLIOGRAPHY

A. THE SPIRIT

GUNKEL, H., *Die Wirkungen des heiligen Geistes*, Göttingen 1909.
HEHN, J., "Zum Problem des Geistes im alten Orient und im A.T.", *ZAW*, 1925, p. 210.
IMSCHOOT, P. VAN, "L'action de l'esprit de Jahvé dans l'A.T.", *RScPhTh*, 1934, p. 553.
    "L'Esprit de Jahvé, source de vie dans l'A.T.", *RB*, 1935, p. 481.
    "Sagesse et Esprit dans l'A.T." *RB*, 1938, p. 23.
KOEBERLE, J., *Natur und Geist nach der Auffassung des A.T.*, Munich 1901.
KOCH, R., *Geist und Messias. Beitrag zur biblischen Theologie des A.T.*, Vienna 1950.

[1] Instead of speaking about foreign influences it is better to see in the analogous expressions and speculations the mark of a fundamental structure of the primitive mind according to which the life of a person shows itself in the form of breath and word, dynamic realities *par excellence*.

[2] It is evident that in a text like Ecclus. 24.3 where Wisdom says, in speaking of itself: " I came forth from the mouth of the Most High " and in Wisd. 7.25 which represents wisdom as a " breath of the glory of the Almighty ", the rôle attributed to wisdom is literally proper only to the word or to the spirit.

LAMORTE, A., "La notion de ruach chez les prophètes", *EThR*, 1933, p. 97.

MOWINCKEL, S., "The spirit and the word in the pre-exilic prophets", *JBL*, 1934, p. 199.

SNAITH, N. H., "The spirit of God in Hebrew thought", *The Doctrine of the Holy Spirit, Headingley Lectures I*, London 1937.

B. THE WORD

DÜRR, L., *Die Wertung des göttlichen Wortes im A.T. und im antiken Orient*, Leipzig 1938.

GRETHER, O., *Name und Wort Gottes im A.T.*, *BZAW* 64, 1934.

HEINISCH, P., *Das Wort im A.T. und im alten Orient*, Münster 1922.

RINGGREN, H., *Word and Wisdom*, Lund 1947.

SZERUDA, J., *Das Wort Jahwes*, Lodz 1921.

II. GOD THE CREATOR OF THE WORLD

A. HISTORY AND CREATION

IN the volume of his *Dogmatik* devoted to the doctrine of creation Karl Barth characterizes the Old Testament idea of creation very appropriately in these words: "The covenant is the goal of creation, creation is the way to the covenant" and he arranges his material under two main headings: (a) the covenant, the internal basis of the creation; (b) the creation, the external basis of the covenant.[1] This means that the idea of creation is secondary to that of covenant, of which it is both the condition and the consequence. Faith in God the creator holds a less important place than that of God the saviour, and the God who made the heavens and the earth is less often and less directly the object of faith than the God who brought his people out of Egypt.[2] But the covenant is only possible within the framework of creation. The Old Testament is not unaware of the idea of a Cosmos, that is, of a universe organized with wisdom where each thing has its place and is produced in its own time. The author of the Priestly creation narrative shows God setting the elements in order like an architect intending to build a house[3] inside which new inhabitants should be entirely at their ease; this house must be substantial, sheltered from dangers, pleasant, with a measure of luxury not forbidden there. God himself takes pleasure in the construction: "Elohim saw all that he had made and behold it was very good" (Gen. 1.31). The architect is not confused with the creation, God makes his creation so far independent of himself that he exercises his sovereignty to the

[1] "Die Existenz und das Wesen des von Gott gewollten und gesetzten Geschöpfs ist der Gegenstand und insofern die Voraussetzung seiner Liebe. So ist der Bund das Ziel der Schöpfung, die Schöpfung der Weg Zum Bunde" (*Dogmatik* III/i, p. 106).

[2] Faith in God as creator is not mentioned in the earliest credo of Israel: Dt. 26.5ff.

[3] The comparison with a house, which is only hinted at by the Priestly author, is explicitly developed in the book of Job (38.4-7) where all the acts of the architect are attributed to God: marking off of the land, laying of the foundations and the corner stone. Egyptian and Mesopotamian texts speak in the same way of the construction of temples which are always thought of as a representation of the universe.

profit of man, who in his autonomy must nevertheless remember that he is only the image, that is to say the representative, of God. This autonomy which God confers upon the whole creation and more particularly upon man alone makes possible a covenant, for there can only be a covenant where the autonomy of the two contracting parties is maintained. In order that man might suitably fulfil his function of partner, God subjects the framework of nature to certain fixed laws or to certain unforeseen movements and the normal aspect of the cosmos, as shown in the regular succession of days and seasons, is quite as much directed towards man and thus towards the covenant, understood in a wide sense, as its extraordinary and catastrophic aspects. After the flood, when God is ready to make a covenant with a new humanity, he sets out in these terms the conditions which render its existence possible: "As long as the earth shall remain, seed-time and harvest, cold and heat, summer and winter, day and night shall not cease" (Gen. 8.22). Still more often nature is there in the form of a miracle and offers a suitable setting for the fulfilment of the covenant: the Red Sea allows the Israelites to pass and engulfs Pharaoh's host, the waters of the Jordan retreat to allow the conquest of Canaan, and the Song of Deborah records that the stars in the heavens fought alongside the Israelite troops and that, at the critical moment, God caused the Kishon to overflow in order to produce utter panic amongst the enemies of Israel. If the first covenant is only possible within a cosmic framework, it will be the same with the new covenant which will mark the arrival of the last days. The classic passage about the new covenant stresses the necessity of this setting: "I will sow Israel and Judah with the seed of man and with the seed of beast" (Jer. 31.27) and the certainty of the new covenant is compared with the fixity of the laws of nature which are its indispensable condition (Jer. 31.35ff.). Second Isaiah speaks in a similar way of the transformations on a cosmic scale which will precede or accompany the return of the exiles: rivers will spring forth in the dry places, trees will give shade in the desert (49.17ff.), Yahweh will renew the promises made to Noah after the flood (54.9), but the prophet at once adds that cosmic realities can disappear without any consequent shaking of the covenant (v. 10). To the question: Why had God created the world? the Old Testament would answer: He has created it for the covenant, that is to say because of his plan of love and salvation for humanity by means of Israel;

in creating the world God already had the covenant in view, and it is this motive which gave to the idea of creation its specific orientation.

B. THE UNIQUENESS OF THE ISRAELITE IDEA OF CREATION

The creation is more than the setting in which the covenant is unfolded; it is already a prefiguring of that covenant; it is not something from another period of time but itself forms part of time. That is why, when we speak of a creation myth in the Old Testament, this term has not the same meaning as in other religions. Ancient Israel knew one or perhaps several creation myths whose traces can be detected less in the Genesis narratives than in certain passages of the prophets and of the poetic books. In texts such as Job 7.12ff.; 26.10-13; 38.8-11; Ps. 74; 89.11ff.; Is. 51.9ff., we can gather that these ancient myths told of Yahweh's struggle with rival powers, with sea monsters like Rahab and Leviathan, and doubtless Babylonian traditions of the victory of Marduk over Tiamat and Canaanite traditions of the struggle of Baal with the sea were not alien to the composition of these myths. But in the narratives of Genesis and their poetic parallel in Psalm 104, which are the only passages where theological reflection about the creation is exercised, mythological elements are clearly subordinated to history, so that we are here in the presence of a history of creation and not a myth of creation; the features characteristic of myth are absent from it. There is no trace of theogony or theomachy; furthermore, there is a lack of what is increasingly considered to be the essence of myth, namely repetition. A myth only lives in the measure in which it is repeated and actualized in ritual, thus the Babylonian myth of creation was recited and represented in the New Year festival, because each year it was necessary to celebrate the cosmic power of Marduk if one wished to assure the prosperity of men and things and above all that of Babylon, of which Marduk was the national god. To Babylon—and the case holds for other civilizations—creation, remaining limited to the domain of myth and ritual, was not able to become the point of departure for a movement in history, so the world of the gods and historical reality remained closed to each other. For Israel creation marks a commencement. The word *reshit* (Gen. 1.1) is a whole plan of action, because it shows us that God's plan in history has creation as its starting point. The same Priestly author uses the term *toledot* for the creation of the heavens and the earth (Gen. 2.4) as well as for the genealogy of the patriarchs and still to-day the Jews express this unity of creation and history by dating their calendar from the creation of the world. The Yahwist, less explicit on the subject of creation proper, applies to his presentation of the early ages of mankind for which he had no historical information, the plan of the covenant, that is to say the succession of judgments and restorations which he had discerned in the history of Israel, so that for him also creation appears as a consequence of the covenant.

Creation, being a commencement, has a sequel. No doubt God completes the creation at the beginning, he makes everything (*hakol*), he gives them independence and fixes laws for them which should automatically ensure their maintenance in virtue of a decree (*choq*) proclaimed once for all: Gen. 1.11, 22, 28; 8.27; Jer. 5.24; 31.36; 33.20, 25; Ps. 104.9; 148.6; Job 14.5; 38.10; but other texts, generally more ancient, draw much less distinction between the creation and the conservation of the world and make it possible for us to speak of a *creatio continua*. "Between the creation and what follows it," says Karl Barth, "there is no *metabasis eis allo genos*. The former does not end when the history of the covenant begins and continues. What we think of as the providence of God, namely the conservation and governance of men and of the world, is just as much creation, *creatio continua*; but the other statement is quite as true: history itself commences with the creation,[1] creation has the character of history, it is an event which occupies time" (Dogm. III/i, p. 64). The origin of the people of Israel, even the birth of each individual, are presented as creations of God, who does not act as a first cause but who ceaselessly intervenes by his spirit and word to guarantee the preservation of creation. Here again it is appropriate to notice the analogy between creation and covenant, for it is equally by the spirit and word, of which the prophets are the principal agents, that history takes place. Spirit and word are not independent forces acting *ex opere operato*, but only become effective by express order of the creator: "Thou sendest forth thy breath and they are created" (Ps. 104.26). The direct action of

---

[1] G. Östborn, *Yahweh's Words and Deeds*, UUA, 1951, has also stressed this identity, but he sees there, wrongly as we think, proof for a cyclic view of history.

God in creation is seen at each birth, for it is Yahweh who opens the mother's womb (cf. Gen. 4.1, 25; 18.10), it is he who forms the plants and gives the animals their food (Ps. 145.15; 147.8; Job 38.39) and it is he again who gives light each day (Amos 5.8). This direct intervention of God in nature is not only a proof of the lordship with which he makes use of all the elements; it sometimes takes the form of a veritable struggle, because in spite of its perfection creation is unceasingly menaced by two forces which have not been created by Yahweh but have simply been subjected to him, namely darkness and the sea, residues of the chaos which existed before creation.   Darkness is a power hostile to Yahweh, whose essence is light.   "Are thy wonders known in the dark, and thy righteousness in the land of forgetfulness?" asks a Psalmist (Ps. 88.13), feeling that the answer can only be negative because the essence of darkness is different from that of light; and the prophets stigmatize the confusion between light and darkness as a lack of discernment between what comes from God and what comes from chaos (Amos 5.18; Zeph. 1.15).   The sea constitutes a still graver menace.   *Tehom*, whose name recalls that of Tiamat in the Babylonian myth, is originally the power against which Yahweh had to struggle in order to tear away from his control the solid earth, of which Genesis 1.9 gives an echo, though faint it is true. The vast domain of waters was not conquered by Yahweh, but only more or less neutralized by being confined within certain limits assigned to them: "At thy rebuke they fled; at the voice of thy thunder they hasted away; they scaled the mountains, they went down into the valleys unto the place which thou hadst assigned for them; thou hast set a bound that they may not pass over, that they turn not again to cover the earth" (Ps. 104.7-9).   Once subject to Yahweh the waters can become a source of blessing, both those which come from the ocean above in the form of rain and dew, as well as the rivers which arise from the ocean beneath (cf. Gen. 49.25; Dt. 33.13; Ps. 148.7).   But the water, though driven back, has only one desire, to return and take up again the place it originally occupied.   In obedience to the general tendency of giving all mythological elements historical significance, the theme of the sea as Yahweh's enemy only faintly appears as a figure of speech used of the enemies of Israel, yet in such texts as Is. 17.12: "the uproar of many peoples, which roar like the roaring of the seas; and the rushing of nations, that rush like the rushing of mighty waters; but he rebukes them, so that they flee far away and are driven away", and Jer. 6.23: "Their noise (i.e. of the peoples of the north) roareth like the sea", it is easy to perceive underneath these figures the theme of the chained, rebellious sea. Without doubt it is no mere chance that the great miracles of Yahweh in the world of nature are victories won over the waters (the Red Sea, the Jordan, and in some measure Jonah's fish). Concerning the miracle at the Red Sea one Psalmist exclaims: "The waters saw thee, O Elohim; they were afraid, the depths (*tehomot*) were moved" (Ps. 77.17), a trembling of revolt as much as of awe. It is not without reason that the Israelites did not become a seafaring people and that they always showed a kind of instinctive horror of the sea and its dangers; Psalm 107 mentions sailors along with travellers in the desert, prisoners and the sick as people in especial peril. Darkness and the sea will only disappear at the coming of the new heavens and the new earth, and we have to wait till the last page of the Apocalypse of John to read that there will be no more night and that the sea will be no more (Rev. 21.1; 22.5). The sin which comes from man is a still graver threat weighing down upon the creation; created to be king of creation, man, by his disobedience to the divine command, has drawn into his fall this creation which was entrusted to him. In Genesis, the trees of Paradise are replaced by thorns and thistles, and the soil will only be a source of blessing at the expense of painful effort. Many a time the prophets depict the birds of heaven, the beasts of the field and the fish of the sea which had been entrusted to man's dominion as pining away because man by his wickedness has opposed God and become the victim of powers placed originally at his service. The relation between the fall and the creation also helps us to understand the exclamation of the Psalmist, so surprising at first glance, which ends his praise of God the creator: "Let sinners be consumed out of the earth, and let the wicked be no more" (Ps. 104.35), for sin involves the danger of undermining the integrity of the creation and of leading to a return of chaos.

Creation which has a commencement and a history has also an end. Ludwig Koehler appropriately writes of this:[1] "To the beginning there corresponds an ending, to creation a completion, to the 'very good' here the 'perfect' yonder; they correspond, each to each; in the theology of the Old Testament, creation is

[1] *Theol. des A.T.*, p. 71.

an eschatological conception." Eschatology is a return to the beginning, but with something additional which was absent at the first creation. This is why interest in the new creation goes hand in hand with the intensity of Israel's hope, which becomes the more eager as sin has more increasingly turned the earth into a chaos (cf. Amos 7.4; Jer. 4.23ff.; Zeph. 1.2, 14; Is. 51.6). The new heavens and the new earth will not be essentially different from the first creation, but they will be freed from the forces of chaos which threaten its integrity and security. This hope does not mean, however, that God desires at all costs to preserve his creation: God has no need of his creation in order to be God, and he can do what he pleases with creation; he is able to make the sun set at noon and to bring darkness upon the earth contrary to all expectation and all evidence in the sight of man (Is. 13.10; Amos 8.9); the earth can be shaken and the mountains totter (Jer. 4.24). These are not merely figures of speech; rather must we see there the assertion that creation can only subsist by God's will, for even the fixed laws which God allots to his creation depend upon time, of which he alone remains master.

C. THE PRINCIPAL MODES OF ACTION OF GOD THE CREATOR

To express the direct and personal intervention of God in creation Old Testament writers have at all times had recourse to anthropomorphic language, which moreover harmonizes very well with a most spiritual conception of God, particularly in Second Isaiah (Is. 40.12f., the hand of God, and Is. 45.12; 48.13). Yahweh is compared with an architect who lays the foundations of a building and who supervises the various stages of construction (*yasad, banah, qanah, konen*: Ps. 24.2; Amos 9.6; Is. 45.18; Ps. 119.90), with a potter who moulds the clay (Gen. 2.8; Amos 4.13; Is. 45.18) and even with a father who begets children (cf. Job 38.28; Ps. 90.2), an idea correlative with that of Mother-earth of which Israel was never able to rid itself entirely (cf. Job 1.21; Ps. 139.15; Ecclus. 40.1). However, the specific term for the creative act of God was not borrowed from anthropomorphic speech: the verb *bara'*,[1] both

---

[1] P. Humbert, "L'Emploi et la portée du verbe *bara* dans l'A.T.", *ThZ*, 1947, pp. 404ff., and less recently F. M. Th. Böhl in *Alttestamentliche Studien für Rud. Kittel*, 1913, pp. 42ff.

in the Qal and Niphal forms, is only used of God and designates an activity peculiar to God and to him alone; the object of the divine *bara'* is the world, but Israel also—another mighty work of God (Is. 43.1, 7, 15)—the new heavens and the new earth, the new heart and the new spirit, and in a general way all that is original, unforeseeable and not realizable by man (Jer. 31.22; Is. 48.7; 65.7; Ps. 51.12; 104.30). The superiority of the divine *bara'* over human creations is also shown in the fact that the object of this verb is never a substance, an intermediate stage, but always the result, the completed and perfect work. The originality inherent in this term does not, however, prevent its association with expressions borrowed from anthropomorphic speech; it is used as parallel to *'asah* in Gen. 1.26, 27, with *yatsar* and *konen* in Amos 4.13; Is. 43.1; 45.18, so that no more than these can it be used as evidence in favour of the conception of *creatio ex nihilo*. This idea is foreign to the Old Testament, where God is content to mould matter without creating it, though the sovereignty he shows in this moulding and the readiness with which the elements bend to his orders compel us to recognize that *creatio ex nihilo*[1] was the only possible issue from the thought of the Old Testament in which the action of God increasingly tends to take a less material form, namely that of the word. Creation by a word is not an idea peculiar to Israel, but by presenting the diverse works of creation as a simple order from God, the Priestly writer gives unequalled expression to the divine sovereignty and to the marvellous character of creation, and texts such as Ecclus. 42.15; Apoc. Baruch 21.4ff.; Hebs. 11.3; 2 Pet. 3.5, 6 show sufficiently the extent to which the line starting from Genesis 1 determined the teaching of Judaism. Creation by the spirit is not opposed to creation by the word; for language allowed the establishment of a very close relation between them. Since the spirit is the breath in which the air comes out of the mouth just like the word, the synonymous use of the two is easily explained: "By the word of Yahweh were the heavens made, and all the host of them by the breath of his mouth" (Ps. 33.6). "His word [here the Messiah's] is the rod which smites the violent, the breath of his lips slays the wicked" (Is. 11.4). But this parallelism is the result

[1] *Creatio ex nihilo* is found explicit affirmed for the first time in Second Maccabees (7.28); "Consider the heaven and the earth . . . and know that God has not made them from existing things", οὐκ ἐξ ὄντων ἐποίησεν αὐτά ; the reading presupposed by the Syriac version and the Vulgate was ἐξ οὐκ ὄντων which accentuates still further the creation *ex nihilo*.

of a development: originally the spirit was a force more dynamic than moral, more destructive than constructive; so, to become a power serviceable in creation it had to be subjected to the word. Probably it is in this way that the reference to spirit at the beginning of the creation narrative must be understood; the *ruach Elohim* which moves over the water of chaos is not a violent wind,[1] although the translation is permissible, for it seems very unlikely that the Priestly writer who uses the term *Elohim* for the creator God should have used the same word for a reality opposed to the creation, the more so since he could have found less ambiguous expressions for the violence of the wind. The spirit (we translate: *but* the spirit of Elohim moved upon the face of the waters) is the first act of creation, it is indispensable to the word, but the word alone allows the spirit, a terrible and dangerous force, to become a constructive power.[2] In the wisdom literature word and spirit are sometimes replaced by Wisdom, yet in spite of the attempt at hypostatization of which Proverbs 8.22-36[3] and Job 28 bring us echoes, wisdom was always regarded rather as an attribute of God than as a form of his activity.

D. THE INFLUENCE OF FAITH IN GOD AS CREATOR UPON THE PICTURE OF NATURE AND THE COSMOS

The cosmological conceptions of the Israelites do not seem to have been directly influenced by their religious beliefs. In a general

[1] For a justification of this point of view cf. Eissfeldt in *Forschungen und Fortschritte*, 1940, pp. 1ff.

[2] Evidently we must regard Gen. 1.2 as a parenthesis which seeks to describe the condition before creation and 1.1 as the heading of the whole chapter. Jewish theologians who have taken Gen. 1.1 as referring solely to the first act of creation have had to admit the creation of chaos by God and so have reduced its significance, like Jubilees 2.2 and 4 Esdras 6.38ff., by misunderstanding the sense of the expression *tohu wabohu* which wherever it is met (Is. 34.11; Jer. 4.23), denotes the contrary of creation and not merely an inferior stage of creation. By seeing in Gen. 1.1 a heading we also discard the reading of the medieval theologian Rashi, who sees in the three first words the temporal complement of a sentence the main part of which commences only at verse 3.

[3] The verb *qanah* is only attested six times in the O.T. in the sense of to create: Gen. 14.19, 22; Dt. 32.6; Ps. 78.54; 139.13; Prov. 8.22; it seems to have been more frequent in the Canaanite world; we find in Ugarit (Keret 1, 57; Danel 11.6, 41; 2 AB 1.22, 23; 3.25, 28-30); to the evidence of El Elyon's being the creator of the heavens and the earth in Gen. 14 we must add the reference to *El qn 'rts* in the Phoenician inscription of Karatepe. Cf. for the verb *qanah* the study of P. Humbert, "Qanah en hébreu biblique" in *Festschrift A. Bertholet*, pp. 258ff.

way the Israelites shared the ideas common to the ancient world, conceiving the world as a three-storey building, the heavens above, the earth below and the waters under the earth (Ex. 20.4), a representation which rests as much upon observational data as upon certain mythical concepts.

The sky is not an immaterial reality but a solid construction, a *raqia'* ($\sigma\tau\epsilon\rho\epsilon\omega\mu\alpha$= firmamentum), which indicates literally a smooth surface. Resting upon pillars the sky forms the dome of the earth; by its solidity the celestial vault can separate the terrestrial ocean from the celestial and its rupture would be equivalent to the return of primeval chaos. Above the celestial ocean a high chamber is constructed, supported by beams, where God has established his throne (Ps. 104.3). Other texts compare the celestial vault to a tent which Yahweh has pitched (Ps. 19; Is. 40.22; 44.24; Job 9.8; Ecclus. 43.12) or to a mirror of molten metal (Job 37.18). The columns which support the vault seem to be identical with mountains; they can be shaken by thunder, which is the voice of Yahweh, or by earthquakes (Ps. 18.8; 29.5; Job 26.11). The stars move according to laws of which God himself guarantees the fixity (Ps. 89.38; 104.19; Eccl. 1.5); according to a tradition of which we have an echo in the book of Job the stars were anterior to creation (38.7), though it is advisable to ask what parts are played in such representations by belief and by mere poetic imagery respectively. The stars have a place reserved for them somewhere behind the celestial vault for the time when they are invisible (Hab. 3.11; Ps. 19.6), just as there are in heaven containers for certain atmospheric forces such as the snow and the hail (Job 38.22) which God opens at will and which he holds in reserve for the day of judgment (Is. 28.17; 30.30); the rain and the other celestial products pass to the earth through the doors and lattice windows arranged in the celestial vault (Gen. 7.11; Is. 60.8; Ps. 78.23-25). The name by which the Israelites referred to heaven shows that they recognized a plurality of heavens whose importance increased with their distance. The "heaven of heavens" was the veritable divine abode (Dt. 10.14; Ps. 148.4). At the time of St. Paul Judaism admitted the existence of at least three heavens (2 Cor. 12.2) and indulged in speculations about the respective value of each of them, probably under the influence of conceptions arising in Babylonia.

The earth is a flat surface resting upon pillars whose bases go down into the waters of the great ocean, waters which feed the

F

terrestial oceans by means of subterranean conduits. Thus the earth appears as the first floor of a gigantic building of which heaven is the higher floor (Ps. 18.16; 24.2; 75.4; 93.1; Prov. 8.29). The mountains which are a kind of framework of this building form the connection between heaven and earth, and this explains the religious esteem with which they were regarded (Ex. 24.9f.). In one passage alone is there touched upon the idea of an infinite space in which the earth may be suspended: "He stretched out the north over empty space (*tohu*), and hung the earth over nothingness (*'al belimah*)" (Job 26.7). Mention of the four corners of the earth suggests that the Israelites did not think of it as a disc but as a square surface (Is. 11.13). Yahweh makes firm the pillars of the earth to set a limit to the fury of the watery elements which seek only to arise and submerge it (Job 38.10; Prov. 8.28).

The subterranean world lies under the ocean (Job 26.5; 11.8; Jonah 2.6; 2 Sam. 22.5). It is the place of darkness, full of dangers which make it, for those who go down there, the place of destruction and the country from which no one returns (Job 7.9; 16.22). Nevertheless, *Sheol* is not always so clearly distinguished from the earth; it bears the same name *'erets* (Jonah 2.7). At the time of the revolt of Korah's sons against Moses (Num. 16.32ff.) the earth opens and the rebels go straight down to *Sheol*, and the phenomena of necromancy also seem to show that *Sheol* was not separated from the earth by an ocean.

This conception of the world is so little influenced by religion that it was rather an obstacle than an aid to faith. Yahweh was not at the outset the god of heaven and to become so he had to dethrone other deities and it took him several centuries to extend his power over *Sheol*. But it is impossible to reduce the cosmological ideas of the Israelites to a single type and even if they had a coherent system it is certain that we only know of it by allusions, a properly scientific interest being outside the concern of the biblical writers. What we can say with certainty is that the men of the Old Testament were interested in the world less from a theoretical angle than with an essentially practical aim: the term *tebel*, of Assyrian origin, the universe (*tabalu*), gave way to *'adamah*, the soil; this soil God has placed at the disposal of man for him to rule over it and to enjoy within the limits of his condition and not in order for him to reflect upon the laws which govern it, which are known only to God.

If faith in God the creator did not overthrow these cosmological ideas and was content to rely upon traditional beliefs, at least it succeeded in creating a view of the world which we can call coherent. The Israelites always regarded the universe as a whole. Affirmation of the unity of the world is already found heavily under-lined in the Yahwist account of creation which refers all the works of creation to God their author on the one hand and to man as their beneficiary on the other, for before the creation of man the earth was a desert—it is drought and not water which constitutes the element of danger in this account—and the garden of Eden was only planted to put there the man whom Yahweh forms before the other works of creation (Gen. 2.8); what a commentator of a later period expressed in the words: "Thou wouldest make man the administrator of thy works, that it might be known that he was by no means made on account of the world, but the world on account of him" (Apoc. Baruch 14.18).

The unity of the universe is still more evident in the account by the Priestly writer. There the works of creation are less directly attributed to God than in the Yahwist narrative, for God is there freed from all features which might suggest the figure of a demiurge; so the elements do not arise directly from the hand of God but from one another. Yet this *generatio* is only possible through an order issued afresh each time by the creator. This inter-dependence which unites together the works of creation shows that all things belong together and that nothing is useless and nothing incomplete, and it must be said that the need our writer feels to arrange the ten works of creation in the space of six days hardly diminishes the imposing character of his description.

The third account, which in some respects is the most complete and which equally emphasizes the unity of the creation, is in Psalm 104, which expresses in less solemn but much more picturesque language the interdependence binding together the various parts of the cosmos. For this poet the antinomies still apparent in the first chapter of Genesis are resolved, there is no more opposition between the earth and the sea, the latter personified by Leviathan is no more than a plaything with which Yahweh amuses himself and the ships ply there without risk of being swallowed up by chaos. The universe is not only a house solidly built, it is also a work of art.

The idea of the unity of creation did not come to Israel from the mere observation of nature, but from a contemplation of nature in the light of faith in a God who was the sole God and the God of the covenant. By its monotheism the Old Testament surmounted all mythology, that is to say all the traces of dualism inherent in every mythology; while the covenant idea allowed the Old Testament to oppose the belief in a distant god who might be reduced to the function of *prima causa*.

Along with unity the Israelites were deeply conscious of the aspect of finality in their conception of the universe. Since creation itself is an eschatological concept it is natural that this feature is also reflected in their conception of nature. Everything in creation is well done, but perfection in the creation is entirely directed towards Yahweh's final aim, which is the salvation of humanity. The creation of man as the Bible thinks of it belongs to the order of redemption rather than to the order of creation; the whole theology of Second Isaiah envisages the creation[1] only in its relation to the final salvation, itself presented as a creation. It is the certainty that everything conspires to the final goal which makes the Israelites able to admire the creation without reserve and to announce that the heavens declare the glory of God, that is to say that they are a visible form of his presence (Ps. 8; 19; 136.5; Prov. 3.19; Jer. 10.12; Eccl. 3.11; 7.29). To read some of these passages it might seem that nature is the clearest and most perfect revelation of God, and it is true that in the wisdom literature the whole of divine revelation seems to centre upon the creation of the world and of humanity. Even moral laws are bound up with the creation: "Whoso mocketh the poor insulteth his creator" says the sage in the book of Proverbs (17.5),[2] and one of the last represen-

---

[1] No prophet insists as much as Second Isaiah on faith in God as creator, but for him also creation remains subservient to the covenant; yet instead of being condition and consequence the two are merged (see particularly Is. 51.9ff.), so that the covenant is presented in the language of creation (cf. the terms *bara'*, *tsemach*, *parah*) rather than in that of election. The prophet's teaching about God the creator can be summarized by saying that God is the creator God because he is the God of the covenant and he is the God of the covenant because he is the creator God.

[2] Comparable ideas occur in the wisdom literature of Egypt, such as Amenemope (chap. 25): "Do not mock a blind man and do not slight a dwarf; for man is clay and straw, the god is his maker, he is tearing down and building up every day." It is very probable that the texts which insist on order and plan in the creation betray Egyptian influence and a tradition about creation which knew nothing of the chaos (Prov. 8.22-26 is unaware of the chaos, everything is done by wisdom, that is to say with perfection from the start); but it must be recognized

tatives of this tendency says explicitly that it is from the contemplation of his works that we arrive at a knowledge of the artificer (Wisdom 7.17ff.). In the Old Testament itself creation never became the mirror in which the wise providence of God might be reflected plainly and, so to speak, rationally. Rather does creation witness to a mysterious, hidden God and even if an Israelite succeeds in discovering in creation and its order a wise and just God, for others it is an object of fear. In fact nature contains subjects for wonder and even for scandal in which man discovers no purpose and before which he can only bend in fearful adoration (Job 42.3; 40.9), or glorify the mighty and holy God who does what he pleases (Ps. 115.3; 135.6). Yet because of the priority of the covenant man can look creation in the face, for the covenant is eternal whilst the creation will come to an end. "Therefore the material universe is only the temporary and removable setting of the divine-human drama. It does not possess permanent worth. To-morrow the heavens will be rolled up like a book and all the host of heaven will fall ' as the leaf falls from the vine, as the fading leaf from the fig tree ' (Is. 34.4)."[1]

BIBLIOGRAPHY

Böhl, F. M. Th., " Bara als Terminus der Weltschöpfung im alttestamentlichen Sprachgebrauch ", *Alttest. Studien* (Kittel Festschrift), Leipzig 1913, p. 42.

Brongers, H. A., *De Scheppingstradition bij de Profeten*, Amsterdam 1945 (gives in conclusion a summary in German).

Galling, H., " Die Chaosschilderung in Genesis I ", *ZThK* 1950, p. 145.

Gunkel, H., *Schöpfung und Chaos in Urzeit und Endzeit*, Göttingen 1895.

Herner, S., *Die Natur im A.T.*, Lund 1941.

Humbert, P., " Emploi et portée du verbe bara dans l'A.T.", *ThZ* 1947, p. 410.

　　　　　" Qana en hébreu biblique ", *Festschrift A. Bertholet*, 1950, p. 259.

Labat, R., *Enuma elish. Le poème babylonien de la création*, Paris 1935.

Lambert, G., " La Création dans la Bible ", *NRTh*, 1953, p. 252.

that the picture of creation as the result of a struggle was far more in keeping with the lines of Israel's religion; so it must not surprise us to find it even in texts inspired by Egypt, as, for example, Ps. 104.26.

[1] Victor Monod, *Dieu dans l'univers*, Paris 1933, p. 16.

LINDESKOG, C., *Studien zum neutestamentlichen Schöpfungsgedanken*, Uppsala 1952 (a third of this volume treats of the O.T. and Judaism).

VAN DER PLOEG, J., " Le sens du verbe hébreu bara, étude sémasiologique ", *Le Muséon* lix (Mélanges Th. Lefort), Louvain 1946, pp. 1-4.

RAD, G. VON, "Das theologische Problem des alttestamentlichen Schöpfungsglaubens", *Werden und Wesen des A.T.*, *BZAW* 66, 1936, p. 138.

III. THE NATURE AND DESTINY OF MAN

THE first affirmation of the Old Testament about man and one which underlies all the rest is that he is a creature and as such shares in the feebleness and limitations of all creatures; his existence is ephemeral and ends inexorably with death: "Man that is born of a woman is of few days, and full of trouble. He cometh forth like a flower, then he withereth; he fleeth as a shadow and continueth not" (Job 14.1-2), "As for man, his days are as grass; as a flower of the field, so he flourisheth; let the wind pass over it, and it is gone, and the place thereof knoweth it no more" (Ps. 103.15-16). The feebleness of man inherent in his creaturely estate is one of the reasons why God is moved to pity and to pardon: "God is compassionate, he forgives their sin and destroyeth them not; yea, many a time he turneth his anger away and giveth no course to all his wrath. He remembereth that they were but flesh, a breath that passeth away and cometh not again" (Ps. 78.38-39). The opposition between God and man is defined by the prophet Isaiah as that of flesh and spirit (31.3), flesh being synonymous with feebleness and spirit with power; therefore the trust man places in his fellow man is vain and illusory: "Cursed is the man that trusteth in man, and maketh flesh his arm, and whose heart departeth from Yahweh" (Jer. 17.5). This is how the Chronicler represents the antagonism between Judah and Assyria by putting into the mouth of king Hezekiah the words: "With him is an arm of flesh, but with us is Yahweh our God to help us and to fight our battles" (2 Chr. 32.8). Nothing obvious distinguishes man from other creatures;[1] according to the Yahwist creation narrative man is created from the dust of the earth and animals are formed from the 'adamah (Gen. 2.7, 19). At the time of the flood men and animals, creatures of the same creation, are objects of the same condemnation (Gen. 6.7), with the same promise following for both (Gen. 9.15). The final end of man and beast is the same: death for the one and also for the other (Eccl.

[1] L. Koehler, *Theol. A.T.*, p. 143: "According to the revelation of the Old Testament, animals share the same fate as men."

151

3.19) and Ecclesiastes looks with extreme scepticism upon attempts to speculate about a fate reserved for man different from that for animals (12.8). Plant life and social life do not differ essentially from animal life: to maintain and propagate life is their common function. Man's limitations are also shown in the limited nature of his knowledge. God is the one who knows, while man remains eternally ignorant. This last opposition is shown in a particularly dramatic light in the last chapters of the book of Job and this it is which is given as the answer to the problem debated in that book.

Alongside the statement of man's ephemeral and limited nature the Old Testament proclaims unceasingly the eminent dignity conferred upon him by his peculiar association with God. The link is not a relation of kinship, man is no fallen god, he is not as in the Babylonian myth partly composed of divine substance; he is placed by God as an independent and autonomous creature to whom as God's image dominion over the rest of creation is entrusted. This is why man, although subject to the laws which govern the realm of created things, is yet nearer to God than other creatures: although man and the animals were created the same day—which stresses their family relationship—an impassable barrier separates them, for the principal function of the image consists precisely in domination of the animals and maintenance of the distance which separates them from the human sphere. Because of this distance the Old Testament regards any sexual relation with an animal as a fault worthy of the severest penalty: Ex. 22.18; Lev. 18.23; 20.15; Dt. 27.21. The worst punishment a man can suffer is to be reduced to the state of an animal: Dan. 4.13, 29; Ps. 73.22. But in no way does this difference in rank weaken man's obligations towards animals. Since God " preserveth man and beast " (Ps. 36.7) man in the image of God must take care of the animals: " A righteous man taketh care of the life of his beast but the tender mercies of the wicked are cruel ", says the wise man in the book of Proverbs (12.10) and the legislation of the Code of the Covenant does not fail to stress the duties of men towards those who are indeed by virtue of their original kinship their inferior brethren. Opposition between man and the animals, already marked at the time of creation, has been accentuated by the fall: in the garden of Eden and up to the time of the flood man forbore using animal flesh for his food (Gen. 1.29; 2.16); the fall of man involves that of the animals and is the cause of their wickedness (cf. Jer. 12.4; 14.2), as also in the time of his restoration man will draw the animals into his salvation; once again the wolf will dwell with the lamb (Is. 11.6); they will stop devouring each other (Is. 11.7) and the benefits of the covenant will extend to the animals (Hos. 2.20). Man's superiority is shown in a general way over all nature. In the oriental world as a whole, nature was deified and the presence of gods and spirits in its midst induced men to make them harmless by devoting a cult to them. In Hebrew religion there is no bond between man and nature. Thus salvation for man will not consist in the adoration of nature but in dominion over it; in a sense man looks upon it with the eyes of God, although of course that does not mean that he knows all its secrets; God alone possesses absolute wisdom: Prov. 8.22; Job 28.12ff.; 38. Man's position of sovereignty is also to be observed in other realms: work, marriage, use of the good things of the earth; man should do all that is in his power and fully enjoy all the pleasures of existence, while remembering that he is only a stranger on the earth and that his supreme dignity consists in belonging to a Lord who is the creator and owner of all things.

The third point of which account must be taken for a sound grasp of Israelite anthropology is the way in which the Semites regarded the relation between the individual and society. Numerous works applying the results of sociology to the study of the religion of Israel have made plain the primary importance of society and the group. Amongst all peoples the group had primacy over the individual, but in Israel purely natural solidarity based on blood, cohabitation and a common history receive a singular stress by the fact of divine election. Examples of solidarity both in good and evil are too numerous in the Old Testament for the point to be laboured: when one member of a clan has committed a fault punishment falls on the whole clan; thus for the fault committed by Achan not only himself but all his family and his possessions are consumed by fire (Jos. 7.24). David delivers seven descendants of Saul to the Gibeonites to avenge the blood of their ancestors who had been massacred by Saul (2 Sam. 21.9). Punishment is always collective; the iniquity of the fathers extends to their children (Ex. 20.5); no one is concerned to challenge the justice of such a principle and it is always thought that the one who is punished is really culpable. The same solidarity holds for rewards: Noah, who was righteous,

saves all his family, who were plainly not righteous to the same
extent as he was (Gen. 7.1); the house of Obed-edom is blessed
because he gave shelter to the ark (2 Sam. 6.11). Yahweh's benefits
are always conferred upon the people as a whole and it seems at first
sight that the quality of the members forming it is of no consequence. That shows that the distinction between the individual
and the group cannot be made according to modern criteria. Are
we to say that the group was the only reality and that in practice
the individual was sacrificed to it? Must we repeat Wellhausen's[1]
classical statement: "The wheel of history passed over the individual; nothing was left to him but hopeless submission. He had
to find his reward in the well-being of his people." The attempt
often made to divide the history of Israel into two periods, the one
governed entirely by collective retribution and the other inaugurated
by the great champions of religious individualism, Jeremiah and
Ezekiel, who were the first to announce the promotion of the individual, does not do justice to the historical development of Israel.
In fact we find from ancient times the coexistence of a collective
mentality and of a more individualistic way of thinking, and the
examples of solidarity which we have mentioned are in themselves
the best proof of this.[2] That an individual is able to implicate the
whole of his group in his reprobation or his blessing is a very
different matter from the totalitarian idea in which the individual
may be "sacrificed for social ends". This blending of individualism and socialism, both of them thorough-going, and their
organic relationship, have been explained in recent years by the aid
of the concept of corporate personality whose classical formulation
has been given by Wheeler Robinson:[3] "The whole group, including its past, present and future members, might function as a single
individual through any one of those members conceived as representative of it." Applying to the Old Testament the results of the law
of participation as Lévy-Bruhl has defined it three aspects of this

[1] Wellhausen, *Israelitische und jüd. Geschichte*, 1914, 2nd ed., pp. 69, 107.

[2] Cf. J. Hempel, who very soundly writes that "the awakening of the individual
to self awareness lies behind even the most ancient sources" (*Gott und Mensch im
A.T.*, p. 192). An intermediate position is taken up by A. Causse, "Following
the cultural crises of the period of the kings the individual tended to assert himself
independently of the primitive group, whilst by the evolution of morality and of
ideas the hard law of collective responsibility lost its force" (*Du groupe ethnique
à la communauté religieuse*, p. 106).

[3] In *Werden und Wesen des Alten Testaments*, BZAW 66, 1936, p. 49:
"The Hebrew conception of corporate personality."

notion become clear : (*a*) the idea of corporate personality is uncon-. cerned with our conception of time; Amos addresses his contemporaries as if they had been present at the Exodus from Egypt; to live in the present is at the same time to embrace all the past and all the future; (*b*) corporate personality is something essentially realistic and it would be false merely to see in it a moral ideal or a literary personification; Moab is the ultimate unity of which the Moabite is only a part, likewise Israel or Adam who show themselves in numerous sons : ben Israel, ben Adam; (*c*) the relation between the individual and the group is extremely fluid : the individual can be thought of in the community and the community in the individual. Wheeler Robinson has applied this principle to two questions which have always perplexed exegetes, to the "I" of the Psalms and to the Servant of Yahweh. Through the idea of corporate personality the I and the Servant can be understood both in an individual and a collective sense at the same time : the Psalmist who speaks in the first person is an individual, but as a member of the community he incarnates in his own person the whole community, so that in a re-reading of these Psalms the community can apply to itself the experience of that individual. For the Servant of Yahweh it was rather the inverse movement which took place : originally collective this figure ends by being restricted to a single individual. Prior to Wheeler Robinson an analogous point of view had been defended by Otto Eissfeldt,[1] who had insisted upon the fact that in communities based upon blood relationship the ancestor continued to live and to determine their destinies.

The best solution is probably of this kind, yet it must never be forgotten that, although the individual incarnates in himself the group, he is also personally responsible and that the Old Testament never thinks of the people as a neutral entity but as the assembly of individuals, each one of whom has a personal link with God. Every birth is presented as a personal intervention of God and the wisdom literature, which is only the development of a tendency that existed in Israel from the beginning, corrects the too rigid idea of collective election by that of creation, which can only be interpreted in an individual sense. Even a text like the Decalogue, which belongs to the realm of election and covenant and which is

---

[1] *Der Gottesknecht bei Deuterojesaja im Lichte der israelitischen Anschauungen von Gemeinschaft und Individuum*, Halle 1933.

addressed to the nation as a whole, sets out its commandments in such a way that their execution is only possible by individuals.

A. SOME SEMANTIC CONSIDERATIONS

Hebrew uses several terms to designate man. The one that corresponds most closely to the Latin *homo* is *'adam*, which means he who has been brought forth from the *'adamah*, that is the earth. According to Lidzbarski before it denoted man *'adam* had been the name of god: having found in a Punic inscription mention of a goddess *Hawwat* (*rabbat chawwat 'elat malkat* = the great, queen goddess Hawwat) he attempts to find the associated god who, by biblical analogy, can only be Adam. Several inscriptions mention *ba'al melek 'adam*,[1] but it seems that we should see in *mlk 'adam* a function of baal rather than the title of another god. Lidzbarski's reading becomes quite improbable since there has been found in Ugaritic texts the expression *El 'ab 'adam*. The basic meaning of the root *'adam* is probably that of the colour red which man has in common with the earth, an association which facilitated the myth of man brought forth out of the earth.

The term *'ish* probably goes back to a root that means in Arabic to be powerful and which is found in the biblical name *Yo'ash*. So *'ish* would denote man as a being endowed with power. While *'adam* stresses his origin and his external appearance, *'ish* expresses his power of will and choice; choice is particularly present in the case of marriage; so a man is the *'ish* in the presence of the one he chooses. This meaning appears in several passages, notably in Psalm 49.3, which mentions the *bene 'adam* and the *bene 'ish*, humble folk and powerful nobles; the same meaning appears again in Ps. 4.3; 62.10, and Lam. 3.33.

The root *'anash* from which the term *'enosh* comes, is attested in Accadian and Hebrew in the sense of being weak, wretched. So the use made of the term *'enosh*, principally in poetic writings, stresses the feeble and mortal aspect of man and connects it with *'adam*, with which it is also often used in parallel: Ps. 8.5; Ps. 90.3; Dt. 32.26; Job 10.4, 5; Is. 13.12; 24.6; 33.8. It is probably to this same root that the term *'ishshah*, woman, must be attached, the popular etymology of which given by the Yahwist is philologi-

[1] The text in question is published in *Ephemeris für semitische Epigraphik* I, p. 34.

cally impossible (Gen. 2.23), for it means not she who is drawn from man but the feeble creature who needs support.

The term *geber* lays stress on power and is often used of a man to distinguish him from a woman or child (cf. Ex. 10.11; 12.37; Jos. 7.14), it is also used of one who by his power thinks he can oppose God (Ps. 12.5; Job 15.25).

From these terms some conclusions can be extracted about the nature of man and his vocation. If it is true that *'adam* insists on the human kind, *'enosh* on his feebleness, *'ish* on his power, *geber* on his strength, then we can say that added together they indicate that man according to the Old Testament is a perishable creature, who lives only as the member of a group, but that he is also a powerful being capable of choice and dominion. So the semantic enquiry confirms the general teaching of the Bible on the insignificance and the greatness of man.

Outline of Israelite anthropology

To attempt to present the anthropology of the Old Testament with the aid of current concepts and modern speech will lead to certain failure. Opposition between body and soul is not to be found in the Old Testament, nor even a trichotomy (body, soul and spirit). Man is a psycho-physical being and psychical functions are bound so closely to his physical nature that they are all localized in bodily organs which themselves only draw their life from the vital force that animates them. The fluidity of the relations between individual and group has its repercussions in anthropology: indeed the human body is conceived in the image of the greater body that constitutes the people of Israel. It is not a collection of separate organs but an organism animated by one single life and each organ can give expression to the life of the whole. Hebrew expresses this truth by speaking of a heart, a soul,[1] a spirit for the Israelite people, for the only life is that of the nation. The fundamental idea of Israelite psychology is that of an animated body, and moreover it can only be understood in its practical and experimental aspect. In presence of this reality of the body, the beauty and harmony of which the majority of texts are pleased to stress, the Israelites applied themselves to a few

---

[1] *Nephesh* in the singular is used in a collective sense: Lev. 26.15; Num. 21.5; Is. 46.2; 47.14; Ps. 124.7, 10b; Jer. 7.24; 17.1 etc.

reflections about the life that animates it, without always succeeding in expressing in a logical analysis the sometimes contradictory impressions they experienced.

B. MAN IS A CREATURE OF FLESH

It was the impression which most forcefully presented itself. Possibly the term *basar* originally meant, as in Arabic, the skin and then the outward appearance and ended by signifying the whole man. Flesh is what man has in common with other living beings; in its narrow sense flesh is distinguished from bones: "My bones cleave to my flesh" (Ps. 102.6). More frequently flesh denotes the entire body: 1 Kings 21.27; 2 Kings 6.30; Num. 8.7; Job 4.15; Prov. 4.22, and it can be the seat of spiritual faculties as well as of genuinely fleshly desires, both of which are bound up with the body. So the flesh is consumed with desire for God (Ps. 84.3), it is able to rejoice (Ps. 16.9) or to fear (Ps. 119.120); but more often it is connected with more purely animal functions, as the satisfaction of thirst (Eccl. 5.11) or the sexual instinct (Eccl. 11.10; Ez. 23.20). The idea that the flesh might be the principle of sin is foreign to the Old Testament[1] and is expressed for the first time, clearly under Greek influence, only in the Wisdom of Solomon: "The perishable body weighs down the soul and oppresses the spirit" (9.15), but the weakness of the flesh is a very favourable ground for sin, as is shown in the early pages of Genesis. In the Old Testament flesh is always what distinguishes man qualitatively from God, not in the sense of a matter-spirit dualism, but of a contrast between strength and weakness (Gen. 6.3; Is. 31.3; 40.6; 49.26; Jer. 12.12; 17.5; 25.31; 32.27; 45.5; Ez. 21.4; Ps. 56.5; 65.3; 78.39; 145.21; 2 Chr. 32.8).

C. MAN IS A LIVING SOUL

"Yahweh Elohim formed man of the dust of the ground, and breathed into his nostrils the breath of life; and man became a *nephesh chayyah*" (Gen. 2.7). This passage, highly important for

---

[1] Ed. König, *Theologie des A.T.*, p. 237, goes so far as to suppose that the three roots of sin, egoism, sensuality and weakness, correspond to three aspects of *basar*.

Israelite anthropology, contains several essential statements. The term *nephesh chayyah* which is applied to men and animals (Gen. 2.19) places animate beings on the same plane and distinguishes them from plants which only have a vegetative life that they draw from the soil to which they are fixed; living beings on the other hand are characterized by their mobility. However, there is an important difference between man and other living beings: man alone receives the vital breath in his nostrils direct from Yahweh, which is proof that Yahweh considers him an individual, whilst animals are created in conformity with, and with a view to, the species. The text then clearly affirms that the *nephesh* is not given to man as a soul which might be considered as deposited in a body, but as the final result of divine activity which is a reality at once physical and spiritual; so the most adequate translation of *nephesh chayyah* is "living being". But the question is complicated by the fact that the term *nephesh* in the Old Testament proliferates into many realities. The first task of the Hebraist in the presence of a word is to recover the original meaning from which others were derived: since Hebrew terms all originally have a concrete meaning it seems to some[1] that the Accadian *napistu* = throat is the desired key, but since already in Accadian this term also denotes the immaterial reality we are accustomed to translate by "soul", the wiser course is to admit a multiplicity of meanings for *nephesh*, that is to say a plurality of senses from its origin up to at least the point to which we can reach back, which have in common the fact that each expresses a particular aspect of life.[2] The *nephesh* is the life, not in a theoretical sense but in its external and visible aspect, whilst heart and spirit denote life in its interior and hidden aspect.

(*a*) *Nephesh* has the general meaning of life in the following expressions: *nephesh tachat nephesh* = life for life (Ex. 21.23); *nephesh benephesh* (Dt. 19.21), to make an attack upon someone's *nephesh* (life) (Ex. 4.19; 1 Kings 19.2; Job 2.6).

[1] Cf. the article by L. Dürr, *ZAW*, 1925, p. 262; although this sense suits many passages, others are mentioned in favour of the meaning in which *nephesh* seems rather connected with the nose as Is. 3.20 where the *battè banephesh* are more likely to be flasks of perfume than "Häuschen am Hals".

[2] According to Mandelkern and Gesenius the idea of breath was expressed by the two fundamental letters *n* and *sh* which by combining with various labials gave birth to such words as *nashab*, to blow, *nashaph*, to breathe, *naphash*, to take breath, *nasham*, to respire, cf. the graphic presentation in J. H. Becker, *Het begrip nefesj in het oude Testament*, Amsterdam 1942, p. 100.

(*b*) Life reveals itself most especially in certain parts or functions of the organism, for example the throat (cf. the Accadian *napishtu*), "waters are come up unto my *nephesh*" (Ps. 69.2), or the breath; the verb *naphash,* used of rest for God or man, literally means to breathe, to take breath (Ex. 23.12; 31.17; 2 Sam. 16.14) and when Job speaks of the *nephesh* of the crocodile which burns like glowing coals he is evidently alluding to its breath.   To the most primitive observation the breath is always reckoned the most important manifestation of life.   So death is interpreted as the departure of *nephesh*: the *nephesh* leaves Rachel and she dies (Gen. 35.18); the *nephesh* returns into the body of the widow of Zarephath's son (1 Kings 17.22); the *nephesh* that "shortens" itself is similarly based upon the observation that the breath becomes spasmodic at times of great emotions like fear (Num. 21.4) or impatience (Jg. 10.16;16.16).   Other texts bring *nephesh* into relationship with the blood, which was the other most obvious manifestation of life along with the breath.   In legal texts the formula often recurs: *hadam hu hannephesh* = the blood is the life (not the breath!): Gen. 9.4; Lev. 14.11; 17.14; Dt. 12.23, and the figure of the *nephesh* poured out can only be understood by the association of *nephesh* with a liquid substance: 1 Sam. 1.15; Ps. 141.8; Is. 53.12.

(*c*) Life also reveals itself in certain non-organic functions such as aspiration and desire: the *nephesh* of his enemies from which the Psalmist asks to be preserved (Ps. 27.12; 41.3) is the eagerness they show in desiring his ruin.   Desire to eat or drink is also expressed by the *nephesh*, the man with a good appetite is a *ba'al nephesh* (Prov. 23.2) and particularly voracious dogs are *'azze nephesh* (Is. 56.11), that is to say ones which are strong in *nephesh*. When reading such expressions we cover the whole range of difference that separates biblical realism from Greek spirituality. The *nephesh* can be lifted up or stretched in a certain direction (Ps. 24.4; Hos. 4.8; Ez. 24.25).   The desire expressed by *nephesh* is in general violent.   In character as well as in piety passion prevails over meditation and it is with the same ardour that Old Testament man desires to satisfy his hunger, have vengeance upon his enemies or enter into communion with God (Is. 26.8, 9).

(*d*) The Israelites realized that bodily organs and functions were incapable of expressing the full reality and dynamism of life; so *nephesh* often has the sense of living being and of person.   The members of a tribe or inhabitants of a city are *naphashot*, persons:

Gen. 14.21; 46.18; Num. 5.7; Jer. 43.6; Ez. 33.6. In numerous passages—135 have been counted—the most adequate translation of *nephesh* is the reflexive personal pronoun with which moreover it is sometimes used in parallel: "Our *nephesh* is escaped out of the snare of the fowler and we are free" (Ps. 124.7; cf. also Num. 23.10; Jg. 16.31; Job 30.25); when, however, it is a question of the *nephesh* within someone (Ps. 42.5, 7; 131.2) or when one speaks to one's *nephesh* (Ps. 42.6) it seems that more may be meant than the personal pronoun, some kind of superior or inclusive ego, the *nephesh* is the self and all that this self embraces (Ps. 103.1). It may be that sometimes we are simply confronted with rhetorical hyperbole, as in the case where Yahweh judges by his own *nephesh* (Jer. 5.9, 29; Amos 6.8).

(*e*) It is also on the idea of "person" that the stress falls when *nephesh* is used to denote the dead. The complete expression *nephesh meth*[1] clearly does not mean the "soul of the dead", but by analogy with *nephesh chayyah* a dead being (Lev. 21.11; Num. 6.6; *nephesh* only in Lev. 21.1; 19.28; Hag. 2.13). In post-biblical Hebrew, Aramaic, Palmyrene and Syriac the word *naphsa* means the funeral monument. This use takes us far from the primitive meaning, since it is used for the very contrary of life, yet the monument representing a person guarantees, at any rate for a limited time, the continuance of his presence.

D. MAN HAS A SPIRIT

Nephesh is what results when *basar* is animated by *ruach*. This last comes from without, only Yahweh possesses it in its fulness, since occasionally he can be identified with it. All the texts speaking of the spirit of God stress its power, which creates life wherever it acts; penetrating within man this life reveals itself with various degrees of intensity. There is no life without spirit, as Gen. 2.7 clearly says; but there are instances when the spirit comes upon beings who are fully alive in order to give them the power to accomplish extraordinary actions, from martial exploits in the time

---

[1] We must reject as utterly fanciful the interpretation put forward by Miriam Seligson, *The meaning of nephesh meth in the O.T.*, *Studia orientalia fennica*, 1951, who starts from the sense of power which is a fundamental sense given to *nephesh*, and sees in *nephesh meth* the demon of death prowling round the corpse.

of the Judges (Jg. 13.20; 14.6, 19; 15.14; 1 Sam. 10.6; 18.10) to manifestations of prophecy (Joel 3.1). When the spirit disappears, for it only acts sporadically, these people again become normal folk and continue in full life; in other cases, on the contrary, the absence of spirit produces a decidedly inferior grade of life, a kind of loss of strength or even unconsciousness. In presence of Solomon's wealth the Queen of Sheba is deprived of breath (1 Kings 10.5) and the spirit of Jacob revives when he learns that Joseph is still alive (Gen. 45.27), so we can say that an individual without *ruach* is not dead but is not a genuine *nephesh* either; its absence, when it is not simply identified with the vital breath (Ps. 104.29) does not bring about the death of a creature but only diminishes its vitality. In this last sense *ruach* ceases to be regarded as a power lent to man and becomes a psychological reality residing in man in a permanent manner and like *nephesh* able to be the seat of faculties and desire. In the latest texts there is a tendency to identify the two terms with *ruach* predominating; where the earliest expressions use soul, spirit is found (Is. 57.16) whence the phrase: the God of the spirits of all flesh (Num. 16.22; 27.16). In spite of this tendency to merge there remains a perceptible difference. It has been well defined by Johs. Pedersen[1] when he says that " the spirit is the motive power of the soul. It does not mean the centre of the soul, but the strength emanating from it and, in its turn, reacting upon it." The feelings that are connected with the spirit are the particularly violent ones which by their effects seem to be the result of possession: Isaac and Rebekah experience bitterness of spirit because of Esau's marriage with foreign women (Gen. 26.35, cf. also 1 Kings 21.5); the spirit of jealousy (Num. 5.14, 30) which seizes a man through a suspicion of his wife's adultery is a feeling which moves him with such violence that he cannot resist it; often the spirit is said to be stirred up (Hag. 1.14; 1 Chr. 5.26; 2 Chr. 36.22), so it is not easy for a man always to keep control of his *ruach*. It is harder to control the *ruach* than to capture cities (Prov. 16.32; 25.28); thoughts which mount up into the spirit (Ez. 11.5; 20.32; 18.31) are always ripe for passing into action. Though the spirit can be the seat of manifestations whose violence sometimes threatens to rupture normal equilibrium, it is all the more important for it to be controlled by the spirit of God; Psalm 51, speaking of the action of God's spirit on that of man, shows it steadying,

[1] *Israel*, I-II, p. 104.

making firm (v. 12) and breaking (v. 19) the spirit of man (cf. also Ps. 34.19; Is. 57.15; 66.2). Since man is incapable of controlling his spirit it is God who must put a brake upon it and reduce man to his true status. When this control is assured to the extent of man's spirit being possessed by God's, spirit becomes the principal religious organ, the seat of the genuinely spiritual faculties. This evolution prepared the ground favourably for an alliance between Greek dualism and Hebrew thought.

E. MAN HAS A HEART

Whilst for *nephesh* and *ruach* localization in one definite part of the body remains vague, the heart is a distinct organ whose entire psychical functions are closely conditioned by its place in the human body. To the Israelites the heart appears as the chief instance of an invisible and hidden organ; it is within the body, so the terms *leb* and *qereb*, the middle, are often linked: 1 Sam. 25.37; Jer. 23.9; Ps. 64.7. Moreover, we find the same parallelism in the Babylonian world: the creation poem describes in these words the final blow with which Marduk killed Tiamat: "He cut her inward parts, he split open her heart." The heart, inward and hidden, is contrasted with the face; the *leb hashamayim* (Dt. 4.11) is contrasted with the face of the heavens; the heart of the sea into which Jonah laments he has been cast is contrasted with the face of the waters (Jon. 2.4). The heart of man also is contrasted with his face, although the face often reflects the thoughts of the heart. Since it is invisible it is mysterious, unfathomable, man cannot know it, only God who sees everything, because he has created everything, sees the heart (1 Sam. 16.7; man looks at the outward appearance, but Yahweh looks at the heart).

The Hebrews deduced from its movement that this hidden organ might have a life and a function the full scope of which they were far from suspecting. The heart seemed to them a concentration of all the vital powers, as Johs. Pedersen is impelled to write: "*Nephesh* is the soul in the sum of its totality, such as it appears; the heart is the soul in its inner value."[1] Without having modern physiological knowledge, the Israelites were able to observe that impressions and emotions coming from outside influenced the heart,

[1] *Israel*, I-II, p. 104.

retarding or accelerating its movement. They were also able to prove that life depended as much on the heart as on the breath and thus were led to make the heart the "source of life" (Prov. 4.23). From that double assertion they made the heart, understood in a psychological sense, an organ both receptive and active, an idea which is perfectly suitable for the seat of knowledge: knowledge arrives at the heart from without and especially by the channel of the ear;[1] oral tradition was the basis of all teaching amongst the Semites: the pupil had to gather up the words of his wise teacher, and the better he listened the more his intelligence would be developed. From the ear a canal ran straight to the heart (Prov. 23.13; Ez. 3.10), which itself also must be wide open (*rachab-leb*); Accadian texts also say that the heart must see a long way, corresponding to the remoteness of wisdom (Eccl. 7.23, 24). Intelligent men are men of heart (Job 34.10, 34) and in order to say that he is not more stupid than his interlocutors Job exclaims: "But I have a heart as well as you" (12.3). On the other hand, the unintelligent man lacks a heart (*chasar leb*, Prov. 6.32; 7.7) and to condemn a people one says they are without heart (Hos. 7.11; Jer. 5.21); and the figurative expression "to steal someone's heart" (Gen. 31.21, 26; 2 Sam. 15.6, 13) means to rob him of his intellectual faculties to the point of destroying his capacity of judgment. Since in large measure intelligence is a matter of memory, the expression "to come up into the heart" usually refers to remembering: "Remember Yahweh from afar, and let Jerusalem come into your heart" (Jer. 51.50; cf. also Jer. 3.16; Is. 33.18; 65.17; Ps. 31.13; Dt. 4.9, 39, etc.). Because it is by the heart that man is aware of external impressions, it is natural that consciousness itself should be termed the heart.[2] David said to Shimei, "Thou knowest all the wickedness which thine heart is privy to, that thou didst do . . ." i.e. you are fully conscious of the wrong (1 Kings

---

[1] The Egyptian wisdom books, in particular chapter 125 of the Book of the Dead, give frequent evidence that the heart is the organ by which man can receive and understand the divine commandments; an insane man is a man without a heart; it is not impossible that the "listening heart" asked for by Solomon in his prayer at Gibeon had some connection with Egypt (cf. H. Brunner: "Das hörende Herz" in *ThLitztg*, 1954, col. 698).

[2] In a study on "Suneidesis, une pierre de touche de l'hellénisme paulinien", M. H. Clavier has made clear that even when hellenistic Judaism was flourishing the idea expressed by συνείδησις corresponds on the whole to what is called the heart, meaning thereby the totality of the states of consciousness (*Athènes*, Extrait du volume jubilaire du 1900ᵉ anniversaire de la visite de saint Paul en Grèce, 1953).

2.44); remorse of heart is remorse of conscience (1 Sam. 25.31), the table of the heart is the conscience (Jer. 17.1), the wise man in the house of mourning takes to heart, i.e. becomes conscious of, the meaning of life (Eccl. 7.2) and above all Eccl. 7.22: "For thine own heart knoweth how often thou thyself hast cursed others" (Vulgate: *conscientia*). In short, we may say that the receptive functions of the heart place it between conscience and memory.

But in Hebrew thought consciousness is more active than receptive; the heart does not only receive the thoughts which mount up into it, it also forges new and original constructions. According to von Meyenfeldt, the heart plays the part of a "planensmid",[1] that is to say an organ by which impressions and ideas are transformed into projects which must end with action. It is still the heart which devises plans (2 Sam. 7.3; 1 Chr. 22.7; Est. 7.5); these plans are good (Ps. 20.5; 1 Chr. 12.38), or more often evil, since the fall created a congenital propensity for evil (Gen. 6.5); in this last passage there is talk of the imagination (*yetser*) of the heart of man. The heart therefore has the power to create and its function joins up with that of the image of God without, however, being able to be identified with it. Man moves in the direction determined by his heart (Is. 57.17); all the feelings which express a direction or pull towards an object have relation to the heart, which in this sense is often an alternative for spirit: hunger, thirst, arrogance come from the heart: Jer. 49.16; Prov. 21.4; 2 Chr. 25.19; 26.16; 32.26; Est. 6.6, even love and hate; true love has its seat in the heart (Jg. 16.15). Nevertheless it must be noted that the heart plays a lesser part in the affective life than it does in our conceptions and language.

Organ of knowledge[2] in general, the heart is likewise the seat of religious knowledge. Being the source of the body's life, it is natural that it should be related to what is the ultimate source of human life. With the heart one loves God and in the exhortation to love God in Deuteronomy the heart takes first place (Dt. 6.5);

---

[1] *Het hart (leb, lebab) in het oude Testament*, Leiden 1950.

[2] An animal has no heart and this is its principal difference from man, even more than the way in which the *ruach* is communicated to the one or the other. The "heart of a lion" (2 Sam. 17.10) is to be understood in the sense of courage. It is true that in Daniel (4.16 and 5.21) it is said that the heart of Nebuchadnezzar became like that of beasts, but is a heart devoid of knowledge still really a heart?

but as man can truly make real only what God works within him, the heart must be tested and known by God. God weighs the heart (Prov. 21.2), he fortifies it, establishes it and, to show that of all the organs the heart is the one which belongs to him alone, he circumcises it (Lev. 26.41; Dt. 10.16; 30.6; Jer. 4.4; 9.25; Ez. 44.7, 9). But when the heart turns away from God, when it is hardened, then Yahweh himself hardens it, as a temporary measure only, since the goal of Yahweh's work is the new heart which will be given at the end of time (Ez. 11.19; 36.26) and which believers ask to receive in the present as a guarantee of what must come (Ps. 51.12).

The heart holds so great a place in Israelite anthropology, it is so far the quintessence of the man, that we may be tempted to assimilate it to *nephesh* and say: man is a heart. The precise location of the heart prevents our going so far, but at least we can fully subscribe to Dhorme's judgment that a "man is worth what his heart is worth".[1]

F. MAN CREATED IN THE IMAGE OF GOD

The theme of the image of God, which has figured so large in the development of theology, only appears in the Old Testament in a solitary book, and more particularly in only one of the documents of this book: Gen. 1.26, 27; 5.1, 3; 9.6; all belong, in fact, to the Priestly source. From the position of these texts an immediate conclusion of considerable significance can be drawn; it is that neither the fall nor the flood destroyed the image of God, and this from the outset puts the concept into the domain of anthropology and not into that of soteriology. The principal text of Gen. 1.26-27 says that man was created in the image and after the likeness of Elohim. Must we regard these terms as in opposition, or as complementary, or as merely hendiadys? In the Old Testament the first term *tselem* means a fashioned image, a shaped and representa-

---

[1] Here is the full quotation: "Particular passions or emotions will be localized in other internal parts (kidneys, liver), the heart contains them all. It sums up the inward man in opposition to the flesh which is the outward, tangible man. A man is worth what his heart is worth" ("L'emploi métaphorique des noms du corps", *RB*, 1922, p. 508). It is in this study of first rank importance that we already find the essential ideas systematized later by Pedersen in his work *Israel, its life and culture*, 1926.

tive figure (2 Kings 11.18; Amos 5.26; Ez. 23.14), something eminently concrete, so that after an exhaustive semantic investigation Paul Humbert comes to the following conclusion: "The semantic verdict is perfectly definite: man, according to P, has the same 'outward' appearance as the deity of whom he is the tangible effigy, and the noun *tselem* refers to no spiritual likeness in this case any more than in the others."[1] The term *demut* can have the same concrete sense as *tselem* (e.g. Is. 40.18), but as its original force was that of resemblance its use by the author of Genesis in effect curbs and tempers the excessively material and plastic meaning that the first word might suggest. Be that as it may, it is proper to keep a realistic sense for the expression and before asking in what the image consists (bodily resemblance, spiritual capacity, intelligence, speech, will, freedom, differentiation or reciprocity of the sexes, etc.) it is necessary in the first place to start from what is initially given in the text, that man is created as an image of God.

The ancient orient shows us with ever increasing clarity that the purpose and function of an image consists in representing someone. An image, that is to say a statue of a god, is the real presence of this god; prayers are addressed to it and its destruction is equivalent to the destruction of the life of the one it represents. The king had his image set up in the remote provinces of his empire which he could not visit in person. Assyrian inscriptions often repeat the ritual phrase: "I will set up my statue in their midst." The ancient orient also shows us that the title of image was applied to the living person of the king; a hymn of Thutmose III puts these words into the mouth of the god Amon: "I am come, I give you to walk on the princes of Djahi (the population of Palestine or Phoenicia), I spread them out under your feet across their land, I cause them to see your majesty like that of a lord of glory, while you shine in their face like my own image."[2] The term image applied to man in general is rare; it is reserved for kings, whose place was nearer to the gods than that of ordinary folk. Notice, however, an Egyptian text also dating from the reign of Thutmose III: "How wise was God when he arranged the condition of men, God's flock. He made the sky and the earth for their sake,

[1] *Etudes sur le récit du paradis et de la chute dans la Genèse*, 1940, p. 157.
[2] Quoted from J. de Savignac, "Interprétation du Psaume 110" in *Oudtestamentische Studiën*, IX, p. 111.

he drove back the darkness of the abyss. He made the breath of the heart as the life of their nostrils; they are his images coming out of his flesh. He shone in the sky for their sake. He made for them the plants, the cattle, the birds and the fish as their food."[1] This reference to man as an image of God is first conceived in Egypt where humanity is supposed to have originated by way of generation from the divine world;[2] but that it is found in the Old Testament and in a document which otherwise stresses strongly the divine transcendence is at first surprising, the more so as the central place it occupies shows that it is not a truth mentioned in passing but a quite fundamental reality. The representative function which the term image implies is not exercised by a particular person, the king for example, but by man, who is, according to a particularly happy expression, the "vizier"[3] of God on earth. Man is a representative by his entire being, for Israelite thought always views man in his totality, by his physical being as well as by his spiritual functions, and if choice had to be made between the two we would say that the external appearance is perhaps even more important than spiritual resemblance. The Old Testament teaches in fact that in man's exterior aspect there is a beauty and dignity found in no other living being. According to L. Koehler[4] the image of God could consist in man's upright posture (*die aufrechte Gestalt*) which separates him from the animals and which would find its commentary in a verse of Ovid's Metamorphoses (1/85):

> Os homini sublime dedit, caelumque videre
> Jussit et erectos ad sidera tollere vultus.

The solemnity with which the Priestly writer speaks of the *imago Dei* seems to prove that he did not restrict it to this single aspect; it is none the less true that the Old Testament affirms that the human ideal always includes external beauty, and when Second

---

[1] Quoted from Podechard, *Les Psaumes*, commentary on Ps. 8.

[2] In the epic of Gilgamesh, Enkidu is created as the image of Anu, but the translation of *zikru sha Anim* by image of Anu is doubtful; interesting information on the identity of the image with the god will be found in the work of H. Schrade, *Der Verbogene Gott. Gottesbild und Gottesvorstellung in Israel und im Alten Orient*, Stuttgart 1949; the proper name Ur-Tsalmi, servant of the image, which we find in Babylonian hymns, clearly expresses the identification of the god with his image.

[3] The expression is from J. Hempel, *Ethos des A.T.*, p. 201.

[4] *ThZ*, 1948, pp. 17ff.

Isaiah speaks of a servant who has neither attractiveness nor beauty he introduces to Israel such an original idea that he takes care to stress its paradox and offensiveness. It is true that no Old Testament text expressly connects bodily beauty with the image of God; but a passage in Rabbinical literature shows that the connection was made at least once in Hebrew thought: in Midr. Lev. R. 34, referring to Prov. 11.17: "The merciful man doeth good to his own *nephesh*", we have the following comment: When Hillel (20 B.C.) took leave of his disciples he usually accompanied them far along the road, and as they asked him: Rabbi, where are you going? he answered: I am going to fulfil a commandment.—Which one?—I am going to take a bath at the bathing place. When his disciples asked: But is that a commandment? he replied: Certainly, for if the man appointed for the statues of kings set up in the theatres and circuses washes and rubs them down and for that work is not only provided for but honoured amongst the great men of the realm, how much more must this duty be incumbent upon me who am created after the image and likeness of God? "[1] It is also to a rather physical sense that we are directed by the passage in Genesis which refers to the image of God over the matter of blood vengeance (9.6): to touch man is to touch God himself, of whom every man is the image; God will not require account of animal blood, but man's blood is in some measure God's, even though there may not be the bond of physical kinship between God and man, as in Babylonian myth.[2]

If the representative function is the specific quality of the image, it is clear that man can only exercise it in connection with other creatures in whose eyes he represents God. Man's place in the bosom of creation is that of an intermediary: whilst in neighbouring religions, particularly in Canaan, distinctions between God, nature, the animal world and man were exceedingly ill-defined and it was very easy to pass from one to the other of these domains, the Old Testament draws a clear distinction between man and his environment. Now, straight after the creation of man in God's image, Genesis speaks of his dominion over the animals. This dominion over the animals is not itself the *imago Dei*, but it is the

---

[1] Quoted from Strack-Billerbeck, t. I, p. 654.

[2] This inviolability of man is already recognized in earlier texts; for this reason the Code of the Covenant (Ex. 21.28) lays down that an animal which kills a man shall be stoned and its flesh not eaten; the impurity of the animal throws into relief the holiness of the man.

first opportunity for the image to be exercised in a definite way and Psalm 8, which is the best commentary on Genesis 1, also sees the particular sign of man's superiority in his dominion over the animal world. This same Psalm says that man was created only a little inferior to Elohim; what man lacks to be equal to Elohim is what the Priestly Code expresses when it tempers *tselem* by *demut*. To mark clearly the limit which must not be transgressed the Psalmist, speaking of man's rôle, avoids the name Yahweh which is, however, used at the beginning, for the name Yahweh is a personal name and for that reason the inalienable property of the one who bears it, and cannot be associated with any creature. To this being, clothed with glory and majesty—and the figure of speech of clothing is again an allusion to man's physical aspect— God has given dominion over nature.

This ruling of man over nature is a privilege: the beasts of the field must serve for his food, make his life easier, increase the product of his work and his wealth; but this privilege can only be maintained at the price of effort for although the animal world is subject to man it remains a perpetual temptation into which he is in danger of falling either by overestimating it and worshipping it or by underestimating it through not recognizing the hostile and dangerous element which characterizes it. From the serpent of Genesis to the beasts of Daniel, the forces of evil are symbolized by animal powers; and this is why we think that the image of God and dominion over the animals also implies to some extent dominion over evil. Not far from the passage proclaiming man's dominion over the animals is this other order of God: "If thou doest not well, sin coucheth at the door: and unto thee is its desire, but thou shouldst rule over it" (Gen. 4.7). This passage differs from Genesis 1 both in origin and terminology; yet it is hard not to see a connection between these two orders given to man about the dominion which he must exercise as God's representative. Domination through struggle reproduces God's own action: the earliest traditions about creation of which we have traces in certain poetic texts represent it as a struggle and victory of Yahweh's over the powers of chaos, which have not, however, been totally destroyed but only bridled. These powers of chaos, which people liked to picture in animal forms, could even be an obstacle to God's just government of the world. This is why when God desires to reply to Job's bitter complaints and questions he chooses the apparently ridiculous way of describing to him two beasts, Behemoth and Leviathan. Commentators usually put this reply of God down to the irony which the Old Testament and the book of Job in particular often uses to express divine sovereignty. There is probably a still more profound reason: God wants to show Job how difficult the conduct of the world is with creatures so extraordinary and so mysterious which fear nothing (Job 41.24) and against which he has to wage incessant war. By transposing that to his own plane, Job will be able to draw the conclusion not only that God is not unjust by his lack of concern for him since he himself on a much higher plane struggles against evil, but that Job will only find a solution for evil by mastering it; then the words of Job 40.7-11 would be less an order to keep silent and be humble than a call to the struggle, a call to the image of God himself: "Deck thyself now with excellency and dignity; and array thyself with honour and majesty. Pour forth the overflowings of thine anger: and look upon every one that is proud, and abase him. Look on every one that is proud, and bring him low; and tread down the wicked where they stand. Hide them in the dust together; bind their faces in the hidden place. Then will I also confess of thee that thine own right hand can save thee."

Such interpretations might leave the impression that the Old Testament presents an ideal for man akin to that of a superman. Far from it, for the *imago Dei* means for man a relationship with, and dependence upon, the one for whom he is only the representative. To wish to be like God, the temptation suggested by the serpent, is to desire to abandon the rôle of image and on several occasions the Old Testament shows that in behaving thus man degrades himself and falls to the animal level instead of raising himself: to desire to become an angel is to prepare to become a beast.[1] To remain an image man must maintain his relationship with God, he must remember that he is only an ambassador and his dominion over creation will be effective only in proportion as that relationship becomes more real.

This theme, which has only a very limited place in the Old Testament, simply expresses in theological dress a truth admitted in Israel long before the time of the Priestly writer: the Yahwist, in showing the direct intervention of Yahweh in the creation of

[1] The respective positions of these different creatures can be described by saying that the animal lives in the present, the angels in eternity and man in history.

man, already brings to light his royal function,[1] but since his thought is directed entirely towards the fall he stresses the contrast more than the resemblance; it is the same with the prophets, though their persistence in speaking of man's sin and the necessity of his return proves that they expected much from man. It is only in apocryphal literature that explicit reference is made to the theme of the image of God:

"He gave into the power of men what is on the earth. He clothed them with power like his own; in his image he created them. He put the fear of man on all creatures" (Ecclus. 17.2-4).

"God created man for incorruption, and made him an image of his own proper being" (Wisdom 2.23). The last passage points forward to the developments which will extend this theme far beyond its particular Old Testament attachments.

G. MAN IS CREATED MALE AND FEMALE

Man's destiny is only fully realized within the unity of the married couple. Marriage is always regarded as the normal state and celibacy is only considered as an exceptional vocation, necessary for the fulfilment of a mission, as in the case of Jeremiah. The breaking of the unity of the couple by the decease of one partner is regarded as a misfortune because one of the two is reduced to solitude; to be a widow is synonymous with abandonment and the requirements of the law aimed at easing this misfortune. The most developed reflection on the unity of the married couple is in the Yahwist creation narrative, from which we can extract the main contentions which the whole Old Testament makes on this subject. Since the woman is taken from man's body she forms with him a single flesh; this is why man and wife unceasingly seek and call upon each other. The joy of reunion and the sadness of parting are celebrated in an incomparable way in the Song of Songs. Alongside this unity all the Old Testament insists on the subordination of the woman to the man. Man by himself is a complete being, the woman who is given to him adds nothing to his nature,

---

[1] It would be wrong to follow Wellhausen, *Prolegomena*, 5th ed., 1899, p. 312, and oppose the conception of man in Genesis 1 to that of the Yahwist narrative; the equality with God that man wants to attain is something quite different from the image of God which is given him by God at the time of his creation.

whilst the woman drawn forth from man owes all her existence to him, though man only assists passively in her creation, which is the work of Yahweh alone and before the outcome of which man utters a cry of admiration: "This is now flesh of my flesh" (Gen. 2.23). The bond of the man to the woman is not an indication in favour of a matriarchal order;[1] if there were traces of a matriarchate it was before the Yahwist period of Israelite religion. The Old Testament always assigns the woman an inferior rôle, in the religious domain as well as in social life, though this does not prevent her fulfilling on occasion the functions of military leader or prophetess; but generally the place of the woman is the home, where she is called to devote herself to tasks whose dignity is recalled by the author of the book of Proverbs (chap. 31). It is in the setting of the home that the woman can exercise her double vocation of 'ishah and chawah, by giving man all the help she can and by bringing sons into the world who will assure the continuity of the generations. This ideal of the unity of the married couple is only intelligible in a society where monogamy was the normal condition,[2] but in this realm, as in others, the reality no doubt often fell far short of the ideal.

H. THE IMITATION OF GOD, THE PRINCIPLE OF THE MORAL AND SPIRITUAL LIFE

If man's nature can be defined by the theme of the image of God, his function can be qualified as an imitation of God. This involves a double obligation for man, we might say a double outlook: one eye turned towards God and the other towards the world. The Old Testament re-echoes both a piety in which communion with God reaches the highest intensity (Psalm 73) and a realism which underlies much social legislation. This does not mean they are two mutually exclusive parallel lines; the apparent duality belongs to man's own position within creation: as a creature man receives his life from God only, but as an autonomous and

---

[1] The arguments which have been used in favour of a matriarchal period in Israel have little substance and on the whole historians reach a negative conclusion, cf. L. G. Lévy, La famille dans l'antiquité israélite, Paris 1905, p. 125.

[2] For the evolution from polygamy towards monogamy, cf. the study of A. Gelin in Mélanges Podechard (Études de critique et d'histoire published by the Faculté de théologie catholique de Lyon, 1946).

free creature he is capable of initiative and dominion: " In the Yahwist's religion communion with God means to experience in the personal life the creative sovereignty of God and to express it positively in one's own action and one's own sufferings."[1] What this contemporary author says of the prophets is true for every individual, for each man is called to enter into God's plan.

To enter into communion with God is to enter into a movement, to participate in a history which is of God. Participation by man in God's plan is, first of all, faith; and it is not by chance that Isaiah, who is the prophet of God's plan, is also the prophet of faith. To believe is to share in the stability of God, to see things as God sees them with security and confidence. Faith has a three-fold aspect in the Old Testament: [2] it is knowledge, and the phrase knowledge of God expresses one of the essential features of Israelite religion; it is trust, and Isaiah defines it as an attitude of calmness (7.4; 30.15; 28.15) because it is submission to an all-powerful and good master; and finally, it is active obedience, for the believer, far from abandoning himself to fatalism, must struggle along with God for the fulfilling of his plan. This entering into God's plan is illustrated by the use of the same word or at least of the same root for both divine and human activity: 'emunah and 'emet denote at the same time the faithfulness and veracity of God and the faith of man. It is the same with the use of the term chesed which, in spite of the numerous studies made of it, still remains difficult to render into any of our western languages; the word is used at one and the same time for the attitude of God to man, of man to God, and of man to his fellow. By chesed man best attains to the imitation of God and the chesed he shows to his neighbour is always chesed Elohim (2 Sam. 9.3; 1 Sam. 20.14); the more complete expression 'asah chesed we'emet is used of God and of men (2 Sam. 2.6; 15.20; Gen. 24.12; 2 Sam. 10.2) and every Israelite's ideal to become chasid is realized in a perfect way by Yahweh himself (Jer. 3.12; Ps. 145.17). The requirements of righteousness and holiness are already partly implied in that of chesed, but nevertheless are not explicitly formulated there: " Ye shall be holy, for I am holy " (Lev. 11.44). It could also be asked whether the formula " I

---

[1] I. P. Seierstad, *Die Offenbarungserlebnisse der Propheten Amos, Jesaja, Jeremia,* Oslo 1946, p. 22.

[2] On faith in the O.T., cf. the article of P. Michalon, " La foi, rencontre de Dieu et engagement envers Dieu dans l'A.T.", *NRTh,* 1953, p. 587.

am Yahweh" which serves as conclusion to many of the laws of Leviticus does not also signify that the principle of imitation lies behind all the legislation; this legislation which culminates in "Thou shalt love thy neighbour as thyself" (Lev. 19.18) applies in the human realm God's own method who, by creating man in his image and clothing him with a dignity like his own, loved him as himself.[1]

The bond subjecting man to God and the freedom which gives him dominion over the world also give direction to the entire devotion of the faithful Israelite. The humility characterizing it is no blind submission, but a walking with God (Mic. 6.8). The believer who has seen in history a manifestation of divine righteousness and *chesed* can only involve his own existence humbly in the wake of that history. Humility will be accompanied by fear, for nothing else is possible before a holy and sometimes terrible God; yet, important as fear is in Israelite religion, it does not occupy the central place, joy far outweighs it; joy belongs to God. A God who laughs, a God who indulges so largely in humour, is a joyous God: the morning stars (Job 38.7) and wisdom (Prov. 8.22-31) which utters cries of joy before him are a poetic personification of the feelings which animate God himself when he takes pleasure in his created works (cf. Gen. 1 and Ps. 104.31: that Yahweh delights in all his works). "There is no word," writes L. Koehler,[2] "which is more central in the Old Testament than the word joy." God gives man a considerable share in his joy (Eccl. 2.26; 8.15; 9.7; 11.9ff.), joy forms the centre of the cult, which consists in rejoicing before Yahweh and in communion with him (Lev. 23.40; Num. 10.10; Dt. 12.7; 14.26; 16.11) and when the future kingdom arrives its advent will be marked by great joy (Is. 9.2). In a joy which does not merely show itself in inward feelings, God and man express the domination and the victory, experienced by God and hoped for by men, over all the powers capable of attacking their liberty.

The principle of imitation appears in the two cultic manifestations of piety—prayer and sacrifice. In the Old Testament there are traces of purely eudemonistic and egocentric prayer, but under the

[1] Hempel, *Ethos des A.T.*, p. 201, speaks of the theomorphism of man and stresses its ethical consequences, which are shown particularly in man's dominion over nature and other beings.

[2] *Theol. A.T.*, 1936, p. 137; cf. also the fundamental article of P. Humbert, "Laetari et exulter dans le vocabulaire religieux de l'A.T.", *RHPR*, 1942, pp. 185ff.

influence of Yahwism and of the prophets it became primarily prayer for the work of God. Israelite prayer only shares with mystical prayer a certain similarity of terms; in reality they serve different ends: mystical prayer seeks to separate the individual from the world and from himself by submerging him in the absolute, while Israelite prayer aims at uniting the will of man with God's will so that the individual, abandoning himself entirely to God, also finds himself fully in God. "Israelite prayer," says Fernand Ménégoz,[1] "tends to make the believer an energetic co-operator and not a beatified enjoyer of God. The expression and driving-force of a will active in holiness shows itself to be in the last analysis a result of God's redemptive work such as takes place age after age in men's hearts." Imitation of God is to be understood as the continuation of God's action. In Israel, as with all religions, sacrifice had an aim like that of prayer; yet even more than prayer it seems to us to be the expression on the level of ritual of the fundamental attitude of *chesed* which governs all Israelite life; it does no violence to the texts to discover in them the three aspects of *chesed* we have defined above. Sacrifice is a manifestation of God's presence made perceptible on earth; therefore it expresses the *chesed* of God towards men which is a gift symbolized by the sacrificial elements. In the second place, sacrifice is a gift of man to God, the offerings symbolizing the life of man submitted to God, and finally, by the rite of fellowship and the common meal, *chesed* is realized on the horizontal plane in the form of the great brotherhood of Israel. Looked at from this angle, sacrifice approximates to the symbolic actions of the prophets which were revelatory and also set in action the divine purposes.[2] If there is a relation between sacrifice and *chesed* the celebrated words of Hosea: "I desire *chesed* and not *sacrifices*" (6.6) do not underline the opposition between the two, but imply that a sacrifice not inspired by *chesed* lacks the spirit to make it effective.

The sabbath is also an invitation to act like God, who rested on the seventh day.

The imitation of God does not remain limited to the specifically

---

[1] *Le problème de la prière*, 1st ed., p. 246.
[2] For the relation between sacrifice and symbolic action, cf. H. Wheeler Robinson, *Redemption and Revelation*, p. 250, and *Old Testament Essays*, 1927, pp. 1-17, as well as Rowley, "The meaning of sacrifice in the O.T." in the *Bulletin of John Rylands Library*, 1950, p. 74. Cf. also G. Fohrer, *Die symbolischen Handlungen der Propheten*, Zürich 1953.

religious life. The theme of conjugal love was widely used to express the relationship between Yahweh and his people. It is not unduly rash to suppose that the religious use of this figure rebounded upon the idea of marriage and that the Israelites saw a reflection in the mutual love of man and wife of Yahweh's love for his people; indeed we have proof of it in the Song of Songs, which celebrates conjugal love in terms borrowed from the metaphorical language of the prophets. Wisdom—that is to say, the art of succeeding in life—and the work of man find in God both their inspiration and their pattern. In short, the two great realms of divine revelation and action are also offered to man: creation and the covenant. Man must be a creator and do everything of which his hands are capable (Eccl. 9.10); but his creative work must be directed because of the covenant by the bond of *chesed* which he must show particularly to those whose vitality is menaced by their weakness; service of one's neighbour is the basis of the social and economic life.[1] With the pride and harshness of King Jehoiakim the prophet Jeremiah contrasts a portrait of his father, Josiah. "He judged the cause of the poor and the orphan. Was not this to know me? saith the Lord" (Jer. 22.16). The "knowledge of God" which sometimes in the Old Testament has an echo which we shall gladly call mystical, is here identified with action on behalf of the poor. The Gospel will show in a still more complete way how encounter with God can simply be encounter with one's neighbour.

I. THE DESTINY OF MAN: LIFE

Life in the Old Testament has many aspects. Whilst breath and blood are its most evident manifestation they are far from exhausting its content, for life is not only the exercise of organic functions but is the sum of the ways by which man realizes his destiny of *nephesh chayyah* and of *imago Dei*. God has created Man as an independent being, as his partner, but man only attains that independence by ever-renewed contact with the one who is the source of his life and the source of all life. To define what that life is the Old Testament has recourse to a number of comparisons and

---

[1] "L'économie est le service du prochain", writes W. Eichrodt, *Die soziale Botschaft des A.T.*, 1946, p. 51.

pictures, each of which suggests life in its characteristic aspect, namely motion; it is by immobility in the first instance that death differs from life, the dead no longer do anything and Sheol as a land of silence is in contrast to the land of the living. Life is compared to a tree, a spring, a roadway; and these comparisons conceal ancient myths which, apart from the tree of life in Genesis, have left no trace. Only God possesses this life in its fulness, and he concentrates it in certain objects or places so that man can possess the portion to which he has a right. In the East, water is the source and condition of life; it is water which in the Yahwist creation narrative makes life possible on earth (Gen. 2.5) and lack of rain and dew was always regarded as a grave message threatening vitality; but as water in its maritime aspect was also thought to be an element of chaos, it could only partially express the power of life. It is otherwise with light,[1] which is always connected with life; light in its proper sense is synonymous with health (Is. 58.8), salvation Ps. 27.1; Mic. 7.8; Is. 60.1, 3), happiness (Amos 5.18; Is. 9.1; Ps. 112.4; 97.11); to make someone's face shine is to renew his vital power (Ps. 13.4; 19.9; Prov. 29.13) and the absence of light distinguishes Sheol from the earth. The earth itself is charged with life, it makes the plants spring up without which man could not maintain his life, but in place of the mythical idea of an animated and generative earth there is substituted, through the general process of historization, that of an earth which is the source of life because of a special manifestation of God in time and space. At a given time in history salvation is bound up with the possession of a certain land, for the land is indispensable for the maintenance of the covenant and the community. Even when the community replaces the land as the source of life, even in the eschatological promises, salvation will be associated with dwelling in safety in the land. In this land Yahweh chooses certain places where he reveals himself with greater reality and where man can meet with him: the sanctuaries and particularly the Jerusalem temple were the places where life could be found,[2] and the Psalms bear many echoes of a piety for which remoteness from the holy place meant separation from the source of life.

---

[1] On this subject, cf. the work of Sverre Aalen, *Die Begriffe "Licht" und "Finsternis" im A.T.*; particularly pp. 63ff. In some passages light is synonymous with salvation: Ps. 36.10; Is. 9.1; 50.10; Mic. 7.9.

[2] The more so as the Jerusalem temple probably had a cosmic significance.

Then wherein does this life consist? A life such as the Israelite ideal conceived it could only be a long one; for man to realize his destiny he must have time; for the king, who is in some measure responsible for the life of his subjects, the wish was expressed that he might live for ever, that is to say for a very long time (1 Kings 1.31; Ps. 21.5; 61.7ff.); the prayer the righteous man addresses to Yahweh is for the gift of long life or for the maintenance of his life (Ps. 34.13; 91.16; Prov. 4.10; 9.11; 10.27), and the greatest misfortune that can happen to him is to be removed in the midst of his days (Ps. 55.24; 89.46; Prov. 10.27; Is. 38.10).

It is the content of time which gives it its value, but since according to the faith dominant in Israel long life was already a reward it could not be anything other than an uninterrupted train of happiness. The idea of happiness attaching to the word life is explained by the terms *berakah* and *shalom*; the man who possesses life is a blessed man; just as the knees (*birkayim*) maintain the balance of the body, the *berakah*[1] maintains the equilibrium of life. At an early period when religion was still infected with magic, when it could be thought that God needed the blessing of men, particularly of influential people (Gen. 9.26) the word to bless used of men was very soon reduced to that of praise and give thanks. The blessing which has weight is the one bestowed by God. With Pedersen we distinguish three fundamental aspects:[2] (*a*) it consists in numerous offspring; "be fruitful and multiply" says Elohim to the first men after having blessed them (Gen. 1.28; 9.1); this is also the basic element of the blessing given to Abraham (Gen. 12.1; 13.16) and David receives the promise that his dynasty will be eternal (2 Sam. 7.29). (*b*) Riches are the second sign of blessing: the blessed man has many possessions (Gen. 24.35). Job is an example of a man blessed by a large posterity and abundant wealth, and one of the closing chapters of Deuteronomy similarly expresses the constant connection between blessing and prosperity (Dt. 28.1-13). (*c*) Blessing finally consists in being victorious over one's enemies, as appears from many texts belonging to the heroic age of the early tribes (Gen. 27.29; 49.8-12, 22-26; Dt. 28.7).

In conclusion we may say that the blessing is the power by which life is maintained and augmented. The result of the blessing is the

---

[1] We believe that the root *brk* embraces the ideas of firmness and extension, the first in the words from *barak*, to kneel, the second in *berekah*, an expanse of water.
[2] *Israel*, I-II, pp. 205ff.

condition defined by the word *shalom*,[1] which suggests the idea of abundance, prosperity and peace; this state will only be fully attained in the last times, but for the righteous it can be a present reality, so true is it that there is nothing hoped for which cannot be translated immediately into actual life.

Refinement of the religious sensitivity and the lessons of experience created doubts in serious minds about the identification of life with length of days and earthly success, and led to a view of life as no more the possession of God's gifts but of God himself; so we find in the Old Testament an ideal of life which neither premature death, trials nor poverty are capable of shaking, but which rather even gains in intensity by contact with suffering. Psalmists such as the authors of Psalms 16 and 73, put to the test of sickness and poverty, found in communion with God a life to which death itself could set no limits. According to a thinker whose faith did not attain the profundity of the Psalmists', the old equating of life with prosperity is likewise destroyed; life for him is merely a synonym for mortality; the living who are still alive know they will die (Eccl. 4.2; 9.5), and this attitude has probably been more common than that of the Psalmist who accepts the loss of his life in order to find it again on a higher level in God: "Thy *chesed* is better than life" (Ps. 63.4).

Life, having its source in God, can only be a gift, yet this gift, just like God himself, is the object of a choice on man's part; it is only by choosing life (Dt. 30.19) that man truly becomes what he is.

BIBLIOGRAPHY

BACHMANN, "Das Ebenbild Gottes", *Das Erbe Martin Luthers, Festschrift L. Ihmels*, Leipzig 1928.

BARTH, KARL, *Kirchliche Dogmatik* III, 2, §46.

BECKER, J. H., *Het begrip nefesj in het oude Testament*, 1942.

BRIGGS, C. A., "The use of nephesh in the O.T.", *JBL*, 1897, p. 17.

CASPARI, W., "Imago Divina Gen. I", *Festschrift Reinbold Seeberg*, t.I, 1929, p. 190.

---

[1] *Shalom* is the outcome of righteousness (Is. 32.17) or wisdom (Prov. 3.2, 17) which are only fully realized through Yahweh or his most eminent representative, the messianic king (cf. Is. 9.5).

CRESPY, G., "Le problème d'une anthropologie théologique", *EThR*, Montpellier, 1950, pp. 1ff.

DELITZSCH, F., *System der biblischen Psychologie*, Leipzig 1855.

DHORME, P., *L'emploi métaphorique des noms de parties du corps en hébreu et en accadien*, Paris 1923.

DÜRR, L., "Nephesh = Gurgel, Kehle", *ZAW*, 1925, p. 262.

EICHRODT, W., *Das Menschenverständnis des Alten Testaments*, 1947. Études carmélitaines, *Le coeur* (recueil collectif).

GALLING, K., *Das Bild vom Menschen in biblischer Sicht*, Mainz 1947.

GELIN, A., "L'homme biblique", *Lumen Vitae*, 1955, no. 1, p. 45.

HEHN, J., "Zum Terminus Bild Gottes", *Festschrift Ed. Sachau* 1915, p. 46.

HEMPEL, JOH., *Das Ethos des Alten Testaments*, Berlin 1938.
Gott und Mensch im A.T., Stuttgart 1926.

JOHNSON, A. R., *The One and the Many in the Israelite Conception of God*, Cardiff 1942.
The Vitality of the Individual in the Thought of Ancient Israel, Cardiff 1949.

KOEBERLE, J., *Natur und Geist nach der Auffassung des Alten Testaments*, 1901.

KOEHLER, L., *Der hebräische Mensch*, Tübingen 1953.

KORNFELD, H., "Herz und Gehirn in altbiblischer Auffassung", *Jahrbücher für jüdische Geschichte u. Literatur*, 1909, p. 81.

LICHTENSTEIN, MAX, *Das Wort nephesh in der Bibel, Schriften der Lehranstalt für Wissenschaft des Judentums*, Bd. IV, 5-6, Berlin 1920.

MEYENFELDT, VON, *Het hart (leb, lebab) in het oude Testament*, Leiden 1950.

PIDOUX, G., *L'homme dans l'A.T.*, Neuchâtel-Paris 1953.

ROBINSON, H. WHEELER, "Hebrew Psychology", *The People and the Book*, ed. A. S. Peake, Oxford 1925.

RUST, E. C., *Nature and Man in Biblical Thought*, London 1953.

RYDER SMITH, C., *The Bible Doctrine of Man*, London 1951.

SCHMIDT, K. L., "Imago Dei" (*Eranosjahrbuch* 1948).

SCHWAB, J., *Der Begriff der nefesch in den heiligen Schriften des A.T.*, Munich 1913.

VOLZ, P., "Die Würde des Menschen im A.T.", *Glaube und Ethos (Festschrift G. Wehrung)*, pp. 1-8, 1940.

VRIEZEN, TH. C., "La création de l'homme d'après l'image de Dieu", *Oudtest. Studiën II*, p. 87, 1943.

WRIGHT, G. E., *The Biblical Doctrine of Man in Society, Ecumenical Biblical Studies* no. 2, S.C.M. Press, 1954.

ZIMMERLI, W., *Das Menschenbild des A.T.*, *Theol. Existenz heute*, N.F. 14, Munich 1949.

I. THE DESTINY OF MAN: LIFE

AALEN, SVERRE, *Die Begriffe Licht und Finsternis im A.T., im Spätjuden-tum und im Rabbinismus*, Oslo 1951.

BAUDISSIN, W., "Alttestamentliches 'chayim' Leben in der Bedeutung von Glück", *Festschrift Ed. Sachau*, 1915, p. 143.

DÜRR, L., "Die Wertung des Lebens im A.T. und im antiken Orient", *Vorl d. Akad. Braunsberg* 1926-27.

GÜNZIG, J., *Das jüdische Schrifttum über den Wert des Lebens*, Hanover 1924.

HEMPEL, J., *Das Ethos des A.T.*, Berlin 1938.

KLEINERT, P., "Zur Idee des Lebens im A.T.", *ThStKr*, 1895, p. 693.

RATSCHOW, C. H., *Werden und Wirken. Eine Untersuchung des Wortes hayah als Beitrag zur Wirklichkeitserfassung des A.T.*, BZAW 70, Berlin 1941.

IV. GOD THE LORD OF HISTORY

A. FAITH AND HISTORY

(a) Generalities

"HISTORY might be called the sacrament of the religion of Israel; through the history of Israel, she saw the face of God and endured as seeing him who is invisible. But the details of that history with which we shall be concerned—the words and deeds, the thoughts and emotions, and above all the persistent purposes of the Israelites—these were the bread and wine of the sacrament, which the touch of God transformed into both the symbol and the instrument of His grace for all time." This definition of Wheeler Robinson's,[1] while bringing out the importance of history as a revelation of God, underlines at the same time what might be called the supra-historical aspect of the history of Israel; for from early times and already in the Old Testament history was interpreted in a typological manner,[2] and in the Rabbinic and ecclesiastical tradition, thanks to allegory understood either in a mystical or ethical sense, believers read their own history in the pages of the Old Testament. It is none the less true that the nature of history is its inability to repeat itself. If, therefore, God reveals himself in history, he does so through very precise events in time,

---

[1] *The History of Israel*, 1938, p. 12.

[2] Typology is already to be found in the Old Testament. The Exodus, in the entirety of Israelite tradition, is handled as the symbol of salvation and more particularly certain episodes within the Exodus: the gift of manna in the account given by the priestly writer (Ex. 16.6-13a, 16b-26) is not only a unique event, but a reality which is ever being freshly reproduced in the life of God's people; the Flood, the Temple, the possession of the land are interpreted as symbols of catastrophe, salvation and rest. The process of typologization can also be noticed in the way in which certain figures represent in themselves the totality of the functions of government: Samuel, Moses and, to some extent, the Servant of Yahweh are the most striking examples of this. But *always* the type is an historical reality; the historicity of a figure or of an event is ever the condition of their typological application; this idea is already expressed by Joh. Gerhard (1762), " Typus consistit in factorum collatione. Allegoria occupatur non tam in factis, quam in ipsis concionibus, e quibus doctrinam utilem et reconditam depromit ", quoted from Goppelt, *Typos*, p. 8.

the historicity of which is in no way weakened by the typological meaning acquired by those events.

History, however, is not made of events alone. To speak of history and revelation through history, two realities must be brought together: raw facts and their interpretation. The latter is even more important than the facts, for it is one's idea of an event which assures for it its quality as an historical fact, that is as a decisive fact in the course of events. In general this interpretation reveals the true significance of a fact, but it also happens, even in the Old Testament, that it gives a presentation of facts that is quite the opposite of strict historical truth.[1] The Old Testament is a clear example of the priority of the interpretation of history over its presentation, for the narration of history implies for the Israelite an interpretation of it, because he views God's action through faith and not by the methods of the archivist or the archaeologist. If by history is meant knowledge of the past, it is fair to recognize with L. Koehler that the Hebrew mind has little awareness of the notion of history,[2] for it is interested in history only to the extent in which it is *hic et nunc* a present and dynamic reality. There is a double relationship between history and faith: on the one hand history provides faith with its object. The most ancient confession of faith recorded in the book of Deuteronomy (26.5ff.) is a purely historical *credo* to which any metaphysical affirmation about God is foreign. On the other hand faith gives to history its orientation through the prophets, who bring on Yahweh's behalf the word which provokes events, and through those who in various degrees deserve to be called historians and who by making a selection from the facts envisaged history in the light of God's plan of salvation taken as a whole and who considered that only what was used in that plan's fulfilment was worth retaining.

(b) The events

The great stages in the history of the people of Israel

Real history is born only when a religious or philosophical principle establishes some relationship between the course of events.

[1] The clearest example of this is given to us by the author of the book of Chronicles whose testimony, for the interpretation of history, is for this reason all the more interesting to study.

[2] *Der hebräische Mensch*, 1953, pp. 126 and 129: "Geschichte als zeitlichen Abstand gibt es nicht."

Yet certain circumstances of a geographical or ethnic nature already ensure a certain continuity among the facts and maintain certain common features in their unfolding. A country's history is to a large extent a function of its geographical position. Now Palestine's situation is characterized on the one hand by being at the cross-roads of three great cultures, Asiatic, Egyptian and Semitic, each of which has left its mark on Palestine, and on the other hand by its nearness to the desert. Throughout the whole of Israel's history we can find the antagonism between civilization and the desert, the first representing the elements of dissolution, the second the reservoir of young and vital forces. The second constant is of a sociological nature : it concerns what has been called "corporate personality" and the primacy of the group. To neglect the principal rôle of the group is to expose oneself to the danger of understanding nothing concerning the rites, the ethics, or the institutions of the Israelites.

The origins of Israel's history date back to the vast movement of peoples which brought the Aramaeans from the Syrian desert, the cradle of origin, down to the shores of the Persian Gulf and the Mediterranean. Certain of these Aramaean tribes, to which are linked the names of Abraham, Isaac, Jacob and Joseph, move into Palestine, whence certain clans go down into Egypt with the object of pursuing their penetration by means of the usual process of raids widely practised by the Habiru, of which the Hebrews are probably a branch. This very involved history is reduced by the Old Testament to the simple proportions of a family of 70 men who became a great nation (Gen. 46.27; Ex. 1.7). All the Hebrew tribes were not in Egypt, but only those of the Rachel branch and some isolated elements of the Leah tribes, among whom was Levi, from whom Moses descended. In Egypt the tribes suffered a period of oppression which was ended by the intervention of Moses. Concerning the Exodus itself we know little, and we cannot even date with certainty this event which the body of Israelite tradition holds to be fundamental.[1] After escaping from the Egyptians by a coincidence of circumstances in which faith saw a miracle, the tribes set off for a mountain of which we know for sure neither the correct name (Sinai or Horeb) nor the exact situation (Sinai peninsula, Arabia or Qadesh). Having arrived at this moun-

---

[1] On the present state of the problem, cf. the study by E. Drioton, "La date de l'exode" in *RHPR*, 1955, p. 36.

tain they concluded a covenant with Yahweh, who had revealed himself to Moses, receiving from him a revelation and laws and undertaking to observe the terms of this covenant. After a period of half-nomadic, half-settled life at the Qadesh oasis, the tribes set off for the conquest of Canaan, joining forces with other elements that had not been in Egypt; this conquest was carried out simultaneously by war and by peaceful penetration through pacts with the native population. Soon the Israelites, thanks to the permanent contribution of the desert, proved stronger than the Canaanites (cf. the song of Deborah, Jg. 5). But later a greater danger was to jeopardize the still very precarious foothold of the Israelites in the promised land. To the south-east the Ammonites launched powerful assaults and to the west the Philistines, a branch of the sea-peoples, by cutting the land into two had proved before the letter the Roman adage: *divide et impera.* The Philistine danger obliged the Israelites to re-examine and to consolidate their own organization.

The bond, in the beginning a purely religious one, which held the tribes together in a sacred association of the same kind as the Greek amphictyonies, became with the adoption of a monarchy a primarily political and social bond, which did not prevent the first experiment of kingship under Saul from ending in setback. With David we see the tribe of Judah, which hitherto had lived rather at the edge of the Israelite confederacy, rise to the zenith of history. Thanks to his personal ascendancy and also to the support of the prophets, David succeeded in uniting the tribes of north and south about a single new capital, Jerusalem, which he made into a religious centre by bringing the Ark thither. After establishing peace within the country, David neutralized the neighbouring powers. With Solomon, civilization, with its accompanying forces of corruption, took precedence of the forces of the desert, to such an extent that at the end of his reign, rich as it was in grandiose achievements, all was again thrown into the melting pot. Henceforth the northern kingdom, where the specifically Israelite traditions had all along been observed, became the centre of gravity of the historical development. A particularly brilliant period was marked by the reign of Omri, about whom the Old Testament says very little at all and, in that, very little good, but whose creative rôle is attested by the excavations of Samaria and by Assyrian inscriptions. The policy of alliance with neighbouring peoples carried out by the Omri dynasty was not unanimously approved; the reaction came from Transjordania, from that area where the nomadic spirit was still deeply rooted. Elijah's success was certainly less great than the Bible states, for the prophet was forced to flee and his zeal did not prevent the presence some years later of prophets of Baal in the court of Samaria. The policy of the Omri dynasty was so skilful that it succeeded in maintaining the relative independence of the kingdom of Israel after the crushing, at the battle of Qarqar (853), of the anti-Assyrian coalition in which Ahab seems to have played a predominating part. For a century Israel, and as a result Judah also, which in its mountains was less directly aware of the surge of world politics, enjoyed a period of relative calm when Amos came and announced that the threats proclaimed by Elijah were to be carried out. With increased rhythm, disasters followed one another until the fall of the kingdom of Samaria (722). This event was for Judah the opportunity to regain awareness of its mission; the live forces, urged on by the prophets and the Yahwist elements that had sought refuge from the northern kingdom, were all to create a favourable atmosphere of resistance to Assyrian influence, an atmosphere considerably strengthened by the events of 701, which were greeted as a manifestation of divine protection. The action of the prophets, to whom kings like Hezekiah and Josiah gave sympathetic hearing, ended in the Deuteronomic reform, which was not without political repercussions.

It was thus that Josiah, moved by religious motives, attempted to regain dominion over all Palestine and to restore to the empire the frontiers of David's time, and in so doing opposed Pharaoh Necho, who was going to the help of the rest of the Assyrian Empire. The relative independence of Judah came to a final end in 605, the date of the battle of Carchemish, which marks the advent in the whole Near East of Babylonian power and which led for Judah to the fatal dates of 597 and 587. The history of that period is dominated by the figure of the prophet Jeremiah and the attitude, by turns favourable and hostile, which the authorities adopted towards him is a proof of the important rôle attributed to him in the course of events. We have available very little information about the Israelitish groups which during the exile came into existence in Egypt and in Palestine itself; the influential elements of the nation were in Babylon and it was there that, under the direction of men like Ezekiel, there were outlined the reflections on the disaster they had suffered and the plans of restoration to which the edict of Cyrus allowed a concrete form to be given. The successive efforts of Nehemiah and Ezra ended in the reconstruction of Judaism into a theocracy about the two poles of the Law and the Temple, but within this theocracy we see developing two quite different currents: a strongly nationalist current which showed hostility to all that was not Jewish and a wider current which aimed at making Judaism accessible to the nations and whose most typical echoes are shown in the books of Ruth and Jonah. Henceforth Palestine was not the only centre of Judaism; important diasporas grew up in which great capacity of assimilation was generally shown and in which there grew up also new forms, in particular synagogue worship. But as soon as its very existence was questioned, Judaism always showed itself uncompromising: thus, when Antiochus Epiphanes made his attempt at Hellenization, a few members of the aristocracy were the only ones to declare their agreement, whilst the people rose with fierce energy. It was at this precise moment that the author of the book of Daniel, reflecting on the vicissitudes of history, disentangled its essential lessons and grasped its fundamental unity.

(c) The historical foundation of Israel's faith

The idea that God is the initiator of events is not specifically biblical. "From the time of primitive totemism," writes R. Niebuhr,[1] "until the time of the great imperial religions, the notion prevails that there exists a power superior to all human will which acts on the destiny of the tribe, the nation or the empire." But the special characteristic of biblical revelation is that God binds himself to historical events to make them the vehicle of the manifestation of his purpose. The holiness and uniqueness of Israel's God confer on him a power superior to that of any other god. While the powers of the gods of the nations cease at the frontiers of their territory, Yahweh directs universal history, and a declaration like that of Amos that Yahweh directs not only the destinies of Israel, but also that of the Philistines and of the Ethiopians, provides a good illustration of the specific power of Israel's God, all of whose potentialities were developed by the prophets. Yahweh is not only a powerful God but a wise sovereign who leaves no place

[1] *Foi et histoire*, p. 109.

either for dualism or for chance: all is initiated and willed by him (Amos 3.6; Is. 47.7; Lam. 3.37), which does not mean that history is only the unfolding of a plan fixed in advance, for Yahweh holds the destinies of men in his hands, not in the way of a marionette operator, but by leaving them with the freedom of decision; and so history always appears to be a drama in which the two protagonists, God and men, call one another, flee from one another and finally become reconciled.

In the directing of universal history, Yahweh did not choose the way of the providence that assures equilibrium and stability, from the starting-point of the universal laws of creation. Yahweh's action goes from the particular to the general; universal history is made by means of the election of a little people whose destiny it is to become the light and leaven of the nations, and even within the history of Israel God's presence is not always clearly revealed. Yahweh is certainly present in that history and that is why it may rightly be called holy, but the events of the history are far from being confused with God's presence itself; events tell God's glory but, like the heavens and the stars, they are not confused with him. Israel's religion had too lively a conception of God's personality to reduce it to events. God's presence in history is that of the hidden God whose intentions always remain full of mystery in men's eyes (Is. 45.15; 55.8), but the hidden God is also the one who comes at certain moments in time to demonstrate through certain events the totality of his being and of his action. This coming of God into history—we prefer the term coming, as being more dynamic than presence—is on God's side an action and at the same time an interpretation. The origins of Israel's history as God's people may be traced back to the Exodus, but the event of the deliverance of the tribes from Egyptian servitude was preceded by the revelation of Yahweh to Moses, who receives the assurance of God's coming and the announcement of the actions which will make that coming manifest. Before acting, Yahweh tells Moses what he is about to do and when the events take place they will only be the confirmation of that word: and so the people believe, not merely because of the events, but also and especially because of the word which has set those events in motion and which has been entrusted to Moses (Ex. 4.31; 14.31). This is the truth expressed by Amos when he says that " the Lord Yahweh does nothing without revealing his secret plan to his servants the prophets " (Amos 3.7).

History's moments of revelation are in fact always marked by the appearance of one or more prophets; not that they must be considered as the politicians of the time responsible for directing events, but when God wishes to reveal himself through an act of history, he first makes sure of the choice of a prophet to whom he entrusts his word before that word is enacted in events. The Exodus would not have been the moment of revelation without the prophet Moses. At a time when the events of world history were seriously compromising the universal sovereignty of Yahweh Isaiah was charged by Yahweh to proclaim and to interpret his plan. Jeremiah and Ezekiel are contemporary with the fall of the kingdom of Judah and at the time of the great turning-point marked by the advent of Cyrus, Second Isaiah is there to show its true meaning. Sometimes the prophet is ahead of the events, thus Amos announces Israel's ruin at a time when nothing immediate gave reason to expect it; at other times he is contemporary with the event or appears after it, but always his message is nothing other than an interpretation of those events. The presence of these men of God was of itself a sign that something was being unfolded, that there was a crisis in history that was about to burst in catastrophic form but which might also be the starting point of a new awakening. Consequently it was enough to see the prophets proclaim the word and carry out their symbolic actions to grasp the divine action in history, for they were themselves a word of God in action.

Out of the events which manifest God's coming into history faith has selected and, as a faithful interpreter of Yahweh's plan, has retained two main ones, the first at the beginning, the second at the end of history—the Exodus and the Day of Yahweh: [1] between these two extremes there are, of course, many interventions of Yahweh but they only serve to confirm and make explicit the initial revelation of the Exodus or to announce the future kingship of Yahweh. Since the object of history is to make Yahweh known to the people of Israel and to the nations (cf. the formula: " You shall know that I am Yahweh ", Ez. 6.7, 10, 12; 7.27; 11.10,

---

[1] We give a treatment of eschatology in another chapter but we wish to stress here and now that there is no contradiction between eschatology and history; in using the term eschatology (doctrine of last things) in connection with the Old Testament, it is important to bear in mind that for Israel it is less a matter of the end than of the coming of Yahweh which marks the end of a period but which, because he is essentially the living God, inaugurates a new beginning; the former things must pass away solely to give place to the kingship of the God who comes.

etc.), there could be no better method for God to give his teaching than time and again to turn people's eyes afresh to the time when he first showed himself to Israel and to the eyes of the peoples. It was at the time of the Exodus that Israel had felt the experience of a God sovereign in his grace and judgments who was capable of calling forth a new creation out of the most desperate situations. And so we must not be surprised to find the fact of the Exodus at the head of a passage which by common consent is recognized as one of the most ancient "creeds" of Israel's faith,[1] the confession that the Israelite had to recite at the offering of the first-fruits (Dt. 26.5ff.). At the Passover feast, the departure from Egypt was enacted through the ritual, so clearly that it may be said that at least once a year the Exodus ceased to be a fact of the past and became a living reality, and that never, even after five centuries, did the Israelites consider themselves different from their ancestors who, under Moses' guidance, had experienced the deliverance (cf. Amos 3.2).[2] References to the Exodus are too common for us to be able to consider them all, for they are not found only where the event is explicitly mentioned, but the theme underlies the many images of the God who leads, who delivers, who feeds, who quenches thirst and gives light. The *credo* of Deuteronomy 26 mentions the entry into Canaan as a second article; the deliverance of the Exodus was only made with a view to the possession of the country; although there are variants in the texts concerning the rôle of the promised land, all agree in the assertion that it is a gift of God to his people that they may have a place of security and rest (Ex. 3.8; Dt. 12.10-12), so that Yahweh himself may have a dwelling-place (Deut. 11.10-12) and that the wicked nations who occupy the land may be dispossessed of it (Deut. 9.5). To the

[1] Two other "creeds" are found in Deut. 6.20-24 and Jos. 24.2-13 with the same fundamental assertions. We may also conveniently add certain Psalms which present the great facts of history in the double form of praise and teaching: Ps. 77.12ff.; 78; 105; 136. It seems more and more probable that the recital and confession of history in worship constituted the nucleus from which the historical books were formed.

[2] Paul's speech in the synagogue at Pisidian Antioch (Acts 13) takes up the same themes as the Old Testament credos; the history of salvation stops with the coming of David; the whole of history between David and Jesus Christ is passed over in silence as though it were only the deepening or repetition of previous events. The movement of the history of salvation would be more adequately represented by a spiral which has depth while following certain fixed points than by a straight line (cf. O. Strasser, "Les périodes et les époques de l'Histoire de l'Eglise" in *RHPR*, 1950, pp. 290ff.).

two historical themes of the Exodus and the conquest, there were joined two memories which were considered as subordinate and whose links were of a sacred rather than an historical nature: the Sinai theme, originally independent of that of the Exodus and absent from the *credo* of Deuteronomy 26, was introduced to extend the latter by the motif of the theophany and the law, these being particularly important to remind the people of God's greatness and the necessity of conforming to his requirements. The temple theme was fused with that of the conquest, the more easily since the temple was considered as the centre of the country; thus the temple becomes very clearly the object of the Exodus and, by giving Jerusalem to the Israelites, David only continues the rôle of Moses, who promised a country to the people. It is quite probable that, in the popular belief which is always prone to become attached to static realities, the temple and Sinai themes may have been more preponderant than that of the Exodus, but all theological reflections on history always returned to this initial theme.

The important place held by the theme of the past among the prophets is at first surprising in men who had from God direct and immediate revelations and visions. It is quite clear, however, that the prophets never considered their own revelations as superior to those given in the early days of the people and that they always thought in terms of the election and the covenant. That Yahweh chooses and saves the people is a reality that the prophets never doubted, but for the election and the covenant to remain valid, they had to be manifested through the judgment that was brought upon the people by their all too frequent unfaithfulness. That is why history becomes for them a sequence of deliverances issued from a series of judgments, while all those judgments only anticipate the great final judgment. It was important to the prophets to show that disasters, deserved or not, did not invalidate the ancient *credo*, and that God's plan was simultaneously accomplished by destruction and construction, as Isaiah expresses in a famous parable (Is. 28.23-29). The Exodus theme with its accent on deliverance had a new flowering when the events of the exile were considered as the final point of Yahweh's judgments. The two great prophets of the exile, Ezekiel and Second Isaiah, again take up the theme of the Exodus and the possession of Canaan; certainly, both stress the point that the temporary loss of national independence is the result of multiple disloyalties to the covenant, but the punishment is only transitory, while the promise will have a still finer flowering than in the time of Moses. By emphasizing the wilderness theme and by introducing into it the idea of punishment, they reconcile judgment with the promise: Yahweh will once more lead Israel into the wilderness of the peoples and will perform a judgment there (Ez. 20.35), for, through the dangers that it presented, the wilderness was a place of temptation rather than an idyllic setting. Ezekiel sees his own rôle in the light of that of Moses: as a sentinel with the duty of warning the people, he will proclaim the coming of a new shepherd, a new David, who will take up on a vaster scale the work of Joshua. The people will be restored: just as in former times they had crossed the Red Sea and the Jordan, which in each case had been a passage through death—think of the lasting association of the sea with chaos—they will again pass from death to life (Ez. 36-37) and the Temple rebuilt in the centre of the country will be the guarantee of the dependability of this promise. So Ezekiel proclaims nothing which is not to be found already in the ancient *credo,* so convinced is he that the faithlessness of the people does not cancel the faithfulness of God. Second Isaiah insists on the fact that the events of history have exceeded in severity that of a strict punishment. The trials of the exile have been for God himself a suffering in the face of which he could only remain silent (Is. 42.14; 47.6) and a profanation of his name (Is. 52.4-5). So it is high time that the silence should be broken and that Yahweh's arm should once more be made manifest as at the time of the Exodus. The deliverance of the people will be a new Exodus followed by a new covenant (Is. 54), and an invitation to come and drink at the well of living water (Is. 55.1ff.) is a synthesis of the fountain springing forth in the desert at Moses' call and the river coming from the new temple (Ez. 47); and the servant of Yahweh will be a recapitulation of all the deliverers, kings and prophets who have assured the permanence of election and of whom Moses was the first.

History has never ceased to inspire and to give direction to faith, for all the events of that history went to confirm the great facts of God by showing that history was not only a revelation by which God showed itself to men, but a redemption by which he saved them.

(d) The theological aspect of the presentation of history

Faith in a single God who directs events according to the laws of justice for the purpose of establishing his kingdom was the basis of all presentations of Israel's history and produced methods and results whose originality and value historians of antiquity are pleased to stress. The religious foundation of historiography allowed a quite marked independence with regard to the compilatory method from annals and allowed the development of a literature where the accumulation of facts yields pride of place to an interpretation of the essential events. In the life of a people, all periods are not equally favourable to historical composition: in a general way history is written under the dominion of striking events which by their creative nature constitute a turning point and which are the opportunity for reflection and exhortation. These notable events may be of two kinds: a people which has reached the peak of its power feels the need of looking back over the way it has come to reach it;[1] on the other hand national disasters are also appropriate times, for the trial opens people's eyes to the causes which have occasioned it and the reflection which it suggests may be the cause of a salutary reawakening. Historical works in Israel show the mark of this double origin. The governing idea of the biography of David (2 Sam. 9.20 and 1 Kings 1-2), which by common consent is regarded by historians as a model of the narrative type, is expressed not by commentaries linked to the presentation of the facts but by the presentation of the facts themselves arranged with the object of showing up David's personality, whose kingship endures in spite of his own infidelities, which are in no way passed over in silence, and in spite of the obstacles of his enemies, for the disappearance of the three legitimate claimants to the throne, Amnon, Absalom and Adonijah, does not prevent the monarchy from being firmly settled in the hands of Solomon (1 Kings 2.46). The stress given to the rôle of individuals, which is one of the originalities of Israelite historical writing, also constitutes one of its limitations. While seeking the cause of events in the fluctuations

---

[1] On the interpretation of history in the Old Testament, cf. the more detailed studies of North, *The Old Testament Interpretation of History*, London 1945; G. von Rad, " Theologische Geschichtsschreibung am A.T.", *ThZ*, 1948, p. 161; Ed. Jacob, *La tradition historique en Israël*, Montpellier 1946, and " Histoire et historiens dans l'A.T." in *RHPR*, 1955, p. 26.

of character of dominant individuals, the writers forget that other things of a more general nature, reasons of a political or social kind, are also determining factors in history. There is thus good ground for supposing that the opposition of the northern tribes to Judaean supremacy was as important in Absalom's revolt as the desire to avenge the outrage to his sister. The Yahwist, embracing a much vaster period than the writer of David's biography, seeks to write a work of synthesis. Having at his disposal much written or orally transmitted material, he makes a selection and retains only what serves his fundamental theme, which is to show that history is the fulfilling of a promise or, which amounts to the same thing, the putting of a word into practice. The promise is that of a land to possess, a promise made formerly to Abraham and renewed to Moses. It is at the moment when this promise seemed to have been fully carried out, probably in the reign of Solomon, that the Yahwist undertakes the composition of his work; he reviews the road travelled, in order to find in the march of events towards the goal of the promise, reasons for thankfulness and faith. Around the fundamental nucleus based on the Exodus from Egypt and the march through the wilderness, whose memory was made present in the cultic ritual, the Yahwist groups other elements, first the patriarchal traditions and then the traditions of the origins. It is in connection with the latter that the theological thought of the Yahwist has the opportunity to assert itself with more freedom by his insistence on the theme of the promise to which man should respond by faith. All the accounts illustrate this fundamental theme. The religious bias of the Yahwist appears again in the way he binds together cycles of tradition that were originally independent. The wretched condition of the Israelites in Egypt after the glorious period of Joseph is explained by the coming to the throne of a "Pharaoh who knew not Joseph" (Ex. 1.8) and he has an equally happy touch in linking the patriarchal traditions to the story of the origins by the episode of the tower of Babel, the destruction of which allows Yahweh to create a people for himself.

Some centuries later, at the time of the exile, the work known under the name Deuteronomic, while paying a greater respect to the documents that had been handed down, presents history according to certain outlines which sometimes grasp the essential point, but which at other times pass reality by. Since the kings are judged in the light of their attitude to the temple at Jerusalem, our writer sometimes omits important events in their reigns; on the other hand, he has fully grasped the unity of the history represented by an uninterrupted line of prophets (Dt. 18.15ff.), through whom the word of God becomes a vital power. All that happens is the result of a divine word and no word of God falls to the ground (cf. 1 Kings 11.29-12.15 and 2 Kings 1.6-17). Although he undertook his work under the blow of most tragic circumstances for the people, it would be wrong to consider his presentation of history as catastrophic in contrast with the optimistic view of the Yahwist, for at the heart of and above the operation of the law of strict retribution there subsists a promise which von Rad said served as a κατέχων : [1] it is the perennial continuity of the promise made to David concerning the eternity of his dynasty; as long as the lamp of David lasts (1 Kings 11.32, 36) nothing is irretrievably lost. The exile itself does not erase this promise; and so the Deuteronomist's work comes to its end with an apparently quite trivial event, the rehabilitation of King Jehoiachin in the depths of the captivity (2 Kings 25.37-39); but, as often happens, endings are rich in meaning for faith. It is not too rash to suppose that this gesture aroused among the exiles a resurgence of hope of national restoration. It is the same theme of the perennial continuity of the promise to David which constitutes, but in a much more unilateral way, the main thread of the Chronicler's work. Although this writer made a wide and conscientious use of sources, the theologian in him takes precedence of the historian and he has no hesitation at times in presenting a distorted version of events. This point of view is explained, however, when account is taken of the Davidic viewpoint destined, in the writer's thinking, to galvanize the people's hope and not to let them meekly accept national humiliation. Two centuries later the historical synthesis will find expression, not lacking in greatness, in apocalyptic literature.[2] The unity and finality of history are at the basis of the visions in chapters 2 and 7 of the book of Daniel; but by regarding history as purely determined, following the manner of the Priestly writer, apocalyptic deprives it of its substance so that no more is seen in history than what is ordered to disappear at the coming of the king-

---

[1] *Deuteronomiumstudien*, p. 63.

[2] The words determinism, dualism, pessimism provide a quite good definition of the conception of history in the apocalypses. The unfolding of history is of little importance; thus in the vision of the statue, the four empires which come one after another are all present at the end of the last empire (Dan. 2.35, 44).

dom of God. The great historical productions cease with the great wave of prophetic utterance; revelation found its best interpreters in the prophets.

(e) Historicization, an expression of the faith

In the Old Testament history is the most characteristic channel through which thought is expressed; the historical mode of thinking, moreover, spreads far beyond the category of truly historical works. Only two books of the Old Testament are completely apart from history—Job and Ecclesiastes. Although their writers strove to give them an historical background and to give their characters location in time, revelation through history is wanting in them; also, lacking this essential mainspring, the religion that is expressed in them leads either to an attitude closely verging on scepticism (Ecclesiastes) or to a submission to the mystery of the hidden God (Job). Everywhere else history is so fundamental that not only does it inspire everything, but by subjecting them to itself it even succeeds in transforming realities that are originally foreign to it. This process of historicization is most apparent in three fields:

(a) Like all the peoples of antiquity, Israel knew many myths which came from its own background or from neighbouring peoples with whom Israel had been in contact, but the majority of these myths no longer exist except in a fragmentary form or in allusions, for history has caused them to undergo a transformation which sometimes went as far as complete disappearance. It was thus that Israel knew some creation myths which, like Babylonian or Phoenician myths, spoke of an original struggle between two opposing deities; through certain poetic texts we can picture this myth as a struggle between Yahweh and two sea monsters, Rahab and Leviathan, the victorious outcome of which allowed him to organize heaven and earth (Ps. 74.12-17; 89.10-13; Is. 51.9-10; Job 26.10-12; 38.1-11; Ps. 104.26). But faith in the God of history made Rahab into an historical reality, Egypt; Leviathan became a beast that Yahweh made completely subject to his authority (Ps. 104.26); the Tiamat-of the Babylonian myth became the *tehom*, that is, the sea. In the well known text of Isaiah 51.9-10: "Awake, awake, put on strength, O arm of Yahweh; awake, as in the days of old, the generations of ancient times. Art thou not he that cut Rahab in pieces, that pierced the dragon? Art thou not he who dried up the sea, the waters of the great deep; that made the depths of the sea a way for the redeemed to pass over? "—the last words are clear proof that the prophet deliberately put at the service of history the traditions of the cosmogonic myths; God's action at the time of the Exodus from Egypt is more striking because it is nearer than his work of creation. It is worth noting that all these mythical references are found only in relatively late texts, which otherwise insist so strongly on the sovereignty of Yahweh that these allusions constitute no danger of Israel's falling back into mythology. The same thing can be said of the eschatological myths. Cosmic images, such as the shaking of the earth's foundations or invasion by the waters, clearly pass into the background and the great final cataclysm is presented as a battle. The day of Yahweh, says Isaiah, will be like " the day of Midian " when Gideon won a particularly resounding victory (Is. 9.3) and in Second Isaiah the great change comes about without disturbance, so far has eschatology been penetrated by history, of which it is no longer the opposite, but the conclusion.

All religions give great importance to the problem of the dwelling-place of the gods. In undoubted imitation of the Canaanites, the Old Testament is acquainted with the picture of the gods dwelling at the top of a high mountain which was situated in the extreme north and whose peak penetrated the sky, which allowed the celestial rôle of the deities to be reconciled with their earthly presence. The myth of the mountain of the gods in the north is also met in the Old Testament (Is. 14.13); but in Psalm 48.3, it is Jerusalem that is called the extremity of the north, a point which can only be explained by the transference to Jerusalem of the myth of the mountain of the gods. According to the cosmography of Gen. 2.10-14 paradise was also found in the north, but the north is already conceived as a geographical reality and the rivers which rise there may be situated in a known background. Sinai has also in a certain degree been substituted for the mythical mountain, but it is the temple which has become God's mountain *par excellence*, making the presence of God among his people a possibility open to all.

Genesis has preserved the fragments of a myth which told of relationships between celestial beings and the daughters of men which resulted in the birth on earth of beings originally divine (Gen. 6.1ff.), but in the adaptation of this theme by the biblical historian the fault of the angels became men's and it is men who undergo the punishment (Gen. 6.5ff.). The *Helal ben Shachar*, the shining star, son of the dawn, the title by which Isaiah ironically calls the king of Babylon (Is. 14), was certainly, as the Ugaritic texts confirm, a divine being reduced to the proportions of an historical figure, in the same way as the guardian cherub hurled from God's mountain because of his pride (Ez. 28), and the man who presents himself to Joshua as the chief of the armies of Yahweh is only a slightly humanized picture of the local god of Jericho (Josh. 5.13). To-day it is no longer possible to argue reasonably in support of the primitively mythical character of the Patriarchs and to speak of historicization in their case, but it must be realized, however, that the historical spirit has been at work on these admittedly rather shadowy characters in order to establish genealogical links between them. On the other hand, the possibility of historicization could well be envisaged for the characters of Samson and Esther, in whose names those of Shamash and Ishtar can be seen quite clearly. If this hypothesis were verified, we should have a further proof of the art with which the Israelites subordinated myth to history by creating from mythical elements perfectly credible historical tales. Lastly we must notice how far the constituent features of the myth about man (Urmensch) have been shifted on to historical figures: Noah (Gen. 5.29) and Abraham (Gen. 12.3) must convey the consolation and blessing that was expected from the first man, and the ideology of kingship is another indication of the general tendency to seek the activity of God in history rather than in myth.[1]

(*b*) The cultic field was not unaffected by this general process of historicization. Although markedly indebted to the Canaanites in all that concerns ritual and the organization of things sacred, the Israelite tradition was, however, strong enough to repress the mythical elements with which Canaanite religion was abundantly provided. Thus while adopting the holy places of Canaanite worship they made a point of bringing them within Israelite tradition by presenting the venerable sanctuaries of Bethel, Beersheba and Penuel, whose origins for the Canaanites was lost in the darkness of time, as founded by their own ancestors. Jerusalem certainly had a very ancient cultic tradition, but the Israelite spirit

---

[1] We are thinking here only of the specifically Israelite aspect of kingship which, contrary to what happened elsewhere, is a movement in history and which attaches equal importance to the perpetuity of the dynasty and to the person of the sovereign.

strove to prove that the temple had been built on a virgin site and had become a holy place only after an express theophany of Yahweh (2 Sam. 24). The calves set up by Jeroboam at Bethel and Dan are the usual symbols of the fertility cults, but, in their desire to satisfy the rights of history, they are related to the Exodus from Egypt (1 Kings 12.28). It is in the significance of the great feasts that the process of historicization is most apparent: the Passover, originally the feast of offering of the first-born of the flock, became at a very early date, by reference to the Exodus, the commemoration of that event. The New Year Feast, the annual feast *par excellence*, became, through the theme of the kingship of Yahweh revealing himself in history, much more the time of renewal of the nation's destinies than the renewal of nature.

(c) The laws, too, bear the mark of this historicization; the common expression "that is not done in Israel" (Gen. 34.7; Dt. 22.21; Jos. 7.15; Jg. 19.23; 20.10; 2 Sam. 13.12; Jer. 29.23) to rebuke an action contrary to good conduct proves that the moral sense was subordinate to the historical sense. All the rites have an historical foundation; thus the institution of circumcision, which the Israelites doubtless practised from very early times, like their neighbours, is recorded three times (Ex. 4.24ff.; Jos. 5.7; Gen. 17) and is ascribed to Moses, to Joshua and to Abraham. Generally speaking, the laws are all attributed to Moses and lose their character of ancient taboos to become ordinances of the God of the covenant who is unwilling to have anything that concerns his people outside his sovereignty. The decisions that the people are called on to take are always dictated to them by the circumstances of the moment, but as in the precise circumstances the will of God may be manifested in its totality, these decisions assume the force of laws. That is why Israelite law is not expressed in formulae fixed once for all, but undergoes the repercussions of every new divine intervention in history. Comparisons of the Elohist and Deuteronomic versions of the Decalogue is the clearest illustration of this and the variations are still greater for laws whose "historical" character is more solidly based. Attacks directed against the Old Testament in the name of ethics would do well to remember that the Old Testament does not set out to give general principles without taking account of the concrete circumstances in which they were promulgated.

This historicization was not without its dangers. The mythical

elements might take their revenge and give a mythical appearance
to historical realities.   Apocalyptic literature marks a renaissance of
myth: not only is there a resurgence of old elements which had
been repressed—creation myth, fall of the angels, etc., but historical
events themselves receive mythical trappings: Jerusalem becomes
a celestial reality before descending to earth and the Law exists in
heaven from the beginning in its totality and in its perfection.   But
it must be said that such a reversion deprived Israel's religion of
what was its specific character; cut off from its source, Judaism was
to be a body of doctrine and ritual, but it was no longer a history.

In conclusion it must be noticed that Israel's faith was subjected to
a quite radical "demythologization"; it is none the less true that
the profound essence of myth, the direct intervention of God
in the world, has still been preserved and that the coming of God
into the world represents the main power line of Israel's religion.

B. ELECTION

Election is one of the central realities of the Old Testament; even
though it is less frequently mentioned than the covenant it is
however the initial act by which Yahweh comes into relation with
his people and the permanent reality which assures the constancy
of that bond.   Every intervention by God in history is an election:
either when he chooses a place in which to make more especial
manifestation of his presence, or when he chooses a people to
carry out his intentions, or when he chooses a man to be his representative of his messenger, the Old Testament God is the one
who has universal sovereignty at his disposal, and shows it by the
free use that he makes of it.   The technical term to designate the
fact of election is the verb *bachar* which expresses a choice among
several possibilities.[1]   The particular aspects and the deep motives
of this election are made explicit with the help of other roots, each
of which brings out in full one of the particular aspects of the
election: this *qara'* brings out the idea of the call; *qanah* that
of belonging; *hibdil* that of separation; *hiqdish* that of setting

---

[1] The main idea expressed by the root *bachar* is that of free unmotivated choice;
only in two passages, Is. 48.10 and Job 34.4, is the verb used to designate a choice
following an intensive examination; it seems then that, in the evolution of this
word, there was such an attenuation of the idea of free choice, that in Aramaic
and in Syriac *bachar*, to choose, and *bachan,* to test, are to end up by being
confused.

apart and finally *yada'*, which shows that the election is accompanied by interest and solicitude for those who are its object.[1]

The important place held by the election theme is also expressed by the rich variety of images used in the Old Testament to show the union of Yahweh with his people. The commonest and the one that found most favour is incontestably the one of marriage union.[2] First used by Hosea, it was taken up by Jeremiah (2.1-7; 3.11-22), Ezekiel (16 and 23) and Second Isaiah (50.1; 54.5, 8, 10; 62.4-5). Just as in marriage the wife becomes the property of her husband who has purchased her for money, Yahweh has taken possession of the people, like a faithful husband he assures them fertility and prosperity; the wife owes obedience and faithfulness, her infidelity would be a refusal to acknowledge the grace of election. Marriage is in effect an election before being a covenant and that, much more than Israelite law, gave to the husband the right to repudiate his wife.

Another image borrowed from the realm of natural relations is that of father and son; the Yahwist calls Israel " the first-born son of Yahweh " (Ex. 4.22) and gives as realistic a sense to the idea as to the Pharaoh's family relationships—the idea to which this election is compared and contrasted. The numerous proper names in which Yahweh is called " father " witness to the same truth. We must not draw from the use of this image the conclusion that Israel regarded its relationship with Yahweh as a bond of the natural order; in biblical language, the son is the one who was created by the father and who consequently is in a relationship of dependence in regard to him; that is why the divine fatherhood is endowed with a sovereignty which was vainly sought for in human relationships (Is. 63.16; 64.7).

The image of the clay and the potter might suggest that election is made in an arbitrary way; in reality something very different from God's fancy is involved. God does not create for the pleasure of destroying; he always acts according to a plan, but the materials he uses in its accomplishment are diverse and occupy the places for which they are individually suitable; in the interpretation that he gives to the parable, Jeremiah preserves human liberty: man is so

---

[1] The verbs *chashaq*, to be attached to, *'ahab*, to love, *racham*, to have pity are also words belonging to the language of election.

[2] The marriage image is specifically Israelite; it is possible, however, that the image of the union of Baal with the earth, which is nowhere explicitly attested, but which seems to underlie the nature myths, may have provided the biblical language with some expressions.

free that his conversion can lead God to review his intentions (Jer. 18.8). The idea is also met in Is. 29.16 and 64.7.

The vineyard theme is a variant of the marriage theme. When Hosea meditates his going in search of the unfaithful wife, the gift that he means to offer to seal the pardon consists of vineyards: " I will give her her vineyards " (Hos. 2.17). The well-known word of Isaiah 5 is only the religious adaptation of a love-song. The vineyard expresses the hope of God and the obedience that he has the right to expect from his people. At the origin of this hope there is the devouring love of one who is jealous, which is shown in unwearying perseverance, but when the hope is dashed it changes to cursing; a vine which bears no more fruit is only fit for uprooting. The image of the inheritance is particularly applied to the land of Israel which Yahweh, its legal owner, gives to the people that he has chosen; to some extent he gives up his sovereignty to the people, who also take the title of " Yahweh's inheritance " (Ex. 34.9; 1 Sam. 10.1; Jer. 12.7, 8, 10; Ps. 28.9; 33.12; 74.2; 78.62, 71; 94.5 and 106.5, 40). Still more than the marriage image, that of the inheritance is a two-way one: if Israel is Yahweh's inheritance, Yahweh is also Israel's inheritance, in a particular sense for the Levites (Num. 18.20; Dt. 10.9; 18.2), in a general sense for the body of the faithful (Ps. 16.5-6).

The image of the shepherd and the flock which by its frequency bears witness to the central place of the Exodus theme (Ps. 68.52; Is. 63.11; Hos. 11.1-4) insists on the utter dependence of the people with reference to their God.

The terms which designate the people of Israel themselves express, each in its own way, divine election. The name Israel itself[1] was probably from the beginning that of a group of tribes united by a religious and cultic bond, like the amphictyonies in

[1] The explanation of the name Israel by the root *yashar* receives not unimportant confirmation from the fact of the existence of the noun Yeshurun, which certainly derives from the same root and which in the four passages where we meet it (Dt. 32.15; 33.5, 26; Is. 44.2) is a poetic designation of Israel; the *sepher hayashar*, one of the oldest collections of national songs (Josh. 10.13; 2 Sam. 1.18) could be understood as the book of Israel, understood as the righteous one, the hero of God. The explanation given in Gen. 32 is philologically untenable; this text could at the most justify the translation: El fights. It is none the less a testimony to a theology which saw expressed in the name of Israel all that made the reality of the chosen people. For the exposition and discussion of all the problems relating to the name of Israel, we refer the reader to the work of G. A. Danell, *Studies in the name Israel in the Old Testament*, Uppsala 1946.

Greece; this name contains a distinctive meaning, either "El is Right" or "the Righteous one of El". In chapter 32 of Genesis, the name is interpreted as "he who wrestles with God" and the object of this story is to transfer this collective name on to the ancestor of the twelve tribes. From the time of the Judges, Israel is designated as the *'am Yahweh* (Jg. 5.11). The appellations "holy people" and "the people who belong"[1] are not met earlier than Deuteronomy, for the well-known passage of Ex. 19.5 must probably be attributed to a Deuteronomic editor: "If you hear my voice and keep my covenant, you shall be to me a *segullah* among all peoples, for all the earth is mine. And you shall be for me a kingdom of priests, *mamleket kohanim*, a holy nation, *goy qadosh.*" But what is expressed in this verse certainly represents a more ancient opinion. The prophets had the sole object of giving back to the people the consciousness and sound understanding of their election, such as existed in the beginning. Since it is holy, Israel belongs to Yahweh and since it belongs to Yahweh, it is different from other peoples on earth. Election confers on him who is its object a particular dignity, but, so that this may never harden into a haughty conceit, election carries service as its necessary corollary; to be the *'am* of Yahweh involves being his *'ebed*: the two terms are sometimes put in parallel: "Yahweh will do justice to his people, he will take pity on his servants" (Dt. 32.36). "Rejoice with his people for he avenges the blood of his servants" (Dt. 32.43) and association of the terms "elect" and "servant" is particularly frequent in Second Isaiah (41.8-9; 42.19; 43.10; 44.1-2; 45.4). When the Old Testament gives to certain individuals the title of *'ebed* it means to assert that a great privilege has been granted to them: the patriarchs are servants (Gen. 26.24; Ex. 32.13; Dt. 9.27; Ps. 105.6, 42); Moses is called by this title forty times; the kings, David in particular, are servants of God (1 Kings 18.26; 2 Kings 9.7; 17.13; Jer. 7.25; 26.5; Ez. 38.17; Amos 3.7; Zech. 1.6; Dan. 9.6; Ezr. 9.11). This term's link with election is made more evident by the frequent use of the noun *'ebed* with the pronoun of the first person. In giving to a people or to an individual the title of "my servant", Yahweh meant to put the accent less

---

[1] The expression *'Am Yahweh* (Elohim) is also met in 2 Sam. 1.12; 14.13; 1 Sam. 2.14, *'am segullah* in Ex. 19.5; Dt. 7.6; 14.7; 26.18; Mal. 3.17; 1 Chr. 29.3; Eccl. 2.8. This term has sometimes been compared with the Accadian *sukallu*, vizier, minister, which would bring out the dignity attached to the title (cf. Caspari, *NKZ*, 1921, p. 202).

on his obedience than on his belonging, and when in moments of national distress the Israelites call on Yahweh by describing themselves as his servants, they mean by that to remind Yahweh of the reality of election and not to rely on the services that they had performed (Is. 63.17; Ps. 79.2; 89.51; 90.13). But to be a servant necessarily implies a mission to fulfil; the servant should love Yahweh, should cleave to him, fear him, requirements which in Deuteronomy return at least as frequently as the assertion of election, and this mission will always be exercised in a specific task.

The witness of history confirms that of language. No one could seriously contest that election is closely linked to the work of Moses. On the other hand the election of the patriarchs set a problem to which K. Galling a quarter of a century ago devoted a scholarly monograph.[1] Examining the two traditions relating to Israel's election, he came to the conclusion that the patriarchal traditions are a late creation whose object was to justify by a closely linked genealogical line the ideal of a great Israel at a time when the unity of the people was being called in question.

The almost total absence of patriarchal traditions from the pre-exilic prophets seems to be a pointer to their later origin, although all allusion to these traditions is not absent. It is quite probable that in Amos 3.2 and Jer. 4.2 we have an allusion to the promises made to Abraham concerning the blessing that all families on earth are to have in him (Gen. 12.3). The problem is complex and cannot be resolved by simple considerations of dating. Historical research has made the existence of the patriarchs more and more certain. Even if they came far short of playing the religious rôle that tradition ascribes to them, there was in the movement that brought them from Haran to Canaan something which corresponded to an election and it seems impossible to see in the religion of the patriarchs a simple projection into the past of forms and of beliefs that were only current five centuries later. There is then ground for recognizing two elections, the first at the time of Abraham, the second at the time of the Exodus, two elections that we might qualify by the terms of being and of doing. With Abraham, Yahweh declares the existence of the people, and so he throws the whole weight on the permanence of the race, a natural phenomenon, undoubtedly, but which in the precise cir-

[1] *Die Erwählungstradition Israels*, Giessen 1928.

cumstances none the less assumes the appearance of a miracle. For Moses on the other hand, what matters is the accomplishment of a work for which the existence of the people was indispensable. Rowley very rightly defines this relationship by saying that the people was elected " *in* Abraham " and elected " *through* Moses ".[1] Through Moses the people received their consecration as God's people. Whatever may be thought of the hypothesis that Yahweh was originally a God of the Kenites who, at some given time, turned to a people other than his own, it is certain that Moses had a revelation of Yahweh and that his work of liberation is linked to this revelation; it is because he experienced the activity of Yahweh in his own life that he can interpret events as the work of that same God. The departure from Egypt and the crossing of the Red Sea would not have become such fundamental facts without the interpretation given to them by Moses and, after him, by the prophets. The person of Moses plays a part of the first importance in the forming of the elected people, it is the reality which cements the unity and the faith of the people; when the leader is present, the people go forward, when he disappears, they relapse into waywardness; but, important as his rôle may be, Moses is only the intermediary, it is the people as a whole that is the beneficiary of election.

The fact of election is then earlier than the theology of election. The Yahwist presents his historical work according to the principle of election; that is why in his work the history of the patriarchs is preceded by the history of the origins as the background against which the election of Abraham is picked out. Yahweh is the universal God yet one who chooses a people, obeying in this nothing but his own plan. This election is not envisaged by him, as an initial act which sets a mechanism in motion—it is constantly being renewed and always freely and in a way that cannot be foreseen. The existence of the people is called in question, the younger is chosen to the detriment of the elder without there being an idea that the notion of choice automatically implies the notion of rejection, as L. Koehler[2] rather arbitrarily asserts, for if certain ones are left outside the election it is only for the time being, in order

---

[1] *The Biblical Doctrine of Election*, p. 31: " The election in Abraham and the election through Moses."

[2] *Theologie des A.T.*, 1936, p. 66. Koehler believes that the notion of election only appeared at a time when Israel had ceased to be a nation to become a religious community and that it occupies only a very secondary place in the Old Testament. At the opposite extreme to Koehler, H. H. Rowley makes election

to make more readily possible the accomplishment of God's plan. The prophets, as elected to be the servants of Yahweh, made a large contribution to the theology of election: "You alone have I known out of all the families of the earth" says Amos 3.2. By choosing Israel, Yahweh has conferred on them a privilege and has given proof on their account not only of grace but of love, which is made clear by the verb *yada'* (cf. also Is. 1.2; Hos. 11 and Jer. 2). For the people, election implies the duty of loving Yahweh with a love worthy of that with which he has loved them, otherwise election will be turned to judgment; but the insistence that the prophets place upon the continuance of a remnant proves that neither acts of disobedience nor judgment mean in their view the end of election. The Deuteronomist found the ground well prepared for a more systematic elaboration of a doctrine of election. Impressed by the preaching of the prophets on the imminence of judgment, he sets out, by returning to the sources, to reconstitute the reality of the holy people as it existed in Mosaic times. To prove the perennial nature of the election, frequent mention is made of the promise to the patriarchs (Deut. 1.8; 6.10; 9.5; 10.11; 30.20) for the patriarchs received a word and for the Deuteronomist the Word is the supreme divine revelation. But in order to become God's people once more, only the return to Moses will be effective. In the legislative parts of Deuteronomy only the Exodus is under discussion (Dt. 30.1; 24.18, 22; 26.5ff.) and Josiah's reformation is ratified by a solemn celebration of the Passover (2 Kings 23.21), the old nomadic feast which had for some time previously been connected with events of the nation's history. With a force that is expressed in the Hebrew language by repetition, the Deuteronomist lays the foundations of the theocracy which he means to make a reality: the people of Israel is separated from other peoples, the idea of separation is more heavily stressed than in the Yahwist's writings, other people are left outside his horizon and delivered over to false gods by Yahweh himself (Dt. 4.19). Separation implies the demand of belonging to Yahweh and of serving him with all one's heart and with all one's being. The exile was needed to set free all the potentialities that were implicit in the idea of election. For the first time, no doubt, the election itself was called

the centre of the Old Testament. Vriezen occupies an intermediate position; according to him, election is secondary to the covenant and only made its appearance from Deuteronomic times.

in question. That Yahweh had forsaken his people (Is. 40.27; 42.18; 49.14) must have been the state of mind of the majority of the exiles. To restore the certainty of divine election to the people was the message of Second Isaiah. The election stands, for Israel is always the servant of Yahweh, that is to say, the object of a privilege that a restoration more wonderful than past times will show, but this privilege is accompanied by an obligation and it is this second aspect that the prophet brings to complete expression. Since the light of Yahweh is risen upon it, Israel in its turn must be a light to the nations and must not be content to let the nations come to itself. Henceforward the theocratic ideal of the Deuterono-mist is raised to a universal plane, and by making this ideal of the servant real in the person of an individual belonging to the future, Yahweh gives to Israel the pledge that its election remains sure and that its missionary duty can be a reality when, through the forgiveness received, it will be in a position to realize it fully. While envisaging the election of the people as a whole, Second Isaiah is interested in the lot of individuals; the example of Abraham, who was chosen when he was alone (Ez. 33.24) is fre-quently invoked to show what Yahweh can do with a single individual and to make it clear that for his power nothing is impossible (Is. 41.8; 48.19; 51.2).

All through the Old Testament the election of the people is accompanied by the election of individuals. The king is always one of the elect, a *bachir* (1 Sam. 10.24; 16.6ff.); in the first instance David, but also his descendants right down to that mysterious Zerubbabel, on whom at one time the hopes of the people were based (Haggai 2.23). But the object of election may also be found outside Israel: the Pharaoh of the Exodus and Nebuchadrezzar are the servants of Yahweh (Jer. 25.9; 27.6; 43.10). Cyrus even receives the title of "messiah" (Is. 45.1, 3). But each time an election of this type takes place, it is done with a view to the punishment (Assyria the rod of Yahweh's anger) or to the saving of Israel. The election of Jerusalem, and more especially of the temple, answers to a slightly different theology, although in Deuteronomy it goes hand in hand with the theology of the election of the people (1 Kings 8.48; 11.13, 36; 2 Kings 21.7; Dt. 12.5; 2 Chr. 33.7; Zech. 3.2). The temple and the people must show clearly the universal character of election: the temple of Ezekiel's vision (Ez. 47), from which flows the spring that brings life, and the servant of Yahweh bringing salvation to the nations, are both in the service of one cause—the manifestation in the world of God's presence and the permanence of his grace.

The election of which it had been the object was for Israel the most powerful of stimulants. Thanks to the covenant and the law which were its visible expressions, election maintained Israel's separateness apart from which it would have been unfaithful to its destiny. But there was also in this notion a danger to which Israel sometimes succumbed, that was to confuse the fact of election, of which God alone is the subject, with the feeling of being elected, which Vriezen expresses by using the terms *Erwählung* and *Erwähltheit*.[1] The prophets always gave fresh reminders that the notion of election was to be set right again in opposition to its deviations. In a word election has no effective value except when it is understood in the spirit of the exhortation that Deuteronomy proclaims with the same solemnity as the reality of election: Thou shalt love Yahweh and shalt seek him with thine whole heart . . . (Dt. 6.5; 8.6ff.), with all the obligations and all the risks that this response could involve.

C. THE COVENANT

Election constitutes the fundamental event, but, so that it may be a dynamic reality, it is exercised within the framework of a covenant.[2] The covenant makes a restriction of the election, for, if the latter keeps Israel's looks turned towards the other people from among whom and for whose salvation Israel was chosen, the covenant insists on the bond which unites the people to their God.[3] For the etymology of the term *berit*, the door remains open to

---

[1] *Die Erwählung Israels nach dem Alten Testament*, p. 115.

[2] The character of the covenant as a relationship of belonging between two contracting parties has been well brought out by the work of Johs. Pedersen, *Der Eid bei den Semiten*, 1914, and *Israel*, I-II, pp. 265ff.

[3] A. Neher, who in his book on *Amos* (Paris 1950) devotes some very thought-provoking pages to the *berit*, considers it as a synthesis of the ideas of hiatus and participation, the hiatus being the difference between the given and the perfect, which the Alexandrine translators felt in translating *berit* by διαθήκη instead of by συνθήκη which would have been the exact translation; as for the participation, it appears especially in the various images that recall marriage union (cf. on this last point, the same author: "Le symbolisme conjugal, expression de l'histoire dans l'A.T.", *RHPR*, 1954, pp. 30ff).

H

several possibilities,[1] among which the one that derives the term from the root *barah*, to eat, seems to us to be best supported by the evidence; but in any case the term became separated from this root at an early date, which proves once again that Old Testament concepts must be studied more in the light of their internal evolution than their etymology. On the plane of human relationships, the truth almost always points to a covenant between two partners who are on an unequal footing; it is the stronger who proposes the *berit*. The Israelites grant a *berit* to the Gibeonites who manage, by a trick, to place themselves under their protection (Josh. 9), Nahash, king of the Ammonites, grants a covenant to the people of Jabesh-gilead (1 Sam. 11.1ff.), Ahab grants it to Benhadad his prisoner (1 Kings 20.34), Abimelech makes a covenant with Isaac (Gen. 26.28) and Abner asks David to grant him his *berit* (2 Sam. 3.12). It is the stronger alone who takes the initiative in acts which accompany the conclusion of a covenant, such as the oath (Jos. 9.15), the shared·garment (1 Sam. 18.3) and the meal, apart from which there can be no real bond between the two partners (Gen. 26.30; 31.46, 54; 2 Sam. 3.20). One of the most ancient rites, and one which lasted a long time, was for the participants to pass between the two halves of one or of several beasts that were killed, a gesture by which the participants undertook to suffer the lot of the victims in the event of their transgressing the claims of the covenant (cf. Gen. 15 and especially Jer. 34.10ff.). It is to this practice that we can trace the origin of the expression *karat berit*, to cut a covenant, the term *berit* denoting the result of the action, the cutting being in this case only the means of attaining an agreement. The grant of a *berit* is not made, however, without the observance of certain conditions on the part of the recipient: David is quite willing to make a covenant with Abner on condition that he return Michal his wife to him (2 Sam. 3.13), so that the *berit* also becomes a contract. The two partners observe together the rites that are to make it effective; and so, parallel with the expression *karat berit*, we meet the more specifically contractual *heqim berit*, followed by *'im* or *beyn*: "Now come," said Laban to Jacob, "let us make a covenant, thou and I"

---

[1] The proposed etymologies are many; if we keep to Hebrew roots only, that of *barah*, to eat, seems to have the greatest probability on its side. L. Koehler, *LVT*, p. 152, favours this etymology. Recourse to other Semitic languages has suggested the Assyrian *birtu*, bond, fetter or *beritu*, separation, or the Arabic *beraat*, ordinance, edict; none of these comparisons seems more conclusive than the explanation by a Hebrew root.

(Gen. 31.44, cf. also 2 Sam. 3.21; 1 Kings 15.19; Ez. 17.13). The two aspects are met with side by side; it is thus that in 1 Sam. 18.3 the covenant is imposed by Jonathan on David, while in 1 Sam. 23.16 that same covenant is concluded jointly by the two partners. These covenants between men are not devoid of religious significance; they are accompanied by sacrifices and very often the divine presence and guarantee are explicitly invoked. God is the witness of the covenant between Laban and Jacob (Gen. 31.50), he is, in some degree, the third partner and it is his presence that gives the covenant its binding strength. He could not indeed be anything else in a religion where the aspect of the parent-god held so important a place. Every covenant is concluded before Yahweh (1 Sam. 23.18; 2 Sam. 5.3; 2 Kings 23.3).

When God is one of the two partners of the covenant, obviously there can be no question of a bilateral contract. We are acquainted with some examples of covenants concluded by deities outside Israel : the king of Lagash, Urukagina (c. 2400 B.C.) imposes on his subjects " the word that his king Ningirsu had pronounced " and ends the list of his laws with these words : " with Ningirsu Urukagina concluded this treaty " and the Old Testament itself mentions the local god of Shechem *El Berit* or *Baal Berit* (Jg. 9.4, 46), whose characteristic was probably to be bound by a covenant with the people of the sons of Hamor. But in spite of these analogies it is certain that the notion nowhere took such a central place as it did in the religion of Israel. In the same way as election, of which it is at once the form and the content, the covenant is due only to the initiative of Yahweh and is in no way the reward of Israel's merits. This free character of the covenant is the condition of its moral aspect, for the covenant is valid only if the people respond to it by obedience and faithfulness (cf. particularly Dt. 7.7-10).

All the accounts of covenant-making between Yahweh and the people show three aspects of the covenant, though the accent is sometimes differently placed : (*a*) the covenant is a gift that Yahweh makes to his people; (*b*) by the covenant, God comes into relationship and creates with his people a bond of communion; (*c*) the covenant creates obligations which take concrete shape in the form of law.[1] The covenant, mentioned in the stories about the

---

[1] Begrich, *ZAW*, 1944, p. 7, seems to us to put a little too much emphasis on the difference between the covenant and the law when he writes that the premises of legislation cannot be understood by beginning with the notion of *berit*.

beginnings and in the patriarchal traditions, is probably largely a projection into the past of the Mosaic covenant, though it is very probable that the covenant already held a certain place in the essentially family religion of the fathers, such that the covenant with the fathers, sealed by an oath that the Old Testament mentions quite frequently, might preserve a memory of historical events (Dt. 4.31; 7.12; 8.18; 9.5; Jer. 11.5). The most detailed account telling of the Sinai covenant (Ex. 19-24) has been retouched many times and the various traditions are " so entangled that it would be very difficult, if not impossible, to separate them and restore them ".[1] The following elements may, however, be put forward as certain: the Sinai covenant includes a revelation granted to Moses, a rite of blood-sprinkling, a reading of the laws and a sacramental meal. The meaning of this covenant is expounded in the introductory verses of chapter 19: the covenant is an *election*, "you belong to me from among all peoples"; it is a *bond*, the people will have with Yahweh the particularly close bond of belonging which characterizes the priestly function; it is an *obedience*, for if Yahweh is king, the members of the people can only be the subjects who will follow him everywhere he leads (Ex. 15.18; Num. 23.21; Dt. 33.5; Jg. 8.23). Covenant-makings later than Sinai are renewals, or extensions to a wider association, of the covenant: the laws listed in the book of Deuteronomy (12.26) are interpreted as the clauses of a new covenant concluded by Moses with the people of the land of Moab to the East of Jordan (Dt. 28.69). The covenant concluded by Joshua's mediation at Shechem (Josh. 24.25) probably has as its aim the extension of the Sinai covenant to certain clans who were not yet members of the Israelite amphictyony. Following the discovery in the temple of the book of the covenant (2 Kings 23.2), King Josiah, after giving a reading of it, "made the covenant before Yahweh" and undertook to put into practice the words of that covenant and all the people entered into the covenant (2 Kings 23.31). In the covenant made in the time of Ezra (Neh. 8.10), the people undertake to "walk in God's law and to observe and to keep all the commandments" (Neh. 10.30).

Within Yahweh's covenant with Israel there is a place for individual covenants which generally have the object of confirming and guaranteeing the covenant with the people: the everlasting

---

[1] For the account of the Sinai covenant, cf. the study of M. Haelvoet, in *Analecta lovaniensia*, no. 39, 1953, p. 28.

covenant made with David (2 Sam. 23.5; Ps. 89.4, 29) expresses in its quintessence, according to Procksch's[1] happy expression, Yahweh's covenant with the people; the particular relationship of the king with God only serves to symbolize the relationship of the people as a whole. The relationship with Yahweh of the messianic king of the future is also presented as a covenant (Is. 49.6). These characters, beneficiaries of the covenant, are at the same time and especially its mediators. It would be going too far to assert that the covenant always requires a mediator, but it is certain that, as the concept of covenant becomes more precise, the person of the mediator, past (Moses), present (the King) or future (the Messiah) tends to increase in importance. The mediatorial function can also be fulfilled by a group; thus in the post-exilic period, priests, who take in almost all fields the kingly succession, become the mediators of the covenant and make its benefits possible for the people (cf. the covenant with Levi, Num. 18.19; Jer. 33.20-26; Mal. 2.4ff.).

It was natural that such an essential reality should be exploited by all those historians, prophets and thinkers who strove to give literary expression to the fact of the close relationship of the people with Yahweh. The covenant has its origin in history and more especially in the event of Sinai, but how does it come about that, outside the accounts which concern it directly, this fundamental event is mentioned only very rarely later on? This absence should not make us suspicious of the historical truth of the events, it is explained rather by the fact that faith, in Israel, while having an historical foundation, does not bind itself to the historical events themselves, but to the objective realities created by those events. Now by the Sinai covenant a close relationship was created with Yahweh and henceforth the covenant is envisaged only under the form of that relationship, which remains as close and as vital as in the days of Moses; the memory of the covenant was, moreover, kept going by the ritual of the great feasts. That there was an annual feast of the covenant, as A. Weiser[2] thinks, is an hypothesis that is more theologically than historically founded, but it is certain that, at the time of the feast of Tabernacles, the reminder of the covenant kept the memory of its origin alive among the people.

---

[1] *ThAT*, p. 529.

[2] Weiser insists on this feast in all his recent publications, particularly in the introduction to the commentary on the Psalms in *ATD* and in "Die Darstellung der Theophanie in den Psalmen und im Festkult", *Festschrift A. Bertholet*, pp. 513ff.

The eclipse of the Sinai theme by the Exodus one probably has a still deeper reason: the Exodus theme, being the commencement of a movement, illustrated in the most expressive way that Yahweh's revelation was made through history, while to stress the Sinai covenant might easily have led to a static conception of revelation and to a mythologizing against which Israelite religion always protested. The subordination of the covenant to history explains the variations that the notion of the covenant has undergone in the course of the ages.

From the time of the settlement in Canaan of the Israelite tribes, the covenant was to be subjected to a serious crisis: in an environment in which religion was a realm apart, that of the sacred, unconnected with everyday life, the covenant ran the risk of being reduced to cultic practices instead of being the bond that linked every aspect of life; the frequent taking over by Israelites of Canaanite sanctuaries opened wide the door to this danger. Furthermore, the adoption of the monarchy ran the risk of making the covenant into an institution whose stability would be guaranteed only by the presence of the sovereign. The purely institutional side of the covenant threatened to become more important than the event itself. However dangerous this crisis may have been, the covenant idea did not thereby lose its particular quality: against the danger of departmentalizing that would ascribe to Yahweh the mission of guiding the people, but would leave the realm of agricultural life under the protection of the *baalim*, the prophets forcefully declared that the products of nature were not independent of the God of the covenant and of the moral conditions demanded by him. As the settled life became more and more the nation's normal way of life, it became clear that the Sinai and Shechem covenants no longer altogether answered the situation thus created; in particular, all the legislation which had issued from that covenant needed to be re-examined. Faithful to their method of returning to the first source, the great prophets of the eighth century insisted on the foundation of the covenant, that is on the free election of Israel and on the responsibility laid upon them by that election. It was the task of the Deuteronomic reform to outline upon this foundation of election a new framework which was to allow the message of the prophets to filter through into the institutions. One of the happy results of the critical work of recent years is to have shown the importance of Deuteronomy. The

Deuteronomic reform is at the same time reactionary and revolutionary; this code sets out to be only a reminder of the single covenant conceived by the mediation of Moses, but by sanctioning the state of things created by the settlement and monarchy Deuteronomy marks the taking up of a stand in history that is both political and religious. At the moment of its promulgation the very existence of the people was seriously in question; the northern kingdom, the more important, had ceased to exist more than a century before; the kingdom of Judah was so strongly vassalized and paganized. that it was going to fall at any moment the prey of the Assyrian conqueror. And so the new constitution was going to give to the people, not only the opportunity to survive, but even to reorganize. To the Deuteronomist, faithful to the spirit of the prophets, election is the fundamental message; by virtue of this election Yahweh is the master of nature and the master of the nations. But Israel is the people of Yahweh, that is a people set apart whose particular character must be shown by separation from the pagan environment and by a renewal of awareness of the bond which unites the members of the people to Yahweh and to one another. Like the Sinai covenant, this covenant will find expression in a law, but this law will not be far away, hidden by the brilliance of the divine glory, it will be practicable and everyone will be able to have access to it by turning to the book in which it is recorded (Dt. 30.5ff.). If Israel conforms to the words of this law, it will be able to stand as God's people, even though it should pass through the severest of trials.

After Deuteronomy, the term *berit* is again used by the prophets; thanks to this reformation they can speak of it without its evoking an archaic and faded reality, but we can pick out, according to the religious temperaments that used it, a twofold orientation of the concept of covenant. For the author of the priestly code, the *berit* becomes the foundation and the goal of the nation's whole life. By stressing its character of *foedus iniquum*, given and established by God, as is suggested by such expressions as: *natan berit* and *heqîm berit*, and of everlasting ordinance *berit 'olam*, the theologians of this school are satisfied with the primitive sense, the limit of which they pass, however, by making of *berit* the only religious concept: all is *berit*, all is fixed once for all,. creation is envisaged in the light of *berit*; according to the analogy of the people whose characteristic is their separation from all that is impure, the essential characteristic of the creation is its separation from chaos (Gen. 1.28; 8.21; 9.9). The law is the present and concrete expression of that covenant with which, moreover, it becomes more and more confused. To remain within the covenant is to conform to the letter of the law; finally, in a last stage, the term *berit* will come to signify the people or the Jewish religion (Zech. 9.11; Dan. 9.27 and especially 11.28). Alongside this priestly current in which the covenant becomes a static reality, the prophets, particularly Jeremiah and Second Isaiah, retained the "provisional" character of the covenant by stressing that the narrow framework of the covenant could be broken, when election flourished afresh. According to Jeremiah, the new covenant (31.31-34)[1] will be made according to the Mosaic mode. It aims only at maintaining the ancient ideal: Yahweh Israel's God and Israel Yahweh's people (v. 33); but, thanks to the extension of this ideal to all, and to the interiorization of the law, which in no way signifies the abolition of the written law, and thanks especially to the forgiveness by which God forgets the whole past, it will make fully real the ideal of a holy people. Ezekiel (36.23-28) gives more weight to interior regeneration and ascribes it to the action of the spirit without which no creation is possible. Second Isaiah goes still further, by announcing that Yahweh's servant will be at the same time the people's covenant (Is. 42.6) and the light of the nations (42.7), which means that the privilege of the covenant granted to Israel is to become the portion of the nations.

These two currents each in its own way helped to keep alive in Israel its specific inheritance: the priestly current, by insisting on the present and immutable character of the covenant, allowed the people to stand firm and to "walk before God" (Gen. 17.7-8, 19); the prophetic current, at the basis of which is found the eschatological hope of the perfect union of God and his people and of all the peoples in the kingdom to come, allowed the people to envisage history in the light of its end, and gave them, so far as events are concerned, an attitude of freedom and detachment which never gave way.

It may be asked how it happens that a religion so far removed from the juridical spirit as the religion of Israel should have designated one of its essential aspects by a term taken from juridical

---

[1] The all-important passage of Jeremiah on the new covenant probably inspired the other texts that mention it: Jer. 32.38, 40; Ez. 16.60; 34.25; 37.26; Is. 42.6; 49.8; 55.3; 59.21; 61.8; Mal. 3.1.

language. It was because the language was particularly suitable to express the reality of a fact and the presence of divine action in visible things. Just as the Old Testament shows the election made visible through the covenant, the New Testament is not content with speaking of God's love for sinful man, but insists on its reality by turning again to the juridical term of justification. The covenant expresses that election is true and that Yahweh now and in truth is consistent with what he is; and so we think that it is not going too far to define the relationship of election and covenant as that of word and sacrament.

D. THE MISSION

The election of Israel was to lead of necessity to a missionary duty, but this fact, which was the most powerful lever, was at the same time to reveal itself as the most tenacious of brakes as soon as it was envisaged only under its first aspect of separateness. The Yahwist presents Abraham's election as an episode which, standing out against the plan of universal history, is to pour forth as a blessing upon it. Yet it could be that the promise, several times repeated, that all the peoples of the earth will be blessed or will bless themselves in Abraham (Gen. 12.3; 18.18; 22.18; 26.4; 28.14), is not so definite concerning the missionary duty as it seems at first sight, for, according to the similar grammatical constructions of Gen. 48.20; Jer. 29.22 and Zech. 8.13, the blessing of Abraham is to be understood in an exemplary sense as being among the peoples the prototype of blessing, without their being direct beneficiaries of the blessing. But the solemnity of the formula and especially the general plan of the Yahwist's book provoke us rather to see between Abraham and the peoples a relationship of cause and effect and the assertion of the universal mission of the people of Israel. From the beginning the religion of Israel was convinced of the superiority of its God Yahweh over the gods of the nations; even though his action was limited to his own people, it can be said that Moses was a missionary for the Egyptians[1] by demonstrating to them the weakness of their gods. The conversion

---

[1] Before being a missionary to the Egyptians, Moses is a missionary to those of his own people who did not yet know Yahweh, at any rate under the form that he had revealed himself to Moses. One of the merits of H. H. Rowley is to have stressed the rôle of Moses in the development of a missionary sense (cf. *The Missionary Message of the O.T.* and *The Biblical Doctrine of Election*).

of the nations to the God of Israel, ordered by the election, was done by ways that often seemed to go counter to this fundamental intention. At the time of the conquest, Israel must, with a view to obtaining the country linked with the promise, exterminate the nations who occupy it. Later, settled and organized according to the laws of all the peoples, in order to be able to maintain itself as a people, it will adopt relationships of good neighbourliness with the surrounding nations without trying to interfere with their religion. The following period will be marked by vassalization to two great peoples who will gravely compromise its existence. By keeping Israel almost always on the defensive, historical circumstances created great difficulties to any missionary attempt by Israel to the nations. This does not prevent the faith of Israel from being still more strengthened and deepened by stressing the unique and jealous nature of Yahweh, who could not bear other gods beside him. This faith finds theological expression in two reflective passages on the relations of Israel with the nations: the table of nations in chapter 10 of Genesis presents all the peoples as issued from one common ancestor and destined to find harmony in spite of racial and linguistic differences which are a sign of the Creator's bounty, but which, when pride supervenes, change into a mass and can no longer understand one another and who make war on one another. The other passage is limited to a single verse (Dt. 32.8)[1] which must be read according to the Greek version: "When the Most High divided the lands among the nations, when he separated the children of men, when he fixed the boundaries of the peoples according to the number of the bene El, Jacob was Yahweh's share, Israel the lot that fell to him." Other gods are not denied and in another text Deuteronomy even equates them to the stars (4.19). Under the influence of an even more thorough-going monotheism, the gods of the peoples are presented as subject to Yahweh and reduced to the rank of angels who exercise over the peoples subject to their dominion a right of protection—protection which is often badly carried out, a point which emerges from Psalm 82, which shows the bene El, chiefs of the peoples, receiving from the God of Israel a sentence of condemnation for having failed in their

---

[1] According to the reading of the Massoretic text "according to the number of the sons of Israel" the text is rather puzzling; we should have to assume that there were as many peoples as descendants of Jacob (12 or 70 according to Gen. 46.27); in any case it expresses the idea that Israel is the standard of the nations.

essential charge, the exercise of justice. From powers auxiliary to Yahweh, these beings can, like all angels, degenerate into opposing powers. Such a reflection bears witness of a great solicitude with regard to the nations. If there is a veil of mourning over all the peoples (Is. 25.7) the fault lies with the host on high and with the kings appointed by the gods, by the punishment of whom judgment will begin and whose disappearance will free the peoples from their yoke (Is. 24.21; Jer. 46.25). Freed from this tyranny, the peoples will be ready for the worship of Yahweh. The final triumph of Yahweh over all the peoples belongs only to eschatological times, but even at this time Yahweh had given in history enough proofs of his superiority to inspire the respect and even the confidence of pagan peoples who politically, in comparison with Israel, were in a position of domination. The extraordinary vitality of Israel amid ever-increasing difficulties was in itself a missionary testimony to the pagans, the power and mercifulness of Israel's God was talked about abroad[1] and people came to him to receive the benefit of it. The story of the Syrian general Naaman is a striking example of this: this officer does not accept the worship of Yahweh to the exclusion of other gods but gives him an honoured place beside his own national gods, and Naaman was certainly not the only proselyte. The rules decreed by the Deuteronomic Code concerning the admission of foreigners to the congregation of Yahweh proves that the admission of proselytes was no exception (Dt. 23.2-8). Yet at this period the mission is only centripetal. Naaman, and after him all the foreigners, come to Palestine, and more particularly to Jerusalem, which, under the influence of Isaiah and Deuteronomy, becomes the unique and necessary point of attraction for all those who desire to have a share in the benefits of the worship of Yahweh. A prophecy reproduced both by Isaiah (2) and by Micah (4) asserts that one day all nations will come and adore Yahweh in his sanctuary and that Zion will be the centre of the world towards which all peoples with one accord will make their way.[2]

---

[1] The kings of Israel had the reputation of being very merciful kings (*malke chesed*), 1 Kings 20.31.

[2] Tolerance never leads to mission. The gods of the Egyptian, Mesopotamian and Canaanite pantheons tolerated other deities beside themselves, even when a single god tended to wield the supremacy. The only exception in antiquity is constituted by Akhenaton's movement, which manifested itself by active missionary propaganda which, however, found little lasting echo among the masses.

The same hope is found in Zephaniah, who, after describing the catastrophe of the last day, goes on: "Then will I give to the peoples pure lips so that they may call upon the name of Yahweh and serve him with one accord. From beyond the rivers of Kush they will bring sacrifices and offerings unto me" (3.9-10). Jeremiah (16.19-21) also shows the nations recognizing the vanity of their idols and seeking refuge in Yahweh. Jerusalem holds an important place as the centre even in the work of the one who is rightly called "the missionary prophet of the Old Testament". Zion will be restored and its splendour will attract the peoples (Is. 54.1-3), but, beside this power of attraction, Israel will exercise a more active mission, it will be the light of the nations and the Servant will go to the peoples who are, moreover, waiting for his coming, and he will not only bring the revelation of Yahweh's crushing majesty but also the revelation of the love that wills their conversion and which, to that end,[1] accepts the suffering of death. The prophet's faith, more exclusively monotheistic than that of his predecessors, does not lead him to pronounce a final judgment on the value of pagan religion. Certainly he had depicted with remarkable irony the foolishness of the worship of idols (e.g. 44.9), but precisely because the gods of the pagans are nothing, the peoples are ready to accept Yahweh, who is the creator of all men and towards whom their aspirations unwittingly carry them. Never was the missionary ideal expressed in the Old Testament more profoundly. By sacrifice and death, the servant rediscovers the election and its indispensable corollary, the mission. The promise made to Abraham is henceforward made real. In its attempts to put its missionary programme into practice, Israel was not always able to maintain itself on the summits glimpsed by the prophet of the exile. The prophet's book itself underwent some retouching of a nationalist kind, and chapter 47, proclaiming Babylon's punishment, is very different from the passages of the Servant's mission. Necessities of the organization and defence of the post-exilic community brought a stiffening of Israel's position; having had to experience the fact that brotherly contact with other peoples led to syncretism, the rigorist policy of Nehemiah and Ezra, while delivering a salutary blow, also put an end to missionary possibilities or envisaged them

---

[1] By his death, Yahweh's servant became the martyr of his mission. Now the idea of martyrdom is incompatible with tolerance; that is why we only meet it in the realm of the religion of the jealous God, Judaism, Christianity and Islam.

only as a submission by force: the nations which will not submit will be severely punished, and certain prophets invoke upon them the worst of scourges in case of refusal of obedience (Joel 3.12-14; Zech. 14.16-21). The figure of the Servant gives place to that of the Tyrant and Inquisitor. Israel is the chosen people, that is, the privileged people which has the right to expect other peoples to humble themselves and to sacrifice themselves on its behalf; the Chronicler, in places, and the book of Esther are the most outstanding examples of this exclusiveness. However, the line inaugurated by Deutero-Isaiah was never altogether abandoned; it is continued particularly in the Psalms, which see in Jerusalem, not the place where the nations will be tolerated as slaves of Israel, but the place where they will enjoy civic freedom absolutely equal to that of the chosen people. "All were born in Zion," cries a Psalmist (Ps. 87.4). In practice, fulfilment proved difficult and it was not clear how foreign peoples could be won over to Israel's faith without at least accepting the Sabbath and circumcision. But the eschatology remained universal in outlook and never gave up the hope of a day when all peoples will adore Yahweh. Beside the eschatology, the missionary ideal is expressed, but only implicitly, in the bulk of the wisdom literature: wisdom is always presented as universal and cosmopolitan, she addresses herself to all men without reference to their national adherence, for all men issued from the same creator share a great number of common traits and identical possibilities. But in passing from the level of theory to that of accomplishment wisdom reveals itself incapable of creating anything but a moralism, and so it was absorbed by legalism, which showed itself superior for the training of man and of society but closed the door to tendencies of a universal nature.

Nevertheless, these tendencies found ways of showing themselves: the importance for the missionary ideal of the book of Jonah cannot be overstressed. Not for a single moment does this little book forget the religious superiority of Israel. The unique power of Yahweh blazes forth even to the eyes of the sailors, but all Israel's prerogatives are placed at the service of the nations; as in the case of Yahweh's servant, the mission is carried out to the detriment of Israel, the spoliation of whom is to enrich the heathen and, by presenting the most serious truths in a form full of irony, the author makes it clear that the only unsympathetic character is an Israelite and even a prophet. The nations will know in their turn that Israel's God is not only the master of universal history, but that he is merciful and compassionate and that his kingship is fulfilled in his love. From that point onwards there is no need to go to Jerusalem; it is possible to be at the same time a citizen of Nineveh and a worshipper of Yahweh. More briefly, but with an accent that speaks volumes about the progress of universalism, we find the prospects of salvation opened to the nations in prophetic passages. The prophet Malachi, a lucid and stern critic of cultic formalism, contrasts the temple sacrifices with the sacrifice of incense and the pure offering presented to the name of Yahweh in any place among the nations from East to West where his name is great[1] (1.11). Whether we must interpret this verse of a heathen cult which, under cover of its own gods was in fact addressed to Yahweh or see in it a prophecy of eschatological times, it is the testimony of a state of mind for which the wall of partition is broken down. The universal outlook of Is. 19.16-25 is based on the same viewpoint: Israel will be reconciled with its great oppressors of former days, Egypt and Assyria, and the three together will serve Yahweh.[2] When such texts are compared with the majority of oracles on the nations, the extent of the way travelled can be measured. So that Israel should get outside its national limits and forget the insults and sufferings it had undergone, it had to win a victory over itself, but by this victory it rediscovered its real

[1] An outline and discussion of the various interpretations of Malachi 1.11 will be found in the typewritten thesis of Th. Chary, *Le culte dans la littérature prophétique exilienne et postexilienne*, p. 195. Four solutions share the critics' favour: (a) allusion to the worship of proselytes; (b) worship of the Jews of the diaspora; (c) a syncretistic ideal; (d) an eschatological view. We feel that the solution must be sought in a combination of solutions (c) and (d). The prophet saw among other nations, particularly in the worship of the god of heaven Ahura Mazda, a pure offering, and such manifestations were for him the sign of the near approach in eschatological times of a worship that would surpass all that was at present observed; that is why we can subscribe to the assertion of a contemporary scholar who calls this verse "a saying whose universalism could only be further surpassed by the word of Jesus about the worship of God in spirit and in truth" (De Liagre Böhl, "Missions- und Erwählungsgedanke in Alt Israel", *Festschrift A. Bertholet*, p. 94).

[2] The text of Isaiah 19.16-25 is probably earlier than that of Malachi, who was moreover able to get inspiration from it as well as from Jonah and from Isaiah 66.20-21, and might date from the end of the Persian domination (fifth century). The prophet's viewpoint is not purely historical; Assyria had long ceased to exist; these nations are then types of the mass of pagan nations called to share in the benefit of the covenant formerly concluded with Abraham (Ps. 47.10). Cf. A. Feuillet, "Un sommet religieux dans l'Ancien Testament", *Recherches de Science religieuse*, 1951 (Mélanges J. Lebreton), pp. 65f.

self with an awareness clearer than ever of its election for the service and glory of God alone.

E. MIRACLES

Since nature and history are both creations incessantly renewed by God, there is no room in the Old Testament for miracles in the sense of a breaking of the laws of nature or history. The only miracle is God himself, who is ever a wonderful God and whose works inspire either dread, or gratitude and joy, and as there is no limit to God's power everything is miraculous. Sayings in proverbial form gave popular expression to this faith in Yahweh's limitless power: "Is there anything too wonderful for Yahweh?" (Gen. 18.14). "Nothing prevents Yahweh from giving the victory, whether by small or by great means" (1 Sam. 14.6) and when Israel reached a conception of the universe governed by fixed laws, those very laws did not fail to arouse more admiration than rational reflection (Jer. 5.24; 8.7; Ps. 8.4; 19.5-7; 104.5-9; 148.6; Job 5.9; 38.16): God "filling the heavens and the earth" (Jer. 23.24) could, it was thought, subject these very laws to his pleasure. Still further, history is never envisaged as the unfolding of events by virtue of immanent laws, but as a perpetual creation of God. The history of the people of Israel as a whole is always considered as the only and the great miracle: "I shall make a covenant with thee. In the sight of all the people, I shall perform wonders (niphla'ot) such as have not been performed in any land or in any nation. The people which surrounds thee shall see what Yahweh is able to do, for it is a terrible thing that I shall do for thee" (Ex. 34.10). The chosen people is the most obvious sign of God's presence; but at certain moments this presence is more intensely manifested and it is then that what we popularly call a miracle takes place. Within the revelation miracles mark culminating or turning-points. This aspect of miracles, as wide as it is diffuse, is confirmed by the language. The fact that Hebrew has not one but several terms to signify miracle attests its frequency, but also its fluidity. Everywhere where God is found, there is miracle; that is why the latter is called beri'ah, creation (Num. 16.30; Ex. 34.10; Jer. 31.22; Is. 48.7), it is the manifestation of the holy and terrible God, nora' (Ex. 34.10; 2 Sam. 7.23), it is the effect of the sovereign and powerful God, a gedolah or a geburah (Ps. 20.7;

106.2) or of the transcendent hidden God whose very name is wonderful, a *pele'* (Ps. 77.12-15; 78.12; 88.11; 89.6) or more often *niphla'* (plural *niphla'ot*). This term is applied by Job to the miracles of nature (Job 9.10; 37.19) and by the Psalms and Isaiah to the miracles of history, mainly to those of the Exodus already interpreted as types (Ps. 78.4, 11, 12, 32; 105.5; 107.24-31; Mic. 7.15; Is. 28.19; 29.14) and, in one passage, to the divine prerogatives of the Messianic sovereign (Is. 9.5).

For the Old Testament the essential mark of a miracle does not lie in its "miraculous" character, but in the power of revelation that it contains, two realities which, as we show elsewhere, did not necessarily overlap; and so the two terms which most frequently designate miracle insist less on its nature than on its function: the word *'ot*, whose primary sense is one of sign, does not in any way evoke the idea of a miracle, and *mophet*, which is often associated with it, evokes the revelatory intensity which may be linked with a sign and which according to the circumstances provokes admiration or fear. So the scope of the miracle is determined by its significance as a sign. Quite ordinary facts or phenomena can become signs: the almond branch seen by Jeremiah (1.11) was a thoroughly natural spectacle, but, through the word given to the prophet and the faith which this word creates, it assumes the value of a sign. The crossing of the Red Sea only became a miracle by a concatenation of circumstances, firstly the presence of the Israelites at that particular moment, and still more that of Moses who gives to these circumstances a religious interpretation. This is a point whose importance must be stressed: a fact is not a sign and a miracle except as a function of the time in which it takes place; now in the Old Testament there are times of miracles which coincide with a crisis and consequently call for an intensification of revelation. The times when miracles flourish are found at the time of the Exodus, at the dawn of the prophetic age with Elijah and Elisha, when the power of Yahweh had to be asserted against that of the baalim, at the time of Isaiah, when the advent of a world empire made the establishment of Yahweh's kingdom improbable for many, finally during the exile when the promised deliverance was to be in proportion to the suffering endured. The link of the miracle with the time assures it in the course of history certain common features.

(*a*) The aspect as a sign is apparent in the close connection between miracle and prophet. Even though it is probable that sometimes a miracle was invented to express the very strong impression aroused by a prophet or to increase the prophet's greatness—this is what happened in the case of Elisha, whose disciples wished to raise him to the same level as his master Elijah—the person of the prophet is almost indispensable to the miracle. The prophet, being a man of God, can perform to some extent in God's stead miracles of which God is the author: Isaiah allows it to be understood that he could perform on the spot the sign suggested to Ahaz (Is. 7.11), but the greatest miracle is the person of the prophet himself.

(b) The miracle is a sign to strengthen faith (Ex. 4.1ff.; 7.8ff.); the power of miracles is granted to Moses only with a view to confirming the promise.

(c) The miracle serving as a sign and as a testimony requires the presence of witnesses; the witnesses are at the same time the people of Israel and other nations. Whether it be the Egyptians at the time of the Exodus, the Assyrians under Sennacherib before Jerusalem, or the Babylonians at the end of the exile, at the sight of the superiority of Israel's God the heathen must be convinced or hardened (Is. 40.5; 42.12; 45.6; 48.20; 52.10).

(d) A sign foretells what is going to happen. The miracles of the Old Testament all have an eschatological bearing, they are signs announcing new heavens and a new earth and the real habitation of Yahweh among his people which was expected with the coming of God's kingdom. If faith produces the miracle, absence of faith does not, however, bring its suppression, just the contrary; when the period of prophetic inspiration is considered closed, we see a resurgence of miracles, and seeking for the miracle then becomes a substitute for faith. This tendency, already very obvious in the book of Chronicles (e.g. 2 Chr. 20), grows steadily in apocryphal literature (2 Macc. 1.19; 3.23; 2 Macc. 2.21; 4 Esdr. 13.44-47) where the spectacular character of miracles shows that instead of being superimposed on faith they were an object of research.

The following classification of the Old Testament miracles can be given:

(a) The majority of them are due to the coincidence of natural phenomena:[1] the miracle of the Red Sea is due on the one hand

---

[1] According to Phythian-Adams, *The Call of Israel*, p. 180, there was in the Exodus miracle a threefold coincidence; material—the one we have already pointed

to the ebbing of the waters which allowed the Israelites dry passage and to the flowing back which caused the drowning of the Egyptians, and on the other hand to a sandstorm which concealed the Israelites from the sight of their enemies. Similarly the crossing of the Jordan (Josh. 3.16) is the crossing of a ford which tradition has amplified, and at the basis of the fall of Jericho there is probably an earthquake. In none of these cases does the miracle break the order of nature; in the majority of them there is rather a question of returning nature to its original state, as in the miracles of cure and resurrection.

(b) However, it does happen that the miracle contradicts the most elementary cosmic laws: the most typical case is the one told in the book of Kings (2 Kings 20.10). It was certainly known from the most ancient times that a body's shadow was always seen on the side opposite the light, and that a shadow going in the other direction was going counter to the natural order; nor could anybody seriously think that an iron axe could float by the simple power of a piece of wood (2 Kings 6.2-7).

(c) In certain cases the miracle can be a simple creation of language. The most extraordinary of the Old Testament miracles, the staying of the sun at Joshua's command, is due to the literal interpretation of a poetic flight: "Sun, stand thou still upon Gibeon" (Josh. 10.12). In exhortation ready use was also made of images which enlarged events to the level of miracles (e.g. Josh. 24.7). We can thus state that in Israel the action of language was never used in the direction of rationalization of miracle.

F. PROVIDENCE AND THEODICY

In using the term Providence, we must avoid interpreting it in the light of the rationalist conception, of a god as impersonal as possible who directs events from afar while ensuring balance and harmony everywhere. The personality and holiness of the God of the Old Testament are too dynamic to be satisfied with an aloof ordering of things, but precisely Yahweh's intervention in the world and his will to leave nothing outside his sovereignty give

out; spiritual—the presence of a prophet-interpreter of the events; finally sacramental—because in the nature of the phenomena there was a reservoir of spiritual significance.

us the authority to speak of a biblical notion of providence which is exercised at the same time in creation and in history.

The creation is maintained, not by virtue of autonomous laws, but by Yahweh's free will; its duration is eternal only in so far as Yahweh is pleased to preserve it. On the whole the biblical view is not directed towards the preservation of the world, but towards its transformation. The teaching of the prophets concerning creation is dominated by the hope of new heavens and a new earth, so that they see in the present world, before all else, the signs of catastrophe, foreshadowing the great change. Even the book of Job, which is unaware of eschatology, gives a vision of creation which is far from making equilibrium and harmony obvious, as happens in Psalm 104 for example. From the sight of the irrational and frightening, man should draw lessons of faith in providence, for in God the display of power is always a manifestation of life, and consequently a source of hope. Another sage, Ecclesiastes, after putting the divine providence into momentary doubt, finally succeeds, in the discovery that God does all things at the right time, in finding a solution which allows him to accept life not only with resignation, but even with joy.

Divine providence in history is exercised, first and foremost, in favour of Israel and is implied by the very fact of election and of belonging; but Yahweh's interest in Israel obliges him, to some extent, to glance also at the nations, either by punishing them when they oppose the realization of that election (for example the Canaanites at the time of the conquest) or by using them to chastise his people when the latter forgets the conditions attached to its election (Amos 3.2). At other times Yahweh's intervention among the nations is motivated by his justice (Amos 1); the Yahwist shows us the iniquity of the inhabitants of Sodom, who were not Israelites, calling forth Yahweh's intervention (Gen. 18.20-21). This defence of justice was not specially peculiar to Israel's God, but what gives the particular tonality to the biblical affirmation of providence is the eschatological foundation of its message. Before the vision of the kingdom that is coming, sectional barriers fall and the coming of that kingdom is so certain that all present history can have no other purpose than to be used in its coming, and even the most open opposition to this kingdom will be used for its triumph (e.g. Gog and Magog's assault in Ez. 38). Faith in Yahweh's universal providence found less dynamic expression, but expression which however does not lack greatness, in the priestly theology, which by presenting all things as fixed and maintained by divine decree expresses in its own way that nothing could happen outside the eternal plans of God.

Just as there can be no chance in the life of peoples, so individuals taken one by one are the object of the divine providence. The Old Testament is not unaware of chance, but by calling it an encounter (*miqreh*) it registers its objectivity and does not put it outside God's plan. Moreover, for a God who shows so little rationality as Yahweh, the element of chance is almost normal and ignorance of second causes also makes apparently contradictory actions to be attributed to Yahweh. Providence, in the life of individuals, is most frequently manifested at certain particularly outstanding moments of that life, but the Old Testament is also acquainted with several examples of lives which are in themselves a manifestation of providence. Thus Joseph's life is entirely destined to illustrate the theme of the plan of God who thwarts the designs of men; Jeremiah's life, which existed as a thought of God's before being manifested in history, has no unity or sense apart from the carrying out of that plan; finally the life of Yahweh's servant must, through the most mysterious of wayfarings, carry out God's redeeming plan. But besides those precise examples, conceptions such as the " bundle of life "[1] (*tseror hachayyim* : 1 Sam. 25.29) and the book of life (Ps. 69.29) and especially prayers like Ps. 139 give sufficient evidence of how far individual life was considered as directed by a higher will.

The assertion of the government of the world and of all history by God is so evident for the Old Testament that the recognition of evil does not succeed in throwing serious doubt upon it. Misfortune itself comes from Yahweh : " Is there misfortune in the city without God being the author of it ", cries Amos (3.6). In the Yahwist religion, which we distinguish from the popular religion which had a strong admixture of pagan elements, the evil spirits are subject to Yahweh, who uses them at his will with the object of chastising those who deserve his anger, for the ethical stress of Israel's religion puts suffering in relationship with sin; historians, prophets and wisdom writers are agreed in declaring that sin brings

---

[1] This expression is also found in one of the Qumran hymns, the Hodayoth: " I praise thee, Adonai, that thou hast placed my nephesh in the *tseror chayyim* " (cf. *ZAW*, 1949-50, p. 258; cf. also Ecclus. 6.16).

suffering, whilst a return to God brings happiness. Since this assertion is, however, often contradicted by the facts attenuations were introduced into it which never brought harm to faith in providence and did not open the door to a dualist conception. The misfortune of the righteous could be a means of education; this point of view, already stated by the book of Proverbs (3.12 : God chastens the one he loves), is developed at length by the author of Elihu's speech (Job 33.19ff.; 36.7ff.). It was considered also that in certain individuals suffering could have the value of substitutionary expiation, for example with Hosea, Jeremiah and especially the Servant of Yahweh. It even happened that the most inexplicable and unjust misfortune brought the one who was struck by it to a deeper understanding of the intentions of the divine providence[1] (Job and Ps. 73) for God's power and saving intention could, in the end, only make all things work together for the triumph of his glory.

BIBLIOGRAPHY

A. FAITH AND HISTORY

CRIADO, R., *La teologia de la historia en el antiguo Testamento*, Madrid 1954.

DIETRICH, DE S., *Le dessein de Dieu*, Neuchâtel et Paris 1946.

EISSFELDT, O., "Geschichtliches und Übergeschichtliches im A.T.", *ThStKr* Bd. 109 H. 2, 1947.

HEMPEL, J., *Altes Testament und Geschichte*, Gütersloh 1930.
    "Die Mehrdeutigkeit der Geschichte als Problem der prophetischen Theologie", *Nachrichten der Göttinger Gesellsch. d. Wissensch.*, 1936.
    Glaube, Mythus und Geschichte im A.T., Berlin 1954.

HÖLSCHER, G., *Die Anfänge der hebräischen Geschichtsschreibung*, Heidelberg 1942.

---

[1] These believers, whom we can link to the stream represented by "the poor " of Israel, found in the *qirbat elohim* (Ps. 73.28) the solution to the problem of providence and through that closed the way to the problem of theodicy. This attitude re-echoes the one that has been defined by Karl Jaspers, *Introduction à la philosophie*, French trans. 1951, p. 54: "When living in the world one has struggled towards the good believing that one is allowing oneself to be led by God, and when one finally runs into a setback, there remains only this single immeasurable reality: God Is." The subject of the poor in Israel has received its most recent treatment in a very suggestive manner by A. Gelin, *Les pauvres de Yahweh* (coll. Témoins de Dieu, 14), Paris 1953.

JACOB, ED., *La tradition historique en Israël*, Montpellier 1946.

JIRKU, A., *Die älteste Geschichte Israels im Rahmen lehrhafter Darstellungen*, Leipzig 1917.

NIEBUHR, R., *Foi et histoire*, Neuchâtel et Paris 1954.

NORTH, C. R., *The Old Testament Interpretation of History*, London 1946.

NOTH, M., "Die Historisierung des Mythos", *Christentum u. Wissenschaft*, 1928, p. 265.

    Überlieferungsgeschichte des Pentateuch, Stuttgart 1948.

    Geschichte und Gotteswort im A.T. Bonner Akadem. Reden 1949, English translation in *Bulletin of the John Rylands Library, Manchester* 1950, pp. 194ff.

    Das Geschichtsverständnis der alttest. Apokalyptik, Cologne 1954.

ÖSTBORN, G., "Yahweh's Words and Deeds. A preliminary study into the O.T. interpretation of history", *UUA* 1951.

PROCKSCH, O., *Geschichtsbetrachtung und geschichtliche Überlieferung bei den vorexilischen Propheten*, 1902.

    "Die Geschichte als Glaubensinhalt", *NKZ*, 1925, p. 485.

RAD, G. VON, *Das Geschichtsbild des Chronistischen Werkes*, BZAW, Stuttgart 1930.

    Das formgeschichtliche Problem des Hexateuchs, 1938.

    "Theologische Geschichtsschreibung im A.T.", *ThZ*, 1948, p. 161.

    Deuteronomiumstudien, 1948.

RIEGER, J., *Die Bedeutung der Geschichte für die Verkündigung des Amos und Hosea*, Giessen 1929.

ROBINSON, H. WHEELER, *Redemption and Revelation in the Actuality of History*, London 1942.

RUST, E. C., *The Christian Understanding of History*, London 1946.

SENARCLENS, DE J., *Le mystère de l'histoire*, Geneva.

SÖDERBLOM, N., *Dieu vivant dans l'histoire*, Paris 1937.

TROELTSCH, E., "Glaube und Ethos der hebr. Propheten", *Gesammelte Schriften IV*, p. 34.

WEISER, A., *Glaube und Geschichte im A.T.*, Stuttgart 1931.

B. ELECTION

CASPARI, W., "Beweggründe der Erwählung nach dem A.T.", *NKZ*, 1921, p. 202.

DAHL, N. A., *Das Volk Gottes*, Oslo 1941.

DANELL, G. A., *Studies in the name Israel in the O.T.*, Uppsala 1946.

EICHRODT, W., *Israel in der Weissagung des A.T.*, Zürich 1952.
GALLING, K., *Die Erwählungstraditionen Israels*, BZAW 48, Giessen 1928.
HESSE, FR., *Das Verstockungsproblem im A.T.*, BZAW 74, Berlin 1955.
HERTZBERG, H. W., *Werdende Kirche im A.T.*, *Theol Existenz heute*, Munich 1950.
LINDHAGEN, C., *The Servant Motif in the O.T.*, Uppsala 1950.
PORTEOUS, N. W., "Volk und Gottesvolk im A.T.", *Theol. Aufsätze Karl Barth zum 50. Geburtstag*, 1936, p. 146.
POWIS SMITH, J. M., "The Chosen People", *American Journal of Semitic Language*, 1928, 29, p. 73.
RAD, G. VON, *Das Gottesvolk im Deuteronomium*, Stuttgart 1929.
ROST, L., *Die Vorstufen von Kirche und Synagoge im A.T.*, Stuttgart 1938.
ROWLEY, H. H., *The Biblical Doctrine of Election*, London 1950.
SCHOEPS, H. J., "Haggadisches zur Auserwählung Israels", *Aus frühchrist-licher Zeit*, 1950, p. 184.
STAERK, W., "Zum alttestamentlichen Erwählungsglauben", *ZAW*, 1937, pp. 1ff.
VRIEZEN, TH. C., *Die Erwählung Israels nach dem A.T.*, Zürich 1953.

C. THE COVENANT

BEGRICH, J., "Berit. Ein Beitrag zur Erfassung einer alttestamentlichen Denkform", *ZAW*, 1944, pp. 1ff.
GEHMAN, HENRY S., "The Covenant. The O.T. foundation of the Church", *Theology to-day*, 1950, p. 26.
HOEPERS, M., *Der neue Bund bei den Propheten*, Fribourg en Br. 1933.
IMSCHOOT, P. VAN, "L'esprit de Yahweh et l'alliance nouvelle dans l'A.T.", *Eph. th. lov.*, 1936, p. 201.
          "L'alliance dans l'A.T.", *NRth*, Louvain 1952, p. 785.
KARGE, P., *Geschichte des Bundesgedankens im A.T.*, Alttestamentliche Abhandlungen 2, 1-4, Münster 1910.
KRAETZSCHMAR, R., *Die Bundesvorstellung im A.T. in ihrer geschichtlichen Entwicklung*, Marburg 1896.
LOHMEYER, ERNST, *Diatheke*, Leipzig 1913.
PEDERSEN, JOHS., *Der Eid bei den Semitem*, Leipzig 1914.

D. THE MISSION

BERTHOLET, A., *Die Stellung der Israeliten und der Juden zu den Fremden*, Freiburg i.B & Leipzig 1896.
BERTRAM, G., "Das antike Judentum als Missionsreligion", *Rosen: Juden und Phönizier*, Tübingen 1929.

BLAUW, JOH., *Goden en Mensen. Plaats en Betekenis van de Heidenen in de heilige Schrift*, Groningen 1950.

BÖHL, F. M. TH. DE LIAGRE, "Missions-und Erwählungsgedanke in Altisrael", *Festschrift A. Bertholet*, p. 77.

CAUSSE, A., *Israël et la vision de l'humanité*, Strasbourg 1924.

EICHRODT, W., "Gottesvolk und die Völker", *Evang. Missionsmagazin*, 1942.

EISSFELDT, O., "Gott und Götzen im A.T.", *ThStKr*, 1931, p. 151.

LÖHR, M., *Der Missionsgedanke im A.T.*, Leipzig 1896.

LUBAC, DE H., *Le fondement théologique des missions*, Paris 1946.

MORGENSTERN, J., "Deutero-Isaiah's terminology for 'Universal God'", *JBL*, 1943, p. 269.

RAGUIN, Y., *Théologie missionnaire de l'A.T.*, Paris 1947 (La sphère et la croix).

ROWLEY, H. H., *The Missionary Message of the O.T.*, London 1944.

SCHMÖKEL, H., *Jahwe und die Fremdvölker*, Breslau 1934.

SELLIN, E., "Der Missionsgedanke im A.T.", *Neue allgemeine Missionszeitschrift*, 1925.

STAERK, W., "Ursprung und Grenzen der Missionskraft der alttestamentlichen Religion", *Theol. Blätter*, 1925.

E. MIRACLES

BALLA, E., "Das Problem des Leidens in der Geschichte der isr.-jüd. Religion", *Eucharisterion (Gunkel Festschrift)*, 1923, p. 214.

EICHRODT, W., "Vorsehungsglaube und Theodizee im A.T." (*Festschrift O. Procksch*), 1934, p. 45.

KELLER, C. A., *Das Wort OTH als Offenbarungszeichen Gottes*, Bâle 1946.

KNIGHT, H., "The O.T. conception of miracle", *Scottish Journal of Theology*, 1952, p. 355.

PEAKE, A. S., *The Problem of Suffering in the O.T.*, London 1904.

ROBINSON, H. WHEELER, "The nature miracles of the O.T.", *JTS*, 1944, p. 1.

ROWLEY, H. H., *Submission in Suffering*, Cardiff 1951.

V. GOD IN INSTITUTIONS

A. MINISTRIES

THE people's election does not create among the members of that nation an equality that removes all precedence. The Old Testament has strong convictions on the necessity of leaders. One ancient Bedouin poem from Arabia, which compares leaders and led with the poles and pegs of the tent,[1] reflects quite faithfully the feelings of Israel which, despite all the developments that took place in the course of history, was always able to avoid despotism by the chief and dictatorship of the people. The various offices that we see exercised among the people and in which religious and secular elements are mingled as well as institutional and charismatic elements, are primarily representative offices: whether it concerns leadership, justice or teaching, the ministry's objective is to show in concrete form an activity which is assumed in a perfect form by God himself. To exercise a ministry implies a more direct relationship with God, an individual election within the general election; by virtue of this election the chosen individuals are not aloof from the people; as the latter's representatives before God they point out to the people the way that it is right to follow in order to remain faithful to their vocation. And so the elect have a great responsibility before God, whose representatives they are, and before the people, which behaves in accordance with the example that the elect provide. That is why the prophets apportion the chief blame to the leaders, kings, priests and prophets who take advantage of their superior position to lead the people astray instead of being its servants, for their worth resides only in the call which they have received and not in some personal quality which distinguishes them from the ordinary run of mortals (e.g. Jer. 5.29ff.).

[1] " A people that lacks leaders will inevitably fall, and leaders are short where the people reigns. A tent cannot be put up only with poles, and the poles are of no value if there are no pegs. Where poles and pegs are in correct union, there only what is set up stands, complete " (quoted by Nöldeke, *Delectus*, p. 4, II, 8-10, from A. Bertholet, *Histoire de la civilisation d'Israël*, French trans., p. 139, E.T. London 1926).

(a) The King

Among the human beings set apart by God to be his more especial representatives and the mediators of his gifts, the king occupies the most important place. According to one tendency which has a wide following, the king is the only channel by which divine realities are accessible to men. In a series of studies which appeared twenty years ago and which were devoted to the general subject of myth and ritual, several English scholars, taking up the ideas put forward by the great Norwegian exegete S. Mowinckel ten years earlier, insisted on the dramatic character of the cult and on the need of dramatic representation for the efficacy of the myth which underlay it. Taken up in their turn by other Scandinavian scholars, these ideas gave birth to what is already called the Uppsala school, and which has no other ambition than to set a new interpretation of the Old Testament, founded on the priority of ritual and tradition, against historical and documentary interpretation.[1] The essential points of this cultic drama, traces of which can be found, it is thought, in texts apparently far removed· from any cultic viewpoint, have been summarized in the following way: (a) struggle of the god represented by and incarnate in the king and ending in the king's victory over opposing mythical forces; (b) proclamation of the king's victory through the whole world; (c) adjuration to the king to reign justly; (d) assumption of the regalia; (e) the king receives sacramental food, baptism by water and unction of oil; (f) proclamation of the king as the son of God;

---

[1] The subject has given rise to a considerable literature; the most complete bibliographical material is to be found in the book of J. de Fraine (1954). In speaking of the Uppsala school, we must not forget that the work that it has produced would not have seen the light without that of the English school, the Myth and Ritual group whose principal representative is S. H. Hooke. The methods of this school have been applied to the study of quite diverse subjects, particularly to several prophets (Isaiah, Obadiah, Joel); one of the most systematic applications has been made by H. Riesenfeld, *Jésus transfiguré* (published in French, Lund 1947); the reading of this book permits us to form an idea of the value and also the exaggerations of this method. It must be pointed out that even in Scandinavia these ideas did not meet with unanimous agreement; in his last work, *Han som Kommer* (He that cometh), p. 47, Mowinckel insists on the fundamental importance of the Yahwist religion, that is on a religion with a historical foundation, in order to understand the Israelite monarchy. One of the best criticisms of this method is that of M. Noth, who points out the excessive simplifications and the disregard of historical results of which this school unfortunately gives too many examples ("Gott, König und Volk", *ZThK*, 1950, pp. 157-191).

(g) the king's installation on God's throne; (h) the sacred marriage of the king. The initial and final acts of this drama may be summarized by the terms death and resurrection, for in the background of this drama there is the rite of the dying and rising god about whom we know to-day the extent to which he formed the centre of the Sumerian, Babylonian and Canaanite religions, and whose main purpose was to explain the mystery of life and to assure, by means of rites, the upkeep of that life in the realms of nature and of human life, which were almost always intermingled. In these religions, kingship is part of a fixed framework and the person of the king is of secondary importance in relation to the pattern which he incarnates and whose continuity he is to assure. Now it is impossible to find this pattern as such in the Old Testament. There is no doubt that Israel had mythical traditions, with corresponding rites, and the kingship, David's particularly, is one of the places where this heritage is particularly noticeable; but to see in the kingship the simple transposition on to the historical plane of a mythical pattern would be to do violence to the texts. The monarchy in Israel has its history and that history, so human and so full of vicissitude, has nothing in common with the rigidity which myth requires, and it is far from expressing always God's will. The history of Israel begins with the election of a people and with the covenant entered upon by God with the mass of that people, of which every member is clad with royal and priestly dignity. The chiefs who lead this people owe their higher rank to their gifts and to their noteworthy actions, and especially to the fact of having been chosen by the people to safeguard its interests and energies. It is also the people that chose the kings, when political and military considerations led the people to opt for this régime, which had so little in common with its social and religious structure. The king is chosen by God and by the people: "I will belong to him who has been chosen by Yahweh, by this people and by all the men of Israel", as one of the king's servants expresses himself (2 Sam. 16.18); the anointing[1] which accompanies the choosing of a king is not the communication of an extraordinary

---

[1] Anointing is also the communication of a power by the gift of the spirit; thanks to the anointing the spirit rests permanently on a man instead of acting intermittently (1 Sam. 16.13; 2 Sam. 23.2; Is. 11.2). But the spirit is never presented as a force which transforms the man's nature; it always remains a grace which God is free to withdraw at any moment. Cf. North, *ZAW*, 1932, p. 30, and D. Lys, "L'onction dans la Bible", *EThR*, 1954, p. 3.

power of life, for objects also were anointed (Gen. 31.13; Ex. 30.26; Dan. 9.24), but rather a gesture expressing the king's belonging to Yahweh and consequently his close dependence; being a ritual gesture it requires the presence of a specially qualified person, priest or cultic prophet, but it is none the less conferred by the entire people (2 Sam. 2.4). The divine and at the same time popular origin of kingship is a feature common to the entire Israelite monarchy, though the latter developed quite differently in the northern and southern kingdoms. In the kingdom of Israel, the king is a charismatic figure chosen by Yahweh, or by the people on Yahweh's indication, his charism is not transmissible and at his death he is replaced by a person whom the spirit will raise up at that moment. It can be asserted that this was the specific form of Israelite monarchy and the one which was most in harmony with the notion of an elect people; for such a mentality monarchy was neither necessary nor indispensable, and a prophet like Hosea considers that it is better to remain without a king than to establish kings to preserve the principle of the monarchy while doing without Yahweh (8.4ff.). The only attested dynasties for the northern kingdom, Omri's and Jehu's, had merely an episodic character because of this order of things. In Judah, on the other hand, the Davidic dynasty lasted for more than four centuries, thanks in part to a divine promise made to David, and partly, also, to the support of the people, who took the side of the legitimate claimant each time that the throne became vacant and consequently favourable ground for a palace revolution (2 Kings 14.21; 21.24; 23.30). The circumstances in which the biblical books were composed mean that we are much better informed about the Jerusalem monarchy. The Psalms, which are the most valuable source, deal with this monarchy only, which answered only distantly to what was peculiar to Israelite tradition. The Jerusalem monarchy bears the mark of the Canaanite heritage and in it the king plays a part very like the one he holds in neighbouring countries, yet without being absorbed into a common pattern. The term son of God is currently given to the king, though it must be understood in the sense of an adoption and not of a begetting (2 Sam. 7.14; Ps. 2.7; 89.26). In a passage which the exegetes have emended often with more ingenuity than scruple, the king is even called god. In the present state of the text the words of Psalm 45 can only be addressed to the king: "Thy throne, O Elohim, is an eternal throne"; royal ideology reaches its highest point in this passage, but doubtless it is entirely right to remember in connection with this text that "one swallow does not make a summer",[1] and that Old Testament teaching viewed as a whole always clearly asserts the king's subordination to Yahweh. The king is the channel of divine blessings; it is he who really assures the life of the people, which would be doomed to disaster apart from his presence (Lam. 4.20), he is the lamp of Israel (2 Sam. 21.17), he is responsible for the country's prosperity and for its calamities, he, thanks to his righteousness, which must be understood in a religious rather than a moral sense, causes the corn to grow (Ps. 72.16; 2 Sam. 21.1); to him is ascribed as to a god the power of healing (2 Kings 5.7); his knowledge is like that of one of Elohim's angels, that is to say supernatural (2 Sam. 14.17); he is the people's shield (Ps. 84.10), and it is significant to notice that in one and the same text the same title is simultaneously applied to the king and to God (Ps. 84.12; 47.10 and 89.19). The picture of the king's religious rôle may be completed by ascribing to him certain prerogatives of the high priests who, after the exile, continued his functions.[2] But despite the interest that they offer, none of these texts permits us to draw the conclusion that in the temple at Jerusalem there existed an annual feast coinciding with the New Year Festival, and including a dramatic representation of Yahweh's struggle against the powers of chaos and in the course of which the king played the part of the servant, at first humiliated and then victorious over the kings of the earth. On the other hand, it must not be forgotten that if the king could incarnate and express the consciousness of the nation, he was not the only one who could do so. By virtue of the principle of "corporate personality" and of the fluidity of the relationships between the individual and

---

[1] This verse has always intrigued the exegetes; without mentioning the many textual corrections, sometimes very cavalier, let us mention the possibility in the present state of the Massoretic text of translating: Thy throne is divine (as in 2 Chr. 9.8) or: thy throne is like Elohim's, the preposition "like" being understood. Even in admitting that the king is treated as Elohim—which seems to us the correct reading—it must be borne in mind that the term *'elohim* has a variety of shades of meaning which forbid our speaking of a real deification.

[2] Many other elements in the royal ritual had a religious significance, such as the seven steps of Solomon's throne, the number seven representing the divine perfection (1 Kings 10.18). But on the point of the monarchy in Jerusalem it is difficult to define where the idealization of the king lies, and on the other hand where the reaction of eschatological messianism on the monarchy is manifested; in the reckoning by which the king only typifies the Messiah, his person is honoured by reference to another person.

society which such a principle implies, each individual could typify the people in his own life;[1] that is why behind the individuals who pray in the Psalms there lurks no rite of a democratized and decayed ideology of kingship as is declared by disciples of the Uppsala school, but the real experience of an individual—who on occasion may be a king—who because he belongs to Israel, can incarnate in himself the whole of his people.

The Old Testament observes and always stresses very strongly the limit which separates the king from God. The true king and the true throne are to be found in heaven, from where Yahweh directs world history (cf. Ps. 33.13; 29.10; 103.19), and if the Chronicler speaks of Solomon as "sitting on the throne of Yahweh" (1 Chr. 29.23) instead of the throne of David, he is less intent on insisting on the religious rôle of the king's person than on that of the Davidic dynasty from which the Messiah will come as a guarantee of the presence of God on earth. The king's duties are, moreover, no less great than his privileges. The king can only be God's representative if he observes in his life absolute obedience to God, for the fact that he sits on the throne and even that he has the advantage of a promise does not *ipso facto* confer on him righteousness and equity. Prayers on his behalf by his subjects are indispensable to him (Ps. 72.15) and Deuteronomy, which is a new charter of the people and which completes that of Sinai by introducing kingship as a necessary element in the people's life, insists very strongly on this subordination. The king's foremost task will be the study of the words of the torah; he will thus avoid "growing proud beyond his brethren" (Dt. 17.20) and Jeremiah declares that there is no other knowledge of Yahweh, that is to say no other bond with Yahweh than by exercising justice and doing right to the poor (22.16). Throughout history the prophets reminded royalty of its duties and its bounds; even David was not exempt from the censure of prophets. Confronted by the textual evidence we must recognize that in Israel's religion, apart from a few very localized attempts, the king never became a god, and to remember in this connection the definition of an historian of encyclopaedic vision:[2] "Elsewhere the king was a god, in Israel

[1] Pedersen, *Israel*, I-II, p. 23, points out that the monarchy has left almost no trace in the laws and that consequently it must have been only indifferently assimilated by the people.

[2] Henri Berr in the preface to the work of A. Lods, *Les prophètes d'Israël* (coll. L'évolution de l'humanité), 1936, p. XX.

it was God who was king." Indeed Yahweh's kingship over the people as a whole, and the figure of the ideal king projected from the earliest times into the eschatological future, were quite powerful brakes in preventing religion from ever being confused with the cult of the king's person.

(b) The Prophet

The prophet is the man of God *par excellence*; with the exceptions of Moses, David and Samuel, who participate in all the mediatorial functions at once and who were claimed by the people as a whole, the title *'ish ha 'elohim* is given to the prophets only; the reason is that the prophet stands in a particularly close relationship with God, a relationship expressed by the term "knowledge of God";[1] although this is demanded from all men, the prophets are the only ones who realize it in a perfect and exemplary way. The direct bond with God which characterizes the prophet leads us to place the prophetic centre of gravity in the individual experience of each prophet and to speak of individual prophets rather than of prophetism, but it must also be noticed that the prophets as a group form an institution which, in the course of great changes of history, presents a certain number of common features. When they first appear on Israel's historical scene, the prophets are grouped into brotherhoods and it is probably in the strongly communal life of the *nebi'im* in the times of the Judges and of Elijah that the monastic tendencies of late Judaism, one of whose aspects we can reconstitute from the Qumran documents, have their deepest roots. This communal spirit is cemented, if not created, by the presence of a sanctuary, the schools of prophets developing around the cultic centres of Ramah, Gibeah, Bethel and Gilgal. Although the recruitment of the sons of the prophets was made by spiritual affinity and not by bond of blood and although their prerogatives were different from those of the priests, it is none the less true—and it is true also for prophetism in general—that kinship with the priestly

---

[1] The fullest study of the knowledge of God among the prophets is by J. Haenel, *Das Erkennen Gottes bei den Schriftpropheten*, 1923; Mowinckel's study, *RHPR*, 1942, pp. 69ff., is shorter, but gives a clearer insight into the content of prophetic knowledge. On the same subject, cf. G. J. Botterweck, *Gott erkennen im Sprachgebrauch des A.T.*, 1951; W. Reiss, "Gott nicht kennen im A.T.", *ZAW*, 1940-41, pp. 70-98, and W. Zimmerli, *Erkenntnis Gottes nach dem Buche Ezechiel*, 1954.

functions was infinitely greater than anything that separated the two.[1] The prophets' bond with the cult appears in their frequent association with the priests, as in Hos. 4.5; Is. 28.7; Mic. 3.11; Jer. 4.9; 26.7; 29.1; Lam. 4.13, and in the fact that several of the great prophets like Jeremiah and Ezekiel actually belong to priestly families. The freedom that Amos enjoys to express his message inside a sanctuary seems to speak clearly in favour of a bond and common objective of the two functions, and it is not too rash to suppose that belonging to the priesthood constituted a ground favourable for a more complete revelation of the divine holiness and for a more intimate knowledge of the hidden God who did not readily release his mysteries. So it must be recognized that the antithesis, so often stated, particularly among the Wellhausen school, between prophets and priests, is historically highly questionable. We must not, of course, rush to the opposite extreme and make all the prophets into cultic agents, a thing that would singularly limit the freedom of prophetic inspiration, but we can say with A. R. Johnson[2] that all through history, the prophet exercises, alongside the properly prophetic function which is to transmit a message, a priestly activity through his intercession before Yahweh on the people's behalf.

The institutional aspect of prophetism is further apparent in the quite close bond which unites the prophets and the royal court; charged by the king to make God's will known to him, they are in his service and receive their subsistence from him. If this bond might sometimes be an obstacle to the sincerity of their message, as in the case of the 400 prophets at the court of Samaria (1 Kings 22.5ff.), it is more usual to find them enjoying considerable freedom with reference to the royal authority; already the prophets concerned in the Mari texts[3] express a different opinion from the king's, which the latter, moreover, hastens to follow. It is because of the reciprocal association and interaction of the two spheres, royal and prophetic, that the prophets were able to be the nation's conscience throughout the centuries.

[1] The Uppsala school would like to make all the prophets into cultic prophets (cf. particularly A. Haldar, *Associations of Cult Prophets*). It is true to say that the prophets use cultic means, but they are not enslaved by them and for certain prophets the means of access to their ministry is not through the cult.

[2] *The Cultic Prophet in Ancient Israel*, Cardiff 1944.

[3] On prophetism at Mari cf. Ad. Lods: *Studies in Old Testament Prophecy presented to Professor T. Robinson*, Edinburgh 1950, pp. 103ff.

All these sociological bonds are, however, of secondary importance to the direct and immediate calling of the prophet by Yahweh. Whether the term *nabi* is interpreted as active: he who proclaims, or as passive: he who has been called,[1] it is certain that it is the call that he has received which characterizes the prophet and which differentiates him at the same time from other men and from false prophets. The election of which he has been the object—and the prophet is always a chosen one, despite the rare use of the classical term *bachar* in connection with him—puts him in a particular relationship with God that the Old Testament calls knowledge of God. This knowledge is manifested, according to time and temperament, in various ways. In origin the *nabi* is the successor to the seer, the *ro'eh* (1 Sam. 9.9), and the visionary element under its divinatory aspect will never disappear completely from prophetic activity in which inspiration will readily lend support to a minimum of technique. The vision may assume the form of a dream, Samuel is called in a sort of dream,[2] but the great prophets are generally very wary about the type of revelation thus obtained. Jeremiah even questions whether the dream has any authority (Jer. 23.25; 27.9; 29.8), but in the book of Zechariah we find nocturnal visions which by the splitting of the personality that they seem to imply are really nothing other than dreams. Recourse to the phenomena of hypnosis and hallucination can only occasionally throw some light on prophetic experience, when a prophet is called he is not found in a state of semi-consciousness, on the contrary his sensitiveness is heightened rather: with eyes fully open on to the outside world, the prophet takes as the starting point of his vision real objects which come before his sensitive perception. Thus Jeremiah's almond branch (1.11) and Amos's basket of fruits (8.1ff.) are not set before a visionary gaze, but before normal perception; but the particular bond of knowledge, which at that moment unites the prophet to his God, charges these objects with a deeper content. We may, in this case, speak of the sublimation of a real perception.

---

[1] The etymology of *nabi'* = called was suggested by Albright, *From the Stone Age to Christianity*, p. 231; and before him by Torczyner, ZDMG, 1931, p. 322. Albright connects it with the word *nabitu* given to the king in the Hammurabi code. For more details on the etymology and the relations of the nabi with the *ro'eh* and the *chozeh*, we refer readers to H. H. Rowley, " The nature of prophecy in the light of recent study " in *Harvard Theological Review*, 1945, pp. 1-38, and reproduced in *The Servant of the Lord and other essays*, pp. 91ff.

[2] On the dream, see now Ehrlich, *Der Traum im Alten Testament*, BZAW, 1953.

Isaiah's famous vision (chap. 6) is the sublimation, that is the transformation into a celestial sanctuary and cult, of rites that were enacted before his eyes in the temple at Jerusalem. At other times, the prophetic vision is explained by the sublimation of sentiments: the prophet must be put into the category of individuals with fixed ideas, but, in his case, the fixed idea is not the result of a morbid state of mind, it is imposed on him from without by a transcendent power and henceforward forms part of his psychic background. Thus certain visions must probably be interpreted as the actualizing of sentiments that slumber in the depths of consciousness: the image comes to mind when the sentiment rises from the subconscious to assume a concrete form and to strike with a force which for the prophet takes on the value of certainty. According to all that we reckon to know about the links of the prophets with tradition, it seems quite improbable that in the majority of cases the prophetic vocation always assumed the aspect of a sudden and radical turning point. Before being called, the majority of the prophets led a life of obedience and even intimacy with God; the moment of their call is that when communion with God takes on such a constraining aspect that in the form of a vision it imposes itself as a new reality. Let us add that the kinship of many of the images with mythical representations, such as the sea, the serpent, the lion, proves that they originate, like myths, less in literary reminiscence than in certain fundamental structures of the human spirit. The great variety of the visionary element must not, however, make us neglect the other aspects that make the prophet into a man of God. It is not only through his sight and his feelings that the prophet knows God, his whole being is seized by God; very often we read that Yahweh's hand seizes the prophet (Is. 8.11; Jer. 15.17; Ez. 3.14) or that the spirit takes possession of him, making him into an 'ish haruach (Hos. 9.7), so that sometimes he finds that he is outside himself in a state of ecstasy,[1] which can be manifested as abnormal excitement, or on the other hand

---

[1] All depends obviously on the sense that is given to the word "ecstasy". If by the word the disappearance or the absorption of the subject by a superior power is understood, it is not suitable for defining the prophets' experience; but if one understands by ecstasy the concentration of a subject on an object, to a point where that object alone impinges upon him to the exclusion of all others, the use of the term seems legitimate. Lindblom, "Einige Grundfragen alttestamentlicher Wissenschaft" in Festschrift A. Bertholet, 1950, distinguishes between ecstasy of fusion (Verschmelzungsekstase), that of Plotinus and St. Teresa of Avila, and ecstasy of concentration (Konzentrationsekstase) of the prophets and of St. Paul.

by a state verging on apathy. Without awarding it pride of place in the explanation of prophetism, we cannot exclude the ecstatic element. Elijah, as though moved by a strange power, sets out to run before Ahab over a journey of several miles (1 Kings 18.12, 46), and his disciples consider it as in-no way impossible that the spirit should have caught him up and dropped him in some secluded valley so that he might die (2 Kings 2.16). Jeremiah com-pares himself to one in a drunken state (23.5), Ezekiel, more than all the others, was shaken in his psychical balance, and the simul-taneous mention of the prophet and the fool (*meshugga‘*) (e.g. Jer. 29.26) leaves no doubt about the frequency of the manifestations which it would be difficult to refuse to qualify as ecstatic. Rare, however, are the cases where this ecstasy is expressed by a real loss of personality: possession by a superior power does not prevent a conflict with the prophet's own feelings and he is never " possessed " to such a point as to be unable to hold further conversation and to enter into prayerful relations with him by whom he is addressed.[1] The particular knowledge God grants to the prophet when he takes possession of him is destined to make him into a participant and representative of that supernatural force. Prophetic knowledge is certainly of a different order from mystical union, but the two have in common an element of participation which in the case of the prophets can be quite safely defined by the term *pathos*,[2] *pathos* being the characteristic of the divine activity itself as it is mani-fested by love and by anger; and so the prophet must, in his whole bearing, make God's presence perceptible. The extraordinary, not to say extravagant, actions performed by the prophets[3] have a

[1] The technique necessary for the inspiration of the ancient *nebi'im* of Samuel's day was not altogether abandoned by the great prophets; in the main it is limited to the most spiritualized form, prayer; often the revelatory word is only com-municated to the prophet after prayer (cf. Is. 37.4, 6ff.; Jer. 11.18-20, 21ff.; 12.1-4, 5ff.); prayer may also be the starting point of the vision (Dan. 9.20); in the form of patient waiting (Hab. 2.11) or of passionate struggling with God (Jeremiah), prayer is for the prophet the condition of his ministry and the reality indispensable to its fulfilment (Jer. 15.19). It is possible that some asceticism was linked to this life of prayer; but absolute proofs are lacking.

[2] The term *pathos* for the prophet's relation with God goes back to Abram Heschel, *Die Prophetie*. This work did not have, in its time, all the attention it deserved; notice, however, that the importance of the element of pathos has been stressed by C. R. North, *The O.T. Interpretation of History*, 1946, p. 173.

[3] By symbolic actions the prophet represents events before they actually take place; it is an actualization comparable with that of past events in the cult. Externally these symbolic actions are hardly distinct from magical gestures with which they

symbolic value which not only serve to illustrate their preaching by matching deeds with words, but which must act in a determining way upon events, which they represent. Jeremiah's yoke and water-jar (chaps. 19 and 27) show that punishment is inevitable and that Yahweh has no intention of deferring it, and Hosea's marriage is for the prophet, who actually entered upon it, not only a representation, but also a participation in the suffering and the love of God, and therefore a gesture of redemption. It is not going too far to speak of the sacramental value of the prophets' symbolic actions. They are, in any case, a *verbum visibile* which might yet be unintelligible without the word proclaimed by their mouth, for it is first and foremost by what he says that the prophet reveals himself as the man of God.

"Thou shalt put words into his mouth, he shall be a mouth unto thee and thou shalt be as God to him," says Yahweh to Moses in speaking of Aaron (Ex. 4.15-16).

"Balaam said to Balak: I shall speak the words which God put in my mouth" (Num. 22.38; 23.5, 12, 16).

"I will raise up a prophet like thee and I shall put my words in his mouth" (Dt. 18.18).

"Behold I put my words in thy mouth" (Jer. 1.9 and 5.14; 15.19). The word he proclaims has been communicated to him by God in a mysterious and secret way; that is probably the sense of the word *sod* which Amos makes the first condition of all prophecy (3.7). This word is not given to the prophet once for all at the beginning of his activity. The prophet Jeremiah is typical of the accomplished disciple to whom Yahweh opens his ear each morning (Is. 50.4; Jer. 1.11, 13; 2.1; 11.9) and Ezekiel's vision of the roll does not indicate a new development in prophecy characterized by a complete and written inspiration, but simply the objective and transcendent aspect of his words. It is in the faithful reproduction of the message entrusted to him that the prophet discharges his mission and makes it authentic in the eyes of his audience. It

---

have in common a realistic, effective and often frightening character; but while magic is an initiative of man to constrain the deity, the symbolic action of the prophets is an initiative of God's. The discovery of the realism of the Old Testament (cf. especially the works of Pedersen) has again brought to light the importance of these symbolical actions which rationalistically inspired exegesis attempted to reduce to the level of literary fictions or of pathological manifestations. The subject has received very full treatment by G. Fohrer, *Die symbolischen Handlungen der Propheten, Abhandlungen zur Theologie des A.u. N.T.*, 1953.

is in this, too, that he is distinguished from the false prophets.[1] These, too, had visions and performed symbolic actions, but they spoke without receiving a word. We may compare them with demagogues who attempt to flatter the crowds by repeating words that they wish to hear and which they order by payment. The distinction was less easy when the false prophets were perhaps true prophets who, instead of ceasing to prophesy when they had no further word to pass on, ended, when they continued to speak, in being no longer the interpreters of Yahweh's plan. The prophets to whom Jeremiah is opposed and who proclaim *shalom* and the inviolability of Jerusalem, faithfully reproduce the message formerly proclaimed by Isaiah but, given the very different conjuncture of events in Jeremiah's time, their message has a false ring. It is the word that acts as the distinguishing criterion, not so much in the agreement between the prophecy and its fulfilment, but in the aspect of constraint and certainty which it is impossible to escape (Jer. 23.21). The prophetic word is always conditioned by historical circumstances and by the environment in which it is delivered;[2] it is so lacking in timelessness that certain oracles such as the book of Nahum are only pamphlets composed for the occasion; it is, therefore, difficult to speak of prophetic preaching.[3] Nevertheless, since the prophet is always seized in his totality by God and since God's action is exercised in accordance with certain constants, the preaching of the prophets is never irrelevant to the great themes of the holiness that condemns sin, and of the promise which culminates in salvation. The preaching of all the prophets could be summarized in the Decalogue's exhortation: "Thou shalt have no other gods beside Yahweh". Anything that attacks that sovereignty

[1] On false prophets, cf. the book of G. Quell, *Wahre und falsche Propheten*, Gütersloh 1952, p. 218.

[2] We feel that the strictly historical character of certain oracles should be upheld, contrary to the thesis of the Scandinavian school, which discovers traces of myth and a common pattern everywhere.

[3] The words of the prophets are to a large extent an interpretation of contemporary history and it is quite normal that they should have been led to take part in politics, but as the interpretation of history consists for them essentially in bringing a word from God, they take a stand above the course of events; what is for them an absolute certainty is partly the realization of God's plan by means of Israel's election and partly the punishment of sin. This double certainty leads them to speak sometimes of wars and invasions, at a time when the human agents of this punishment were not yet present on the historical scene; sometimes they also announce events which in actual fact took place rather differently; this in no way lessens their authority as men of God.

falls under the lash of their censure; their opposition to military alliances is not dictated by a pacifist ideology, but by the exaltation of man and human resources that they encourage. The stern words that certain prophets pronounce against cultic practices[1] are not a condemnation of the cult itself but of the measures of a magical and meritorious nature which man had introduced into the cult in order to launch an attack on God's sovereignty. But to proclaim God's sovereignty was first and foremost to lay on earth in the concrete life of the people the foundations on which his kingdom of righteousness and peace will be built. By identifying the remnant of Israel with the community of his disciples, Isaiah gives a good illustration of prophecy's constructive rôle through which the divine kingship has never ceased to be promulgated on earth. Although clearly set apart, the prophets are also a sign and an example; it can even be stated that, in the history of prophetism, knowledge always becomes less a revelation made to an initiate (e.g. Balaam, Num. 24.4-16) than a communication of God's will to all the people; the aim of the divine ways is not only to ensure a line of prophets, but to make sure that "all are taught of God" (Is. 54.13; Jer. 31.33; Jn. 6.45) and that all should be prophets (Joel 2.28f.; Num. 11.29). Then the people of Israel will be in a position to be before the other nations what the men of God had been for them.

(c) The Priest

The importance of the priests in the relationship between God and man appears throughout the history of Israel, but it took on a broader scope in more recent times, when sacerdotalism imprinted its specific mark on the whole of Israel's religion. The complex history of the priesthood, made up of diverse currents harmonized in the precincts of the temple at Jerusalem with a view to the latter's greater glory, is, however, unanimous in the affirmation of the origin and the Mosaic or Aaronic filiation of the priesthood as a whole. All the functions that we meet in the Old Testament

[1] The question of the "anti-cultic" preaching of the prophets has often been examined in the course of recent years; it seems that opinion is taking a middle position, the prophets being neither cultic agents nor systematic opponents of the cult, but the heralds of God's sovereignty which the cult could express, but which it could also on occasion cause to be forgotten (cf. Hertzberg, "Die prophetische Kritik am Kult" in *ThLitzg*, 1950, p. 219).

as characteristics of the priests can be found, in the most ancient texts, as being already exercised by Moses: he communicates God's oracles (Ex. 33.7), he sprinkles the blood of sacrifice (Ex. 24.6), he intercedes for the guilty people with the object of obtaining its pardon (Ex. 32.20). The link with Moses appears in the predominance of Levi over the other priestly families. It is doubtless difficult, in view of texts such as Gen. 34.30 and 49.5, to argue against a period of warrior activity in the history of this tribe on the same footing as all the others, but it must be recognized that this memory was erased at an early date and the name passed from the tribe to the office. Originally itinerant, the Levitic priesthood shared in the general evolution from nomadism towards a sedentary way of life, by becoming the consecrated personnel of the sanctuaries, where its presence was all the more necessary as the settling of the children of Israel in what were originally Canaanite sanctuaries ran the risk of creating cultic forms which had little conformity with the Mosaic ideal. The dignity and office of the Levites are well characterized in Moses' blessing in chap. 33 of Deuteronomy (vv. 8ff.): The Levite is there emphatically described as a man of an office and not as a member of a family, he must teach Yahweh's laws and the juridical ordinances (*torah* and *mishpatim*) and officiate at the offering of the sacrifices; these functions originally had to be practised only in a curtailed way. In earlier times and until the time of the Judges the celebration of the cult did not require a specially organized consecrated personnel; the patriarchs, who were certainly not priests, bless, build altars, offer sacrifice, practise intercession. In the time of the Judges the head of the family is still priest at the same time; but the presence of a Levite gave a greater prestige to the religious celebration, as arises in the adventures of the Levite attached to the service of Micah and carried off by the Danites (Jg. 17); on his side the Levite, as is shown in the same narrative, had every interest in giving up his itinerant ministry and in attaching himself to a sanctuary, unless he were willing to be reduced to depend on other people's generosity like the widow, the orphan and the stranger. The priests follow an evolution parallel to that of the ark, which finds shelter in the sanctuary, after accompanying the tribes on the battlefield.

It is in the sanctuary that the priests carry out their twofold duty of teaching and intercession. The *torah*, which characterizes the priests' ministry (Jer. 18.18),[1] was given in the sacred place; it consisted of revelations from God from the most rudimentary form of the *urim* and *thummim*, which corresponded in origin to a yes and a no, to more highly developed instruction. The *torah* was sought by the people as a body when it went on pilgrimages to the sanctuaries (cf. Is. 2.3; Mic. 4.2), and the reading of the law every seven years at the feast of Tabernacles (Dt. 31.10ff.) represents the most highly evolved stage of a custom firmly established for generations. When it was the answer to a consultation concerning a more precise case, it might initiate the development of details, the discussion of which mentioned by Haggai (2.11) on the contagiousness of holiness shows the degree of subtlety it could attain. It is not improbable, and the last text seems to confirm it, that the priests' teaching could give proof of originality, but in the main their teaching consisted in the transmission of customs and traditions, and in seeing that the rites are correctly performed. Israelite law did not issue from this priestly *torah*, for the most ancient legislative document, the Code of the Covenant, never mentions the priests, but it may be supposed that the sanctuaries carried out a kind of supervision, so that the law should always be referred back to its religious foundations, in proportion to its progressive secularization.

The increasing importance of the office caused the person of the priest to be surrounded with certain prerogatives intended to make clearer his rôle as God's representative. In the exercise of his duties the priest is clad in a special costume, the *ephod*; this word also being that of a cultic image (Jg. 8.26; 17.5; 1 Sam. 21.9), we can conclude from it that, by putting on the *ephod*, the priest put himself for his part and in the eyes of the people in the position of the god in whose name he acted and in whose name he pronounced the benediction, whose presence or absence was a question of life or death (Num. 6.22-27). The High Priest's costume is

---

[1] The priest is, like the prophet, in a special relationship with God which Hebrew expresses by the term knowledge (*da'at*). Hosea reproaches the priests with having despised knowledge (4.6) and Malachi (2.7) considers that the duty of the priests is to preserve knowledge, in order to be able to let the people know the difference between the sacred and profane (Ez. 22.26; 44.23); this knowledge, which is at the basis of their torah, makes the priests akin to the prophets; we think, however, that they can be distinguished by calling the priestly knowledge a mediated knowledge, which only arises in the framework of an institution, and the prophets' knowledge a direct knowledge (cf. H. W. Wolff, "Wissen um Gott bei Hosea als Urform von Theologie." in *Evangel. Theologie*, 1952-53, pp. 533ff.).

charged with symbolic significance: the gold and precious stones represent God's glory; the breastplate with the names of the twelve tribes means that he assumes the responsibility of the people as a whole; the diadem comparable to the headdress of the Nazirites symbolizes the integrity of the vital force, on which Levitical prescriptions lay such stress, for reasons which were probably not altogether of a ritual nature. Yet never in his representation of God does the priest attain a degree equal to the king's, or the prophet's; these had an immediate link with God, the first through his enthronement, the second through his calling; the priest's link with the deity is only one of an institutional nature. Further the priest's human side only rarely appears with a few details; except for Zadok and Eli we know little about their life, and Ezra owes his biography less to his priestly function than to his rôle as doctor of the law. Within the sacred area in which their activity takes place, the priests are in the service of the head of the family and later of the king (1 Sam. 2.35ff.). The real initiative in the cultic realm lies with the king; thus the priest Urijah can only conform willy-nilly to the directive of King Ahaz, who imposes on him the construction of an altar of Assyrian pattern (2 Kings 16.10ff.). They rarely take part in political affairs; only twice do we see them playing a part other than that of executant of the king's orders: Zadok takes Solomon's side against the legitimate heir (1 Kings 1) and Jehoiada provokes the fall of Athaliah (2 Kings 11). As for the great religious initiatives, such as the removal of the brazen serpent in Hezekiah's reign and the Deuteronomic reformation, they are the result of prophetic preaching.

The priest's mediatorial function is more exercised in the opposite direction, that going from man to God. Behind the increasingly complicated rites which accompany the priestly functions there is always the care to uphold the election of the people who, to be Yahweh's people, must be a holy people. To assure this holiness and to re-establish this holiness, which is ever being freshly compromised, such seems to us to be the priest's essential function, as shown in the specially ritual texts. In a religion that is increasingly insistent on divine transcendence, the priest becomes, through the permanent contact that he has with divine holiness, the only intermediary capable of bearing the weight of the faults committed by the people and of reinstating it into a condition of wholeness (Ex. 28.38; Lev. 10.17; Num. 18.1), his own person being, moreover, in no way sheltered from the need of expiation, as is brought out by the expression *'awon kehunnatkem* = the iniquity of your priesthood (Num. 18.1). This representative function appears again in the classical expression by which the priest's investiture has in all times been designated, *mille yad*, "to fill the hand" (Lev. 16.32; Jg. 17.5, 12; Ex. 32.29) and which probably refers to the gesture which consisted, at the time of the sacrifice, in returning to the priest the share which was to be offered to the deity (cf. also Ex. 29.22), and when the Priestly code sees in the Levites the substitutes for the first-born which belong by right to Yahweh, it also intends to make clear that the priests represent the congregation of the people (Num. 3.12, 41; 8.16, 17).

When the monarchy no longer existed and when prophetic inspiration was beginning to weaken, the priest eclipses king and prophet and dons to some extent their mantles. The priestly monarchy of Maccabean times will be the outcome of this tendency; the covenant with Levi will gain the importance that the Davidic covenant had (Jer. 33.18, 21, a text much later than Jeremiah), and Malachi's diatribe against the priests is all the more severe because the dignity ascribed to them is greater; are they not in effect Yahweh's "angels"? (Mal. 2.4). The Messiah himself will assume a priestly aspect, and in the Zadokite theology the Messiah son of Levi will tend to displace the son of David (cf. Jer. 30.18-21).[1] And since there are no more prophets, the priest may prophesy; Josephus records that the High Priest Hyrcanus, while offering incense in the temple, heard a heavenly voice telling him that his sons had just won the victory over Antiochus (Ant. XIII 10.3), and the writer of the Fourth Gospel appears to consider it normal that the High Priest Caiaphas, by virtue of his position, should have the gift of prophecy (Jn. 11.51). But before drawing all these conclusions from the High Priest's supremacy the people of Israel had already found in the priest's function the expression of its ideal and the model of its vocation: chosen by Yahweh to be a "nation of priests" (Ex. 19.6) it hoped for a time when all the redeemed would be called priests for Yahweh and servants of Elohim (Is. 61.6).

---

[1] The terms *qarab* and *nagash* which in this text characterize the Messiah's activity are current in cultic language (cf. Ex. 40.31ff.; Lev. 21.21; Num. 16.5; Is. 29.13; Ez. 44.16). On the subject of the priestly aspect of the Messiah in apocryphal and pseudepigraphical literature, cf. A. J. B. Higgins, "Priest and Messiah", *VT*, 1953, pp. 321ff.

(d) The Wise Man

The wise men, the *chakamim*, probably formed in the eighth century a special class, distinct from prophets and priests (Jer. 18.18; Ez. 7.26) and, by the same title, formed part of the governing élite of the nation. But even earlier than this we find several references to the wise who, by their counsel (*'etsah*), have an active influence on the course of events. This function was often, it seems, in the hands of women: it is a *chakamah*, gifted with powers of divination, who informs Sisera's mother about her son's movements after the battle (Jg. 5.28-30); it is a wise woman who, through a trick, obtains Absalom's return in peace (2 Sam. 14.14), and it is also a wise woman who obtains the handing over of Sheba (2 Sam. 20.18f.), and the town of Abel beth Maachah, where this episode takes place, seems to have been a centre of wisdom, or at least of good advice (2 Sam. 20.18). We find wise men in David's immediate entourage besides the priests and prophets; it is the counsel of a wise man, Ahithophel, who gives to events the turning favourable to David's final victory, and the narrator does not omit to add that this advice had the same value as the *dabar* of Yahweh himself (2 Sam. 16.23). It is, then, useless to seek the origin of this social class outside Israel, or at any rate outside Palestine, for in this realm, as in many others, Canaan[1] must have been more than a dependency of Egypt. But interest in human problems gave to the wise men an horizon which was not limited by Israel's frontiers. Since we have proof of a direct link between certain wisdom writings and Egyptian documents, we must admit that, among the wise men of Israel, human interest became more important than specifically Israelite interest; precursors of free masonry, they took moreover for patron the least Israelitish and most humanist king of the Old Testament, King Solomon. Solomon gave a fixed organization to a wisdom movement that was already in existence and outlined its programme of action; and so the wise men almost all remained anonymous in order to place themselves under the authority of that paragon of wise men.

[1] One of the patrons of Canaanite wisdom was Danel, who is less well known to us than his son Aqhat, to whom a whole cycle of Ugaritic poems is dedicated; he there appears as a king who metes out justice at the gate for the benefit of the widow and the orphan (1 Aqht, 20-25, 11.5-8); in Ez. 14.14, 20 and 28.3 he is the type of the wise man; this same figure could also be the prototype of the figure of Daniel (Dan. 1-6) who, like Joseph, is conspicuous for his wisdom.

The activity of the wise is shown in three ways which earlier characterized the work of Solomon himself. The first is of a literary and philosophical nature. The wise are writers of maxims, fables and more developed works like the book of Job; Solomon's literary activity, attested by the historians (1 Kings 4.20), cannot be seriously doubted, although his own literary works are not easy to identify among biblical texts. The author of the account of the beginnings, usually called the Yahwist, who was probably a contemporary of Solomon's, is like the prophets in his way of showing the divine directing of events, and like the wise man in the depth with which he approaches the problems of mankind, such as the origin of life, the differentiation of sexes and the peculiarities of language, which have always excited the speculations of philosophers and scholars.[1] This wisdom rarely had a purely non-religious aspect, it is entirely dominated by the fear of God, but the God of the wise men is more the one who created the world and who directs it by his providence than the master of history who views the world's destiny through the destiny of Israel.

The field of pedagogy is the second place where wisdom is practised. There were in Israel, as elsewhere, schools of wisdom[2] where the art of reading and writing was taught, but where the main effort of the teachers was directed less towards instruction than towards the formation of character; through the teaching of the fear of Yahweh, the young were to learn to respect authority, to struggle against pride and to give proof in all their ways of a wise moderation. Yahweh himself, in the garden of Eden, had taught just this to the first human beings.

But it was in the political field that the activity and counsel of the wise was to be revealed as particularly successful. Contrary to the prophets, whose political preaching consisted in stressing the precariousness of alliances, the illusory nature of military technique, and in extolling trust in Yahweh, the only master of events, which in general earned the hostility of the kings, the wise men became counsellors to the king, suggesting foreign alliances, particularly

[1] P. Dubarle's fine book on the *Sages d'Israël* devotes a chapter to the creation narratives.

[2] It may be concluded from texts like Prov. 1.20; 4.5; 8.2; 17.16, that schools of wisdom existed, where the personification of wisdom might have been inspired by the masters of wisdom and by the way they talked; but we know nothing precise about the Israelite schools before the fusion of wisdom with the law, which takes us beyond the Old Testament.

with Egypt,[1] and Isaiah had difficulty in persuading Hezekiah, full though he was of kindly feeling towards him, that nothing could be hoped for from the Pharaoh's help. Even though Israelite wisdom was to a lesser extent than in Egypt entirely directed to the royal circle, that is to future officials, it must be recognized that many of the exhortations of the book of Proverbs were drawn up solely for this purpose; for to no other person were counsels more necessary than to the man whose duty it was to take decisions of an administrative or military nature. And so the disappearance of the monarchy marks a turning point in the orientation of wisdom. Henceforth, the king's adviser gives place to the doctor of the law and in the book of Jesus son of Sirach we see the fusion of the counsels of the wise with the letter of the law (cf. especially Ecclus. 24.8). Yet, despite this promotion of the doctor of the law, Moses never succeeded in ousting Solomon completely; by deliberately taking the great syncretist king as their patron, the wisdom writers set out to strike a universalist note which would allow Judaism to become, despite the barrier of the *torah*, a missionary religion.

The wise, as dispensers of knowledge under its cognitive aspect, but especially under its practical aspect, are one of the channels through which God's presence is communicated to men, and even though their person itself lacks the religious prestige attaching to the king, to the priest and to the prophet, they are none the less a sign, in view of the time when all men will be taught by the author of all wisdom (Jer. 31.34; Is. 54.13).

(e) General conclusion on the ministries

The aim of all four governing bodies is to assure God's presence among his people. The king guarantees God's rule on earth, the prophet expresses by his person and his message God's action in history, the priest, through the administration of sacred things, gives reminders of God's sovereignty over time and space, lastly, the wise man shows and teaches still more that there is no happiness

---

[1] With Isaiah and Hezekiah, we witness the conflict between prophet and sage. Hezekiah, while remaining a faithful worshipper of Yahweh, wished to be a second Solomon, seeking alliance with Egypt and Babylon: we may compare the visit of Merodach Baladan's embassy to Hezekiah (Is. 39) with that of the Queen of Sheba to Solomon. In the political field the prophets' realism showed itself more effective than the idealism of the wise men.

possible outside God's love. The divisions between the various functions were never watertight: the affinity between prophet and priest was very close, the greatest of the sages was at the same time a king, and the prophet, when not proclaiming a precise message from Yahweh, spoke in aphorisms and riddles in the manner of the wise. Only once, at the very dawn of the old covenant, do we meet the four offices brought together in one person. Moses as chief of the people exercises royal functions before the fact, the title of prophet is expressly given to him by tradition (Hos. 12.13), the priests trace back to him the main body of the priestly organization and Yahweh's revelation takes nothing away from the wisdom he had acquired through contact with Egypt. And so Moses, among all those who exercised ministries, is alone in fully meriting the title of mediator *par excellence*; likewise his figure and his work considerably influenced the presentation of the mediatorial work of the Servant of Yahweh and of Jesus himself.

The choosing of an élite by God is not contradictory to the election of the people as a whole, for in addition to the mission of governing and teaching which was entrusted to them, those particular individuals are an annunciatory sign of the kingdom to come and show to the other members of the nation where their vocation lies while helping them here and now to make it real.

B. THE PERMANENT SETTING

(a) The sacred place

Every religion recognizes a tension between the remoteness of God and his nearness. In Israel there existed a very lively feeling of Yahweh's presence in the whole universe, due to his power and spiritual nature, but because of the very personal character of this same God, who was hardly spoken about except in anthropomorphisms, there was a tendency to localize his presence in a fixed place where it was possible to meet him perhaps face to face. The variety of solutions to the problem of the divine presence throws an interesting light on the types of piety which the divine mystery evoked; we meet these types rarely in the pure state and in general the religion and more particularly the place of the cult does justice both to the present God and to the hidden God.

1. The heavenly dwelling-place of Yahweh appears already in the most ancient strata of tradition; we meet it commonly in the Yahwist writings (Gen. 11.5; 18.21; 21.17; 22.11; 24.7; 28.12; Ex. 19.11; 20.22), in Deuteronomy (4.36; 26.15), in the Psalms (2.4; 18.7; 123.1) and in the prophets (Is. 31.4; Mic. 1.2). It is true that, in several of these texts, heaven is only Yahweh's dwelling-place when at rest. To intervene and show himself, he comes down from heaven. This heavenly dwelling-place was occupied by Yahweh in common with many other deities. It was far from being his distinctive feature. Other gods, such as Baal Shamayim,[1] who was, as we know, very widely worshipped in the Near East from El Amarna times onwards, and whose activities were all conditioned by his heavenly rôle, could easily challenge Yahweh's sovereignty over heaven, and the story of Elijah shows us that as late as the ninth century many Israelites thought that it was more worth while to address Baal than Yahweh to obtain the gifts of heaven. It was only from the time of the exile that the temporary absence of the temple and the crisis of the covenant obliged the Israelites to pay more attention to the heavenly dwelling-place of Yahweh. Although Stade's assertion[2] that Yahweh rose into heaven only from Ezekiel's time is certainly exaggerated, it is, nevertheless, probable that it was only from that time that the celestial dwelling-place became a theological problem[3] and an article of faith likely to have the same authority as the divine indwelling among the people or in the temple, themes that were, moreover, never abandoned, for the heaven was always considered less as the symbol of distance than of totality; and so post-exilic texts stress with equal vigour the heavenly dwelling of Yahweh and his presence among his people. It is only among a few isolated individuals such as Qoheleth that we find the idea that

---

[1] On the extent of the worship of Baal Shamayim, cf. the article by Eissfeldt, *ZAW*, 1939, pp. 1ff., we must also now add the testimony of the Karatepe inscription in which *Baal shmm* figures at the head of a triad beside El, creator of the earth, and *Shamash 'olam*.

[2] "Jahweh ist erst zu Hezekiels Zeit in den Himmel hineingewachsen", *Bibli. Theol. des A.T.*, p. 291.

[3] The latest Old Testament books show many traces of this celestial supremacy: the book of Jonah (1.9) calls Yahweh "the God of the heavens who made the sea and the dry land", heaven, as his specific place, is above the works of creation; in the LXX version, we also notice a tendency to lay stress on the celestial dwelling of Yahweh, cf. e.g. 1 Kings 18.36 where the Greek version introduces the words εἰς τὸν οὐρανόν which do not appear in the Massoretic text.

the celestial dwelling of Yahweh makes him more or less insensible to what happens on the earth (God is in heaven, thou art on earth, Eccl. 5.2) and the need of intermediaries only appears in post-canonical literature.

2. Yahweh's dwelling on a high mountain is very close to his heavenly dwelling, since in ancient cosmology mountain peaks communicate directly with heaven. In Israel the theme of the mountain of the gods, mythical in origin and of which we have a few reminiscences, was all the more easily transposed on to an historical plane because the decisive event for the constitution of the people took place on a mountain. Yahweh's dwelling on Sinai left a deep impression, not only among those who had been direct witnesses of the theophany, but also many centuries later Sinai was considered as the pre-eminent place of revelation, and the episode of 1 Kings 19 probably contains an echo of a pilgrimage which the northern tribes continued to make to Sinai. Many texts suggest that it was from Sinai and not from heaven that Yahweh set out at the time of his manifestations (Dt. 33.2; Jg. 5.5; Ps. 68.7ff.).

3. Another tradition makes the whole land of Canaan Yahweh's dwelling-place: the land is Yahweh's inheritance and outside its frontiers it is no longer possible to meet him. When pursued by Saul, David, in banishment from his country, is afraid of being driven far from Yahweh's presence (1 Sam. 26.19-20), and Naaman's gesture in taking a load of earth from Palestine illustrates that this belief held something at once touching and naïve (2 Kings 5.15-19).

4. Among the sacred places made by men's hands, the tent of meeting, 'ohel mo'ed, which accompanied the Israelites during their migration through the desert, reconciled the demands of God's presence and invisibility. To meet Yahweh, Moses set up a tent outside the camp and Yahweh descended in a column of cloud which stopped at the tent's entrance, and Moses spoke with him as a man speaks with a friend (Ex. 33.7-11), particularly when disputes among members of the people made the assertion of the divine presence and holiness necessary (Num. 11.14ff.; 16.19; 20.6ff.).

5. While the tent resolved the problem of the divine presence in the sense of a meeting between God and man, the ark was conceived, at least in the most ancient tradition, as a real dwelling-place of the deity. Whether it had the form of a throne[1] or, as seems

---

[1] If the ark could have been called the throne of Yahweh, it owes it not to

more probable to us, and more in keeping with the textual data, of a chest, it is certain that it was considered as the dwelling-place of Yahweh, to such a degree that the terms Yahweh and ark of Yahweh are sometimes interchangeable. The book of Numbers records the words of invocation, which were addressed to the ark as much as to Yahweh: "Arise, Yahweh, so that thine enemies may be scattered and that those who hate thee may flee before thee." And when it came to a halting-place, Moses would say: "Return, Yahweh, to the hosts of Israel" (Num. 10.35-36). The passage of the Israelites before the ark at the time of the crossing of the Jordan is passage before Yahweh (Jos. 4.5, 13), and when at the time of the Philistine wars the ark is brought into the Israelite camp, the Philistines cry out in fear: "Elohim has come into the camp" (1 Sam. 4.7). During the whole period of the conquest, the ark was sufficient answer to the problem of the divine presence, and if the representation of the ark as a receptacle of the tables of the law is not a concept developed from speculation in priestly circles but corresponds to historical development, we must recognize the very complete appearance of that theology of the ark which, as a sacred chest, contained the mysterious and, on occasion, explosive holiness of God and which as container of the law recalled how God had bound himself to his people. As a symbol of the *deus absconditus* and of the *deus revelatus*, the ark lacked neither dynamism nor objectivity.[1]

6. Sanctuaries, the specific dwelling-places of a deity, could be constituted by natural objects which were endued, for the time being, with supernatural powers. A stone set upright could confer a sacred character on a place and create that thrill which is at the basis of any true religious experience. In the presence of one of these rudimentary sanctuaries Jacob exclaims: "How dreadful is this place; this is indeed the house of God" (Gen. 28.17); and up to the time of David it was held that the noise of wind in the foliage of a tree could be a manifestation of Yahweh (2 Sam. 5.24).

its form, which was quite unlike a throne, but to its association with the cherubim which stood over it and which were considered in certain texts as the bearers of Yahweh (Ps. 18.11).

[1] The disappearance of the ark of the covenant is probably a pre-exilic event; it is officially mentioned for the last time in the Chronicles version of Josiah's reformation (2 Chr. 35.3); Israelite piety does not seem to have been specially affected by it (cf. Jer. 3.16) although the prophet's assertion of its being forgotten was not realized to the letter, as is shown by the legend mentioned in 2 Macc. 2.4-6.

With settlement in permanent quarters and with civilization, the religious object provided by nature gives way to buildings which, with names such as *bet*, *mishkan* or *heykal*, seek to represent the sanctuary as the dwelling-place of the deity and as a place where God's presence was considered to be as real as if he were physically present, even though there was no fashioned image of him. The dwelling of the deity in the sanctuary did not exclude, however, his heavenly dwelling-place; thus in Mesopotamia, the temples which stood at the foot of the ziggurats were places where the deity appeared and which he reached by using those staircases as a way down from heaven to earth.[1] In the whole of the ancient East the building of a sanctuary was an act initiated by the deity himself; the human builders carry out only what is communicated to them by a revelation. Gudea of Lagash received in a dream[2] all the information necessary for the building of the temple for his god; Moses builds the tabernacle according to a pattern (*tabnit*) given by God himself (Ex. 25.8ff.); according to the book of Chronicles, David passes on to Solomon all the data concerning the building of the temple which he received from the hand of God in person (1 Chr. 28.11, 19ff.), and Ezekiel's temple is presented throughout as the content of a vision. Because of these premises, it is permissible to seek the expression of religious realities in the architectural elements of the sanctuaries. Although we know little more than the name of the sanctuaries of Bethel, Nob and Beersheba, we are very well informed about the temple at Jerusalem. This sanctuary is largely modelled on foreign patterns which it is archaeology's business to bring to light; it is none the less certain that the Israelites tried to express through this building their own beliefs about the divine presence.[3] Indeed, in the temple at Jerusalem

---

[1] The archaeology and theology of the ziggurats have received a masterly exposition in the works of André Parrot, *Ziggurats et Tour de Babel*, Paris 1949, and *La tour de Babel* (Cahiers d'archéologie biblique, no. 2), 1953

[2] The text of Gudea's cylinder was published with a commentary by R. Tournay in *RB*, 1948, pp. 403ff. and 520ff.

[3] It is quite probable that the temple at Jerusalem had a cosmic significance. Josephus asserts (Ant. VIII, 3, 2) that the threefold division corresponds to the three parts of the universe: sea, sky, earth; perhaps this shows a desire to read too much into the data, but the symbolic character of certain elements such as the *debir* and the sea of bronze would be difficult to confute (cf. also J. Daniélou, "La symbolique cosmique du Temple de Jérusalem" in *Symbolisme cosmique et monuments religieux*, pp. 61-64, and by the same author: *Le signe du temple*, 1938). Speculations about Jerusalem and the temple as the navel of the world (*omphalos*) express the same belief, the navel being the centre of organic life.

there can be seen a kind of summary of all the answers given to the problem of the divine presence. Yahweh's dwelling in the temple does not contradict his residing in heaven, since because of the theology of the name, which is considered as a sort of double of Yahweh, he was able to be present in both places at once (1 Kings 8.29; 2 Chr. 6.18ff.), and all the texts agree in declaring that the limitation constituted by the dwelling of God in the temple is voluntarily self-imposed. The Sinai theme also finds its place in the temple; the darkness, *'araphel*, in which Yahweh chooses to dwell (1 Kings 8.12) is a reminder of the darkness into which Moses penetrated on Sinai (Ex. 20.21; Dt. 4.11).

The ark, too, helps to give the temple its prestige, but it was reduced quite quickly to the rank of a simple ornament and lost its dynamic power before its finally almost completely unlamented disappearance at a time that is difficult to determine exactly. Even the theme of the land finds its place in the temple, which was the centre, not only of Palestine, but of the entire universe, of which it sought to be a reproduction. Since the temple had thus exercised an attractive function which led to the crystallization of various traditions, it can be understood that piety was determined by it and became centred within its orbit. There was no image of God in the temple, but certain architectural features such as the palm trees and the cherubim constituted a reminder of paradise and gave to the faithful a foretaste of what he hoped to see established. It was in the temple and in the temple only that it was possible to see the face of God and to experience that fulness of power and of joy expressed by the word *shalom*, through which man can rise above time and overcome it, since one day spent in the courts of Yahweh was worth a thousand spent elsewhere (Ps. 84.11 and Ps. 26.6; 27.4; 42.3, 5; 43.4, etc.). The central place occupied by the temple in the Psalms, which in many cases were composed in a milieu of singers and Levites, is not surprising, but the great place that it occupies in the preaching of the prophets proves that the temple theme had a theological importance much wider than the mere cultic observances.

All the prophets agree in declaring that there is a particular and permanent bond between Yahweh and the temple. Even a prophet like Amos, apparently detached from all cultic preoccupations, asserts that "Yahweh makes his voice heard from Jerusalem" (1.2), which he therefore considers as his legitimate dwelling-place. However, the prophets envisage the temple less as a dwelling-place than as the meeting-place of Yahweh and his people; in this they are linked more closely with the theological current represented by the tent than with the popular piety which was centred round the ark. For the prophets, as for the Psalmists, to meet Yahweh is the height of happiness; but for anyone who fails to fulfil the conditions indispensable to entry into the sanctuary (cf. Ps. 15 and 24) this meeting can only be a judgment. The 6th chapter of the prophet Isaiah expresses in the most striking way all the thought of the prophets about the temple. The prophet comes to the temple to meet God and, in his vision, God descending from heaven to the temple manifests himself in his essential aspect, that of holiness, through which the prophet becomes aware of his condemnation and justification. Isaiah's experience in the temple not only summarizes and foreshadows his own ministry, it has value as an example for the whole people. Just as his own destiny is played out in the temple, it is in the temple that his people's lot will be played, a people who will find in that stone in its midst either the salvation which will save or the judgment which will crush (cf. Is. 28.16 and Is. 8.18; 14.32). In order to give concrete expression to this bond of Yahweh with the temple, the prophets delivered their oracles in the very precincts of the temple, thus giving a further sign of the divine authority with which they were endued, by joining the authority of the place to the authority of their message. Since any revelation of God is also a revelation of man—we are still thinking of Is. 6—the divine majesty as it is manifested in the temple places man in his rightful place before God, a position of obedience and faith. If, on the other hand, a man takes advantage of the temple in order to make it a shelter for his pride, that sign of divine protection will be taken from him. As early as the time of Isaiah, the temple had become for many Israelites a sort of talisman which kept them in illusory security and the Deuteronomic reformation had confirmed the people in this feeling, rather than produced a change in depth. It is in this concrete situation that it is fitting to understand Jeremiah's message; he declared clearly, what Isaiah had not dared to proclaim and what was not necessary in his time, that the temple will be destroyed, although not because he considers it as a useless place destined to give way to more spiritual expressions of piety. For Jeremiah the temple remains the " throne of glory " and " the hope of Israel " (Jer. 3.17; 14.21; 17.12), but its destruction is motivated by the sin of the people who by giving offence to God have also profaned his sanctuary (Jer. 23.11). If Yahweh allows the destruction of his dwelling-place, it is to take from the people the illusion of a false security before it is too late, and to force it to go back to the sources and to clear a fresh field (Jer. 4.3; 7.5). In a particularly impressive vision, Ezekiel shows Yahweh leaving his temple and, by so doing, delivering the people over to the most terrible of punishments, that of God's absence (Ez. 8 and 10). The temple, the place of judgment, is also the place of restoration; the nations will go up to the mountain of Yahweh (Is. 2; Mic. 4), the redeemed of Zion will again go up to Jerusalem (Jer. 30.19; 31.4-6, 12) and Ezekiel, who had seen Yahweh leave his temple that had been defiled by idolatry, makes him return to his dwelling-place, the holiness of which will be considerably increased. Even Second Isaiah, anxious to rid religion of its too material attachments, twice mentions the rebuilding of the temple: profaned by sin (43.28) it will be rebuilt by Cyrus (44.28). It is true that in this prophet's writings the place held elsewhere, particularly in Ezekiel, by the temple, is occupied by the figure of Yahweh's servant. In our view, there is here less a difference of essence than of perspective; the prophet's vision goes beyond the sign to its fulfilment, but both the temple and the servant are the concentration of the means by which Yahweh manifests his presence and his salvation. Less animated by the imminence of the new age and obliged to face up to the hard realities of their day, the post-exilic prophets insisted on the temple as the visible sign of the guarantee of the covenant. Haggai reacts against the tendency to pessimism which is beginning to show itself by proclaiming that the temple, still a pitiful place, will become, by the intervention of God himself, a manifestation of glory (Hag. 2.6). With still more force, Zechariah takes up the promises linked with Yahweh's presence in the temple; the presence of Yahweh after returning to his sanctuary will make any other means of protection unnecessary for Jerusalem (Zech. 2.5) and Gentiles, convinced of the power of Israel's God, will rise to adore him in his temple: "I too will go," they will say on all sides (Zech. 8.21). Henceforth, the temple will be more than ever the centre of Jewish piety; many Psalms certainly date from this time and the Chronicler presents a new synthesis of the history of Israel turning on the two poles of the temple and the Davidic monarchy.

Envisaged as a sign, the temple is not in contradiction with the revelation of God in history, for the temple itself takes part in the movement of history, it even takes part in the first place in the succession of judgments and deliverances of which that history is made. But its permanence—as a theological theme—shows that history develops around a fixed point, that of God's presence which, from being hidden, tends to become a dwelling among the people. By showing the fulfilment in his person of the temple sign (Matt. 12.6; Jn. 2.20), Jesus made clear its provisional and at the same time necessary value in God's plan.[1]

(b) The Cult

Any theology finds its expression in the cult: a theology of immanence and a theology of transcendence create particular cultic forms and in any religion the history of changes in the liturgy gives a fairly exact reflection of theological changes. Yet this cultic expression is only partial, for while the cult is governed by the great affirmations of the faith, it is also governed at the same time by remarkably conservative forces which rite and tradition uphold particularly tenaciously long after the disappearance of the thought that inspired them. In Israel the cult did not escape this paralysing influence of tradition and we see only rarely in their pure state the forms which are specific to its religion. In the Semitic world taken as a whole, the fundamental law of the cult was the distinction between the sacred and the profane; it was this distinction that governed the arrangement of the sanctuaries and the development of sacred times and actions. The Israelite cult was never freed from this fundamental law and even developed it in all its breadth at a time when the cult had become for the people the only place where its election could be shown and practised. It must be recognized, however, that the essence of Israel's religion bore it in a different direction; because of the assertion of God's sovereignty over all realms of creation and history, there could be no realm or time set aside for revelation to the exclusion of others. It is probable that if Israel had been free to work out all the consequences of this affirmation it would have finally developed a rather a-cultic

---

[1] Cf. the reflections of S. de Diétrich in the special number of *Semeur*: " Pour comprendre l'Ancien Testament ", 1954, p. 115.

religion in which the permanence of the election and the covenant through justice, war, mission and the law would have taken precedence over truly cultic manifestations. In spite of pointers in this direction implicit in the demands for justice in certain prophets (Amos) on the one hand, and in the humanism of wisdom on the other, Israel did not arrive at a religion which could do without a cultic expression—at least never in the Old Testament. Although much indebted to Canaan, whose ritual and cultic places it adopted to a large extent, Israel succeeded, through the substitution of history for myth, in breathing a new spirit into identical forms. Israel's originality in the cultic field is shown by the priority of history over myth and of time over space. The revelation of Yahweh was not linked to a few natural objects more sacred than others, such as mountains, springs or trees, but he had the freedom to manifest himself where he wished and the famous text in Ex. 20.24: "In whatever place I give reason to remember my name, I will come to thee to bless thee," alludes to the plurality of shrines, historically attested by the books of Judges and Samuel, and whose importance was inversely proportional to their multiplicity. Further, this link of Yahweh with the sanctuary was not regarded as permanent; this is expressed by the use of the verb *shakan*: this term, different in sense from *yashab*,[1] which is never used in connection with the dwelling of the deity in the sanctuary, designates a temporary habitation whose transitory and provisional aspect is well brought out by the figure of the tent. Yahweh's dwelling in the sanctuary is a function of time and the sacred places only exist as a function of sacred times. Everything in the cult was determined by time and at first by cosmic time. In spite of certain opinions to the contrary, it may be considered as an established fact that the Israelites attributed great importance to the year and particularly to the moments that marked its ending and renewal: the year, with its regular rhythm of seasons and lunar phases, provided the cult with its framework and gave assurance that, in the unfolding of time, there would be fixed points, the *mo'adim* without

[1] The term *yashab* is connected with the ark (1 Sam. 4.4; Ps. 80.2; 99.1; Is. 37.16) but in the case of the ark at least at the time of the Judges when it really was the only place of the divine presence, mobility weakens the static aspect which the term contains. It must be said that the theology of the ark represents only *one* current of piety, more or less tainted with Magianism, and that the main current is represented by the theology of the tent which we still find in the New Testament (Jn. 1.14; Rev. 21.3).

which it ran the risk of falling back into chaos (Gen. 1.14). The link between the New Year[1] and the autumn festival of the harvest indicates that one of its essential aspects was the act of thanks for benefits received during the past year and conversely the concern to ensure the same favours for the year that was beginning. The change of year marked indeed a threat of the return of chaos with the unleashing of powers of destruction, and therefore made necessary the affirmation of the forces of creation; and so the thesis which holds the New Year as the *Sitz im Leben* of the creation narrative of Gen. 1[2] in imitation of what happened in Babylon, deserves the most serious attention. The aspect of the feast which looked forward to the future was illustrated, principally, by the rites intended to ensure rain. The scene of Elijah's sacrifice at Carmel, which took place in autumn, might well be a rite of the year's renewal and Isaiah's invitation to come with cries of joy to draw water at the wells of salvation (12.3) seems to allude to a rite practised at a particularly solemn moment of the year. However, nothing permits the statement that the New Year festivities were accompanied by dramatic scenes, in the course of which the death of the god involving the return of chaos and his recall to life were represented by the person of the king. It seems clear, rather, that Israel remained obdurate to this practice, which was so widespread in the ancient East and which was diffused in the biblical environment, as the Ugaritic texts testify. The Canaanite cult consisted essentially in the integration of human life into nature. Now, since nature obeys laws which are to some extent instinctive, that integration was ensured on man's side by the exercise of the natural laws and more especially of sexual functions raised to the level of orgy, in which union with the deity was realized in its perfection. It was thus that the impregnation of the woman by the man was presented as a phenomenon not only similar to, but identical with the generative power of the earth, which was assured by the co-operation of the rain and the seed. In this religion man was only a part of nature which was itself more or less confused with

---

[1] The importance of the year for the Israelites has been contested by Sverre Aalen, *Die Begriffe Licht und Finsternis*, who thinks that the only alternating of time which interested the Israelites was that of night and morning, darkness and light. This over-radical thesis has been refuted by S. Mowinckel, *Zum israelitischen Neujahr und zur Deutung der Thronbesteigungspsalmen*, Oslo 1952.

[2] Cf. P. Humbert, "La relation de Genèse 1 et du Psaume 104 avec la liturgie du Nouvel-An israélite", *RHPR*, 1935, pp. 1-27.

the deity. The Old Testament always regarded this form of religiosity, to which the Israelites more than once succumbed, as a serious aberration, for it led men away from the attitude of faith and obedience, the only fitting attitude before God, and from the attitude of domination and sovereignty, which alone is legitimate before nature. By transferring the metaphors of sexual life into the historical field so as to use them as the expression of a covenant between two unequal partners, the prophets intended to put an end to any mystic connection between man and nature.

The secondary divisions of the year were also the occasion of cultic manifestations. The appearance of the new moon was marked by observances which must have had, on a reduced scale, the same significance as the renewal of the year (Ps. 81.4; Amos 8.5; Hos. 2.13; Is. 1.13). The association of the Sabbath with the moon (2 Kings 4.23; Is. 1.13; 66.23) might suggest the possibility of a relationship between the two which was gradually differentiated into two independent currents; but since the etymological equivalence of the Babylonian *shapattum,* the 15th day of the moon, with the Hebrew Sabbath is improbable, and since the content of the two feasts is very different, a lunar origin of the Sabbath must be considered only with extreme caution. It seems more likely that from its origin[1]—that is, from Mosaic times—the Sabbath was a fixed day set apart, perhaps with the very object of turning the Israelites from the temptation of lunar cults. It would be more readily understood from this why this festival became the supreme holy day. Even the year's smallest division, the day, was considered as a victory of Yahweh over chaos, represented by darkness, with the result that the words for morning and salvation became synonymous (Is. 8.20; 33.2; 58.10; Zeph. 3.5; Ps. 17.15; 46.6). For this reason, the beginning and the ending of the day were marked with cultic ceremonies, the morning burnt sacrifice and the evening offering, by which God's favour was secured while thanks were being offered (1 Kings 18.29; 2 Kings 16.15; Ezra 9.4).

If the cult was a revelation of God as creator and was a reminder that creation must be for ever renewed, it also gave a no less important place to the God of history and to the manifestations of salvation of which that history had been the scene. According to

---

[1] On the present state of the Sabbath question, cf. the article by N. H. Tur-Sinaï, " Sabbat und Woche " in *Bibliotheca Orientalis,* 1951, pp. 14-24, which argues in favour of a purely Israelite origin of the Sabbath.

Mowinckel's suggestions,[1] which were taken up in a modified form by A. Weiser and H. J. Kraus, it is probable that the outstanding events of Israel's history were not only used in the cult as subjects for teaching, but also for real dramatic presentation which had the purpose of making onlookers share in a very real way in those events. At the time of the Passover, the Exodus was represented down to the detail of the appearance of those sharing in the Passover meal "with loins girt, sandals on feet, and staff in hand" (Ex. 12.11). At the time of the feast of Tabernacles the Israelites had to spend seven days living in tents in order to put themselves in the position of their ancestors in the desert period (Lev. 23.43). This feast, which was the feast *par excellence*, commemorated in representational form the Sinai theophany, the granting of the law and the conclusion of the covenant. Ps. 81 is probably a fragment of the liturgy of this feast as it was celebrated in the kingdom of Israel (cf. the reference to Joseph in v. 6) and it shows us that the great acts of God and the exhortation to put the law into practice made the cult into an expression of both prophetic and priestly piety.

The invitation which we read in several places (Dt. 5.3; 26.16-19; Ps. 95.7ff.) to respond "to-day" to God's call is not explained solely by the solidarity which unites the people through successive generations, but supposes some definite act which was to make that solidarity evident; the insistence on the fact that it was not "with the fathers" that God concluded the covenant (Dt. 5.3), but with the present generation, proves that the stress was placed less on the solidarity and the historicity of facts in the strict sense than on their actualization. In the cult celebrated in Jerusalem, the commemoration of events which had marked the foundation of the city was added to events of the Mosaic period. Psalm 132 has all the characteristics of the liturgy of an annual festival which cele-

[1] Several of the suggestions made by Mowinckel were only appreciated at their true value several years after the appearance of his *Psalmenstudien*. The theses of Weiser and Kraus, while offered ostensibly as a criticism of Mowinckel's position, are none the less largely derived from him. Weiser speaks of a feast of the covenant (Bundesfest) celebrated in the autumn which turned mainly on the dramatic representation of the great facts of history (cf. *Einleitung in das A.T.* and *Die Psalmen* in *ATD*). Kraus: *Die Königsherrschaft Gottes*, 1951, reconstructs with a high degree of probability an annual feast of the enthronement of the kings of the Davidic dynasty, thus clearly moving into the historical field what according to Mowinckel belonged to the realm of myth. The exposition of Kraus' ideas can be found in *Die Königsherrschaft Gottes im A.T.*, Tübingen 1951, "Gilgal. Ein Beitrag zur Kultusgeschichte Israels", *VT*, 1951, p. 181, and *Gottesdienst in Israel*, Munich 1954.

brated the ark's removal to Jerusalem and culminated in the oracle addressed to David on the eternity of his dynasty: Yahweh chose Zion (v. 13) and Yahweh chose David—these were the two major themes of the cult in Jerusalem. The conclusion that there was a cultic drama in existence may also be drawn from the invitation to come and "see" Yahweh's works (Ps. 46.9; 48.9; 66.5; 98.3). It is possible that the cult included (cf. especially Ps. 66.5) dramatic representations of the great events of the past such as the Exodus from Egypt and the crossing of the Jordan; but, whether by gesture or simply by word, the recalling of these events had as its object the overcoming of chronological and spatial distance and the real introduction of the onlookers into the presence of the God who not only acted there and then, but who still acts *hic et nunc*. All these reminders, apart from that of the Passover, took place at the time of the great autumn feast, coinciding with that of the New Year, which proves how far the cycle of time was put to the service of history. Thus it is that the creation myth alluded to in Ps. 77 (v. 17ff.) is no more than a figurative way of showing God's intervention for his people's salvation; but by putting the language of myth at the service of history, Israel, consciously or unconsciously, made a new myth out of history, that is to say a fundamental structure of thought which could sometimes lead it far from its anchorage in time.

One theme, however, which did not belong to the history of the past found its way into the cult: though largely directed towards the past, the cult also looked towards the future, towards Yahweh's final consummation of his kingship. In the Old Testament Yahweh's kingship was an object of hope, but for the Israelite hope[1] is a dynamic reality which literally "stretches"— for that is the sense of the root *qwh*—anyone who is animated by it, determining in this way his present behaviour far beyond the cultic sphere, although the cult may have allowed it to manifest itself with maximum intensity, a faithful echo of which is given in the Psalms. That this hope was made concrete in certain rites is quite probable, despite the absence of precise indications, but it should not be concluded that all eschatology found expression in cultic rites. Faith in Yahweh's final triumph was strong enough to do without rites, while in religions lacking eschatology the rite

---

[1] On hope in the O.T., cf. the article by Van der Ploeg, *RB*, 1954, p. 481, which brings together all the material concerning the terminology of hope.

was the only means of ensuring the perpetuation of the revelation.

The representation in the cult of God's past, present and future actions leads us to describe the cult as a revelation of God. This revelation is summarized in Yahweh's name, the invocation of which, moreover, is often synonymous with the cult (cf. 1 Kings 8.43). Linked as it was with the fundamental events of the Exodus and Sinai, this name contained both a command and a promise. Since the revelation of Yahweh could only be the revelation of the holy God before whom evil could not exist, the representation of his acts implied a requirement and a decision to be made: that is what is expressed by the rites of judgment[1] which, from the most distant times, must have formed part of the cult, and the importance of which was stressed by eschatology when it placed them on a universal plane (Ps. 96.13; 98.8). The cult's dependence on history, considered at least by the Yahwist and the Deuteronomist as the history of God's promises and judgments, invested it with an ethical character unparalleled in other religions in which the cult was and at times was forced to be in opposition to ethics. The various decalogues, ritual as well as ethical, probably have a cultic origin intended to state the conditions of entry into the sanctuary (Ps. 15 and 24), and the sometimes complicated Levitical ritual would allow no forgetting that the differences between the sacred and the profane was the expression of the primordial antithesis between the holy God and sin.

This ethical basis of the rite also appears in the legislation on sacrifice. The history of sacrifice in the Old Testament is complex; it is the business of literary and archaeological study to make clear what is truly Israelite and what is adopted from Canaan, what is due simply to the cultural influence of the environment, whether it be nomadic or agricultural, and what corresponds to a religious purpose. Any wish to form an absolutely coherent synthesis in this field would do violence to the Old Testament itself, which never succeeded in unifying either the terminology or the symbolism of sacrifice. While leaving the question open and adopting a very general point of view, we believe that it is possible to distinguish behind the three main forms of sacrifice, gift ('olah, minchah), communion (zebach, shelamin), expiation (chattat, 'asham) three

---

[1] We can only form hypotheses about the way in which those judgments received concrete form in the cult; it is possible that the cult occasionally included rites of ordeal and liturgies of blessing and cursing analogous to those mentioned in Dt. 27.

aspects of a single purpose which was to ensure the revelation of God. And so we think that the sacrifice takes its place in the general purpose of the cult, which is the affirmation of God's sovereignty.

The believer recognizes that everything comes from God, the creator and disposer of all things, and he expresses this by offering to God all or a part of the elements of sacrifice. The cult was the commemoration of the covenant; and so the act of eating together with the invisible but present deity—what the Old Testament calls "eating before Yahweh" (Ex. 32.6; Dt. 12.18; Jg. 9.27; 2 Sam. 15.11)—expressed in the most tangible form that communication of life that God makes to man. To receive life from God became a necessity when human life was threatened either by external dangers (war, epidemic), or by sin. The sacrifice, then, is the means of restoring a broken relationship; it must first appease God's anger justly roused by sin, it symbolizes next, by the victim's death, the death of the guilty sinner, and finally it puts at the sinner's disposal an upright life symbolized by the quality and purity of the sacrificial victims. Without denying the secondary motives, some of which were strongly tainted with magic, we envisage the sacrifice as the act through which God reveals and communicates his life-force, in which man receives infinitely more than he brings and in which it follows that the sacramental element takes precedence of the truly sacrificial element.

Man's participation in the cult can only assume the aspect of a response. To the word, revealed and announced in the form of drama and teaching, there comes in answer from man the word of acceptance. To God's action in going out to his people there corresponds man's answering step: "I come, as it is prescribed in the roll of the book, to do thy good pleasure" (Ps. 40.8). This human word may be a collective or individual confession of sin, a taking of a vow and a confession of faith like the declaration which accompanied the offering of the first-fruits and whose importance we have already pointed out (Dt. 26.1-10). Moreover, the liturgy left much scope for individual initiative dictated by the circumstances of the moment. Since the work of Gunkel and Mowinckel, there is general agreement in recognizing the individual Psalms of lamentation as cultic Psalms, which proves how far the Israelite cult was from being pressed into a single rigid pattern. Flexibility of cultic forms is the necessary corollary of the divine revelation in history, for since inability to repeat itself is characteristic of history, in so far as the cult was an expression of that revelation it could not be reduced to the repetition of an unchanging rite. Music and singing held an important place in the cult, for those were the means through which it was thought possible to give God a response worthy of his power. The Israelite cult was a cult of praise and it always remained so in spite of the insistence on expiation from the time of Ezekiel and the priestly writers.[1] From the most ancient times, praise in the form of brief rhythms beaten out to the sound of the tambourine accompanied the sacrifices; under pressure from David, the part played by music took on fresh scope (cf. 2 Sam. 6.15; Amos 5.23). We witness indeed the unfolding of a type of piety in which praise goes beyond sacrificial symbolism by absorbing it; Psalms 40 and 50 consider the action of thanks as sufficient, whether it be accompanied by sacrifice or not, and in a prophetic flight Hosea expresses himself in an analogous way: "Let us offer thee our lips like bulls" (14.3). And the supremely cultic book, the book of Chronicles, continually makes the point that praise and brotherly joy form the main thread of the Israelitic cult.

(c) The Law

In all religions law represents an element whose importance varies, but whose permanence is generally decisive for that religion's orientation. According to van der Leeuw,[2] the relationship between law and religion may assume four aspects: (a) the law is an object of veneration; (b) the revelation of the law like divine revelation can degenerate into mere observance, as in Judaism and Zoroastrianism; (c) exaggerated observance brings opposition to the law as a reaction; (d) lastly, in mysticism, the law is completely denied.

In the Old Testament the law, like the temple, is one answer to the problem of God's presence; on the one hand it brings out God's transcendence and sovereignty as they are expressed by his word, on the other hand, it shows how God intervenes in the world, leaving nothing, not even the smallest details, outside his

---

[1] Did the Israelite cult include a preaching element? The literary type of preaching is represented in the O.T. by the Deuteronomic exhortations, certain speeches in Chronicles which are put in the mouths of the prophets and by certain passages in the prophetic books themselves, but everything leads to the belief that preaching lay mainly outside the truly cultic realm.

[2] *Phaenomenologie der Religion*, p. 423.

sovereignty. The legalist form of religion appears only at a relatively late period. However, it must be recognized that the law was not grafted on to the religion at one particular time, for it was implied and required by the central notion of the covenant. The covenant being in effect the choice by a superior party of another whom he wishes to associate with his plan, can only be effective if it takes concrete form in a certain number of laws, which have the object of permitting those who have been the object of the choice to lead a life conformed to the new situation into which they have entered. That is why the most ancient texts mention *debarim*, *chuqqim*, *mishpatim*, as having a bearing on cultic or moral ordinances and which, from an early period, were handed on orally as well as in written form. As initiator and surety of the covenant Yahweh continually reminds the people of the conditions necessary for its maintenance. The multiplicity of the terms used brings us an echo of the diversity of the circumstances in which the Israelite had to seek a law in order to live in conformity with God's will. These laws are words, *debarim*, a term which suggests their divine origin and authority, *mishpatim* or *chuqqim*, engraved ordinances which acquire an intangible value through being fixed in writing, or *mitswot*, commandments. The term *torah*, which came to be the supreme term for law, does not have in the Old Testament the sense and scope which it is to acquire in Rabbinic writings; yet its specifically religious origin confers upon it the most important place in the terminology. At first we find it only in the plural. According to the circumstances there are *torot*, divine directives, but already in Hosea 4.6 and especially from Deuteronomic times, the word used in the singular designates the body of legislative measures sometimes summarized in a few brief formulae, of which the best known and most striking is the one in Mic. 6.8ff. The verb *yarah*, to which the noun *torah*[1] is connected, does not originally designate divination by means of arrows shot in a certain direction (2 Kings 13.17; Jg. 18.6), a frequently attested custom in pre-Islamic Arabia, but has the more general sense of pointing out a direction; this sense appears, for example, in such passages as Gen. 12.6 (the indicatory oak tree); Gen. 46.28; Ex. 15.25 (Yahweh shows them a tree); Prov. 6.13 (a worthless person *moreh*—makes signs—with his fingers); Ps. 45.5 (that your right hand may cause

[1] Concerning this etymology of the word *torah*, we are much indebted to G. Östborn, *Tora in the Old Testament*, Lund 1945.

you to see wonders). When this indication is given by a superior, it is also an instruction: Ex. 4.12-15; Is. 28.26; Job 34.32, and when the giver of this instruction is God, it receives thereby an authority that quite naturally appears absolute. This instruction should give to man the means of walking on a straight path. Yahweh points out the road, therefore the verb *horah* is often associated with *derek* (cf. Is. 2.3, Yahweh teaches his paths, and Ps. 25.8-12; 27.11; 32.8; 86.11; 1 Kings 8.36). The term *derek* had a precise sense; it generally refers to cultic practices; Amos speaks of the *derek* of Beersheba (8.14) and, in a passage mistakenly ascribed to Jeremiah, the term is used in the sense of religion (12.6). The *torah*, therefore, is originally a direction which turns people towards a law. The priests who had the main responsibility of promulgating the *torot* (Jer. 18.18) drew either from a traditional background, or from more direct inspiration, the directions required by the cases which were submitted to them. That the direction given by the priest should have been more or less confused with the road to be followed[1] gives no cause for surprise, very often a kind of osmosis is produced between two neighbouring ideas, so much so that the word *torah* is often associated with *halak*, to walk: Ex. 16.4; Is. 2.3; 30.20; 42.24; Jer. 9.12; 26.4; 32.23; 44.10, 23; Zech. 7.12; Neh. 1.10-30; Ps. 119.1; Dan. 9.10. The evolution of the word *torah* can be compared with that of *berit*; in both cases a reality expressing a bond ends by designating a body of rites and customs.

The Old Testament teaching about the law comprises two aspects which correspond to the two successive stages of its development. In the first stage we can define the law as God's revelation to those who are in the covenant. The aspect of revelation of the law appears in the place and manner in which it is presented in legislative texts. The statement of the law's provisions is generally preceded by a reminder of the election and the covenant: "You have seen how I treated the Egyptians, how I carried you away on eagle's wings and brought you to me. Henceforward, if you obey me and respect my covenant, I will keep you as my people . . ." (Ex. 19.4ff.). Moses has a vision, a revelation of

---

[1] The relationship between law and the path throws an interesting light on the Old Testament roots of the word of Jesus: "I am the way, the truth and the life" (Jn. 14.6). The terms truth and life are always associated with the law, which is defined as the way; Jesus represents himself therefore as one who carries out the law.

God's glory, before receiving his instructions; the Decalogue itself is introduced by a reminder of the Exodus from Egypt, of the redeeming act which was for Israel the supreme revelation, and the *Shema Israel* of Dt. 6 is given in that atmosphere of love which unites Yahweh with his people. The frequent use in the laws of the formula (cf. Lev. 18): "I am Yahweh",[1] is a reminder that the law is a revelation, and the "thou shalt" of the Decalogue and of other laws in the apodictic style is intended to express that the law is a revelation before it is an instruction: the "thou shalt" is a corollary of the "I am" of Ex. 3.14, for the revelation of God as a sovereign and present person can only have as counterpart the revelation of man as a dependent and obedient creature. The law is always addressed to a well defined group, to the people and more especially to the people of Israel who were in Egypt, the Exodus from Egypt being understood in a typological more than an historical sense: Dt. 4.1; 9.1; 13.11; 15.1; 20.1; 24.18; Lev. 18.3; 19.34; 26.45 etc. A foreigner or an Israelite without faith in the God of the covenant is incapable of understanding anything about the law. Moreover, there is never any question in the ancient texts of submitting foreigners to the law of Israel; it is given to the elected people as a means of being able to live within the covenant. As this objective needed to be continually renewed, the law too became modified and underwent adaptations so as to fulfil the better its rôle of guide towards salvation. Never in this first stage is the law considered as a sacrosanct reality, fixed once for all. Nevertheless it must be recognized that variations in the law turned only on points of detail and that in its main lines it remained conformed to its first inspiration. The similarity of a text such as Mic. 6.8ff. with the requirements of Moses in the Decalogue makes us realize the continuity of teaching of the *torah* and the fundamental unity between the law and the prophets, for on obedience to Yahweh as the only Lord there was no question of compromising.

The second stage can be characterized by the cleavage between the law and the covenant. The prophets had announced to the people the breaking of the covenant as a punishment for sin: "You are no longer my people, and I am no longer your God"

---

[1] The aspect of revelation in the law is also shown in the frequency of the formula: "I am Yahweh" in connection with legislative texts which were to form part of the cultic observances, cf. on this subject W. Zimmerli, "Ich bin Jahwe" in *Geschichte und Altes Testament (Festschrift Albrecht Alt)* 1953, pp. 179ff.

(Hos. 1.9) and by announcing a "new covenant" Jeremiah and Ezekiel naturally understood that the old one was to be annulled. Events in 587, by temporarily setting aside the covenant and the framework of its normal functioning, also brought into question the value of the law. The dilemma arose: was it necessary to cease using them, to consider them outworn, or, on the other hand, to keep them while attempting to give them a new foundation? It was the last solution that prevailed, for the abolition of the covenant was not considered as final; the prophets had announced a new covenant which was also to include new laws (Jer. 31.33; Ez. 36.27); and so the period of the covenant's rupture was regarded as temporary and, while waiting for God to carry out the promises of the prophets, the people held fast to the observance of the law. The *torah* of Ezekiel (40-48) brings us an echo of that period of transition by showing us how it was put to profitable use in the codifying of a body of law while waiting for the restoration of the covenant. As events gave little authority for a speedy realization of these hopes and as the return authorized by Cyrus was far from corresponding to the re-establishment of the covenant, the representatives of tradition tried, by maintaining and strengthening the law, to restore the lost covenant or rather to find in the law a substitute for the covenant.

This was not less than a reversal of the old order: whereas the law was formerly the expression of the covenant, it now becomes the condition of its restoration. It was normal that the law should assume greater authority from that time forward. Ezra, the man of the law, becomes the great figure of Judaism and it is not impossible that the portrait of Moses in the later strata of the Pentateuch was modelled on him. Henceforward, he who accepts the law becomes part of the community; this system had the advantage over the old one of giving a bigger place to the individual and of allowing Judaism to proselytize. The law is no longer given by merely belonging to the chosen people, but one belongs to that people only by accepting the law. The history of Israel becomes, in this new conception, only a series of examples of men who were faithful to the law. The piety of a Daniel is made up almost entirely of ritual and alimentary interdictions; there is nothing surprising in the law becoming an end in itself, instead of remaining a means of walking in God's way. Having become the foundation of the faith, the law is in certain texts clothed with a prestige and with qualities which in reality are only becoming to God alone; it is often personified; people take pleasure in it (Is. 56.1-8) or take a dislike to it (Lev. 26.43), and the author of Psalm 119 sees no other goal to his religious aspirations than meditation on the law: "I take delight in thy law (v. 70). If thy law had not been my delight, I would have perished in my affliction (v. 92). How much I love thy law. All day it is the object of my meditations" (v. 97). It is fitting to emphasize that this veneration of the law was never felt as a burdensome yoke, but as a very pure joy: the Jews really found in the law the same power as in the covenant or the cult. It was only according as, within the limits of this new situation, salvation became man's work instead of God's, that the religion of the law showed its inability to express God's presence in its full scope.

BIBLIOGRAPHY

A. MINISTRIES

(a) The King

ALT, A., "Das Königtum in Israel und Juda", VT, 1951, p. 2.

ANDERSON, G. W., "Some aspects of the Uppsala school of O.T. study", Harvard theol. Review, 1950, p. 239.

ENGNELL, I., Studies in Divine Kingship in the Ancient Near East, Uppsala, 1943.

EULER, F. K., "Königtum und Götterwelt in den aramäischen Inschriften Nordsyriens", ZAW, 1938, p. 272.

FRAINE, J. DE, L'aspect religieux de la royauté israélite, Rome 1954.

FRANKFORT, H., Kingship and the Gods, Chicago 1948.

GADD, C. J., Ideas of Divine Rule in the Ancient Near East, Schweich Lectures, London 1948.

GASTER, T. H., Thespis. Ritual, Myth and Drama in the Ancient Near East, New York 1950.

GROSS, H., Weltherrschaft als religiöse Idee im A.T., Bonner biblische Beiträge no. 6, 1953.

HOOKE, S. H., The Origins of Early Semitic Ritual, Schweich Lectures, London 1938.

JOHNSON, A. R., "The rôle of the King in the Jerusalem cultus", The Labyrinth, ed. by S. H. Hooke, 1935, p. 73.

KRAUS, H. J., Die Königsherrschaft Gottes im A.T., Tübingen 1951.

KUPPERS, W., "Gottesherrschaft und Königtum in Israel", Internationale kirchl. Zeitschr., 1935, p. 148.

LABAT, R., *Le caractère religieux de la royauté assyro-babylonienne*, Paris 1939.

LINDBLOM, J., "Einige Grundfragen der alttest. Wissenschaft" (*Festschrift A. Bertholet*), 1950, p. 325.

LODS, AD., "La divinisation du roi dans l'Orient méditerranéen et ses répercussions dans l'Ancien Israël", *RHPR*, 1930, p. 209.

MOWINCKEL, S., "Urmensch und Königsideologie", *Studia theologica*, Lund 1948, p. 71.

NORTH, C. R., "The religious aspects of Hebrew kingship", *ZAW*, 1932, p. 8.

NOTH, M., "Gott, König und Volk im A.T. Eine methodologische Auseinandersetzung mit einer gegenwärtigen Forschungsrichtung", *ZThK*, 1950, p. 157.

RAD, G. VON, "Erwägungen zu den Königspsalmen", *ZAW*, 1940, p. 216.

ROST, L., "Sinaibund und Davidsbund", *ThLitztg*, 1947, p. 129.

VAN DEN BUSSCHE, "Le texte de la prophétie de Nathan sur la dynastie davidique", *Eph. th. lov.*, 1948, p. 354.

WIDENGREN, G., *Psalm 110 och det sakrala kungadömet in Israel*, *UUA*, 1940.

The king and the Tree of Life in Ancient Near Eastern Religions, UUA 1951.

(b) The Prophet

BOTTERWECK, G. J., *Gott erkennen im Sprachgebrauch des A.T.*, Bonner bibl. Beitr. 2, 1952.

BUBER, M., *Der Glaube der Propheten*, Zürich 1950.

EISSFELDT, O., "Das Berufungsbewusstsein der Propheten als theologisches Gegenwartsproblem", *ThStKr*, 1934, p. 124.

FOHRER, G., *Die symbolischen Handlungen der Propheten*, Zürich 1953.

GIESEBRECHT, FR., *Die Berufsbegabung der altt. Propheten*, Göttingen 1897.

GUILLAUME, A., *Prophecy and Divination*, London 1938.

GUNKEL, H., "Die geheimen Erfahrungen der Propheten", *Schriften des A.T.* 2, 2.

Die Propheten, Göttingen 1907.

HÄNEL, J., *Das Erkennen Gottes bei den Schrift-Propheten*, Berlin 1923.

HAEUSSERMANN, FR., *Wortempfang und Symbol in der altt. Phophetie. Eine Untersuchung zur Psychologie des prophet. Erlebnisses*, BZAW 58, 1932.

HALDAR, A., *Associations of Cultic Prophets among the Ancient Semites*, Uppsala 1945.

HERTZBERG, H. W., *Prophet und Gott*, Gütersloh 1923.

HESCHEL, A., *Die Prophetie*, Cracow 1936.

HÖLSCHER, G., *Die Profeten*, Leipzig 1914.

JEPSEN, A., *Nabi. Soziologische Studien zur altt. literatur und Religionsgeschichte*, Munich 1934.

JOHNSON, A. R., *The Cultic Prophet in Ancient Israel*, Cardiff 1944.

JUNKER, H., *Prophet und Seher in Israel*, Trier 1927.

KOEHLER, L., *Deuterojesaja stilkritisch untersucht*, BZAW 37, 1923.

LINDBLOM, J., *Die literarische Gattung der prophetischen Literatur*, UUA, 1924.
    "Die Religion der Propheten und die Mystik", *ZAW*, 1939, p. 65.

LODS, AD., *Les Prophètes d'Israël et les débuts du judaïsme*, Paris 1935.

MOWINCKEL, S., *Psalmenstudien III Kultprophetie und prophetische Psalmen*, Oslo 1922.
    "La connaissance de Dieu chez les prophètes de l'A.T.", *RHPR*, 1943, p. 69.

NEHER, A., *Amos*, Paris 1950.
    L'essence du prophétisme, Paris 1955.

QUELL, G., *Wahre und falsche Propheten. Versuch einer Interpretation.* Gütersloh 1952.

RAD, G. VON, "Die falschen Propheten", *ZAW*, 1933, p. 109.

ROWLEY, H. H., "The nature of prophecy in the light of recent study", *Harvard theol. Review*, 1945, p. 1.

SCOTT, R. B. Y., *The Relevance of the Prophets*, 1944.

SEIERSTAD, I. P., *Die Offenbarungserlebnisse der Propheten Amos, Jesaja und Jeremia*, Oslo 1946.

Studies in O.T. Prophecy presented to Professor T. H. Robinson, Edinburgh 1950.

VOLZ, P., *Prophetengestalten des A.T.*, Stuttgart 1938.

WIDENGREN, G., *Literary and Psychological Aspects of the Hebrew Prophets*, Uppsala-Leipzig 1948.

ZIMMERLI, W., *Erkenntnis Gottes nach dem Buche Ezechiel. Eine theologische Studie*, Zürich 1954.

(c) The Priest

BAUDISSIN, W. W. VON, *Geschichte des altt. Priestertums*, Leipzig 1889.

BEGRICH, J., "Die priesterliche Tora". *Werden u. Wesen des A.T.* BZAW, 1936, p. 63.

GAUTIER, L., *Le sacerdoce dans l'A.T.*, 1874.

HÖLSCHER, G., "Levi", Pauly-Wissowa. *REA XII*, col. 2155.

JOHNSON, A. R., *The Cultic Prophet in Ancient Israel*, Cardiff 1944.

KUCHLER, F., "Das priesterliche Orakel in Israel und Juda", *Festschrift W. Baudissin*, Giessen 1918.

Mowinckel, S., "Kultprophetie und prophetische Psalmen", *Psalmenstudien* 3.

Pedersen, J., "The role played by inspired persons among the Israelites and the Arabs", *Studies in O.T. Prophecy presented to Professor T. H. Robinson*, Edinburgh 1950, p. 227.

Press, R., "Das Ordal in A.T.", *ZAW*, 1933, p. 227.

Thiersch, H., *Ependytes und Ephod*, Stuttgart 1936.

Welch, A. C., *Prophet and Priest in Old Israel*, London 1936.

(d) The Wise Man

Baumgartner, W., *Israelitische und altorientalische Weisheit*, Tübingen 1933.

Causse, A., "Sagesse égyptienne et sagesse juive", *RHPR*, 1929, p. 149.

Dubarle, A. L., *Les sages d'Israël*, coll. "Lectio divina", Paris 1946.

Duesberg, H., *Les scribes inspirés*, 2 vol., Paris 1939.

Dürr, L., *Das Erziehungswesen im A.T. und im antiken Orient*, Leipzig 1931.

Fichtner, J., *Die altorientalische Weisheit in ihrer isr.-jüd. Ausprägung*, BZAW 62, Giessen 1933.

Humbert, P., *Recherches sur les sources égyptiennes de la littérature sapientiale d'Israël*, Neuchâtel 1929.

Meinhold, J., *Die Weisheit Israels*, 1908.

Pedersen, J., *Scepticisme israélite*, Paris 1931.

Rankin, O. S., *Israel's Wisdom Literature*, Edinburgh 1936.

Rylaarsdam, J. C., *Revelation in Jewish Wisdom Literature*, Chicago 1936.

Wendel, A., *Säkularisierung in Israels Kultur*, Gütersloh 1934.

B. THE PERMANENT SETTING

(a) The sacred place

Gall, A. von, *Altisraelitische Kultstätten*, Giessen 1898.

Jeremias, Friedr., "Das orientalische Heiligtum", *Angelos. Archiv. für neutestamentliche Zeitgeschichte und Kulturkunde*, vol. 4, 1932, p. 56.

Moehlenbrinck, K., *Der Tempel Salomos*, Stuttgart 1932.

Parrot, A., *Le Temple de Jérusalem* (Cahiers d'archéol. bibl. no. 5), 1955.

Phythian-Adams, W. J., *The People and the Presence*, London 1942.

Rad, G. von, "Zelt und Lade", *NZK*, 1931, p. 484.

Schmidt, Hans, "Kerubenthron und Lade", *Eucharisterion* (*Gunkelfestschrift* 1), 1923, p. 120.

Schmidt, Martin, *Prophet und Tempel. Eine Studie zum Problem der Gottesnähe im A.T.*, Zurich-Zollikon 1948.

Westphal, G., *Jahwes Wohnstätten*, Giessen 1908.

(b) The Cult

ALT, A., *Die Ursprünge des israelitischen Rechts, Berichte über die Verh. d. sächs Akad. d. Wissensch. Phil.-hist.* LI, Leipzig 86 vol., tome 1, 1934, reproduced in *Kleine Schriften*. t. 1, pp. 278ff.
Die Wallfahrt von Sichem nach Bethel, Abhandl. der Herder Gesellschaft, vol. 6, no. 3, 1938, reproduced in *Kleine Schriften* t. 1, pp. 79ff.

HOOKE, S. H., *The Origins of Early Semitic Ritual*, Schweich Lectures, 1935.

HUMBERT, P., *Problèmes du livre d'Habacuc*, Neuchâtel 1944.
"La relation de Genèse 1 et du Psaume 104 avec la liturgie du Nouvel-An israélite", *RHPR*, 1935, pp. 1ff.

KRAUS, H. J., *Die Königsherrschaft Gottes im A.T.*, 1951.
"Gilgal; ein Beitrag zur Kultusgeschichte Israels", *VT*, 1951.
Gottesdienst in Israel. Studien zur Geschichte des Laubhüttenfestes, Munich 1954.

MOWINCKEL, S., *Psalmenstudien*, Oslo 1922ff (6 volumes).
Zum israelitischen Neujahr und zur Deutung des Thronbesteigungspsalmen, Oslo 1952.
Religion und Kultus, Göttingen 1953.

NOTH, M., *Überlieferungsgeschichte des Pentateuch*, 1948.

PEDERSEN, J., "Passahfest und Passahlegende", *ZAW*, 1931.

SNAITH, N. H., *The Jewish New Year Festival. Its Origins and Development*, London 1947.

WELLHAUSEN, J., *Prolegomena zur Geschichte Israels*, 6th ed., 1927.

WENDEL, AD., *Das Opfer in der israelitischen Religion*, Leipzig 1927.

(c) The Law

DAUBE, D., *Studies in Biblical Law*, Cambridge 1947.

NOTH, M., *Die Gesetze im Pentateuch*, Halle 1940.

ÖSTBORN, G., *Tora in the Old Testament*, Lund 1945.

PART THREE

OPPOSITION TO AND FINAL
TRIUMPH OF GOD'S WORK

~~~~~~

I. SIN AND REDEMPTION

"THE idea of sin is the converse of the idea of God."[1] God is strength and his whole action tends only to give strength and life; sin, on the contrary, which assumes the aspect of a hostile force only in the latest Old Testament texts, always produces a state of weakness which is a forerunner of death. God is the one who enters into relationship and who makes the covenant, sin is a breaking of this relationship. "Your sins," says one prophet, "make a separation between you and God" (Is. 59.2). The whole of the sin vocabulary confirms this fundamental aspect of breaking: *chattat* is the missing, the abandoning, of the straight road, *'awon* is to turn aside or to become lost, shown not only in act but in thought, *ma'al* is unfaithfulness, finally *pesha'*[2] expresses open rebellion. Wherever sin shows itself, it destroys communion with God and delivers man to himself or to evil forces.

Although absent from the rest of Israelite tradition, the explanation given in Genesis, concerning the origin of sin, is one that has the greatest theological importance. If the Yahwist connected sin with the serpent,[3] it is not only because this animal symbolized

---

[1] Gelin, *Les idées maîtresses de l'Ancien Testament*, p. 66.

[2] *Pesha'* is always rebellion; in one of the oldest texts in which it appears (Ex. 22.8, Covenant Code), it signifies an attack on the rights of others; cf. L. Koehler, "Ein Beitrag zur Kenntnis des hebräischen Rechts", *ZAW*, 1928, p. 213.

[3] The ambivalent aspect of the serpent is common to many religions; we meet it in Egypt and Babylon as well as in Greece; but while these religions give particular stress to the life-force aspect, the Old Testament, adopting once more the opposite to Canaanite beliefs, stresses its deadly rôle. Furthermore, it seems almost certain

cunning and mystery more than others: in Semitic religions, the serpent was associated with the representations of chaos and death; hostile to life, it carries within it the poison which kills; but the serpent was also associated with the vegetation and fertility cults, in which it symbolized the vital force of the earth. It may be said, then, that sin as it appears in the Paradise narrative is a power of death which definitely deprives man of all possibility of eternal life and at the same time a life-force which, for the time being, assures man of superior knowledge, particularly in the realms of intelligence and sexuality. Sin comes from outside, it is an objective reality, it is the incarnation of forces which are hostile to Yahweh and to which man appealed for salvation. And so the identification of the serpent with Satan which is stated for the first time in the Wisdom of Solomon (2.24) and which passed into the New Testament (Rom. 16.20; Rev. 12.9 and 20.2) only draws the final consequences of what the story-teller in Genesis had already glimpsed. The serpent metaphor seeks to insist on the mysterious and sudden appearance of sin, even more than on its external character, it appears as suddenly as God himself and it seems sometimes that God's presence brings about that of sin as a sort of corollary. The widow of Zarephath, in the presence of the man of God, is suddenly haunted by her sin (1 Kings 17.18) and the prophet Isaiah has a vision of his sin at the very moment of a vision of God. Another Genesis text which is quite difficult to translate also insists on the mysterious quality of sin, comparing it with a demon which lurks in front of a house door

that there was a connection between the name of the serpent and that of Eve. Lidzbarski has pointed out the interest of a Carthaginian votive inscription where these words appear: *chawwat 'elat malkat*=goddess and queen Chawwat, the name of a goddess of the underworld (*Eph. für semit. Epigraph.*, 1, 26ff.); in Aramaic and Syriac the serpent is *chewiya*, in Arabic we meet *chayya* besides other names; in northern Abyssinia a diabolical serpent called *cheway* is known; to all this we may add that Philo says that the serpent was called ἐν πατρίῳ γλώττῃ 'Eva, that is, Eve (*De agricultura*, par. 95, ed. Cohn-Wendland, t. 2) and that Clement of Alexandria holds the same view (*Protrept.* 2, 12, 1-2). In the light of all these parallels, the text of Ecclesiasticus (40.1) takes new point: "God has given much trouble, and a heavy burden is put upon men, from the day when they come forth from their mother's womb to the day when they return to the mother of all the living." The Eve-earth-serpent relationship seems a well established fact, but it is not less clear that the Genesis narrator expressed a deeper truth with the help of these data. Other parallels on the symbolism of the serpent may be found in the work of J. Coppens, *La connaissance du bien et du mal et le péché du paradis*, Louvain 1948.

and lies in wait for the slightest opportunity to rush upon its prey (Gen. 4.7).[1]

There is no contradiction between the external origin of sin and its seat within a man's body. The serpent and man are both taken from the earth, from the 'adamah, and though the serpent has a closer link with sin, man also bears within himself, by reason of his creation from the earth, an innate and permanent propensity towards evil. The Yahwist creates no illusion for himself about man's natural goodness: "The thoughts which are formed in the heart of man are evil from his youth" (Gen. 6.5 and 8.21). The prophet Jeremiah often speaks of the evil inclinations of the heart (16.12; 17.9; 18.12) and looks on sin as a kind of congenital illness in man stemming from his condition as a created being and not from his fall.

There is no man who commits no sin (1 Kings 8.46). None can say: I am free of all sin (Prov. 20.9). There is no righteous man upon earth (Eccl. 7.20). Man, taken from dust, could never be pure before him who created him (Job 4.17-21; 14.4). Certain Psalmists use this state of man as an argument to justify and claim God's mercy; because man is dust God must forgive (Ps. 78.38; 103.10; 143.2) and the author of Psalm 51 asserts the universality of sin by depicting every man as bringing with him, when he enters the world, a propensity towards evil. The same idea is again expressed by a post-exilic prophet: God does not give free rein to the burning of his anger because he created men as feeble beings (Is. 57.16).[2]

The sickness metaphor to designate sin was all the more suggestive as sickness in its proper sense was always considered, according to the classical Israelite idea, as a direct result of sin. We find it in Hosea (5.13; 6.1; 7.1; 11.7), in Jeremiah (3.22ff.), in Second Isaiah (53.5; 57.17ff.), as well as in several Psalms (6.3; 30.3; 107.18; 147.3).

For the most part, however, the Old Testament speaks of man as a sinner, not because he is of human kind, but because he has rebelled against his God.[3] For every man is in relationship to Yahweh and

---

[1] The verb rbts is associated with demons in Isaiah 13.21 and in Babylon rabitsu is the name of a demon.

[2] It is only in the book Ecclesiasticus that we first find the statement of a cause-effect relationship between Adam's sin and that of humanity (Ecclus. 25.24).

[3] What may be termed the finitude of man is distinct from his guilt, even though it prepared ground favourable for guilt. Finitude is based on the difference between

this relationship is not essentially that of creator and creature, but that of two persons: man is God's partner, for whom he has made it possible to respond and before whom he has set the necessity of choosing. Sin is to refuse to choose God and, consequently, the breaking of this relationship. In the Garden of Eden, man could normally have listened and should have listened to the voice of Yahweh, whose prohibition against the eating of one tree was a very little thing in comparison with the pleasures that were granted, and the serpent's temptation, despite its seductive power, was not unavoidable. Sin is presented as a rebellion: finding it unbearable to be content with much when he thought it possible for him to grasp everything, man rebelled against his divine partner in order to seize, as his booty, the gift that had been withheld. According to the Genesis myth, this gift consisted in the knowledge of good and evil, which probably means total knowledge[1] and, since for the Hebrew mentality knowledge is more dynamic than intellectual, a total power which would have made him like Elohim. To know anything is to have power over it; now Yahweh does not wish man to be his equal, because that would rupture the relationship and the filial bond which should remain as the one binding man to God. The sinner always appears as the one who rebels against his God or against his neighbour. Even when the sin is only the transgressing of a prohibition, it is considered by Yahweh as an act of disobedience which provokes his anger, for the divine presence, even in a material form like the ark, is always that of the personal God, at any rate in Yahwist theology. Cain's sin, jealousy of his brother, is the replica of Adam's—jealousy of Yahweh's privilege. The prophets always speak of sin as a responsible act, as a refusal to obey an appeal or an order; the same Yahwist writer, to whom we owe the story of the beginnings, expounds in the Pentateuch how to the initiative of God, to whom they owed their

God and man in the order of creation, while guilt consists in the antithesis between holiness and sin. Cf. on this topic P. Ricoeur, " Culpabilité tragique et culpabilité biblique ", RHPR, 1953, p. 285.

[1] We feel in fact that the mention of two opposed realities expresses some complementary relationship between them. What Yahweh forbids is neither moral awareness nor intellectual discernment, but complete knowledge; this awareness is beyond the reach of the child or of the old man in his second childhood (Dt. 1.39; 2 Sam. 19.36); now what Yahweh requires of man, is unconditional obedience which will keep him inside the limits set for him (cf. on this topic G. Lambert, "Lier-délier, l'expression de la totalité par l'opposition de deux contraires " in Vivre et penser, Recherches d'exégèse et d'histoire, 3rd series, Paris 1944, pp. 91ff.).

freedom, the people replied by repeated refusals, wilfully closing their hearts to the divine appeal, to such a degree as to become finally and permanently insensitive to the call : that is what the Old Testament calls the "hardening of the heart"[1] in which the initiative is from God himself, but of which only those who are themselves already wilfully and consciously hardened are the object. The prophet Jeremiah, to whom we owe the most profound meditations on the subject of man's relationship with God, expressed in a well-known word the power that indefinitely repeated sin can exert in transforming human nature: "Can the Ethiopian change the colour of his skin or the panther eradicate the spots from his hide? Of yourselves, it is impossible to do good, so accustomed are ye to doing evil" (13.23). The habit of doing evil creates a sort of second nature to which there is no other remedy than an intervention by God, who will have to bring in a new circumcision of the heart, which has become infinitely wicked, in order to remove the obstacle which has grown up between man and himself (Jer. 4.4; 17.9). This refusal, according to the prophets, includes different aspects : for Amos, it is ingratitude, for Hosea, unfriendliness, for Isaiah, pride, for Jeremiah, falseness concealed in the heart, for Ezekiel, open rebellion—but always it is the breaking of a bond. Just as on the human plane sin brings the breaking of the social and family bonds, sin against God brings separation from God; every time a man sins, he re-lives Adam's experience and goes far from the face of Yahweh.

Is this sin of rebellion and refusal as universal as the weakness inherent in the created state? Indeed the Old Testament often makes a distinction between the sinner and the righteous man :[2] it sometimes happens that some men claim to be pure from all sin (Ps. 18.24; Job 33.9), and so the "all have sinned" only corresponds in part to the teaching of Israel. However, when the Old Testament considers universal history as a whole, it makes no distinction

---

[1] The main O.T. texts on the hardening of the heart are Ex. 4.21; 7.3; Is. 6.10; 29.10; Ps. 95.8; it is produced less by absence than by excess of revelation, a point which stresses man's responsibility. We must further bear in mind that the O.T. is unaware of second causes and ascribes to God events which depend on the human will and that it draws no further distinction, so important for us, between what God wills and what he allows. On the problem of hardening of the heart, see the study by Franz Hesse, *Das Verstockungsproblem im A.T.*, BZAW, 1954.

[2] When the O.T. distinguishes between sinners and righteous it adopts a sociological standpoint rather than an ontological or moral one; the indispensable distinctions which society makes no longer exist in God's eyes.

between sinners and the righteous; at the time of the flood, it was not said that Noah was sinless but that he had found grace, which rather implies that he was no exception to the general rebellion, and in the pictures of eschatological judgment the Remnant that will be saved is not necessarily composed of the righteous, for upon them too the catastrophe will fall, but it is solely the grace of God itself which determines the composition of this Remnant. The prophets, who had closer relationship than ordinary men with God, never dreamed of denying their own sin (cf. Is. 6; Jer. 1, etc.). On the contrary, they ask to be freed from it, and the fact of being a prophet does not preclude a new conversion (Jer. 15.19).

By sin man places himself in a state of guilt. Among the terms denoting sin *'awon* is the one that most nearly corresponds to what we understand by guilt. "Thou hast taken away," says the Psalmist, "the *'awon chatta'ti*" (Ps. 32.5). This guiltiness generally comes to light as soon as the sin is committed: Adam and Eve are afraid and hide from Yahweh, the guiltiness of Uzzah, who touched the ark in spite of orders to the contrary, is not long in being manifest since he is struck down (2 Sam. 6.6), and the sinner's bad conscience is illustrated by many examples (1 Sam. 24.6). "David's heart smote him because he had cut off the skirt of Saul's robe" (2 Sam. 24.10). The same expression is met in connection with David's census. The fault is often compared with a weight that must be carried by the transgressor (Gen. 4.13; Is. 1.4) or with a measure that will finally overflow (Gen. 15.16; 43.9; 44.16; Is. 40.2). Because of the solidarity which holds all the people together, the punishment falls not only upon the one who committed the evil but also upon those about him;[1] the whole country, even inanimate nature, can be defiled by the fault of one man; but in a general way the fault weighs more heavily on the one who committed the act and gives him the feeling of his sundering from God. Under the increasing influence of a legal conception of life, which did not leave the religious field outside its ambit, the notion of fault tends to become more materialized; sin is no longer the breaking of the bond with God, but simply the transgression of a commandment of the law which can be sufficiently repaired according to the rules of casuistry which make a distinction between

---

[1] Other examples of collective punishment are found in Gen. 9.5; 42.22f.; 2 Sam. 1.16; 4.11; 1 Kings 2.32; 21.1ff.; 2 Kings 9.7.

the various sins. It is obvious that the feeling of guilt takes on a very different aspect when confronted by a catalogue of laws from what it has before the living holy God.

Every fault brings punishment. This is a necessity, firstly because the offence against God must be repaired, then because it is incumbent to eliminate the contagious poison that sin is from the midst of the people, and finally because the sinner himself must be penalized. The punitive action of Yahweh is exercised according to the principle which dominates Israel legislation: the *lex talionis*. "God repays what I have done," exclaims Adoni-bezek when his thumbs and big toes are cut off as a punishment for the same mutilation which he had inflicted on seventy kings (Jg. 1.7). Eve, who, before the fall, guided Adam's desires as she willed, is thenceforward condemned to become her husband's slave, the builders of the tower of Babel who wish to stay together are condemned to be scattered, the people who abandon Yahweh to prostitute themselves before foreign gods will be actually transported to a foreign land, far from Yahweh's face. Man is so far responsible for his rebellions that his punishment appears as the sanction of a state in which he has deliberately placed himself: man has separated himself from God—he will obtain death. The sanction of sin is to involve man still more deeply in sin so that he weaves about himself a web from which it will be impossible for him to escape.

Iniquity is a burden that weighs so heavily on the land that it makes it fall (Jer. 6.19), or a crevice in a wall (Is. 30.13); it means that the sinner's conduct does no harm to God but falls back upon the sinner's own head (Is. 3.9; Jer. 7.19; Ez. 22.31); in the persons of King Saul (1 Sam. 17 to 20) and of the Pharaoh of the Exodus (Ex. 7 to 9), the Old Testament offers two instances which may be considered as typical of the power of sin revealed to its ultimate consequences. God acts according to the *lex talionis*, yet he does not link his punitive action with this legal form. God obeys only those laws that he himself fixes; he is certainly offended by sin but he retains the liberty to react according to the *lex talionis* or the law of anger or of mercy. Cases in which God punishes outside the *lex talionis* are relatively few: when for the sin of one person all the people are struck, Yahweh seems to conform to the principle of collective vengeance; so it is wise to notice that in these cases sins committed by kings are involved and kings are the incarnation of and responsible for the people, so that the king's sin visited upon the people is not a derogation of the *lex talionis*. Further, it sometimes happens that in connection with some particular sin God shows an anger which seems out of all proportion to its gravity; but it must not be forgotten that, when God punishes, he is regarding not a particular sin, but the uninterrupted succession of sins and that the offence can provoke his anger at a moment when man least expects it (cf. Is. 18.4ff.), for what counts before God more even than the punishment of sin is his will to rule and his plan to establish his kingship; although this kingship is manifested only at the price of a rupture, the day of Yahweh, the final judgment is already made partially real in each of the judgments which take place in the unfolding of history.

God also is free to grant mercy. Mercy is not the cancellation of punishment; but it takes away from it its aspect of irrevocable condemnation. In every sentence pronounced upon the first human beings, mercy modifies the punishment: the pains of childbirth, despite their violent nature, are the preliminary to the most beautiful of promises. When driving men from the Garden of Eden, Yahweh is careful to make clothes for them so that they can bear the rigours of a less clement climate. In a general way, it may be said that God acts only rarely in accordance with the violence of his anger, which, moreover, corresponds to strict justice; it is thus that he shows patience, generally intervening only after repeated warnings (Amos 4.6ff.) and that precisely because he is God and not man (Hos. 11.8). There are cases, doubtless, where the death of the sinner is the only means of eradicating the sin, but this represents the exception when logically it should represent the norm: the man who turns his back on God forsakes life for death; if he does not die, it is because God tempers justice with mercy: "God chasteneth but doth not give over to death" (Ps. 118.18). And so the punitive aspect which figures in punishment is counterbalanced and even dominated by the educative aspect. Whether the people or isolated individuals are involved, punishment is intended to set right again and to bring back on the right road the one or the ones who have turned aside from it. The story of Joseph and his brothers illustrates in typical manner this process of punishment by education: the brothers are chastised so that they may recognize the evil they have done to Joseph. To lead to the awareness of sin by way of punishment is the first stage of the divine pedagogy. This awareness is revealed by the confession of sins which, by giving glory to God and by recognizing its own faults, produces a true liberation of which several Psalms bring an echo: 32.3-5; 38.19; 39.2ff. By recognition of his sin, man must learn to hate it, for when confronted with punishment and the mercy which has held back from the full penalty, man will be ashamed of his sin (Ez. 16.59ff.) and especially will the awareness of his sin lead to a renewed awareness of God. " They shall know that I am Yahweh." This phrase frequently recurs in Ezekiel's mouth when he shows God's action towards his people in the form of judgment and of mercy (Ez. 24.27; 25.7; 29.16; 30.19; 32.15; 33.29, etc.). Even when God pardons he does not hide the sins, on the contrary he displays them to the guilty man so that the latter may experience the greater horror of them. The Wisdom writers likewise stress the educative value of chastisement and readily ascribe to God the usual methods of their own pedagogy: to chastise and to set right again (Job 15.17; Prov. 3.12).[1]

What Yahweh seeks to obtain by punishment is the sinner's return and the possibility of a new life. Conversion is the indispensable condition of forgiveness; without it, all the means of forgiveness which God has made available run the risk of being inoperative. This act is expressed by the Old Testament by means of various forms of the root *shub*, which expresses both return and repetition. The common exhortation of prophetic preaching to "return", means Israel's return to its origins, that is to the pure and unalloyed covenant with Yahweh which in the prophetic view has been substituted for paradise as the ideal period. This return necessarily implies a breaking of relationship: to return to Yahweh must bring the forsaking of foreign gods (Hos. 2.9) and of certain cultic and cultural forms incompatible with Yahweh: political alliance and trust in military force are just as much signs of unfaithfulness because they are a challenge to Yahweh's sovereignty. "It is by return, *shubah*,[2] and by quietness that you shall be saved! "

[1] Some interesting information on the pedagogical principles of the wisdom writers is to be found in P. Humbert, *Recherches sur les sources égyptiennes de la littérature sapientiale*, 1929 (chap. 9), and in L. Dürr, *Das Erziehungswesen im A.T. und im antiken Orient*, 1932.

[2] Except for Isaiah 30.15 where we meet the noun *shubah* the O.T. only uses the verb to express the fact of conversion; so conversion can never be considered as a quality that man could possess as his own; in the O.T. there are no converted men, but only beings who are incessantly converted. The term *teshubah* which is to be widely used in Jewish theology from Rabbinic times onwards is used in the

says Isaiah to those who put their hope in an alliance with Egypt (30.15). It was Jeremiah especially who drew from the root *shub* all the overtones of meaning contained in the word. Not only does he stress the moment of breaking by putting the term in relationship with *min*, a construction unknown before his time (Jer. 15.7; 18.8; 23.14, 22; 25.5; 35.15; 36.3 and 7; 44.5), but he shows that the renunciation of certain rites and customs is not enough unless it is done with the heart. Without the heart, the return runs the risk of being a deceit (3.10); he had experienced the fact that the best intentioned religious reforms were incapable of producing a real conversion which would be *be'emet, bemishpat* and *bitsedaqah*. Such a return can only be the business of each individual: before Jeremiah, the prophets address their exhortations to conversion to the people; now—and all the later prophets will adopt this language—this is the order that resounds: *Shubah na 'ish middarko hara'ah*, "Let every one turn from his evil way" (Jer. 18.11; 25.5; 26.3; 36.3, 7). The initiative of this return belongs to God himself; just as he will bring in the great eschatological turning point, the *shub shebut*, he it is who, even now, makes it possible to return to him: "Cause me to return and I will return!" (Jer. 31.18). "Cause us to return to thee and we will return" (Lam. 5.21). In Zech. 1.3 God's return seems to depend on the people's and in the great public prayer which Psalm 80 represents we find three times the request: "*Hashibenu!*"—"Make us return" (4, 8, 20).[1]

Since sin is a separation from God and an offence against God, it can only be effaced by an act of forgiveness. In Israel, faith in the love and faithfulness of Yahweh was so great that the possibility of pardon was never doubted, not that it was thought that laws could be fixed for God who, people knew, would do what seemed good to him (1 Sam. 3.18; 2 Sam. 16.10ff.), but to fall into God's hands (2 Sam. 24.14) was to trust in the Living God who could not in

O.T. in a temporal sense only (return of the seasons, for example) and is never associated with the religious attitude. On this topic, cf. the very thorough study by E. K. Dietrich, *Die Umkehr im A.T. und im Judentum*, 1936, and the more recent study which puts the problem on to a more theological plane by H. W. Wolff, "Das Thema 'Umkehr' in der alttestamentlichen Prophetie", *ZTbK*, 1951, p. 129.

[1] Since the verb is used in an absolute sense, without a preposition to indicate direction, it could also be translated as "Re-establish us"; this is the interpretation adopted by the Jerusalem Bible and by O. Eissfeldt in *Geschichte und Altes Testament, Festschrift A. Alt.*, pp. 65ff.

the last analysis desire the death of his creatures, sinners though they be. Since God created man weak and consequently inclined to sin, he will also have pity on him (2 Sam. 14.14; Ps. 78.38; 89.47-49; 103.14-16; 143.2; 144.3). But the real motive for God's pardon is to be found in the bond by which he freely linked himself with his people, by love, and by what is expressed by the term *chesed*. Sometimes this love is momentarily turned to anger. Nevertheless, it remains God's dominant feeling, a feeling which does not leave him, even when he must chastise (Hos. 11.8ff.) and which through the suffering inflicted upon him by the fact of man's rebellion is still more strengthened by becoming self-sacrifice and self-giving. God's pardon does not have the same scope in all Old Testament texts. In one of the most ancient texts in which God's pardon is mentioned God responds to the request for pardon by an act of repentance (Am. 7.2ff.). God's repentance pushes misfortune away, for the time being, and can, therefore, be considered as an act of deliverance, but, as is evident from the selfsame text in Amos, it does not destroy the deep cause which produced the misfortune. A God who repents of his anger, following the repentance of men or simply obeying his own feelings—such appears to be the main line of pardon in the Old Testament, which insists less on the disappearance of the fault than on its being forgotten. Forgiveness as an individual gesture which removes the sin erected as a barrier between man and God appears essentially in the cultic sphere, where sin is regarded as an objective reality which loads man with the weight of God's anger so long as that weight is not removed by some precise gesture, rite or declaration. If in the main this pardon consists in a limited—and renewable— act the Old Testament also gives a more profound notion of pardon which does not consist in the removal of a fault, but in a single definite act which will allow man to have normal relationship with God. The prophet Isaiah, confronted with the revelation of God's holiness, experiences his own impurity so deeply that he thinks he will die as a result (Is. 6.5); only an act of pardon in which Yahweh himself takes the initiative will provide the possibility of re-establishing the relationship and of giving him a more effective and lasting ability than before his call. Similarly the pardon entreated by the faithful men to whom we owe Psalms 51 and 130 consists not in the re-establishment of a particularly compromised exterior situation, but in the regeneration of heart and spirit. The etymology of the general term *salach*,[1] to express pardon, turns us towards the idea of sprinkling and shows up the ritual element;[2] but much more light is thrown on the Old Testament teaching about redemption by three other roots: the root *ga'al*, which expresses a feature of family law,[3] stresses the protective aspect. The *go'el* is the particular kinsman who has the right—and the duty —to avenge blood (*go'el haddam*: Num. 21.28; Dt. 19.6; Jos. 20.3; 2 Sam. 14.11) or to marry the widow of his nearest relative (Ruth 3.13). This right is spoken of as a redeeming; by asserting that Yahweh is the active party in this redemption, the Old Testament authors mean to show in him the near relative whose protection is made manifest towards the people who are his. This is why the Exodus as well as the return from exile are presented as a redemptive act carried out by Yahweh (Ex. 6.6; 15.13; Ps. 74.2; 77.15; 78.35; 106.10; Is. 43.1; 44.22; 52.9). This function of the *go'el* can also be exercised by Yahweh for the benefit of individuals (Ps. 103.4; Gen. 48.16; Ps. 69.18; Job 19.26). It is clear that, when used of Yahweh, the idea of redeeming takes second place to the more general idea of deliverance, for, in Yahweh's case, there could be no question of paying a ransom; he performs his work of deliverance without effort, but when it is said that Yahweh lays bare his arm (Is. 50.34; 52.10), we can find the idea of a certain effort by which Yahweh pays in person the ransom required by his pardon.

The root *padah* more clearly expresses the payment of a ransom; one of the most ancient cultic laws of Israel demanded the offering of the first-born, but at an early date this offering was done by means of a redemption which allowed the keeping of the first-born while satisfying God's rights (Ex. 13.12f.). This redeeming

---

[1] In Accadian *salachu* has the sense of "to sprinkle"; it is used in a secular sense (medical texts) and in a cultic sense; in Hebrew this concrete sense is hardly apparent, but rites and figures of speech borrowed from the realm of purification are common in the O.T. to denote the reality of pardon.

[2] The verb *salach* can have an attenuated sense, e.g. 2 Kings 5.18 where Naaman asks that Yahweh should be "indulgent" towards him if his duties at court oblige him to go to the temple of Rimmon; and a strong sense, especially when there is a question of pardon at the end of time (Jer. 31.34; 33.8; 50.20).

[3] In an interesting study which appeared in *Supplements to Vetus Testamentum*, vol. I, 1953, A. R. Johnson, "The primary meaning of *ga'al*", considers that the sense of "redemption" is secondary to that of "protection", a sense which itself developed from the concrete significance of "covering" which had a double development, on the one hand to protect, on the other to make unclean, defilement being the covering of the clean by the unclean.

is also shown in other fields: it is thus that the slave can be bought back (Ex. 21.8; Lev. 19.26) and that the Levites carry out the buying back of the first-born (Num. 3.40ff.). *Padah* is often associated with or used in the same sense as *ga'al* and denotes the liberation of the people from Egyptian servitude (Dt. 7.8; 9.26; 13.5; Ps. 78.42; 1 Chr. 17.21), and again we find it used of deliverance from enemies, from sickness and from death (Jer. 15.21; Ps. 44.27; 49.16; 2 Sam. 4.9; Job 33.28).

When we come to the third term, *kaphar*, there is no doubt about the very material aspect of "ransom"; the etymology of *kaphar* has been sought in two different directions: comparison with the Arabic *kaphara* and the quite common association with the term *kasah* suggests the idea of "to cover". In Accadian, on the other hand, the root *kupuru* has the sense of to rub and to "erase"; as in Hebrew the term *kaphar* is also associated with *machah* "to erase", *nasa'* "to remove", *sar* "to set aside", the sense "to erase" is perhaps preferable to the one of "cover"; the very notion of pardon stands in quite a different light, by the adoption of this rendering. The Code of the Covenant (Ex. 21.30) specifies that the master of a bull which has, through negligence, caused a fatal accident should be put to death; but the death penalty may be replaced by a ransom through which his life may be preserved. This ransom is the *kopher* by means of which a man may obtain the *pidyon*, that is, liberation. The redemption is not possible in all cases; there are murders for which no *kopher* is effective (Num. 35.31ff.), sins committed *beyad ramah* "with a high hand" (Num. 15.22-31; 1 Sam. 3.14) cannot be expiated; in a general way, however, expiation is not limited simply to sins committed inadvertently, *bishegagah*, for the sins mentioned (Lev. 5.14-19; 19.20-22; Num. 5.5-8) are perfectly conscious and voluntary ones, yet they are capable of being redeemed. The ransom paid to save one's life is also the meaning of the capitation tax for which the children of Israel were liable according to Ex. 30.12ff. A man can offer a *kopher* to redeem himself in very varied circumstances; in a passage of the book of Job, the *kopher* is offered by an angel (Job 33.24). The *kopher* may also be offered by God: thus when the prophet of the exile announces liberation to Israel, he lets it be understood that Yahweh must give to Cyrus, who allows it, some compensation, a *kopher*, in the form of Egypt, Ethiopia and Seba (Is. 43.2ff.); even though we must make full allowance in this passage for a metaphorical element, it is none the less true that the value and force of the *kopher* are clearly emphasized. Where man can obtain no redemption, God can offer an effective *kopher* because it can consist only in a gift from himself (cf. Ps. 49.8; and especially v. 16).[1]

The idea common to these three forms of redemption is that of substitution; man gives something in order to receive another thing in its place: when sin is concerned, man exchanges sin for a new life.

This substitution found its concrete expression in sacrificial ritual. Without seeking to reduce the body of Israelite sacrifices to a single type, we can affirm that substitution is at the basis of the burnt offering (Lev. 1.4) as well as of the sacrifice for sin, *chatta't* (Lev. 4.20), and of the guilt offering, *'asham* (Lev. 5.16). The victim plays a substitutionary rôle; one Accadian text, coming from a collection of conjurations against evil demons, shows us how widespread this idea was in the Semitic world: " The lamb is the substitute for man; for his life, he shall deliver the lamb: the lamb's head shall he deliver for the man's head. The neck of the lamb shall he deliver for the neck of the man, the breast of the lamb for the breast of the man shall he deliver."[2] In this particular case, it is a matter of a gift to the demons who threaten the sick man as compensation by which he can be free;[3] it is again the substitution notion that alone satisfactorily explains the human sacrifices, which can only with difficulty be regarded otherwise than as the substitution of one life for another. The offering of the firstborn is a ransom for the parents (Ex. 22.23ff.) and each time that the Old Testament speaks of human sacrifice (1 Kings 16.34;

---

[1] We do not think it possible to contrast in the O.T. expiation as a human contrivance acting in a more or less magical way with pardon, a gesture freely granted by God; the means of expiation are always presented as committed to man by God in order to make his pardon real.

[2] Transcribed text in Dhorme, *La religion assyro-babylonienne*, p. 281, and *Recueil Edouard Dhorme*, p. 604.

[3] It is also probably a matter of substitutionary sacrifice in the covenant rite sealing the treaty between Mati'ilu, prince of Arpad and Assur-nirari VI (eighth century). At the moment of the victim's immolation, Mati'ilu pronounces the following words: " This head is not a ram's head, it is Mati'ilu's head, the head of his sons, of his great ones, of the people of his country. If the aforesaid sin against these provisions, just as this ram's head is removed, may the thigh of the aforesaid, of his children, of his great ones, of the people of his land be removed." It is not merely a question of illustrating the oath by a gesture, but the contracting parties symbolically transmit their life to the victim in order to keep it safe.

2 Kings 3.27; Mic. 6.7; Dt. 12.31; Jer. 7.31; 19.5; 32.35; Ez. 20.25-31), the aim of this sacrifice is to safeguard, at the cost of a single life, the life of a whole group. The profound reason for these substitutionary rites is to be found in early beliefs about the mystery of life: the first-born takes upon himself the life of the parents, who, by that fact, are virtually dead; to regain life, they must cause its release by the immolation of the first-born, immolation alone allowing the freeing of the life-principle.

In the beginning, this transmission is purely magical, but in the Yahwist religion this exchange can be effected only by Yahweh, the sole holder of life. Sin, whether it be ritual uncleanness or moral fault, is always a loss of vital wholeness, and, when account is taken of the fluidity of the notions of life and death, a sort of death; the remedy can, therefore, only consist in the restoration of this wholeness. The victim, therefore, fulfils a double rôle; it symbolizes the life of the guilty one, and its death symbolizes the death which is the punishment of sin; but the victim is at the same time the intermediary by which God communicates his life to the sinner, and if the ritual texts insist so much on its purity, its integrity, its youth, its vigour, it is because its life must symbolize the divine life; so the essential point about the sacrifice is not the death of the victim, but the offering of its life. Far from being a magical means through which man may exert a sort of constraint on God, the sacrifice is much rather a means by which man expresses his utter submission and to which God responds by communicating his life. The redemptive rôle of the sacrifice appears in many aspects of the ritual, for example in that of the Passover, in that of the daily burnt offering and of the daily sacrifice, the tamid (Lev. 6.13; Num. 4.16), but nowhere do the various aspects of the expiation and the reconciliation appear so clearly as in the ritual of the yom hakkippurim, in which it is a question of observing " the rite of expiation for the transgressions and all the sins of the children of Israel " (Lev. 16.16). In this passage, which is of a complex literary character,[1] very ancient elements are mingled with obviously

---

[1] All critics, even the most conservative, are agreed in acknowledging the complex character of this chapter; for an analysis of it, we refer readers to the commentaries and to the note in the Bible du Centenaire, p. 155; in its present state the passage is of very late composition, since neither Ezekiel nor Ezra know the feast as it is described here: the most ancient part is probably the sending out of the goat to Azazel (v. 8-10, 20-22, 26) which may spring from the old popular religion and have been absorbed into a more developed and authentically Yahwist ritual.

late provisions. The goat sent into the desert—which with death and darkness is one of the three negative worlds according to J. Pedersen[1]—might well be a survival of the nomadic period. This episode stresses the removal of evil. By the confession of sin (Lev. 16.21) and by the laying of hands upon the victim by the guilty man himself (Lev. 4.15, 24), the people claims to identify itself with the victim and to share its fate; whilst the priest, acting in God's stead, performs the sprinkling of the blood and thus frees the power of life there contained for the benefit of a people who were virtually dead.

Intercession is only another aspect of substitution, more spiritual than the one appearing in the rite and the most frequent use of which is found, not surprisingly, in the prophet Jeremiah. All the prophets exercise their functions of mediation not only by revealing God's will, but also by trying to act according to that will by means of intercession. Just as the prophetic ministry is a gift reserved for an élite, intercession is the privilege of only a few individuals, and never do we find in the Old Testament a general exhortation to intercede for one another. It is also wise to notice that, even among the great intercessors, prayer has nothing magical about it and that it often assumes the aspect of a struggle in the course of which the intercessor offers himself to God until his will shall be in harmony with God's. Abraham does not succeed in arresting the destruction of Sodom by his intercession, Moses has to make repeated efforts before his requests are granted, on two occasions Amos succeeds in delaying God's anger (7.1-9), Jeremiah stood before Yahweh in order to speak in favour of the people (18.20) until the day that he received the command to intercede no more because of the ineluctable approach of judgment (7.16; 14.11). Whether intercession is useless because of the greatness of the sin or pardon is impossible because of the absence of intercession (Ez. 22.30; Is. 59.16), it is important to notice that it depends on the divine liberty and that no human device can bring about God's pardon.

The mediation of celestial beings in the pardon of sins appears only once in the Old Testament: Eliphaz says to Job: "To which of the saints wilt thou speak?" (5.1) and Elihu envisages the possibility that an intercessory angel should offer a *kopher* to God in order to save a man's life from death (Job 33.22); but we have to

[1] *Israel*, I-II, pp. 465ff.

wait for apocryphal literature to find a fuller development of ideas on intercession by the merits and sufferings of the righteous and the saints.[1]

The various aspects of substitution are brought together in the figure of Yahweh's servant: he is the perfect embodiment of the prophet by his election and his obedience which goes to the point of martyrdom, and at the same time he is the sacrificial victim, the 'asham offered for the benefit of the guilty (Is. 53.10); in him the prophetic current and the priestly current come together in a higher synthesis.

Whatever may be the means used by man for reconciliation with God, they are put at man's disposal by God. Pardon is an act of God's mercy. Sin, being a corruption of human nature, will disappear completely only when that nature has itself undergone a radical transformation; so total pardon is part of the gifts of the new covenant in which Yahweh will give to man a new heart which will be so attuned to his own that man will not need to be converted (Jer. 31.34; 33.8; 50.20). This eschatological redemption gives to all the provisional attempts at reconciliation between man and God their real significance in the plan of salvation.

BIBLIOGRAPHY

BENNEWITZ, F., *Die Sünde im alten Israel*, Leipzig 1907.

BOER, P. A. H. DE, " De Vorbede in het oude Testament ", *Oudtestamentische Studiën III*, Leiden 1943.

COPPENS, J., *La connaissance du bien et du mal et le péché du paradis*, Louvain 1948.

DELORME, J., " Conversion et pardon selon le prophète Ezéchiel ", (Mémorial Chaine). *Bibl. de la Faculté de théol. de Lyon*, vol. 5, p. 115.

HERMANN, J., *Die Idee der Sühne im A.T.*, 1905.

HERNER, S., *Sühne und Vergebung in Israel*, Lund 1942.

HESSE, FR., *Die Fürbitte im A.T.*, Dissertation, Erlangen 1951.

HUMBERT, P., *Etudes sur le récit du paradis et de la chute dans la Genèse*, Neuchâtel 1940.

JOHANSSON, N., *Parakletoi. Vorstellung von Fürsprechern im A.T. und im Judentum*, Lund 1940.

KÖBERLE, J., *Sünde und Gnade im religiösen Leben des Volkes Israel bis auf Christum*, Munich 1905.

---

[1] Concerning the intercession and merits of the righteous, cf. principally Tobit 2.12; 2 Macc. 12.42-46; 15.14; Baruch 3.4.

Koch, Klaus, "Gibt es ein Vergeltungsdogma im A.T.?", *ZThK*, 1955, p. 1.

Morris, L., "The Biblical Idea of Atonement", *Australian biblical review*, 1952, p. 83.

Procksch, O., *Der Erlösungsgedanke im A.T.*, 1929.

Satan. Etudes carmélitaines, ouvrage collectif.

Smith, C. Ryder, *The Bible Doctrine of Salvation. A study of atonement*, London 1941.

The Bible Doctrine of Sin and of the Ways of God with Sinners, London 1953.

Staerk, W., *Sünde und Gnade nach der Vorstellung des älteren Judentums, besonders der Dichter der sog. Busspsalmen*, 1905.

Stamm, J. J., *Erlösen und Vergeben im A.T.*, Bern 1940.

Das Leiden des Unschuldigen in Babylon und Israel, Zürich 1948.

II. DEATH AND THE FUTURE LIFE

I<small>N</small> the Old Testament death assumes various aspects, of which the truly biological one is not, perhaps, the most important. There is, in a contemporary author's phrase, a realm of death[1] which breaks into the realm of life, in such a way that man may be involved in it without ceasing for that reason to live. Anything that threatens life, the desert, the sea, sin, disease, chaos or darkness, is linked with death, which remains the hostile reality and which will finally be overcome. Admittedly all parts of the Old Testament do not speak with the same insistence of the destructive power of death. It is, nevertheless, certain that the Old Testament never presents death as a liberation or as a gateway giving access to perfect felicity. Along with the Semitic peoples as a whole, Israel shares belief in the fatal and inevitable character of death which found classical expression in this passage from the Epic of Gilgamesh:

> When the gods created humankind,
> They made death the lot of humankind,
> Life, they retained in their own hands.

This theme that life in its fulness belongs only to the deity is illustrated by the Yahwist in the myth of the tree of life which, in an older tradition, must have been more developed than in the present text of Genesis. Man has never eaten any of the fruit of this tree, of which his mortal state even made him unaware; only after eating of the fruit of the tree of knowledge did man, having acquired the possibility of becoming like an *'elohim*, find the tree of life expressly forbidden to him. Yahweh, through irony and

---

[1] J. Pedersen, *Israel, its life and culture*, I-II, pp. 453ff.; the same point of view is adopted by Chr. Barth (v. bibliog.); the latter applies the principle of the fluidity of the notions of life and death to the exegesis of the Psalms by seeking to show that the quite common expression " to be at the gates " or " in the depths " of Sheol is neither a figure of speech nor a prophecy, but describes the real experience of a man who, through illness, or through some other trial, is under the dominion of the kingdom of death.

also through love, but not through jealousy, returns man to his earthly condition, for divine life, usurped instead of being received, can only bring catastrophe for man. If man had not transgressed the divine prohibition, Yahweh would doubtless have granted him as a grace, added in some degree to his original nature, the power of eating of the tree of life, but by his disobedience man definitively deprived himself of this possibility: he will die; his death, from being potential, will become real and irrevocable and, by this definitive nature, death takes on the appearance of a punishment. We must, however, recognize that this aspect was present only rarely to the mind of the Israelites when they spoke of death. To die old and replete with days is the normal and desirable end of all existence; this fate, which was reserved for Abraham and Job, in whom types of the ideal Israelite were readily seen (Gen. 15.15; Job 42.17), was the hope of every member of the people, who thought that, by being reunited to his fathers, he would continue to share in the eternity of the group. However, this certainty, which considerably weakens the disruptive aspect of death, did not prevent the Israelites from making a number of reflections about the change that death produced in the body of the individual. What becomes of the elements which together constitute the *nephesh* at the moment of death? The dead man is no longer a *nephesh chayyah*, since he is deprived of breath, which is its essential characteristic, but what is he, then? It is difficult to reduce all the Old Testament data into a single viewpoint; but we think that all the reflections about death are the result of two currents of thought. Just as the definition of man as a living being depends on observation, reflection about death does not begin with theoretical considerations, but with the situation that is presented visually. According to the first line of thought, which we shall call the analytical, death is characterized by the absence of breath; the dead person no longer has *neshamah* or *ruach* nor, according to some texts, *nephesh*, either because *nephesh* is used in the restricted sense of breath (Jer. 15.9) or because the fact of no longer being a *nephesh* is presented as a departure of *nephesh* (Gen. 35.18; 1 Kings 17.21). Deprived of *nephesh* and *ruach,* man is left with the *basar* only and, as soon as this ceases to be animated, it is in no way distinct from dust. Death may be considered as a dissolution; as soon as they cease to be held together by the principle of life, the various elements comprising the human being are " as water which runs away and which cannot again be collected up" (2 Sam. 14.14). Man reduced to dust is nothing; he no longer exists, and we must not be surprised that several texts speak of death as non-existence; at least that is the conclusion reached by Job and the Psalmist (Job 7.21; Ps. 39.14)[1] and the Preacher, a man of analytic and scientific temperament, arrives at an identical result: man dies like the beasts, both return to dust (3.20) and, when the spirit returns to its source, the dust returns to the earth and is mingled with it (12.7). This outlook, which has a logical place in Israelite thought, was, however, counter-balanced and finally dominated by a point of view which also started from observation but which reached a different conclusion. The Israelite always looked on the human being less as a collection of various elements than as an organic whole which attained expression in the body or the person. Now, it appeared to observation that at the moment of death the body did not disintegrate into its constituent elements, but, for a certain length of time at least, continued to retain the features of the living being.[2] The individual dies, but he does not cease to exist, yet this existence is only a shadow of the existence of the living, that is why the dead have or are still *nephashot* (cf. Job 14.22);[3] they continue to have the same physical aspect as when they were alive (Gen. 37.35; 42.38; 44.29; 1 Kings 2.6; Ez. 32.27). Death is considered as a state in which the forces of life are at their lowest intensity, a state similar to fatigue or sleep (Job 14.19ff.), a state deprived of what characterizes the living being, the bond of community; the dead man is alone (Job 14.22). According to the first current of thought death is a breaking which marks the brutal and irremediable end of existence; according to the other, death is not in opposition to

---

[1] Gunkel, *Die Psalmen*, p. 165, wrote of this Psalm: "The idea of a life beyond death does not once come into consideration in the entire poem."

[2] The Hebrew term corresponding to body, *gewiyyah*, is often used of a corpse which was regarded as a body even though life was absent (Jg. 14.8, 9; 1 Sam. 31.10, 12; Nahum 3.5; Ps. 110.6). It is quite likely that in Israel a distinction was made between the period when the body still existed as a corpse and the period when it was reduced to dust.

[3] Belief in a double or an exterior soul was not altogether foreign to Israel; it is to be found in certain manifestations of ecstasy among the prophets and in the mention of Elisha's heart which accompanies his servant Gehazi, but we find no mention of it in connection with the dead. The reduction of the dead to the state of shadows in no way conferred greater mobility on them, for having the aspect of a prison, Sheol made any possibility of escape very remote. This does not prevent popular religion having included belief in ghosts—the term *'ob* should probably be interpreted in this way—but it was never exploited theologically.

life. This latter tendency made the passing from life to death a relatively easy one: living beings with their powers much reduced —such was the appearance of the dead in *Sheol,* the place which collected them all together.

None of the etymologies[1] so far suggested for this noun seems to deserve absolute credence. The location of this place is differently presented, for to the Israelites the spatial aspect of the kingdom of the dead is secondary to its dynamic aspect; what is common to all representations is that *Sheol* is to be found in the depths of the earth, the dead go down into the *tachtiyot ha'arets* (Ps. 63.10; 86.13; 88.7; 139.15; Lam. 3.55). This siting of *Sheol* in the depths seems to imply a connection between *Sheol* and the tomb. Tombs generally had the appearance of pits or of wells, several yards deep, at the end of which a door gave access to the burial chamber. It is likely that this aspect of tombs exercised an influence on representations of *Sheol.* According to an interesting passage in the book of Job, it might be concluded that the tomb was a channel giving access to *Sheol*: "He preserveth his *nephesh* from the pit (*shachat* meaning destruction is also applied to *Sheol*) and his life from passing through the channel (*shelach*)" (Job 33.18). But we must be cautious in over-interpreting texts in order to find confirmation of a chronological or spatial link between the tomb and *Sheol.* It seems rather that it was thought at all periods that the dead dwelt in the tomb and in *Sheol* at the same time; the great care lavished upon burial was inspired more from fear and respect for the dead than from the desire to ensure his reaching *Sheol,* otherwise beings deprived of burial would not have been able to reach the abode of the dead; now Jacob does not doubt for an instant that he will find in *Sheol* the son whom he believes to have been devoured by a wild beast (Gen. 37.35) and out of *Sheol* Samuel says to Saul, whose corpse is to remain unburied on the battlefield: "To-morrow thou and thy sons will be with me" (1 Sam. 28.19). Therefore, instead of distinguishing between the tomb and *Sheol,* it is better to con-

---

[1] One of the most recent and interesting etymologies is the one suggested by L. Koehler (*ThZ,* 1946, p. 71): the lamed of Sheol is considered an auxiliary letter, so that the root would be *sha'ah* which, in addition to the meanings of "to bestir oneself, to look at", would also have the sense of "be deserted, ravaged", in particular in Isaiah 6.11 and which has given rise to the word *sha'on*; an expression like that in Psalm 40.3: "he brought me up from a *mibbor sha'on*" favours Koehler's etymology, which, however, is contested by W. Baumgartner (*ThZ,* 1946, p. 233) who sees in Sheol a word of Sumero-Accadian origin in relationship with *Shu'ara,* the dwelling-place of Tammuz in the underworld.

sider them together , and Pedersen's definition of *Sheol* as the "primitive grave"[1] which shows itself in each individual grave could put us on the way to the true solution. If, theologically, *Sheol* was the true meeting-place of the dead, popular piety was more concerned with the dwelling of the dead in the family grave. The expression already quoted "to be reunited with his fathers and with his people"[2] refers to the uniting of the members of the same clan in a common grave, the more so because *Sheol* was in no way reserved for the Israelites only.[3] The term *Sheol* itself does not allow us to throw any light on its nature, but the synonyms used give details of the kind of existence that was supposed to be led there: the kingdom of the dead was called *'abaddon*, destruction (Job 26.5; 28.22; Ps. 88.12; Prov. 15.11; 27.20), and *dumah*, silence (Ps. 94.17; 115.17), or again the land of darkness and dust (Job 10.21-22; 38.17; Dan. 12.2); all these terms go to confirm the view that existence in *Sheol* was the negative replica of earthly existence. From the most detailed descriptions that we read in chap. 14 of Isaiah and chap. 32 of Ezekiel, it seems that social and national distinctions were maintained: kings are seated upon thrones, Samuel continues to exercise upon occasion in *Sheol* his prophetic function without death having added anything to his prerogatives. This existence is always colourless and lacks vitality; it never seems enviable, except to Job who, crushed under the weight of his misfortunes, reaches a point, at one moment, where he sighs for the great repose of the resting-place of the dead (Job 3.17-19). The Preacher, representing as he does a current opinion in Israel, stands by his statement that, however illusory earthly things and activities may be, a living dog is none the less worth more than a dead lion (Eccl. 9.4), for, far from bringing a more complete union with Yahweh, death is equivalent to a separation from him. Death

---

[1] "All graves have certain common characteristics constituting the nature of the grave, and that is Sheol. The 'Ur'-grave we might call Sheol . . . manifests itself in every single grave, as *mo'ab* manifests itself in every single Moabite." *Israel*, I-II, p. 462.

[2] Cf. Gen. 35.29; 49.33; Dt. 32.50; certain passages (2 Kings 8.24; 12.9; 15.38; 16.19; 21.7, etc.) add to this formula the mention of burial in the family grave; but the first expression has a more solemn accent which seems to imply more than simple interment (cf. B. Alfrink, "L'expression *shakab 'im 'abotaw*", *Oudtestamentische Studiën*, II, pp. 106ff.).

[3] According to L. Rost, in *In memoriam Ernst Lohmeyer*, the notion of Sheol is of Babylonian origin, while the return of the spirit to Yahweh leading to total disappearance is the heritage of ancient Hebrew religion.

and *Sheol*—the two terms are sometimes interchangeable, a fact which proves that the stress was laid with *Sheol* upon its function rather than upon its location—are powers opposed to Yahweh or at least neutral in relation to his sovereignty. Since the creation narratives do not speak about the creation of *Sheol*, it may be supposed that in *Sheol* traces were seen of the original chaos—the darkness, while the watery aspect of chaos was represented by the waters of the sea. The Song of Hezekiah, which may be considered as one of the most explicit documents on the attitude of Yahwism with regard to death (Is. 38.9ff.), proclaims: "*Sheol* praises thee not and its inhabitants hope no more in thy faithfulness." Was *Sheol* under the dominion of another deity, *Mot*, for example?[1] or was it this deity himself? What is certain is that this realm remained outside Yahweh's sphere of influence for quite a long time and was only gradually opened to his sovereignty. Beside the idea that Yahweh is a stranger to *Sheol*, and consequently without power over it, there is the idea which speaks of Yahweh's forgetting those who go down to *Sheol*, while they themselves lose all remembrance of Yahweh (Ps. 6.6; 88.13; 94.17; 115.17; Eccl. 9.5-6; Job 26.6; 28.22). This conception was probably born to answer the objection that Yahweh was not all-powerful, since there was a realm which escaped his sovereignty, an unhappy solution, however, for without getting rid of the idea of a powerless Yahweh, it added to it the idea of a wilfully cruel God. The majority of texts know nothing of any differentiation of a moral order among the dwellers in *Sheol*; the only differences are those which existed in their earthly life. We have, however, in the two most explicit texts, an allusion to a division between the righteous and the wicked: in the elegy on the King of Babylon (Is. 14), it is said that he is hurled into the "depths of the abyss", whilst around him the kings of the nations rest with honour in their graves. In the elegy on the Pharaoh (Ez. 32), the distinction is even more

---

[1] Following Philo of Byblos, who identifies the god Mot (Μωθ) with θάνατος many modern authors, because of the Ugaritic texts, have insisted on this connection, e.g. Virolleaud in almost all his published work, Nielsen, *Ras Shamra Mythologie und biblische Theologie*, p. 61, Moret, *Hist. anc.*, p. 619, Sellin, *Theol. A.T.*, p. 80; others such as H. Bauer-Eissfeldt, W. Baumgartner, *ThR*, 1941, p. 92, see in the god Mot the root *mutu*, mortal, man. Note that the Ugaritic texts insist on the destructive rôle of Mot (I AB, II AB 15-20). Whatever the linguistic solution may be, it is certain that the struggle between Baal and Mot represents in the world of nature the conflict between life and death.

pronounced: on the one side are the uncircumcised,[1] that is, those who were buried without ceremony, and on the other the valiant (Ez. 28.10 and 31.18), but it is only from the second century B.C. that the division between the righteous and the wicked within *Sheol* will be taken up and developed in all its breadth.

The distinctive mark of the dwellers in *Sheol* is weakness. Even the *Rephaim*,[2] who constitute the aristocracy of the abode of the dead, are feeble beings who in *Sheol* have lost their terrifying power which they formerly held when they were either auxiliaries to the deity (as in Ugarit), or a population of giants occupying Palestine before the children of Israel settled there (Gen. 15.20; Dt. 3.11; Jos. 12.4). Archaeology confirms the textual testimony to the weakness of the dead, who continue their earthly existence at a much reduced tempo. In structure, the tomb was a reproduction of the dwelling-house. In the Israelite period, it is usually constructed as a chamber roughly hewn in the rock round which are set forms intended for the bodies of the dead; in the middle of this room, some earthenware objects are the surviving traces of the food and other offerings which were brought to the dead. These offerings were not sacrifices and cannot in any way be used as evidence of a cult of the dead, for which the texts themselves offer only the flimsiest basis. The offerings are more like alms and are a sign that the dead needed the living; food, and very specially water,[3] were indispensable to them, and the presence of numerous lamps among the funeral offerings probably corresponds to no other preoccupation than to perpetuate what constituted the centre of the family dwelling. Love tinged with pity might be the motive which inspired all the offerings; but is there not an element of fear mingled with it? It must certainly be admitted that the Israelites shared with many other people the belief that the non-accomplishment of the funeral duties could incite the dead to unpleasant reactions against which it was better to take precautions. This desire to make the dead inoffensive was sometimes able, in times when faith in Yahweh's power was strained, to lead men to devote to them a

[1] On the origin and meaning of this expression, cf. the very interesting study by A. Lods, "Le sort des incirconcis" in *Comptes rendus de l'Académie des Inscriptions et belles-lettres*, 1943, p. 271.

[2] Concerning the Rephaïm in Ugaritic texts, cf. Virolleaud, *Syria*, 22, pp. 1ff., and Dussaud, *Les découvertes de Ras Shamra et l'A.T.*, Paris 1937, 2nd ed., p. 185.

[3] Concerning the theme of thirst of the dead a fairly complete documentation will be found in the work by A. Parrot, *Le "Refrigerium" dans l'au-delà*, Paris 1937.

veritable cult and to ask them for revelations which could come to them through their contact with the mysterious powers hidden in the bosom of the earth (cf. the serpent in the garden of Eden). The dead, and more especially those who called them up, were *yide'onim*, beings who know (Is. 8.19; 65.4; Lev. 19.31; Dt. 18.11).[1] It must, however, be added that the official religion always condemned with great severity the practice of necromancy[2] and that never were the dead as a whole considered to enjoy superior knowledge. The story of the witch of Endor (1 Sam. 28), which the partisans of the cult of the dead in ancient Israel have always called in as their main argument, points rather in the opposite direction, for if Samuel is capable of foretelling the future from *Sheol*, it is solely because he continues to exercise after his death the gifts of divination which he had in life. Rachel, on the other hand, in her tomb, is utterly ignorant of her children's fate and knows it only through a special message from Yahweh (Jer. 31.15-17). It would, moreover, be a vain undertaking to seek to bring funeral rites into line with theology. In our day, as in Israel, the "religion of the dead" is a mixture of pagan customs with perfectly orthodox beliefs. For theology, the dead were in *Sheol*, but in popular belief they lived rather in the tomb, and A. Lods has very correctly said that[3] "the Israelites took no more trouble to reconcile existence in the grave and in *Sheol* than the Christian populations of our lands to reconcile ideas of resurrection, immortality and even survival in the sepulchre". In so far as it was the normal end of a life that has reached its allotted span, death was neither a problem nor a scandal; nothing was more normal than to go, when old and satiated with years, and join one's ancestors. Premature death on the other hand did present a problem: anyone who was taken away "in the midst of his days" (Is. 38.10; Ps. 102.24) or "before his time" (Eccl. 7.17) does not fill the time normally granted to a human life, his life will only have lasted as long as a flower (Ps. 102.12) without reaching the stage of fruition, or as long as the weaver's shuttle-thread which breaks in the middle of the work (Job 7.6), so that the time that he lived will always leave, even in *Sheol*, the bitter memory of something left incomplete

---

[1] The main texts on consultation with the dead are to be found in Ex. 22.17; Lev. 19.31; 20.6, 27; 1 Sam. 28.3, 9-13; Is. 8.19; 19.3; 29.4.

[2] The law stigmatizes recourse to this type of practice as a prostitution, which seems to suggest that it saw the practice as homage to rival deities (cf. Lev. 20.6).

[3] *Croyance à la vie future*, p. 207.

for which he cannot be comforted, especially if he feels that this shortening of his life is not the effect of punishment.

To regard death as separation from God could have led to a dualistic solution, but faith in the omnipotence of Yahweh was to make dualism impossible in Israel. Just as Yahweh had extended his power over realms originally foreign to his own, Sheol could not remain very long outside his sovereignty. "It is Yahweh who causes men to die and to live, who sends down to *Sheol* and recalls thence," sings the author of the song of Hannah (1 Sam. 2.6) and for Amos Yahweh's omnipotence does not stop at the gates of *Sheol* (Amos 9.2). Life and death are within Yahweh's power, but since Yahweh's power was the sovereignty of a living God, death could not manifest it to the same degree as life. Despite Yahweh's dominion over the world of the dead, there is always some incompatibility between him and death; that is why the solution of the problem of death could only be found in the final triumph of life.

Since death was the limit set to human life by Yahweh, it was on him alone that the pushing back or even the complete removal of that limit depended. Before the insistence of Israel's religion on Yahweh's omnipotence, the possibility of escaping death was not excluded, but it is none the less clear that the assertion of his divine transcendence and utter distinction from the created world could leave hope for this privilege only in rare and exceptional cases. Two beings only escaped death, the patriarch Enoch and the prophet Elijah. For the former, "translation"[1] is presented as the reward of his piety, "he walked with God" (Gen. 5.24) and also as a compensation, for his life was noticeably shorter than the lives of the other patriarchs. Enoch continues to live with God, not in an island of the blessed, like *Utnapishtim,* the Babylonian prototype of Noah, but probably in heaven, though we have to wait for apocalyptic literature in order to have any precise information about the place of his abode. Elijah's removal is presented in a more circumstantial manner, he went up to heaven (2 Kings 2.1-11) in a chariot of fire and in the midst of a whirlwind, the classical accompaniment of divine manifestations. The texts are not sufficiently explicit to allow us to state that a similar fate was reserved for Moses; although Deuteronomy expressly states that Moses was buried, there is so much mystery connected with his death and

---

[1] Note, however, that the verb *laqach* which in these passages has a technical sense is elsewhere used in a completely ordinary fashion.

burial-place, which Yahweh alone knows, that tradition associated him with Enoch and Elijah, to whom Ezra and Baruch[1] were added later. These figures, who remained alive though invisible, might return to earth, and Elijah's return was, for Jews, long before the time of Jesus, a belief which had been widely accepted (Mal. 3.23ff.; Ecclus. 48.10ff.). It may be asked whether these translations were considered as strictly individual cases or if they had value as examples. In the Psalms, which are our main source of information on this subject, it sometimes happens that Psalmists ask to be delivered from death. In the majority of cases, death must be understood in the widest sense as anything which threatens human life—disease, persecution and the curses of enemies. It seems, however, that in one case at least the prayer goes to the point of hoping for translation by God: the believer of Psalm 49 is not a sick man, but a " poor man ", scandalized by the prosperity of the rich, a man who glimpses the solution of the problem that torments him in differing final fates reserved for the good and the wicked; while the latter will go straight down to *Sheol,* where they will be the pasture of death (v. 15), he hopes that he himself will be carried away to God; but the text is not sufficiently clear to distinguish definitely whether the Psalmist has in view a translation which would eliminate his passing through *Sheol* or a resurrection from *Sheol* itself; the term *laqach* which is used in connection with Enoch and Elijah and which seems to have quite a solemn ring about it (v. 16) makes us lean rather towards the first solution.

For all believers, death presented a problem and the illumination they had to resolve it more resembles pale gleams than certitude; among some, a more intense faith succeeds in depriving death of its aspect of an agonizing problem or even of a straightforward problem. Job's words: "I shall see God" (19.26) and Psalm 73 (v. 23) are the most advanced expressions of this faith. The writer of the book of Job has little hope for what follows death. Man goes towards *Sheol,* which is the shadowy existence ending in utter annihilation, and the whole drama of Job consists precisely in the

---

[1] 4 Esdr. 14.9: Thou shalt be taken away from among men, and thou shalt dwell beside my son and thy companions. 4 Esdr. 14.49, Esdras was taken away (*raptus est*) and led to the place of those like him. Syr. Apoc. Baruch 46.7: I disclosed nothing to them of what had been told me concerning my removal; 76.2: Thou shalt leave this earth, not for death, but to be kept in reserve for the end of time.

fact that he feels death coming closer without his having been able to obtain an answer to his tormenting problem of God's justice. Yet fear of death is counter-balanced by faith in God and ultimately will be absorbed by that faith. The certainty of seeing God is of first importance for him and it is on earth, before his death, that he expects it. In the well-known word of chap. 19, in which Christian tradition has unanimously acclaimed an announcement of the resurrection, Job expresses the certainty that his *go'el,* who can only be God himself, will manifest himself as his nearest kinsman, the dust on which he must manifest himself is the dust of the earth and not that of the tomb or the corpse. But if Job has the certainty of seeing God, it is because he hopes to enter into a particularly close relationship with him and to share in what constitutes his being, that is, life. To see God, at least in this text, is to share in his life, and, as God himself does not die (Hab. 1.12 according to the original text uncorrected by the Massoretes), for the believer communion with God makes death, if not non-existent, at least powerless to destroy life. An experience similar to Job's was endured by the author of Ps. 16, who declares that *Sheol* will have no power over him, since he is destined to life and since that life is communion with the living God. But it is indisputably in Ps. 73 that this hope of communion with God, in spite of and beyond death, reaches its apogee. The Psalmist, a prey to moral suffering comparable to Job's, finds the solution in the possession of God who cannot be taken from him either by the mocking of his enemies or by his sufferings, or even by death. God will stay with him, even when his body crumbles to dust. We can only make a rather confused survey of what was for these believers an unshakable certainty; it seems, however, that they did not regard this eternal life either as immortality of the soul, or as a reward, or as a resurrection.

Although victory over death by resurrection is the latest Old Testament solution, its antecedents are probably more ancient than the first hopes of eternal life. Yahweh, the living God, could not in his action as creator of life be limited by death, and from time to time he manifested this power by calling dead people back to life. The Old Testament reports three cases of restoration to life, the first two being brought about with the active participation of the prophets Elijah and Elisha, the third by the prophet's bones (1 Kings 17.17ff.; 2 Kings 4.29; 13.21). In all three cases, corpses are recalled to life by Yahweh himself, the prophet being only the instrument and having to ask God for the power to perform the miracle (1 Kings 17.21). The idea of the resurrection of the nation was more familiar. The central theme of eschatology, the *shub shebut*, left the realm of death outside its bounds and interest. Only those living at the time of the great change would be beneficiaries of the paradisal age; but from the eighth century the judgment and salvation of the people are described as a death and resurrection. The prophet Hosea puts into the mouth of the people a liturgy of penitence by which they encourage themselves to return to Yahweh who has "torn and smitten", but who "after two days will restore life to us and will raise us up again on the third day" (Hos. 6.1-2). The terms used, particularly the verb *chayyah*, which often has the sense of healing (Gen. 45.27; 1 Kings 17.22; Is. 38.9), may, however, suggest that the prophet compared the people to a person seriously ill rather than to one dead, although the wide sense of the terms life and death weaken the force of this argument. The text of Ezekiel 37, on the other hand, leaves no doubt. It is well understood that this vision concerns a picture of the people's restoration after the return from exile, but the elements of this symbolism leave it to be understood that the resurrection of the dead was envisaged as a possibility;[1] several clues in the text direct us in fact along this way; the prophet's uncertainty before Yahweh's question: "Shall these bones live?—Lord, thou knowest" can be explained with difficulty if it is a matter only of the resurrection of the nation, which had never been questioned, but is very readily understood if it concerns the resurrection of the dead in general. Moreover, the dead are called *harugim*, those who have been killed (37.9); now later we learn from the book of Daniel that those who have been put to death, the martyrs, will be the first to benefit from the resurrection. Finally, the mention of graves might mean that those who died long ago will share in the re-establishment of Israel; in any case, the precision of the metaphors seems to indicate that the idea of resurrection had made headway between Hosea and Ezekiel. Successive disasters to the people largely contributed to this evolution, but there was added to this

[1] According to H. Riesenfeld, faith in the resurrection had its origin in the pre-exilic period in the rites of the New Year festival in which the victory of life over death and chaos was celebrated; he is, however, obliged to recognize that this notion of life was essentially collective and material (*The resurrection in Ezechiel 37 and in the Dura-Europos paintings*, UUA, 1948, 11).

historical reason a theme of mythical origin which certainly did not have in Israel the importance that one contemporary school ascribes to it, but which, on account of its widespread incidence in the whole ancient East, cannot have left Israel completely unaffected —the theme of a dying and rising god. Through the Ugaritic texts, we know how important a place this myth held in Canaanite religion: the struggle of Aleyin-Baal and Mot is the mythical formulation of the conflict between the two opposing forces of nature, the fertilizing rain of spring and the parching heat of summer. The poems of the Baal cycle express in a particularly dramatic way the death and resurrection of that god: his death entails the disappearance of life from the face of the earth and plunges men and gods into deep desolation until the moment when it is announced that Baal has risen again because of the intervention of the goddess Anat. It is undeniable that the maintenance of life occupied a central place in this religion and that it was not regarded as the simple play of automatic forces but the intervention of the gods, induced it is true by the cultic rites. However, only terrestrial life is concerned, in the form of vegetative life in nature and the exercise of vital functions in man; and so A. Moret's statement: "We take it that the Phoenicians drew from their Adonis rites the hope of a renewal of existence for man after death",[1] is a mere supposition which receives very little support from what the Ugaritic texts otherwise teach us about the sad condition of the dead in a beyond which was no better than the Hebrew *Sheol*.

Since the myth of a dying and rising god, whether among the Sumero-Accadians or among the Phoenicians, led to no positive views on the fate of the dead, only a very secondary root of the resurrection doctrine was to be found in it. The aspects of this myth which touched Israel in the form of the gardens of Adonis (Is. 17.10) and the cult of Tammuz which had penetrated even as far as the precincts of the Jerusalem temple (Ez. 8.14), or the serpent cult, always associated with chthonic powers, did not, apparently, have any connection with beliefs concerning the dead, and must rather have favoured certain instincts of the present life which official Yahwism held in check. Yahweh's transcendence prevented him from being assimilated into one of these gods, but on the other hand it is not altogether impossible that the idea of a dying and rising god was applied to certain men who were considered as

[1] *Histoire ancienne de l'Orient*, t. 2, p. 621.

intermediaries between the divine and human worlds. The funeral dirge intoned at the death of a king, *hoy 'adon, hoy 'achi* (cf. Jer. 22.18; 34.5) strangely resembles the dirges sung at the time of the fictitious death of Adonis, and the special form of the royal tomb in Jerusalem, brought to light by excavations in the City of David, may be proof of a privileged position for a king in the beyond. Finally the idea of David *redivivus* which we find in Ez. 34.23 and 37.24 seems to speak in favour of the king's resurrection preceding the belief in a resurrection extending to a greater number of individuals. Coming through the intermediary of the royal ideology or directly from the myth, the pattern of death and resurrection appears in the figure of the Servant of Yahweh and the confession put into the mouth of the people: "We thought him smitten by God . . ." is found in a very similar form in the Tammuz-Adonis myths. The resurrection of the Servant is in every case presented as an extraordinary phenomenon which could happen to an individual only in very exceptional circumstances. But in the Old Testament all God's extraordinary interventions, such as prophetic utterance, the priesthood, election in general, are called to pass in scope from the particular to the universal, so that the hope of resurrection will spread through the mass from these indications, and all the more because it seemed the only solution to the problem of retribution and to the increasingly frequent crises to which this dogma was subject. In the case of the Servant, resurrection is linked with retribution; it is a reward for offences suffered and for the expiatory work accomplished by his sufferings, henceforth the resurrection will always be presented as a form of recompense. That suffering accepted even to death calls for a compensation is the affirmation of the author of Psalm 22 who, moreover, probably views his own sufferings in the light of the Servant's, and who ends his Psalm with a cry of joy and hope: "Those who sleep in the earth will adore Yahweh and those who have gone down to the dust will prostrate themselves before him" (v. 29).[1] The hope of resurrection which hitherto is only glimpsed as a faint gleam, becomes clear in two fragments which belong to the apocalyptic genre. In the Apocalypse of Isaiah (chap. 24-27)

---

[1] There is reason to distinguish between earth and dust; the first possesses a certain vital force which allows it to produce plants for instance (Gen. 1), while dust acquires positive value only by the use that a living being and especially God makes of it.

resurrection is promised to the righteous only while the wicked are expressly excluded. The seer, who receives inspiration from Ezekiel 37, awaits a manifestation of the spirit; but it is to be more than a national restoration—the dead themselves, the dead of Yahweh, that is, the righteous, will rise again. Concerning the mode of resurrection, the text (Is. 26.18ff.) gives the following details: the righteous will to some extent be brought forth by the earth which will itself be fertilized by a dew of light, the term light having to be understood in a wide sense as a symbol of Yahweh himself, who frequently links himself with this natural phenemonen in order to manifest himself. The idea of the resurrection as a new creation is also found in the second book of Maccabees, where the mother of seven sons expresses the hope that he who presided over their birth will in his mercy return breath and life to them as a reward for their martyrdom (2 Macc. 7.22). In the well-known pericope of Daniel 12, the participants in the resurrection are still more clearly distinguished from the people as a whole; as in eschatology of an earthly or national form, it is only a remnant who will be saved, those whose names are written in God's book; as for the wickedest of the wicked,[1] they will rise again for judgment. Explicit as this text may be in relation to the preceding ones, it leaves in the dark certain points about which we should like to know more. Thus the place where the risen will dwell is not stated; in the light of Dan. 7.27, announcing an eternal kingdom on the earth, this place could only be the earth; but the situation in chapter 12 is slightly differently presented; the resurrection is not a simple return to earthly life, but the raising to a celestial life and the connection of the righteous with the stars might be more than a simple comparison; in the book of Enoch, indeed, the righteous are identified with the stars (Enoch 39.7; 104.2; 108.13), whence we can deduce also that the bodies of the risen will not be like the earthly body, but penetrated with a new luminosity. The transfiguration of which the righteous will be the object will have as a counterpart an exceptional ugliness of the damned which will inspire a horror similar to that of corpses eaten by worms at the city gates.

Because of the law of retribution, the resurrection in Daniel is

---

[1] Outside this passage from Daniel the word *dera'on*, which is used to mean the horror of the damned, is found only in Is. 66.24, where it is used about the horror inspired by decomposing bodies.

more than a hope, it is a veritable necessity. During the wars of independence the flower of the nation had been killed; they had fallen as martyrs of their faith. Many Israelites were hanged, because they vigorously refused to eat unclean things, but they preferred to die rather than eat defiled foods and profane the holy covenant (1 Macc. 1.62-64). The martyrdom of the righteous set an agonizing problem of conscience: the faithful were massacred and the impious and renegade received honour and wealth. What was becoming of Yahweh's promise which assured happiness to the faithful? Wisdom showed itself powerless to resolve this problem: neither Job nor *Qoheleth* gives a direct answer and both are content to pass on to another plane—that of the unfathomable mystery of the divine ways. Ecclesiasticus holds to the old traditional conception (2.10) and declares that inequality and injustice will find a just solution before the death of him who is their victim: "It is easy to the Lord, on the day of death, to render to a man according to his ways. The moment of unhappiness causes pleasure to be forgotten and it is the end of man which reveals his acts. Call no man happy before his death, for it is by his end that a man becomes known" (Ecclus. 11.26-28). But the anguish of the situation required a less superficial consolation and it was thus that there was born the belief that the righteous who had loved truth so much as to die for it would rise at the end of time. "The martyr," says Renan, "was the real creator of belief in a second life"[1] and we will add that the figure of the Servant in Isaiah 53, the prototype of all sufferers and all martyrs, was a powerful contribution to the strengthening of this faith. So it seems clear that internal reasons alone account for the arrival at the doctrine of resurrection out of all the beliefs relative to the beyond. Transcendental eschatology, of which the resurrection is one aspect, is not an Israelite borrowing from Zoroastrianism,[2] but is bound up with a more widespread current of thought which, in the Achaemenian Empire, in Babylon and in the empire of Alexander, aims at freeing religion from its national ties and at creating a terrain favourable for an a-political religion in which the accent is put on the primacy of the individual, without destroying the specific heritage of each of those religions:

---

[1] *Histoire du peuple d'Israël*, t. 4, p. 226 (ed. Calmann-Lévy).

[2] It is difficult to trace the doctrine of resurrection in the Avesta further back than the fourth century B.C., which makes a borrowing by Israel very unlikely. Persian influence seems to have operated rather in the adoption of certain metaphors and representations such as the plurality of the heavens.

thus it was that in Iran the promotion of the individual took place against the background of a cosmic myth of the destruction and renewal of the world, while in Israel it was the result of faith in Yahweh and the consequence of his power and righteousness.

BIBLIOGRAPHY

BAUMGARTNER, W., " Der Auferstehungsglaube im Alten Orient ", *Zeitschrift für Missions- und Religionswissenschaft*, 1933, p. 193.

BARTH, CHR., *Die Errettung vom Tode in den individuellen Klage- und Dankliedern des A.T.*, Zollikon-Zürich 1947.

BEER, G., " Der biblische Hades ", *Theologische Abhandlungen* (Festgabe H. J. Holtzmann), Tübingen 1902.

BERTHOLET, A., *Die israelitischen Vorstellungen vom Zustande nach dem Tode*, 2nd. ed., Tübingen 1914.

DHORME, ED., " L'idée de l'au-delà dans la religion hébraïque ", *RHR*, 1941, p. 113.

FÉRET, R. P., " La mort dans la tradition biblique ", *Le mystère de la mort et sa célébration*, Paris 1952, p. 133.

KARGE, P., *Rephaim*, Paderborn 1917.

LINDBLOM, J., *Das ewige Leben*, Uppsala-Leipzig 1914.

LODS, AD., *La croyance à la vie future et le culte des morts dans l'antiquité israélite*, Paris 1906.

" Les idées des Israélites sur la maladie, ses causes et ses remèdes " (*Festschrift Karl Marti*), 1925, p. 181.

" De quelques récits de voyage au pays des morts ". *Comptes rendus de l'Acad. des inscr.*, Paris 1946, p. 434.

MOORTGAT, A., *Tammuz. Der Unsterblichkeitsglaube in der altorientalischen Bildkunst*, Berlin 1949.

NIKOLAINEN, A. T., " Der Auferstehungsglaube in der Bibel und in ihrer Umwelt ", *Ann. Acad. Fennica*, Helsinki 1944.

NÖTSCHER, FR., *Altorientalischer und alttestamentlicher Auferstehungsglauben*, Würzburg 1926.

PARROT, A., *Le " Refrigerium " dans l'au-delà*, Paris 1937.

QUELL, G., *Die Auffassung des Todes im A.T.*, Leipzig 1925.

RAD, G. VON, " Alttestamentliche Glaubensaussagen von Leben und Tod ", *Allg. evang. luth. Kirchenzeitung*, 1938, p. 826.

RIESENFELD, H., *The resurrection in Ezechiel 37 and the Dura-Europos paintings*, UUA, 1948, no. 11.

ROST, L., " Alttestamentliche Wurzeln der ersten Auferstehung ". *In memoriam Ernst Lohmeyer*, Stuttgart 1951, p. 67.

SCHILLING, O., *Der Jenseitgedanke im A.T.*, Mayence 1951.

SCHULTZ, A., "Der Sinn des Todes im A.T.", *Vorlesungen der Akademie Braunsberg*, 1919.

SCHWALLY, F., *Das Leben nach dem Tode nach den Vorstellungen des alten Israel und des Judentums*, Giessen 1892.

SELLIN, E., "Die alttestamentliche Hoffnung auf Auferstehung und ewiges Leben", *NKZ*, 1919, p. 232.

SUTCLIFFE, E. F., *The Old Testament and the Future Life*, London 1946.

VOLLBORN, W., "Das Problem des Todes in Genesis 2 & 3", *ThLitzg*, 1952, pp. 710ff. (résumé).

III. THE CONSUMMATION

A. THE ESCHATOLOGICAL DRAMA

THE divine presence in the Old Testament may be defined as the presence of the God who comes; but since this presence was linked with the notion of the hidden God, it was never able to satisfy religious aspirations in full in spite of its manifestations in the history, institutions and reality experienced by believers. And so Israel had at an early date the hope of a moment when this divine presence would be made perfectly real, when God would come personally to rule on earth and to fill it with the knowledge of himself as the depths of the sea are filled by the waters that cover them (Is.11.9; Hab. 2.14). Because of these premises, Israelite eschatology presents a unique character, in spite of similar conceptions among other peoples: neither themes of a cosmological nature —affirmation of the ageing of the earth or natural catastrophes—nor themes of a moral order—the need for reward of the righteous and punishment of the wicked—is the basis of Israel's hope, but solely the certitude that their God Yahweh, whose name evokes being and presence, was more powerful than all other gods and that he would come and establish his kingship, an act that would not be a mere restoration of the kingship he held in the beginning, but which would be enriched by all the victories gained in the course of history. Although Yahweh's kingship had been manifested at various times in history with infinite glory, reality fell short of hope and, precisely because of victories won, faith had the conviction that Yahweh could perform things that were still more wonderful. Eschatology was not born, as Mowinckel has suggested,[1] from the disappointment which the realization of Yahweh's kingship as it

[1] Cf. *Psalmenstudien*, t. 2, pp. 211ff.; these are the terms in which the scholarly Norwegian exegete defines eschatology: "Eschatology is to be understood as a flight into the future under the disillusioning pressure of a new, strong and quite unexpected experience of the surrounding world, when the old experiences could no longer be felt with complete reality", p. 324. In a more recent work (*Religion und Kultus*, 1935, p. 80) Mowinckel states that eschatology as a doctrine of last things did not grow out of the cult; but that, just as all that is living and dynamic in religion is expressed in the cult, eschatology becomes a vital force only in the cultic drama.

was exercised in history and in the cultic rites had brought to faith:
it was, on the contrary, the hope which never ceased to be the lever
of faith in spite of all the visible proofs of Yahweh's kingship in
history and in the cult. However, in the oldest conceptions at
least, Yahweh's kingship could only come to pass absolutely at the
cost of a great change which would mark the end of the present
state of things and the establishment of something new. There is
no eschatology without rupture: Israel knew that the present world
was coming to an end, that its days were numbered, though it was
only at a late stage that calculations were made concerning its limit.[1]
Certain natural phenomena were particularly suitable for suggesting
the idea of the end; frequent earthquakes, droughts and the darkness in which Israel could see a residue of original chaos, were reminders to faith that the world subsisted, not because of fixed and
immutable laws, but merely through the good pleasure of Yahweh,
for whom a single moment would be sufficient to reduce to nothingness what he had caused to arise out of chaos (Ps. 102.26; 104.29).
Although the cosmic aspect holds an important place in Old Testament eschatological concepts, it is not the determining factor: the
idea of the end of the world is always secondary to that of Yahweh's
coming and Yahweh does not come because the world is going to
end, but his coming brings, among other things, the end of the
world or more exactly the end of an age, which will be followed by
a new period of the world. And as Yahweh is the God who creates
life,[2] the catastrophic aspect of eschatology could never be the last
word of his coming. The essential place is occupied by the notions
of a new creation and restoration. That is why the cleavage between
history and eschatology is never radical, for on one side the God
who will reveal himself by a grandiose theophany at the end of time
has already manifested himself and does not cease manifesting

[1] According to the chronological system which is at the basis of the Priestly work,
the world will last 4,000 years, that is to say four periods of a thousand years each;
the Exodus, having taken place in the year 2,666 from the creation of the world,
is exactly at the end of the second third of this period, whilst the end of the
world brings us to the time of the composition of the book of Daniel. All O.T.
writings are shot through with the belief in a world of limited duration; but it
was probably only from the time of the Priestly work that this belief became the
object of speculations of an arithmetical nature.

[2] The affirmation of the eternity of Yahweh can already be found in some ancient
texts, thus 1 Sam. 15.29, in which the *nesach Israel* is contrasted with the changeable
nature of man. But it is especially from the time of Second Isaiah that eternity
becomes one of the essential attributes of Yahweh (Is. 40.28; 41.4).

himself in the course of history; and on the other side all historical events are already charged with eternal significance. Such fluidity has had the power to move certain critics to speak of eschatology only at the end of Israel's evolution, at the time when with Ezekiel the apocalyptic movement was germinating—a movement which accentuates the cleavage between eschatology and history.[1]

However, examination of the language and concepts leads us to the conclusion that an eschatology existed from a very early period of Israel's history. At the time of Amos the "day of Yahweh" formed part of Israel's hope and undoubtedly had done so for some time previously. It seems difficult to us to subscribe to the interpretation which looks on this day as a mere feast day,[2] perhaps the day of the next feast in the calendar, for the association of that day with light is an allusion to changes of a cosmic nature. Without being able to say at what date the expectation of this day first arose, it is quite probable to see in it the great means of Yahweh's revelation and action. In so far as it is a day of light, the day of Yahweh evokes the creation of the world, the moment when Yahweh gained the victory over the forces of chaos represented by darkness; more wonderful still than the first creation, when darkness had been merely pushed back by light, that day was to mark the final victory of light over all the obscure forces which would deliver a final assault in order to escape from the subordinate rank to which Yahweh had reduced them (cf. Is. 27.1; 51.9; Amos 9.3; Ps. 74.13-14; 104.26). Yet it was on the plane of history that he was to manifest himself essentially : it was imagined indeed as a great battle in the course of which Yahweh would intervene in person and would subject all the enemies of his people more effectively than he had done at the time of Gideon's victory over the Midianites (Is. 9.3; 10.26; Jg. 9.3). This final victory was also the object of a cultic ceremony which was a kind of anticipatory event. Just as a feast day in Babylon was a day of God (*um ili*),[3] the great feasts of Israel, and not only the probable though hypo-

---

[1] The late origin of eschatology has been asserted by von Gall, *Basileia tou theou*, 1926, and in a general way by the Wellhausen school. Latterly Mowinckel, *Han som kommer*, 1951, likewise defends the post-exilic origin of Messianic eschatology; we refer readers to this book for all matters dealing with the history of the question (English trans. *He that cometh*).

[2] Cf. von Gall, *op. cit.*, and Morgenstern, *Amos Studies*, 1941, pp. 408ff.

[3] Nehemiah speaks of days consecrated to Yahweh (Neh. 8.9), but the day of Yahweh has a unique and unrepeatable character.

thetical enthronement festival, celebrated the coming of God and his victory over all the forces which were opposed to the establishment of his rule.

The expression "that day", *hayyom hahu*,[1] also designates the day of Yahweh: passages such as Is. 2.20; 3.17; 5.30; 28.5-6; Amos 2.16; 8.9; Hos. 2.18, allude to an eschatological reality, though very often, particularly in the historical books, it is simply a past or present reality that is in question (Ex. 32.28; Jg. 3.30; 4.23; 1 Sam. 14.23).

More significant, and allowing no doubt about its eschatological meaning, is the formula "at the end of the days", *be'acharit hayyamim*, or the similar expression "the coming days", *yamim ba'im*, which in Ezekiel and Daniel marks the beginning of the Messianic era (Ez. 38.8, 16; Dan. 2.28; 10.14). Though the expression also has an attenuated sense which allows the translation "in the course of the days", this can be explained by the general tendency to lessen the aspect of the cleavage of the ultimate realities, but proves nothing against its original eschatological significance.[2]

The expression which best summarizes the various aspects of the eschatological drama is *shub shebut*, which can be translated as: the great return, the turning-point or change of destiny. The great resemblance between the two roots (*shub* and *shabah*) led the translators of the Septuagint to render the expression as the return from captivity, a reading which has been adopted by many modern translators.[3] The origin of this term is to be found in the great mythological theme of a return at the end of time of the first things, a theme which Christian theology defines as the ἀποκατάστασις πάντων (Acts 3.21). This great change takes place in two stages: judgment and restoration, hinged together by the idea of the remnant. Judgment constitutes the essential phase of the day of

[1] The eschatological bearing of the expression *bayyom hahu* has been contested by P. A. Munch, *The expression Bajjom Hahu: is it an eschatological terminus technicus?* Oslo 1936.

[2] There are two tendencies present; according to one, history became eschatology, the point of view of the partisans of a late origin of eschatology; according to the other, the view we favour, eschatology was absorbed by history and received from history what constitutes its dynamism, which did not prevent it from determining the interpretation of history.

[3] The translation "to bring back the captives" is manifestly impossible in passages like Ez. 16.53; Job 42.10 and also Ps. 126. Note that Aquila regularly translates it as ἀποστρέφειν τὴν ἀποστροφήν except in Jer. 49.6, in which he follows the LXX reading (ἐπιστρέφειν τὴν αἰχμαλωσίαν); on this topic, cf. the opposing theses of Dietrich and of Baumann (cf. bibliog.).

Yahweh without completely exhausting it, since the day of Yahweh is also and indeed especially the day of the coming of his kingdom, a goal which is never lost sight of in the gloomiest prophetic pictures, which show judgment as operating against Israel—Israel taking the place solely occupied by the nations in popular eschatology. Judgment is not motivated by mythological reasons such as the aging of the world or by national reasons such as the supremacy of Israel, but by sin. Certain scholars like Wellhausen and Smend think that the prophets only announced judgment when they were to some extent forced to do so by the course of events. Certainly the preaching of the prophets is clearly determined by the circumstances of history, but as it appears just as clearly that times of prosperity—for instance in the time of Amos—do not exclude the announcement of judgment, we must admit that the ethical factor triumphs over political opportunism. The prophets' method of announcing judgment is to transpose current practices in lawsuit scenes on to the religious plane.[1] Judgment unfolds in three phases: (a) God presents himself as accuser and enumerates to those with whom he enters into judgment their faults, which are either faults committed against God, idolatry (Jer. 2.23; Ez. 6.3ff.), or offences against neighbours, murder, adultery, calumny (Hos. 4.2; Jer. 7.8-10); (b) God pronounces the verdict of condemnation sometimes introduced by the interjection *hoy* = woe! which through its association with funeral rites indicates that there is no appeal against the sentence (Is. 10.5; Jer. 48.1; 50.27); (c) the execution of judgment is carried out by means of three scourges which Jeremiah summarizes in a striking phrase: "I will destroy them by the sword, by famine and by pestilence" (14.12; cf. Jer. 27.8, 13; 28.8; Ez. 6.12).

Final judgment is not only announced, but is already partially brought to pass by the judgments which are carried out in the course of history, and so its contours only become precise in passages with an apocalyptic flavour in which the divorce between eschatology and history is accentuated. The obviously judicial aspect of judgment, the order and method by which it is carried through, do not permit us to see in it the manifestation of anger of an

---

[1] Note among the principal scenes of judgment: Amos 1.3; 2.16; Hos. 4.1; Is. 1.2, 18ff.; 3.13; Jer. 1.14; 25.15ff:; Mic. 1.2-4; 6.1ff.; Zeph. 3.8ff.; Joel 4.2ff.; Mal. 3.2ff. It is quite possible that certain cultic scenes foreshadowed this judgment (cf. Würthwein, "Der Ursprung der prophetischen Gerichtsrede im Kult", ZThK, 1952, pp. 1-16).

arbitrary God; all Old Testament texts agree that it has the banishment of sin as its goal, although the term sin covers a variety of
things. At the time of Amos sin was identified with the pagan
nations as a whole, the destruction of which appeared necessary
for the triumph of Israel's election; judgment on Israel itself
seemed to be the very negation of that election. In other pronouncements belonging to various periods, the sin to be punished
is identified with the gods responsible for the fate of those nations
(Is. 19.1; 34.4; 46.1; Jer. 10.11; 48.13; 49.3; Zeph. 2.11); but the
main line is represented by the great prophets who show that,
because of the conditions of obedience linked with election and the
covenant, judgment on guilty Israel is the logical conclusion of
God's plan. Whether judgment on the nations or on Israel is
concerned, the law which guides the exercise of judgment is always
the "lex talionis": "Thou hast pillaged—thou shalt be pillaged"
(Is. 33.1); "Those who devour you shall be devoured" (Jer. 30.16);
"Do unto her as she [Babylon] hath done" (Jer. 50.29). The
people forsook Yahweh and so Yahweh will forsake them (Hos.
1.9; 2.4; 4.6). The wicked will reap what they have sown
(Is. 3.10, 11). This is why the prophets were able to see, in the
exile, the just punishment of God against a people who had forsaken
him (Jer. 5.19; 18.10-13).[1]

Eschatology—and this is certainly further evidence in support
of its antiquity—has an aspect which is clearly collective. The
people of Israel as well as the other nations are regarded as a whole.
However, it did not escape the uncompromising moral attitude of
the prophets that there could be, within a single group, guilty and
righteous or at least various degrees of guilt. Already in a well-
known passage of the Yahwist's work we find the idea stated that
the righteous can on certain occasions stop or at least cause the
deferment of the punishment of the guilty; all the prophets took
up this theme (Jer. 5.1; Ez. 22.30) and to one of the greatest of
them belongs the achievement of drawing its final consequences
(Is. 53). The collective aspect of punishment does not necessarily
make it anonymous; the prophets announce that, in the midst of
general punishment, particular punishments are destined to rein-

[1] We must not always see the announcements of the exile by pre-exilic prophets
as prophecy *post eventum*; transportation of people was the normal method applied
by conquerors of antiquity to vanquished populations.

force the judgment—this is the case with the false prophets in Jer. 29.21-23—or on the other hand to temper it—Ebed Melek the Ethiopian will be safe in the midst of catastrophe (Jer. 39.15-18)—for from every judgment Yahweh means to reveal something new which should be a sign of the coming of his kingdom.

A remnant will come out of judgment: the doctrine of the remnant is essential to Israelite eschatology, for it expresses in its own fashion the central message which is the coming of God into the world. Although also used in connection with the nations (the remnant of Babel, Jer. 50.26; of Aram, Is. 17.3; of the Philistines, Amos 1.8; of Edom, Amos 9.12) but solely in a national sense, in Israel the expression has religious overtones, for it reflects very clearly God's will for Israel. The remnant is a concept with two facets, one catastrophic—only a remnant will survive; the other full of promise —for a remnant will escape. The catastrophic sense is basic; a remnant is spoken of only after a terrible catastrophe which has destroyed all but a remnant: by comparing it to two bones and a piece of ear just saved from the lion's mouth, Amos conveys some idea of its smallness (3.12; 5.3). The prophet's hearers could not misunderstand, but they could also remember the word by which Yahweh had announced to the prophet Elijah that he had established a remnant (*hish'arti*) so that his work should continue (1 Kings 19.17-18).[1] This saving and consoling aspect of the remnant has its origin in the mercy of Yahweh, who wishes to uphold his people at all costs: God chooses the remnant, it is the λεῖμμα κατ᾽ ἐκλογὴν χάριτος (Rom. 11.5) and no one can claim to form part of it, although Yahweh exercised his choice on righteous men such as Noah, Lot and Joseph, etc. It was Isaiah who gave systematic expression to the notion of the remnant; like Amos he insists on its catastrophic aspect (6.13; 17.5-6; two olives on the topmost bough) but, however small the remnant may be, it is the germ, the root from which a new plant will be able to spring, for it is in favour of this remnant that the election and consecration granted formerly to Abraham's posterity are renewed.[2] Convinced that what he believes is to be brought about in the immediate future, and anxious also to give concrete expression to his faith by ruling his life in accordance with it, Isaiah tries to make from the

---

[1] In the cycle of narratives concerning Elijah, the notion of remnant is met in 1 Kings 18.22, 40; 19.3, 4; 2 Kings 9.15; 10.11, 14; 17.19, 24.

[2] De Vaux, *RB*, 1933, p. 531.

remnant a reality that is already present: the name given to one of his sons, Shear-yashub = *a remnant will return* (i.e. to Yahweh) signifies not only that there will be a remnant, but that his son will constitute its nucleus. It is possible that in the course of his ministry he more or less identified the remnant with all the things which were the object of God's choice: his disciples, himself, Jerusalem, the community of the 'anawim (14.32) constituted, if not the remnant itself, at least sure signs and pledges of its future coming and triumph, for "the remnant will produce new roots below and fruits above" (37.31), and Micah states that the remnant will be so powerful that it will accomplish a reversal of the situation and that the remnant will in its turn become a lion which tramples and tears, by the power of Yahweh which will reside in its breast (Mic. 5.7-8). In Isaiah the remnant is essentially distinct from a purely political reality; it is essentially an Israel κατὰ πνεῦμα; in Zephaniah, a prophet of progress in many respects, the remnant receives concrete form in the community of the poor (2.3; 3.12) and it is significant that Deuteronomy, which is an attempt to reconstitute the holy people in its entirety, does not speak of the remnant. Jeremiah announces total destruction (5.1; 6.9; 8.3; 9.9; 24.8-9); yet once the catastrophe has taken place a remnant gathers round Gedaliah; but is it God's remnant? For a moment this possibility is envisaged (Jer. 42.10-12), but events were not long in undeceiving the prophet (42.19-22) by inviting him to see the remnant in the basket of figs which symbolizes the exiles (24.4). Ezekiel had hesitated to identify the remnant, but the death of Pelatyah (11.13), whose name, so like that of Shear-yashub, proves the importance of the notion, convinces him that the exiles form the real remnant (11.14-20). After the exile, the community of Ezra was very conscious of being this remnant (Ezra 9.8, 15) and this feeling became current among the last of the prophets. However, the judgment which was brought to pass in the exile and from which the remnant issues does not eliminate the final judgment (Joel 3.5; Obad. 17). The disentanglement of the remnant from its national trappings makes it into a splendid reality open to the heathen, or rather to the remnant among them (Zeph. 3.9; Zech. 14.16). Although with each prophet statements about the remnant are determined by the circumstances of his time, it always appears—and this is the evidence in favour of a supra-historical origin of the notion—as the bridge joining the threat of punishment to the promise of restoration. Proportional to the development in detail of the catastrophic aspect, the remnant becomes disentangled from ancient ties and appears less as the débris of a past that is reaching fulfilment than the germ of a new future in which Yahweh alone will hold the initiative.

The glorious future indeed will primarily be a restoration of the past. In the visions of restoration mythological elements are mingled even more closely with historical memories than in the visions of judgment: the restoration will sometimes be the return of paradise, at other times the return of the particularly glorious periods of Israel's past. Although the terms Eden and the garden of Yahweh are met explicitly only in Isaiah 51.3, the idea underlies all the texts which speak of the felicity at the end of time. The nature of paradise is the nature of fairy tales. There the food comprises wonderful dishes which have the property of conferring immortality and knowledge; at the time of the *'acharit hayyamim* there will be the same luxuriant vegetation as in the beginning (Is. 4.2); there will be a profusion of milk or honey, oil and wine, according as the ideal is regarded from a nomadic or a sedentary viewpoint (Amos 9.13; Joel 4.18); men will live long and death at the age of a hundred years is very premature (Is. 65.20; Zech. 8.4); for those who think absolutely consistently death itself will be abolished (Is. 25.8). Beauty, innocence and wisdom, which were the attributes of the first human beings, will return (Ez. 28.13; 31.3). This transformation of man will be brought about by means of the tree of life, the water of life or the book of life. The tree of life[1] whose fruit confers eternal life is mentioned outside the Genesis narrative only as an image of beauty and particularly of wisdom (Prov. 11.30; 13.12; 15.4), but it again plays an essential rôle in apocalyptic writings (Enoch 32.24-25; Rev. 2.7; 22.2, 24).[2] The theme of life-giving water represented by the four rivers which take their rise in the mountain of paradise (Gen. 2.10-14) reappears in Ezekiel's final visions and an allusion to it can be seen in the ambiguous mention of the river of delights (*nachal 'adanim*) in Psalm 36.9. The notion of the book of life excludes that of

[1] Cf. also 4 Esdras 7.36: "Revelatur iterum paradisus jucunditatum."
[2] In a series of studies devoted to the ideology of royalty Widengren has stressed the importance of the theme of the tree of life in the cult of Tammuz and in that of the king; but apart from Lam. 4.31 there is in the O.T. no connection between this image and royalty (*The King and the Tree of Life in Ancient Near Eastern Religion*, Uppsala 1951).

the food of immortality, for anyone whose name is written in the book of life has no need of special food in order to gain immortality. The transformation will also extend to the animal world; wild animals will be tamed, the wolf will lie down with the lamb (Is. 11.6-8) or they will purely and simply disappear (Is. 35.9; Ez. 34.25; Lev. 26.6); all animals will be beneficiaries of the divine covenant (Hos. 2.20). The Genesis narrative, admittedly, does not insist much on this concord between man and beast, but, by affirming that his food was exclusively vegetarian until the time of the Flood, the Priestly writer seeks to assert that, though called to rule over the animals, man has no right to put them to death. The restored state is quite well characterized by the term *shalom*, which means more than peace as opposed to war, although war also is eliminated in the new age (Is. 2.2-4; Mic. 5.2ff.). It expresses a state of plenitude and perfection in which everyone will attain his maximum intensity in a life freed from all limitations.

Israel's faith was nourished less on myths connected with the beginnings—the absence of allusions to which is quite striking—than on the great facts of the past, on those *tsideqot Yahweh* which were manifested in history. The Exodus was at all times the type of God's interventions; so it is not surprising that the felicity of Mosaic times should occupy more space in eschatology than truly paradisal felicity. Yahweh will recall his people to the desert, to the place of the first betrothal; they will have to cross the desert again but, instead of being an exhausting march, it will be a triumphal procession; wonderful trees will grow there and springs will gush forth (Is. 41.18-20; 51.9-10); along their route, Yahweh in person will be the shepherd (Ex. 15.13; Is. 40.11; 52.12) and will manifest himself in the form of a column of smoke by day and of fire by night (Is. 4.5). The new political and social organization will be like that of the Exodus (Is. 1.26) and Yahweh will proceed to divide the land again. The vision of the new covenant in Jer. 31 is likewise a transposition on to the eschatological plane of one of the essential Mosaic themes. Some sectarians like the Rechabites (2 Kings 10.5; Jer. 35) gave concrete form to this hope by transposing the return of Mosaic times into the immediate present, holding that the fact of ever leaving them was a mark of unfaithfulness. The hope of the return of Davidic times added to the paradise theme and the Exodus theme an element which, in view of the circumstances surrounding the composition of the biblical books, was destined to enjoy great prominence: a large number of the hopes centre round Jerusalem; the route of the new Exodus does not simply lead to the promised land, but to Jerusalem. At the gates of Jerusalem the great drama will be played out, in the course of which Yahweh's kingship over all his adversaries will be declared (Ps. 46; Ez. 38-39). It is very probable that several reasons contributed to give Jerusalem this essential rôle: its sacred character since the Canaanite period, its geographical position and the memory of extraordinary deliverances in the course of history. Israel was conscious of owing all these valuable things of the past to David and, because of the general tendency of Hebrew mentality to incarnate all truths in people, all the glory of Jerusalem came to be concentrated in the person of David.

B. THE MESSIANIC KINGDOM

The eschatology of judgment and of the great return hardly gives a place to the figure of the Messiah; yet it could not be said that it is totally ignorant of him. But the person of the Messiah obviously plays only a subordinate part. Yahweh alone is king and as such the author of judgment and restoration. The Messianic hope, however, has deep roots which go further back than the institution of kingship, though the latter gave it its dominant orientation. Since the return of the golden age formed part of the most ancient religious patrimony of Israel it is quite natural to suppose that it also included the hope of the return of man as he existed in the beginning. Man had been created to exercise the function of dominator and king within the creation (Gen. 1.26; Ps. 8.5). This royal function also appears in certain paradise traditions whose substance had been furnished to Israel by her neighbours. In his well-known elegy on the King of Tyre, Ezekiel (28.13) speaks of a vizier of the great god El, to whom the latter had entrusted guardianship of his seal in the garden of Eden; his wisdom gave him the privilege of being called the protecting *kerub*, the gatekeeper of heaven; but this vizier showed himself unworthy and, because of his sin, he was hurled down to earth, where he built the city of Tyre and founded the most ancient kingdom of the Phoenicians. In an analogous order of ideas, Isaiah applies to the king of Babylon the features of a celestial personage, *Helal ben*

Shachar, shining star son of the dawn, whose pride cost him relegation to earth (Is. 14). Job too knows the tradition of an *Urmensch* begotten before the hills (in time or in place), who was considered to have made fraudulent entry into the council of the gods in order to steal wisdom; this was responsible for his being ejected from the celestial paradise (Job 15.7ff.). Psalm 110, which in its present form is an oracle addressed to the reigning king, greets him as the one who "was begotten on the holy mountain from the womb of the dawn", an expression which probably stems from some myth about the beginning of things; finally it may be remembered that the Babylonian hero Adapa, "seed of humanity", was gifted with a vast intelligence which made him capable of revealing the forms of the earth, that he bore among other titles that of *mshch*, anointed, of shepherd of humanity, and that he had been within an ace of obtaining the privilege of immortality. Original man by whom the fall had come should also be the means of the restoration, and without drawing from the "Protevangelion" all the Christological affirmations which Christian exegesis never ceases to find there, we feel that there is in this text much more than the expression of an everlasting enmity between man and the serpent, for victory belongs to the one who crushes the head and not to the one who will wound the heel[1] (Gen. 3.15). So it is possible to discover behind these fleeting allusions and metaphors the figure of a person who is none other than primitive man; from this man the re-establishment of the compromised situation—in a word—salvation was expected, as is shown by the large number of anthropos myths. But Israel's essentially historical faith always applied this saviour's features to particularly historical figures. Before finding them applied to the Davidic Messiah, we meet them among the first representatives of a charismatic kingship who were themselves called *moshi'im*, that is saviours.[2] These heroes all have

[1] The bibliographical material on this text will be found collected in the article by B. Rigaux, "La femme et son lignage", *RB*, 1954, p. 321. We feel that in this text there is an announcement of the final salvation of man and consequently a "Messianism" which goes far beyond national limitations; this universal aspect never disappeared moreover even when the Davidic current became dominant; the Chronicler again shows how David's kingdom is a universal reality.

[2] Several authors dealing with Messianism prefer the term "saviour" to Messiah, which never has an eschatological sense in the O.T., for example Sellin, *Die israelitische Heilandserwartung*; Dürr, *Ursprung und Ausbau der isr.-jüd Heilandserwartung*; Staerk, *Soter. Die Erlösererwartung in den östlichen Religionen*; Widengren, *King and Saviour*.

common features which can only be explained if it is admitted that their life is cast in the same mould, that of the ideal saviour: (a) their birth is preceded by a long period of sterility in their mother: this is the case of Isaac, Jacob, Joseph, Samson and Samuel; (b) their origin is obscure and modest: Gideon is the poorest of his tribe and the least in his clan (Jg. 6.15), Jephthah is of obscure origin, but this lowliness is responsible for his being chosen by God for brilliant exploits, Saul comes from the smallest tribe (1 Sam. 9.21), and Bethlehem, David's birthplace, is very little among the myriads of Judah (Mic. 5.1); (c) the heroes are filled with God's spirit through which they are capable of performing superhuman actions: Joseph has the strength of an ox (Gen. 49.24; Dt. 33.17), Moses is continually filled with God's power, likewise Samson (Jg. 14.15ff.), Samuel (1 Sam. 15.33), Saul (2 Sam. 1.22ff.) and David (1 Sam. 17.46; 18.7).

It would, however, be a rather fragile hypothesis if we could not support it by what we know of Israel's eschatological hopes in the most ancient times. The date of the Messianic oracles is difficult to determine and, although we think we can find traces of this hope earlier than the establishment of the monarchy, we must admit that all the oracles received their present form only from the time of David. This is true in particular of the oracles of Balaam,[1] but despite their Davidic stamp, these oracles reflect rather the climate of the time of the Judges or the early days of the monarchy under Saul, and their prophetic character, mysterious and veiled, forbids our seeing in them simple *vaticinia ex eventu*. Composed in their present form to the glory of David or one of his descendants, they announce the end of time ('*acharit hayyamim*), but, whereas the eschatological oracles speak only of the coming of Yahweh, here the main stress is put on the person of a mediator who is already endued with the main features which we are to find all through the Messianic tradition: (a) he is called a star (*kokab*),[2] a title which will be one of the constants of eschatological language, since we find it right through to the book of Revelation (Rev. 22.16) and since elsewhere also the coming of the Saviour is found in association

---

[1] The oracles of Balaam have often been re-edited in the course of the centuries, as is shown particularly in the mention of the vessels of Kittim (Num. 24.23) which can only be the Greeks and Romans, but the basis is certainly ancient and characterizes quite well what may be called the heroic age of Israel.

[2] It is particularly interesting to notice the translation of Num. 24.17 in the LXX: Ἀνατελεῖ ἄστρον ἐξ Ἰακωβ, καὶ ἀναστήσεται ἄνθρωπος ἐξ Ἰσραηλ.

with manifestations of a planetary or solar order; (*b*) the Saviour
will be a powerful warrior; he it is who performs the task elsewhere
reserved for Yahweh: to break the skull of his enemies; (*c*) this
Saviour has a universal empire; the earth belongs to him (cf. Dt.
33.13ff.), an echo of Israel's national consciousness and of its mission,
which are as ancient as its election.

Besides the oracles of Balaam our most important literary source
is constituted by Jacob's blessing of the tribes (Gen. 49) and more
especially by the blessing on Judah (v. 8ff.). The mystery of this
passage, which is already partially obscure in itself, is further
increased by the puzzle of the term *Shiloh*.[1] Jews and Christians
alike have always looked on this text as a Messianic prophecy, going
so far as to show that the numerical value of *Yabo Shiloh* and
maschiach were identical. "The sceptre shall not leave Judah nor
the rod of command from between his feet, until the coming of
him to whom dominion belongs." There also, it seems, a saviour
is concerned who will arrive at the end of time, probably issuing
from Judah, but whose arrival will put an end to the authority of
that tribe; he will be different from the saviour of Balaam's oracle
in that he will be pacific, he will be mounted on an ass and will
feed on paradisiac dishes, milk and wine. So, at a time preceding
the monarchy, there may have been, among certain tribes, the hope
that a figure would come with the task of bringing back the golden
age and of exercising again the dominion which had been compromised by opposing forces; but faith never doubted the triumph
of that dominion, nor could faith conceive the return of an age
without the return of a person, for in Israel all truths tend to
crystallize in personalities and not in some abstract principles.

These antecedents do not prevent us from saying that Messianism
in its true sense developed only from the time of the monarchy.
Long before adopting for itself the royal régime, Israel had seen
kings over the majority of its neighbours and had lived for long
enough among Canaanites, who were organized in little kingdoms,
to appreciate the pros and cons of this régime.[2] Throughout the
ancient East, the king was the object of a veneration which sometimes became a real cult: in Egypt, the Pharaoh's divine character

[1] The best analogy to the name Shiloh is provided by Ezekiel 21.32 '*ad bo' 'asher
lo hammishpat,* which cuts short all attempts to seek to interpret the term as a
proper name. Cf. concerning the blessing on Judah Sellin's article in *ZAW*, 1944,
pp. 57ff.

[2] Cf. John Gray, "Canaanite kingship in theory and practice", *VT*, 1952, pp. 193ff.

is always affirmed without reservation, since the Pharaoh is the incarnation of the god and the only true priest through whom the land was assured divine life. In the Mesopotamian world, the deification of the king assumed aspects as numerous and varied as the peoples who mingled in that area, but, as shown in the exhaustive enquiry by H. Frankfort,[1] the idea of the king as servant of the god always and everywhere came earlier than the idea of the god incarnate. Since Syria-Palestine occupies a position midway between Egypt and Mesopotamia, it is not surprising that we find in Canaan a notion of monarchy very similar to Egypt's; the Ugaritic texts, the Legend of Keret in particular, are significant in this respect, while among the Aramaeans of Syria[2] we have no trace of the divine origin of the king or of his deification after death. These variations, in which it is right to see more than differences of detail, make us regard as infinitely improbable the existence of a pattern common to the Semitic world as a whole, of a dying and rising god whose rôle was incarnated in the king. Further—and we must insist upon this—all that the literary sources tell us about the institution of the Israelite monarchy gives very little support to a royal ideology: the monarchy always had a secular character; the constitution of the people by the bond of the covenant into a holy people dispensed with the mediation of the king, who could not be united to God by a closer bond than the people as a whole. The reasons which finally and not without much hesitation led to the adoption of the royal régime were of a political order only, and it is quite probable that kingship would always have remained in the borderland of Israel's life without the person of David. In the history of the Messianic hope David constitutes both a finishing and a starting-point. A finishing-point, for to David, and with better reason than to the heroes of the time of the Judges, features of the final Saviour were ascribed; he was saluted as son of the dawn (Ps. 110.3), as the hero who brings the prosperity of nature with him (Ps. 72.16), as the rising sun (2 Sam. 23.4). It also seems quite probable that by the capture of Jerusalem David inherited certain local traditions connected with this city, which, moreover, we can find in the Old Testament itself. Among the kings who gave brilliance to pre-Israelite Jerusalem, Melchizedek occupies a pre-eminent position. That he exercised royal and priestly functions

---

[1] *Kingship and the Gods*, Chicago 1948.
[2] Euler in *ZAW*, 1938, pp. 272-313.

is in keeping with what we know of ancient oriental custom, but this priest-king, who is invoked in Psalm 110 to establish David's authority, probably held his prestige from something more lofty and more distant than these two functions. Concerning the Messianic king, the same Psalm which mentions Melchizedek speaks of his birth from the womb of the dawn and from the living water of the torrent; these figures of speech form part of a myth of paradise which must have received fairly full expression in Jebusite Jerusalem. Consequently, when David seized Jerusalem, he took over the prerogatives of Melchizedek and through him those of the paradisal king.

In the mythologies of the most diverse peoples, paradise is the impregnable place, the place whose entrance in biblical tradition is jealously guarded by the cherubim with flaming swords; and so anyone who wishes to take paradise by assault exposes himself to an adventure which is doomed in advance to failure. Now the taking of Jerusalem is likewise spoken of as impossible; the Jebusites are made to say to David, "Thou shalt not enter here, but the blind and the lame will force thee to retire" (2 Sam. 5.6). Doubtless the impregnability of the city is partially explained on geographical grounds, but religious considerations are not absent: 'El 'Elyon, who was called "the lord of all the earth", dwelt in Jerusalem (Gen. 14.19) and this presence was a pledge of security for the city. Therefore we should probably consider Jerusalem's rôle as holy city in a rather different way from the one commonly admitted; it is usually thought that Jerusalem's prestige is due to the presence of the temple which, on becoming the depositary of the Ark, concentrated within its walls all the divine presence. It is more plausible to suppose that the temple was built because Jerusalem was already a holy city and that the work of David and his successors was to transfer that holiness from the ownership of the Canaanites to that of the Israelites. David received a considerable inheritance, but for no one is the saying as true as for him: to him that hath shall be given. From all points of view David was a great man. Thanks to a wealth of first-hand documentary evidence, since it comes doubtless from his followers, we can draw a relatively accurate picture of his reign. David could impose his will, he possessed the nature of a chief, but this chief was not a cruel and tyrannical despot using the arbitrary power that his immunity conferred upon him; he was able to take the value of his subjects into account and strove skilfully to win their esteem, by sending for example a share of the booty to the elders of Judah (1 Sam. 30.24). National unity which was brought about in his reign was due less to political contrivance than to his personal prestige, which explains in part why it was compromised as soon as he had died. His military exploits had made him infinitely popular: "Saul hath slain his thousands and David his ten thousands" was a well-known refrain and "all in Judah and Israel loved David, because he went out and came in before them" (1 Sam. 18.7, 16). His poetical and musical gifts put him in the people's eyes in a particularly friendly relationship with the deity, all the more since David was indeed deeply religious. Certainly he did not compose all the Psalms which tradition attributes to him, but it seems certain that this man was capable of humbling himself and of recognizing God's power as much in his victories, in which he never rejoices in the death of his enemies, as in the defeats of his personal life. An oriental despot, considering himself as god, requiring that divine honour should be paid to him, could easily have been incensed at the hope of a king greater than himself; a thousand years later Herod will be bitterly angry when he learns of the birth of a new king. David, however, merely becomes more conscious of his dignity as a precursor of this Messiah. David's attitude towards Messianism can be defined from two texts whose authenticity is more and more recognized by literary criticism: the first is Nathan's prophecy (2 Sam. 7), which takes place at the time when the king is preparing to build a temple to Yahweh. Yahweh declines this offer but gives to David a threefold compensation because of his good intention: (a) I will make thee a name equal to the name of the greatest on earth (v. 9); (b) Israel will attain national independence, it will not be disturbed and the wicked shall no longer oppress it (v. 10); (c) Yahweh shall make thee a house: thy house and thy kingdom shall stand for ever in my presence, thy throne shall be established for ever (vv. 11, 16). Therefore Yahweh gives David the assurance, something he had not done for Saul, that he will found a dynasty and that this dynasty will last indefinitely. From this there opened for Israel, as long as they were governed by a descendant of David, a new prospect of glory. The blessings given to the people and attributed, by Jacob's prediction, especially to the tribe of Judah, were thenceforward concentrated on the royal house of Jesse; from that time, the destiny of God's reign on earth will be linked with that of David's dynasty. Important as this text is, it is, however, only implicitly Messianic, for what is promised in it is not the more or less imminent coming of a saviour, but the eternity of David's dynasty—unless preference should be given to the version of this prophecy given in the book of Chronicles, where the individual sense is clearly brought out.[1]

We find an echo of Nathan's prophecy in the oracle which is usually, but improperly, called the last words of David (2 Sam. 23.1-7).[2] In form this passage recalls the oracles of Balaam (Num. 24.3, 15) and like Jacob's blessing it forms part of the literature of testamentary statements; however there is no question in it of the eschatological Messiah : the *moshel tsaddiq* is primarily David himself and then each of his descendants on his throne; but it is not impossible that there is an allusion to the final victory of the dynasty, which can only be the victory of an individual. This aspect of finishing-point and starting-point is found in several Psalms which, even if they do not come from David himself, at least link up with the current which tended to identify the Messiah with the reigning king. This "realized" eschatology, to use an expression that has become fashionable, very closely resembles, from the formal point of view, the language of royal ideology, and it is quite probable that in certain circles, particularly in Jerusalem, no distinction was made between the reigning king and the Messiah who was to come. This does not mean that all eschatological perspective is absent from those Psalms which are very rightly called royal rather than Messianic. Thus in Psalm 2 the view goes beyond the reign of the present sovereign; doubtless the latter is the one who is meant by the term *mashiach*, but for the Psalmist's faith he is also the sign of the coming king who alone will be able to carry out the mission of victory and universalism which is proclaimed therein. The same point occurs in Psalm 72, which regards the present kingship in the light of the kingship of Yahweh, which is

---

[1] Nathan's prophecy is interpreted in a collective sense by the authors of Psalms 89.30-38 and 132.11-12; it was interpreted in an individual sense by the addition of v. 13 in 2 Sam. 7, in 1 Kings 5.19; 8.16-19 and by the Chronicler: 1 Chr. 17.11-14; 22.10; 28.6; in the latter an individualization of the person of the Messiah is clearly involved.

[2] Cf. Procksch's study, "Die letzten Worte Davids" in *Alttestamentliche Studien Rud. Kittel dargebracht*. In order to show the eminently Messianic character of this passage von Orelli has written: "As he, the old king, departs, the sun does not set but the morning then breaks in unexpected splendour" (*Die alttestamentliche Weissagung*, p. 187).

made real by the Messiah, and this without any need to admit in the post-exilic period a recasting of the royal Psalms with the purpose of making them the vehicle of eschatological Messianism.[1] In a general way, it may be held that Messianism from David onwards enjoyed great continuity, with the stress put sometimes on the dynamic aspect, sometimes on the purely eschatological aspect.

It would, however, be incorrect to state that Messianism forms the centre of the preaching of the great prophets. For the prophets earlier than Isaiah—Elijah, Amos and Hosea—the Messiah plays no part to speak of, though the fundamental theme of eschatology, which is the proclamation of the kingdom, is at the basis of their message, for God's absoluteness and the requirement of justice in social relationships are motivated by their faith in the God who comes to establish his sovereignty after a thorough sifting of the whole world. Even to an Isaiah, the Messiah occupies only a secondary place in his visions of the future; he forms a part of the gifts of the new age far more than being its initiator, but only his coming gives real meaning to the new age, for without his presence God's gifts would risk being ineffective. This Messiah will be a descendant of David, but in all the well-known Messianic prophecies of ecclesiastical tradition, the son of David also bears the stamp of the paradisal man. The association of the various themes appears most clearly in the text of Micah (5.1-5): the Messiah is of the lineage of David or rather he will be David *redivivus* since he will come from Bethlehem, but behind this David looms the figure of the man-saviour who existed at the far-off beginnings of creation and whose birth will be surrounded with mystery and wonder. In spite of the transference on to the historical plane, the mythological background is still clearly discernible; without ignoring the positive values brought by kingship with a view to the actualizing of the hope, the prophets regarded it as too narrow a basis for the coming of the kingdom. A prophet like Isaiah is markedly influenced by the monarchy. More than other prophets, he lived in the immediate vicinity of kings and, by addressing many of his oracles to them, he showed that he considered them as the representatives of the people and responsible

---

[1] Podechard and Steinmann, to quote only two recent French commentators on the Psalms, think that the eschatological Messianism of the Psalms is due to a revision: thus Ps. 2.7; 45.18b; 110.6b, 7b are alleged to have been added in order to bring about this transference.

for them. His pronouncements, however, have nothing in common with the language of courtiers; although he never doubts that the king is installed by God, his own prophetic conscience, which rested on immediate contact with God, assures him of an evident feeling of superiority before the king, for example when in the presence of Ahaz he contrasts his God with the king's (Is. 7.10ff.). It is improbable that Isaiah ever thought that the perpetuity of the Davidic dynasty was enough to establish Yahweh's kingship on earth, for in his eyes the reigning king was only a sign, positive or negative, of the king whom the prophet was awaiting in accordance with the most ancient tradition of his people. A righteous, faithful and pious king, walking in the footsteps of David, was a sign of the Messianic king; on the other hand an unfaithful king evoked, by contrast, the hope and figure of the ideal king. This contrast appears clearly in chapter 7 of this book: on one side is Ahaz, weak and hesitant, seeking salvation in alliances with a foreign power, on the other side Immanuel, the child of mysterious and more or less miraculous origin, who is the son neither of Ahaz, nor of the prophet, and who represents a new age which will put an end to the former order of things.[1] Immanuel's mission, which is only announced there, is given in detail in the oracles of chaps. 9 and 11; his person and work will form part of a new creation, inaugurated like the first with a great light and a great battle which Yahweh, who is always the principal actor, will launch against the powers of chaos. By insisting on the birth of the Messiah, the prophet seeks to declare his complete participation in the course of history, while the attributes with which he is endowed are not conquests due to his genius and activity, but solely gifts from God. His work will consist not only in bringing back the *shub shebut*, but in making it operative through a moral transformation; by founding his kingdom on *mishpat* and *tsedaqah*, the Messianic sovereign must prove that his reign is a faithful reflection of the reign of Yahweh himself, whose means of action are no different (Is. 29.19-20; 32.16; 33.17). The gift of the spirit stressed in chapter 11 is a further reminiscence of what took place at the beginning of creation, when the movement of the spirit hovering

---

[1] *Immanuel* and the *'almah* must have been realities known to the prophet's hearers; the people were waiting for the coming of a divine child of more or less wonderful origin; but in the prophet's mouth this myth becomes present in history and the coming of this Saviour very imminent, in spite of the general situation, which seems unfavourable to the arrival of the golden age.

over the darkness of chaos was the first gesture of God the creator. If this king brings in a new creation, it is obvious that his work goes far beyond the continuity of the dynasty, although it is in Jerusalem and on the throne of David that it must be manifested. Jeremiah, too, envisaged the Messianic kingdom as a contrast and not as a continuation of the earthly kingdom. The righteous seed, *tsemach*[1] *tsaddiq*, is far from being realized by him who bears the name of righteous, that is King Zedekiah (Jer. 23.5) and it might even be that the prophet denies him any link with the Davidic dynasty.[2] The abolition of the monarchy and the exile, while causing a crisis in Messianic beliefs, did not nullify the hope itself, which was founded on faith in the creative power of God much more than on the permanence of an institution. The dynastic current found a way of turning to good account all the signs which could be interpreted as proof that the exile had not put an end to the Davidic line and to the promises connected with it. Thus the Deuteronomic redactor sees, without explicitly stating, a sign of the validity of the promise formerly made to David through Nathan in the reinstatement of Jehoiachin by the king of Babylon (2 Kings 25.27, 30); and at the return from exile the Messianic movement begun by the Davidic Zerubbabel was probably more important than the few allusions in the biblical texts might lead us to suppose.[3]

Yet this current was less dynamic than the specifically prophetic current which is represented by the two men who set their mark on the whole post-exilic development of Judaism—Ezekiel and Second Isaiah. Both proclaim the restoration, not as a return to the past, but as a new creation. Ezekiel, the prophet of the honour of God, presents this restoration as almost exclusively the work of Yahweh, who will conclude a new covenant in accordance with the principles of the first: "Ye shall be my people, and I shall be your

---

[1] The word *tsemach* is a term of cosmic eschatology (cf. Num. 24.17); we find it again in Is. 4.2-3; Zech. 3.6-10; 6.9-15; the Messiah is to inaugurate a new creation.

[2] Messianism holds a very secondary place in Jeremiah's message; its goal is the new covenant under Yahweh's kingship; in a passage which is probably not by the prophet himself (33.14ff.) the name of *Yahweh tsidqenu* is applied to the Jerusalem community, which proves that the Messiah is for him only a means of making fully real the idea of an elected people.

[3] The specifically Davidic current was maintained particularly in the book of Chronicles; we find it used down to the time of the book of Maccabees (1 Macc. 2.57). "David has inherited the throne of the kingdom for ever"; yet the house of David had long ceased to exist.

M

God" (36.28), but this covenant will be new since the people will have passed through a death and a resurrection (37); the David who will reign over this community is less like the king of Israel whose name he bears than the "original man" whose presence is enough to confirm the presence of God, who will be the only king (Ez. 34.23; 37.24). Second Isaiah does not make a clean sweep of the past, on the contrary, he finds in the transformed and purified experience of the past the secret of the restoration. The Servant Songs, far from being fragments of foreign origin inserted into his work, offer us on the contrary the key to his thought which, as has been very rightly stressed, is a theology of history. With the help of this extremely fluid figure, which is used in the Old Testament for the nation and for certain privileged individuals, the prophet recapitulates the whole history of Israel.

Founded upon election and destined to a mission, the people of Israel underwent a long series of trials, due for the most part to their own faithlessness, from which they had always been delivered anew by a not less uninterrupted series of liberating interventions of God. All these themes are used again in the Servant Songs: the servant is the elect, the wretched, the missionary, the glorified one; he summarizes in his person the whole history of his people, but where Israel failed, the servant will succeed: "Behold, my servant will succeed"—thus, as in a superscription the importance of which must not be minimized, is defined his supreme work (52.13). He will succeed by his sufferings and by his death, which have a substitutionary value, for by substituting himself for his people the servant makes their salvation possible; that is why in the last song the figure of the servant can only be understood in an individual sense. To the question which preoccupies him: What are the reasons for the present suffering and how will Yahweh's reign be established on earth? the prophet replies by an interpretation of history in which he grasps, like all historians and prophets, not a few events, but the full scope of the divine plan.[1] From afar or from close by he is present at the fall of Babylon and he enthusiastically greets Cyrus as the providential instrument of the plan of salvation; yet he soon understood that Cyrus was only a conqueror like the others and that a simple political change was insufficient to produce in the people the great change which was to allow them

[1] Cf. J. de Senarclens, *Le mystère de l'histoire*, Geneva. All the biblical part of this book is devoted to an exposition of the theology of Second Isaiah.

to make their vocation a reality. For the prophet, as for his fore-runners, salvation was linked to the event of the Exodus; at the time of the Exodus Yahweh had constituted, saved, redeemed and taught his people, and so any saving intervention in history could be only a confirmation of the Exodus. It is striking to discover how far the Exodus theme dominates the thought of Second Isaiah; it is so central that it forms the introduction and the conclusion to his work (40.3ff. and 55.12-13). The new Exodus will not be a replica of the former: between the type and the antitype there is a relationship of progress and deepening; the terms " to bring back " and "desert" take on a spiritual meaning[1] and the agent of this change is a new figure, the Servant, an eschatological and Messianic figure. This figure, however, has numerous historical connections. Reflection on the Exodus had more than once led the prophet to meditate on the person of Moses, who is called the "servant of Yahweh" in Ex. 4.10; 14.31; Num. 11.11; 12.7; Dt. 3.24; 34.5, a prophet in Ex. 5.5, 23; 6.6 (cf. Is. 49.2), a man of the spirit in Num. 11.25-29; 12.6-9 (cf. Is. 42.1; 50.4-9), the one who becomes an intercessor in Ex. 32.11; 33.12; 34.4; Dt. 9.18-20; 10.10-11 (cf. Is. 53.12), the one who gives a covenant in Ex. 24.8 (cf. Is. 42.6; 52.15), the one who teaches in Dt. 4.10; 7.12 (cf. Is. 42.4; 53.11).

Other features of the Servant figure are borrowed from the royal rites, especially those which dealt with his sufferings and death. An exhaustive comparison of the Servant Songs with the hymns of the Tammuz cult has brought to light the similarity of expressions and metaphors.[2] More conclusive still are the analogies of the Servant's sufferings with certain rites practised in Babylon on the person of the king at the New Year ceremonies: the king underwent a kind of symbolic humiliation; he was struck, his crown was removed and his sceptre and the regalia of royalty were returned to him only after he had made public confession of his sins. In

---

[1] Among reminiscences of the Exodus line of thought, note the theme of the route (40.3, 11), of the Egyptian magicians (41.18, 21), of the prison (42.22), of water in the desert (48.21), of Rahab (51.9), of flight (52.11), of food costing nothing (55.1-7).

[2] The resemblance between certain titles of Tammuz and those of the Servant is quite striking; Tammuz is called the crooked, the ill-treated, the one whose face has lost vitality, the man of tears, the weakling, the lamb who goes into the underworld (cf. the material collected by Witzel, *Tammuzliturgien und Verwandtes* (Analecta Orientalia X 1935), and the very suggestive study of I. Engnell, "The Ebed Yahweh songs and the suffering Messiah in Deutero-Isaiah", *Bulletin of the John Rylands Library*, 1948, pp. 54ff.).

this rite, the king acted as a substitute for the people by taking
upon himself the sins whose burden must not weigh on the new
year.[1] On certain special occasions, the humiliation was not altogether symbolical, but a substitute (*shar puchi*) was actually put
to death, in order to safeguard the king's life. These Babylonian
customs certainly inspired the prophet more than the similar royal
rites in Israel whose existence remains problematical. From the
sole clue in Ps. 89.39: "Thou hast cast off, thou hast rejected,
thou hast pursued thine anointed with thine anger", it seems really
difficult to reconstruct the existence of rites of the king's humiliation
in the Jerusalem temple, the more since in this text the term
mashiach is applied to the dynasty or to the people rather than to
the person of the king. It is improbable, furthermore, that the rôle
of the high priest at the Feast of Atonement was the continuation
of rites which existed before the exile in the royal cult, for the substitutionary rôle of the priest goes back doubtless to the very origins
of the priesthood. Whatever may be the elements borrowed from
tradition by the prophet, it must be recognized that he deepened
and spiritualized them considerably. The Servant does not perform
a seasonal rite, he does not act in a symbolical way, he really dies
and after this substitution, which is also a total gift, he is capable
of bringing salvation. The entirely new figure of the Servant is
made up of elements borrowed from tradition: the *'ebed* is a king
and his sufferings are not contradictory to his royal aspect. This is
one of the important results of the study of the Mesopotamian and
Canaanite parallels, while certain texts from the Old Testament
itself must never have allowed it to be forgotten that humility
formed part of the Messianic functions of the Son of David (e.g.
Zech. 9.9; 13.7). The *'ebed* is a prophet, he fulfils to perfection
all the functions of a prophet: obedience, ministry of the word,
intercession; it is difficult not to admit that the memory of Moses
and Jeremiah haunted the prophet's mind. He is also the priest
and the sacrificial victim offered for the forgiveness of sins. By
borrowing from them most of the features of his saviour, Second
Isaiah seeks to stress the positive values of history and the institutions. All that myth and history taught about salvation he sees
prophetically realized by a man who, because he is a living synthesis

---

[1] On the rites of the New Year festival in Babylon, cf. Zimmern, *Zum Baby-
lonischen Neujahrfest*, 1928; Dürr, *Die isr.-jüd. Heilandserwartung*, and van der
Ploeg, *Les chants du serviteur de Yahwé*, pp. 170ff.

and a concentration of the elected people, will give back to the latter its sense of mission, for in the prophet's thought Israel never ceases to be the real servant. Converted by Israel's example, the nations will in their turn enter the covenant; those nations, out of whom Israel had been called at the beginning of its history, will travel to its light, and the new heaven and the new earth will make a new and final reality of this salvation (Is. 60.19; 65.17).

The Son of Man, who appears in only one text in the Old Testament (Dan. 7.13) is not in absolute opposition to the Messiah, as is often thought, and it is, therefore, not necessary to postulate a foreign origin for this figure. A metaphysical and transcendental aspect already characterizes the Messiah of Isaiah (Immanuel), of Micah, and still more the figure of the Saviour; but while the Messiah, though having celestial features, remains a man whose origin is earthly and who appears in the world by way of generation and birth, the Son of Man is a celestial figure who assumes a human form only when he manifests himself. Here we are in the presence of a new line of thought which is very different from both the Davidic Messianism and the prophetic Messianism represented by the Servant of Yahweh. This original figure, however, is not unconnected with Israelite tradition. Belief in a " primordial man ", as we have seen, constituted the fundamental structure from which other forms of Messianism issued and we think that one of Bentzen's great merits[1] is to have brought to light the unity of the various Messianic currents. In the eschatology of *bar 'enash* we have the return of a concept which had been eclipsed by the prophets, through an anti-Canaanite and anti-mythological reaction, in favour of historical realities. This transference on to the historical plane had made the hope of Israel into an actual and ever-present power, but at the same time it risked opening the door to a this-worldliness and to an identification of religion with politics, at a time when the faith had become less dynamic and less spiritual than at the time of an Isaiah. With this recall of transcendence, which is the main theme, other themes became incorporated which the figure of the Son of Man allowed to reach their full significance: it is said of the divine glory, which the prophet Ezekiel presents as one form of Yahweh's appearance, that it had " a resemblance to a son of man " (Ez. 1.26; 10.16) and this function is stressed by the connection between the glory and the cloud (Ez. 1.4; 10.3-4), the

[1] *Messias, Moses redivivus, Menschensohn,* Zürich 1948.

latter being the normal accompaniment of theophanies and particularly of eschatological theophanies (cf. Nah. 1.3; Ps. 97.2). The coming of the Son of Man on the clouds puts his appearance not in the category of theophanies of the angels, who are never given this dignity (Dan. 8.15; 9.21; 10.5-16), but among those of God himself. The glory is again set in relationship with man in a text which there is general agreement in considering as the best biblical commentary on Gen. 1.26: Psalm 8 celebrates the greatness of man "crowned [man is a king] with glory and majesty" (v. 6). The Son of Man is, then, a real king, his function overlaps the Messiah's, but by giving him the title of man the author of the book of Daniel seeks to disentangle Messianism from national ties and to link it with the universal outlook of Genesis. The identification of the Son of Man with the "people of the saints" (Dan. 7.18, 22) is secondary to the vision of the individual who is "the one whom the Most High has for centuries reserved and by whom he wishes to redeem the creation" (4 Esdr. 13.26). If the Son of Man is a "synthetic figure" who arose to unify the Messianic hopes which broke up into an ever greater multiplicity of varied and often contradictory aspects, according to political flunctuations, it must be recognized that this figure allowed Judaism to safeguard certain specifically religious and transcendent values.

In bringing to an end our study of eschatology, we draw the conclusion that the notion of God's action in history to which the whole content of the Old Testament is referred could not do without his personal presence in men or in certain institutions such as the law and the temple. At the last stage of this history, the synthetic figures of the Servant of Yahweh and the Son of Man, which are among the most perfect creations of Israel's theological thought, will themselves be harmonized in a new unity.

BIBLIOGRAPHY

ALT, A., "Gedanken über das Königtum Jahwes", *Kleine Schriften I*, p. 357.

BAUMANN, EB., "Shub shebut. Eine exegetische Untersuchung", *ZAW*, 1929, p. 17.

BENTZEN, A., *Messias, Moses redivivus, Menschensohn*, Zürich 1948.

BRANDT, TH., "Prophetie und Geschichte in Deuterojesaja", *Wort und Geist*, (Festgabe K. Heim), p. 13.

BUBER, M., *Das Kommende I: Königtum Gottes*, Berlin 1936.

CAMPBELL, J. C., "God's People and the Remnant", *Scottish Journal of Theology*, 1950, p. 78.

CERNÝ, L., *The Day of Yahweh & Some Relevant Problems*, Prague 1948.

COSSMANN, W., *Die Entwicklung des Gerichtsgedankens bei den altt. Propheten, BZAW* 29, 1915.

DENNEFELD, L., "Le Messianisme", *Dict. Théol. cathol.* T.X, 2.

DIETRICH, E. L., *Shub shebut. Die endzeitliche Wiederherstellung bei den Propheten, BZAW* 40, 1925.

DÜRR, L., *Ursprung und Ausbau der isr.-jüd. Heilandserwartung*, Berlin 1925.

EDELKOORT, A. H., *De Christus-verwachting in het oude Testament*, Wageningen 1941.

ELIADE, MIRCEA, "La nostalgie du Paradis dans les traditions primitives", *Diogène* 3, 1953, p. 34.

FEUILLET, A., "Les Psaumes du règne de Yahweh", *NRTh* 1951, pp. 244 and 352.

FROST, S. B., *Old Testament Apocalyptic, Its origin and growth*, London 1952.

GALL, A. VON, *Basileia tou theou*, Heidelberg 1926.

GRESSMANN, H., *Der Messias* (new edition of *Der Ursprung der isr.-jüd. Eschatologie*) 1929.

IMSCHOOT, P. VAN, *Le règne de Dieu dans l'A.T.*, Coll. Gand 22, 1936, p. 253.

JEREMIAS, A., *Die biblische Erlösererwartung*, 1931.

KNIGHT, G. A. F., "Eschatology in the O.T.", *Scottish Journal of Theology*, 1951, p. 355.

KOEHLER, L., "Christus im Alten und im Neuen Testament", *ThZ*, 1954, p. 241.

KRAELING, C. H., *Anthropos and Son of Man*, New York 1927.

LINDBLOM, J., *The Servant Songs in Deutero-Isaiah*, Lund 1951.

MOWINCKEL, S., *Psalmenstudien II. Das Thronbesteigungsfest Jahwes und der Ursprung der Eschatologie*, 1922.

　　　　　　　He that cometh, Engl. trans. by G. W. Anderson, Oxford 1955.

NORTH, C. R., *The Suffering Servant in Deutero-Isaiah*, Oxford 1948 (gives complete bibliog. prior to that date).

OBERSTEINER, J., *Die Christusbotschaft des A.T.*, 1947.

ORELLI, C. VON, *Die altt. Weissagung von der Vollendung des Gottesreiches*, Vienna 1882.

PIDOUX, G., *Le Dieu qui vient*, Neuchâtel & Paris 1947.

　　　　　　　"La notion biblique du temps", *RThPh*, 1952, p. 120.

PLOEG, J. VAN DER, "L'espérance dans l'A.T.", *RB* 1954, p. 481.

344 THEOLOGY OF THE OLD TESTAMENT

PROCKSCH, O., " Christus im A.T.", *NKZ*, 1933, p. 57.

RINGGREN, H., " König und Messias ", *ZAW*, 1952, p. 128.

ROWLEY, H. H., *The Servant of the Lord and other Essays on the Old Testament*, London 1952.

SCHMIDT, H., *Der Mythos vom wiederkehrenden König im A.T.*, 1925.

SELLIN, E., *Die isr.-jüd. Heilandserwartung* (Bibl. Zeitfragen), 1909.

STAERK, W., *Soter. Die biblische Erlösererwartung*, t.I. *Der biblische Christus*, Gütersloh 1933; t.2. *Die Erlösererwartung in den östlichen Religionen*, Stuttgart 1938.

STAMM, J. J., " La prophétie d'Emmanuel ", *RHPR*, 1943, p. 1. " Die Immanuelweissagung. Ein Gespräch mit E. Hammershaimb." *VT*, 1954, p. 20.

STEUERNAGEL, C., " Strukturlinien der Entwicklung der jüd. Eschatologie ", *Festschrift A. Bertholet*, p. 479.

VAUX, R. DE, " Le reste d'Israël ", *RB*, 1933, p. 538.

VOLZ, P., " Der eschatologische Glaube im A.T.", *Festschrift G. Beer*, 1935, p. 72.

VRIEZEN, TH. C., " Prophecy and Eschatology ", *Supplements to VT* 2, 1953, p. 199.

WOLFF, H. H., " Herrschaft Jahwes und Messiasgestalt ", *ZAW*, 1936, p. 168.

INDEXES

GENERAL INDEX

INDEX OF BIBLICAL REFERENCES